Working with and for the Aged

JORDAN I. KOSBERG, editor

National Association of Social Workers, Inc.

7981 Eastern Avenue

Silver Spring, MD. 20910

The articles in this collection were selected from a wide variety of publications with a special view toward their flexible use in one or another combination by students and faculty. The entire collection may be purchased as a total package of articles with Dr. Kosberg's introduction. The articles also may be purchased as individual reprints.

CONTENTS

Introduction/Toward a New Understanding of the Elderly Client
JORDAN I. KOSBERG

WORKING WITH AGED INDIVIDUALS OR THEIR FAMILIES
Attitudes toward Elderly Clients
JORDAN I. KOSBERG AND AUDREY P. HARRIS
Interviewing the Ill Aged
MARTIN BLOOM, EDNA DUCHON, GERTRUDE FRIRES,
HELEN HANSON, GEORGINE HURD, AND VIVIAN SOUTH
Task-Centered Model for Work with the Aged
ELIN J. CORMICAN
Aspects of Sexual Counseling with the Aged
FAYE SANDER
Grandparents and Intergenerational Family Therapy
GERALDINE M. SPARK
The Family Agency and the Kinship System of the Elderly
ANNE O. FREED

WORKING WITH GROUPS OF THE ELDERLY
Group Work with the Aging: An Issue for Social Work Education
NAZNEEN S. MAYADAS AND DOUGLAS L. HINK
Behavioral Group Work in a Home for the Aged
N. LINSK, MICHAEL W. HOWE, AND ELSIE M. PINKSTON
Support Groups for Elderly Persons in the Community
BERYL J. PETTY, TAMERRA P. MOELLER, AND RUTH Z.
CAMPBELL
Group Therapy for High Utilizers of Clinic Facilities
JULIANNE MAIENKNECHT MORRISON

WORKING WITH THE AGED IN INSTITUTIONS
Social Work in the Nursing Home: A Need and an Opportunity
LOU ANN B. JORGENSEN AND ROBERT L. KANE
Individual Psychotherapy with the Institutionalized Aged
JUDAH L. RONCH AND JAN S. MAIZLER

Individualizing Therapy for the Mentally Impaired Aged
      ELAINE M. BRODY, CHARLOTTE COLE, AND MIRIAM MOSS
Social Service Programming in Nursing Homes
      MICHAEL J. AUSTIN AND JORDAN I. KOSBERG

WORKING WITH THE AGED IN THE COMMUNITY
    An Integrated Service Delivery Program for the Elderly: Implementing a Community Plan
      RONALD WEISMEHL AND DANIEL SILVERSTEIN
    Barriers to the Delivery of Psychiatric Services to the Elderly
      CHARLES M. GAITZ
    Outreach and Advocacy in the Treatment of the Aged
      RUTH G. COHEN
    Outreach Services in "God's Waiting Room"
      JEFFREY R. SOLOMON
    Housing for the Well Aged: A Conceptual Framework for Planning
      EPHRAIM F. GOLDSTEIN
    Home Health Care for the Elderly
      JULIANNE S. OKTAY AND FRANCINE SHEPPARD
    Innovative Roles for Social Workers in Home-Care Programs
      TERRY B. AXELROD

WORKING WITH ELDERLY MEMBERS OF MINORITY GROUPS
    Communicating with Elderly Mexican-Americans
      FRANCES M. CARP
    Elderly Asian Americans and Use of Public Services
      SHARON M. FUJII
    Characteristics of the Black Elderly
      DURAN BELL, PATRICIA KASSCHAU, AND GAIL ZELLMAN
    Life Strengths and Life Stresses: Explorations in the Measurement of the Mental Health of the Black Aged
      AUDREY OLSEN FAULKNER, MARSEL A. HEISEL, AND PEACOLIA SIMMS
    A Successor Model for Community Support of Low-Income Minority Group Aged
      SYLVIA K. BARG AND CARL HIRSCH

Introduction/Toward a New Understanding of the Elderly Client

The continuing increase in the number and proportion of elderly persons in our society will affect the profession of social work in many ways. Whether directly or indirectly, practitioners, as well as planners, administrators, educators, and researchers will be affected by this trend in both their personal and professional lives.

The great majority of social work professionals have not been trained for work with aged clients or with the families of such clients. Most workers who hold a position within the field of aging entered that area of practice simply because a job opportunity presented itself and not because they had a commitment to working with the aged. In many cases, however, the commitment has followed. And so, too, has the realization that special training and preparation is needed for working with the aged. A growing number of workshops, in-service training programs, continuing-education courses, and programs in applied gerontology are being made available to those who are already working with aged clients but who are without formal preparation for such work.

There have also been widespread efforts to encourage the study of gerontology within schools of social work. Such efforts can range from the creation of a new course on aging to the development of highly structured programs of specialization or the establishment of centers and institutes for research on aging and old age. Often, these efforts are multidisciplinary, reflecting the fact that neither the problems facing the elderly nor the solutions to these problems are unidimensional, and intervention need not be limited to any one discipline. The use of such a multifocused approach is consistent with the history and practice of social work.

The impetus for this emerging academic and professional interest in aging and old age emanates from various sources. Population studies suggest that the percentage of the elderly in our society will increase significantly as a result of lower birthrates and mortality rates. There is also a growing consciousness, in general, regarding the needs (and strengths) of the aged. This trend is apparent in the increasing interest of social work students in the field of aging, by the growth of programs and services for the aged (which increasingly require appropriate preparation of staff), and by the financial support that the federal government and many private foundations are offering to encourage research, training, and demonstration projects for the benefit of the elderly.

In schools of social work, courses in generic methodology, policy, and sociobehavioral sciences, as well as short-term training courses, often deal with the needs of special groups such as the handicapped, the aged, or the young. For effective training, students, staff, and faculty are all dependent upon case reports and reading material that can assist in the educational process. Often, such material is hard to find or is not available. Social work educators, whether or not they have a background in or a commitment to gerontology, share in the need for gerontological material that can be used in course work and field training. The need is felt as much in the short-term or in-service training of those who are working in the field of aging and old age as it is in connection with formal programs of education within schools of social work.

In the face of the growing demand for social workers who are prepared to work with and for the aged, some would ask whether social work practice with the elderly is different from practice with any other age group. Indeed, some would say that there are no differences. Social workers who disagree with this position have faced the challenge of identifying those characteristics of the elderly that necessitate the use of distinctive forms of professional intervention. But few deliberate systematic efforts have been made to identify the unique requirements of social work with and for the aged.

PROBLEMS OF THE AGED

Despite the lack of formal evidence, work with the aged is generally believed to be different from work with other client groups (although, of course, there are many similarities). In westernized societies, advanced age is associated with many losses. Elderly employees often face mandatory retirement, and they may be subjected to subtle pressures to leave their jobs even when retirement is voluntary. Retirement can result in social, psychological, and economic losses. One of the great questions facing society is what elderly people should do during their nonworking years.

Economic problems are among the most troublesome results of retirement. The loss of earnings combines with inflation to minimize the purchasing potential of savings, pensions, or Social Security benefits. Problems in such categories as housing, nutrition, and recreational needs can follow. Health problems associated with aging are often costly and can deplete one's savings or income.

Whether or not economic problems are a factor, there is a greater likelihood that the aged will develop health problems. Old age is associated with physical im-

pairments and sensory loss in areas such as speech, touch, sight, hearing, and mobility. One's life-style and independence can also be affected by aging. Children inevitably grow up, and their departure from home (possibly to relocate in schools or jobs great distances away) results in a social loss to parents. Furthermore, the elderly face the possibility of the death of a spouse, friends, siblings or—indeed—children and parents. The ramifications of these losses affect the psychological and social functioning of the elderly as well as their independence. Social workers have roles to play in assisting the elderly to work with feelings such as loss, guilt, and depression. A need also exists to permit the elderly to continue to enjoy the same range of opportunities enjoyed by younger age groups. The social worker can help to provide new roles and opportunities for the aged as well as caring for the fears, anxieties, and problems caused by losses.

Professionals should see the elderly as part of a family constellation, for the great majority of aged have families. The belief that aged parents tend to be estranged from their children is a myth. Most elderly parents live in close proximity to at least one grown child, with whom they establish an effective reciprocal relationship. Accordingly, social workers should view the family as a possible means of solving the problems of the aged relative and not only as a potential cause of problems.

In addition to being different from other groups of clients, the elderly constitute the most heterogeneous age grouping in the population. Differences of sex, race, religion, ethnicity, language, health conditions, social setting, economic status—and even of relative age—are but a very few of the many factors that differentiate the elderly from one another. Indeed, chronological age, of and by itself, tells us no more about a person than the number of years he or she has lived or the probability that the person will be subject to certain conditions or events, such as widowhood, physical impairment, institutionalization, or death. It is imperative that social workers not only recognize the differences among the elderly and understand how these differences affect adaptive capabilities and life-styles, but that they also realize that such differences have ramifications for those who plan and practice social work intervention.

SELECTION OF ARTICLES

The articles in this module were chosen on the basis of their practical value to students and practitioners. Articles were assessed as to their potential for providing information on the application of social work skills in practice with and on behalf of aging and aged clients. Excluded from consideration were articles that stressed research, that were heavily statistical in nature, or that were thought to be too theoretical or abstract.

Many journals, monographs, and books published during the last decade were reviewed. The final selection of articles is hardly exhaustive, but it does provide a fairly representative sample of the literature issued in that ten-year period concerning social work with the aged. Inasmuch as the knowledge base and literature in this field of practice is growing, the reader or publisher will be able to supplement the articles in this module with important current articles as well as with "classics" that remain highly relevant to social work.

This module is broken down into five groups of readings, although there is some inevitable overlapping among the groupings. The following discussion contains brief sketches of the readings within each section.

1. *Working with Aged Individuals or Their Families.* Six articles focus upon social work with the aged or their families. Kosberg and Harris point out that professional attitudes toward elderly clients can be negative and can adversely affect the quality of care provided or the type of referrals that are made. The authors explain the reasons for such "ageism" in professional attitudes and suggest methods by which to insure that professionals will hold appropriate attitudes toward the clients they are entrusted to assist. The article by Bloom and associates identifies limitations in physical or mental functioning that can affect the process of interviewing an aged person. A general sensitivity by professionals to the characteristics of the aged is related both to minimizing stress for the aged client and to insuring the effectiveness of professional intervention.

Cormican describes the effectiveness of short-term casework utilizing a task-centered approach. The author provides two case studies to illustrate the benefit of this model of intervention for noninstitutionalized aged clients. Sander, in discussing the relationship between sexuality and self-image in the aged, dispels insidious myths regarding the lack of sexuality among the elderly. She suggests that sexual dysfunctioning can be a reflection of physical, social, or psychological problems of the aged.

Spark discusses the role of grandparents in intergenerational therapy designed to help family members face loyalties and obligations that can result in negative feelings. The author discusses therapeutic techniques and provides a clinical illustration. Freed describes various kinship systems and encourages social workers to consider the function of such systems when working with aged clients. She discusses problems of role reversal and other forms of interpersonal conflict and describes how to create substitute kinship systems for the aged.

2. *Working with Groups of the Elderly.* Four articles in the module focus upon the use of groups in meeting the needs of the elderly. Mayadas and Hink point out the social and psychological benefits of group work for aged persons and suggest that group techniques can also be used to

seek societal change. They caution that the use of group work for the elderly necessitates an awareness of the unique background of individuals as well as their expectations regarding the goals of the group. In their article, Linsk, Howe, and Pinkston investigate the link between empirical research on group behavior and the practice of group work with the aged. They find that the social worker can achieve group participation through the use of interview questions as a part of the treatment procedure.

Petty, Moeller, and Campbell report on the use of support groups to decrease elderly clients' anxiety about the process of aging. In addition to describing group structure and techniques, the authors discuss the general application of their experiences with the aged. Morrison writes of the successful use of short-term, informal group therapy with elderly widows suffering from functional or psychosomatic disorders. The article deals with techniques and goals and with the development of the group.

3. *Working with the Aged in Institutions.* Four articles were selected to be representative of social work efforts within two types of institutional settings: nursing homes and homes for the aged. Such settings pose special challenges for the professional, inasmuch as institutionalized populations are often physically or mentally impaired, and the characteristics of institutions often are in conflict with the needs that aged residents have for individualized care and treatment. Jorgensen and Kane report on a demonstration project using social work within a nursing home. Efforts in this project included education of the staff (through counseling, consultation, and teaching) as well as direct practice. The article also describes functional and behavioral scales that were developed for assessing the capabilities of residents.

Individual psychotherapy for elderly clients within institutional settings is discussed by Ronch and Maizler, who also identify distinctive qualities of therapy with the elderly. The authors discuss issues of dependence, transference, and depression, and they present case material for illustration. Brody, Cole, and Moss report on an effort to provide therapy for a group of mentally impaired and institutionalized aged. The report describes a clinical program in which individualized treatment plans with realistic goals were used to demonstrate that elderly patients with a multiplicity of disabilities could benefit from treatment. Austin and Kosberg propose a comprehensive social service model for nursing homes. The components of the model are presented in an ascending order of complexity from intake, through therapy and counseling, to interagency coordination and development.

4. *Working with the Aged in the Community.* The great majority of the elderly reside within the community, and in many ways it is the quantity and quality of resources the community makes available to them that determines whether their basic and special needs will be met. Elderly persons with multiple or severe mental and physical impairments (the "vulnerable" or "high-risk" aged) pose a special challenge to community care systems, for members of this aged population are frequently referred to various institutions because community-based resources are not available to maintain them within their own dwellings. Social workers have a prodigious number of roles to play in community planning and service provision for the elderly.

The module contains seven articles dealing with past and present efforts to meet the needs of elderly persons residing within communities. Weismehl and Silverstein describe how an integrated service delivery system for the aged was developed and operated in Chicago by the Council for Jewish Elderly. This system was designed to emphasize outreach, coordination, flexibility, and individualization. The article by Gaitz discusses the barriers to psychiatric services for the elderly in terms of the interaction of the client, the service provider, and the milieu. An understanding of such barriers can be helpful to all those who deliver service to the elderly and to all social workers who seek an effective service delivery system.

Cohen discusses three approaches an agency can take in reaching out to the elderly to help them live independently within the community. The first program focuses upon the needs of an elderly population living within a changing area of the city, the second program concerns an elderly population with a need for enrichment of their leisure time, and the third program involves services for elderly who are partially or totally homebound. Solomon discusses two programs through which a home for the aged and a hospital help to maintain community-based living for the elderly in Miami Beach. The first of these programs makes use of a storefront mental health clinic with an active outreach component, and the second involves a day care center within which a variety of service needs of the elderly are met.

The importance of suitable housing to the well-being of the elderly is discussed by Goldstein, with emphasis on the client's need for independence and supportive services and on the significance of comprehensive community planning in this area. The author also presents a framework for appraising the appropriate type of housing for elderly clients, which is related to their ability to care for themselves. Oktay and Sheppard view home health care for the aged as being more humane and less expensive than institutional forms of treatment. The article contains a discussion of the tasks social workers can perform in such programs, including working with the aged and their families, educating members of the home health team, providing advocacy for such resources, and insuring high community standards for home health care agencies.

In the final article in this section, Axelrod describes roles for social workers in a comprehensive health care program designed to maintain and support the elderly within their own homes. The author discusses casework, coordination, and planning as well as the philosophy that provides the overall focus of the program.

5. *Working with Elderly Members of Minority Groups.* Five readings in the module focus upon the obvious fact that racial and ethnic differences exist among the elderly. These differences affect the social worker's approach to treatment and planning. As the readings in this section demonstrate, social workers need to be cognizant of the importance that tradition, history, present values, and language, have in the lives of elderly clients who belong to racial and ethnic minority groups or who are members of the lower-income groups.

The article by Carp deals specifically with problems in communicating with older Mexican-Americans about public housing, but the issues that are raised can be related to work with aged members of other ethnic and racial minority groups. The article includes discussions of the importance of ethnic backgrounds to the channels of communication that are utilized, the role of the family, and the use of formal public and private social service facilities. The author also offers suggestions concerning means of effectively reaching and serving this group.

Fujii states that because of the erroneous impression to the effect that Asian-American families furnish all the care needed by their elderly, this group can be deprived of needed public services. Barriers to service for the aged Asian-American include language difficulties, mistrust, cultural differences, racism, and the structure of delivery systems. Bell, Kasschau, and Zellman present a description of the black elderly, including data on social characteristics, income and employment, education, life expectancy, health, and housing. The authors discuss a number of barriers that the black elderly encounter within service delivery organizations in relationship to cultural, historical, and locational factors.

Faulkner, Heisel, and Simms report on the findings from their pilot study on the perceptions of elderly blacks, and then relate these findings to the identification of mental health problems and the delivery of social work services. The authors' utilization of a questionnaire to canvass the elderly resulted not only in the collection of useful information but also led to greater understanding of the black aged by family consultants who were involved in both the research and the service components of the project.

In the final article, Barg and Hirsch discuss a community-based program that served elderly low-income blacks, Puerto Ricans, and foreign-born whites and that included such activities as advocacy, case referral, and group organization. The article concludes that similar losses and deprivations among groups of the elderly obviate existing cultural differences and that the elderly from disadvantaged backgrounds need political power to help them obtain necessary social services.

CONCLUSION

It is an undeniable fact that social workers will be subject to an increasing professional involvement with the elderly. Therefore, those who educate and train present and future social workers will need educational material that focuses upon the special and unique characteristics, strengths, and needs of the aged. Material of this type should contrast the requirements of the aged with those of younger age groups, and it should identify the diversity that exists among aged individuals. Such educational material can be used in courses and training programs that deal specifically with the problems of the elderly, or it can be used in special sessions that are part of a more comprehensive and generic system of social work education.

This module has been developed to meet the growing need for applied gerontological literature in social work education and training. Social work with and for the aged differs from work with younger clients. This difference is related to the losses associated with aging and to the negative attitudes that society holds concerning the aged. But the elderly also have great strengths and capabilities that they must be given opportunities to express. Social workers can provide such opportunities if they have the appropriate knowledge, skills, and attitudes. The profession of social work has an obligation to furnish society with appropriately prepared professionals. The social work professional, in turn, has a responsibility to understand and help the aged client, hospital patient, or institutional resident. ◄

Attitudes toward Elderly Clients

JORDAN I. KOSBERG

AUDREY P. HARRIS

Many studies have found that social workers often have negative feelings about the elderly. The authors review research findings in this area, offer explanations for the negative feelings of professionals, and provide suggestions for insuring appropriate attitudes among those who work with elderly clients.

IN 1974, 11 PERCENT of the population in the United States was over 65 years of age, and it was estimated that this proportion had almost tripled since 1900 and could grow to almost 20 percent in the next century.[1] In all likelihood, therefore, professionals such as nurses, physicians, dentists, psychologists, and lawyers will become increasingly involved with elderly clients, and this will certainly be true for social workers as well. Future projections indicate that the number of individuals 60 years of age and older will increase by 31 percent by the year 2000, when 43 percent of those over 65 will be 75 years or older.[2] Members of this latter age group often become economically, socially, and psychologically dependent on their families, society, and community resources and frequently require increased health care and social services.

Unquestionably, the need for health services and general social services on the part of the growing number of elderly individuals in this country has been a major factor in the expansion of these areas and has increased the likelihood that more and more social workers will be employed in work directly or indirectly related to older persons. In the past decade, one-tenth of all new social work jobs were created by the expansion taking place in the field of health services, which grew at 3 times the rate of the general economy.[3] Moreover, in a period of 8 years, the number of social workers employed in the mental health field more than doubled.[4] Anticipated increases in funding suggest that the field of health care will continue to be an area of potential growth for social work employment.[5]

PROFESSIONAL ATTITUDES

Ideally, those who work with older clients do so out of concern for the elderly and their problems. However, the jobs professionals take are often a function of what is available to them in the job market. Thus, at present and in the future, social workers involved with the elderly may have been trained to work with other age groups and, indeed, may prefer to work with them. What concerns the authors is not so much that certain social workers are dealing with clients other than those of their choice but that these professionals may hold negative and stereotypical attitudes toward the elderly individuals they are to assist.

Values are among the important factors that determine behavior. Part of the social worker's education involves exposure to the values on which the profession is based, which include a positive orientation toward the client, who is to be respected, individualized, and treated with dignity. Like everyone else, however, social workers hold certain biases and prejudices toward various individuals and groups, and these individual predispositions may affect the outcome of intervention and the type of treatment provided.

Nevertheless, social work education and training generally emphasize methods, procedures, ethics, and technical skills; less attention is paid to attitudes. Moreover, the need for rapport and positive relationships between clients and those working in such professions as medicine, nursing, social work, and psychology is especially great. Positive attitudes toward clients are the foundation of social work practice. Although it is believed that social workers will increasingly be involved with older clients, research findings unfortunately indicate that social workers and others who provide social services and health care often hold negative attitudes toward the elderly in general and older clients in particular. This has been found to be true within institutional as well as community settings.

FINDINGS ON ATTITUDES

A survey of research findings will indicate that the attitudes of both professional and nonprofessional caregivers toward elderly clients are not necessarily positive. The survey is not meant to be a definitive or exhaustive review but a representative sampling of studies on attitudes toward the elderly.

■ Kahana and Coe studied professional staff in a

home for elderly and encountered negative attitudes toward the residents.[6] They concluded that this was attributable to the professionals' view of the elderly as being difficult to work with and to their concern about the residents' manageability. The influence of the attitudes of professional staff on residents was highlighted in this study by the researchers' observation that "staff expectations and attitudes may contribute to the depersonalizing process of institutionalization even when staff evaluations of residents are generally positive."[7]

■ Dealing with the same kind of setting, Wolk and Wolk explored the attitudes of social service workers, psychologists, and nurses working in a home for the elderly.[8] They concluded that positive attitudes were held by nurses in general, that younger professionals held less negative attitudes than older professionals did, and that the atttitudes of those who chose to work with the elderly were the least negative of the individuals surveyed in the home. They thus confirmed the relationship between desire to work with an elderly population and positive attitudes toward such a population.

■ Similarly, the senior author, Cohen, and Mendlovitz studied the attitudes of supervisory staff in a home for the elderly and explored the staff's perceptions of elderly people, humanistic values, the care and service to be provided in the home, and the home itself.[9] The researchers found that the social work supervisors surveyed held more positive attitudes than the registered nurses, whose perceptions, in turn, were more positive than those of supervisors who were nonprofessionals. Although formal education was associated with positive attitudes, chronological age and time employed in the facility were not.

■ In another study dealing with professionals and

> "Ideally, those who work with older clients do so out of concern for the elderly and their problems. However, the jobs professionals take are often a function of what is available in the job market."

nursing homes, the senior author found that social workers were infrequently involved with homes because they viewed such institutions negatively, regarded proprietary settings as inappropriate, perceived elderly clients as too much of a challenge and change as too difficult to achieve, and felt that the elderly reminded them of their own mortality.[10]

■ Investigators of attitudes in settings other than the nursing home have recorded similar findings. Troll and Schlossberg studied the bias of members of the helping professions such as vocational rehabilitation counselors, adult educators, and psychologists against elderly individuals and found that no group was free of bias and that men were more biased than women.[11] The researchers concluded that the age and special training of the individuals surveyed were unrelated to their attitudes, and they speculated that biased attitudes could be reflected in on-the-job performance.

■ Cyrus-Lutz and Gaitz studied psychiatrists' attitudes toward the elderly and found that the individuals in their sample were bored with, impatient with, and resentful of many elderly clients.[12] Many of the psychiatrists felt inadequate in regard to treating older people. However, the researchers indicated that "the extent to which a psychiatrist's personal values directly affect his choice of patients and the quality of his involvement with them [was not] determined by [the] study." [13]

■ In another study, Kastenbaum found psychotherapists reluctant to work with the elderly and concluded that they calculated an elderly person would not live "long enough" to "pay back" their investment of time and effort.[14]

■ In a study conducted in a large general hospital, it was found that psychologists held biases against the elderly and were less likely to refer older persons than persons of other ages for appropriate psychological consultation. The researchers concluded that referring physicians were "less sensitive" to the complaints of elderly individuals requiring referrals and believed "that older people were less likely to profit from psychological intervention." [15]

■ Conte, Plutchik, and Weiner attempted to identify the qualities that contributed to the success of certain aides and orderlies working with institutionalized elderly individuals.[16] They found that staff members who were rated as "successful" by their supervisors were patient, accepting, flexible, tolerant, and respectful and more often failed to support negative stereotypes of elderly people than staff who were less successful.

■ In a report on the attitudes of caseworkers toward elderly clients, Burger assumed that a worker's attitude would influence his or her ability to provide care effectively.[17] Findings indicated that although the attitudes surveyed were basically more positive than negative, workers who were over 30 and had some graduate education expressed the most positive responses. Positive attitudes were not associated with level of employment or experience. Both caseworkers and aides believed the characteristics of their elderly clients rather than something in themselves acted as barriers to communication.

■ Although Burger found that workers over the age of 30 had more positive attitudes than younger workers toward the elderly, Lowy and his associates found that the younger workers they surveyed had the most positive attitudes, followed by older workers, and then middle-aged workers.[18] They measured the cognitive and affective attitudes of social workers and nurses toward aging and the elderly and hypothesized that a relationship existed between the attitudes held by these two profesisonal groups and the morale of their clients. Such a relationship was found. This study decidedly confirms the assumption that the attitudes of professionals affects their clients, or at least the morale of their clients.

■ Thorson, Whatly, and Hancock studied the attitudes toward the elderly of students, registered nurses, social workers, and homemaker–home health aides engaged in delivering services to elderly individuals.[19] The researchers found that negative attitudes increased with the age of the individual being surveyed and that a positive relationship existed between attitudes and years of education completed.

Although the differences in the methodologies, samples, and measurements used in the studies prevent definitive conclusions from being drawn about the characteristics of individuals that accompany negative and positive attitudes toward the elderly, it is apparent that attitudes toward elderly clients vary among professionals. Like other professional and nonprofessional caregivers, social workers have negative attitudes toward elderly clients, and it may be assumed that these negative perceptions can impair their effectiveness with these clients. Indeed, several of the studies found that needed referrals and intervention were not always carried out because of the biases held by some professionals against the elderly. If the reasons behind the negative attitudes of many care-givers were understood, it might be possible to change the attitudes of professionals already in practice and to instill positive attitudes toward elderly clients in prospective practitioners. The authors will therefore explore these reasons in an attempt to help influence professional attitudes toward elderly individuals.

AGEISM IN SOCIETY

In a society such as the United States, which emphasizes attractiveness, productivity, youth, and activity, the elderly are not valued. Rather, elderly people in this country increasingly find themselves without roles and functions as a result of the following factors: social policies such as the institution of work disincentives, low social security benefits, and mandatory retirement; social changes such as those taking place in the family and the greater mobility seen among individuals; and the process of aging, which is characterized by physiological change and, often, the onset of greater health problems. Negative attitudes and ageism have followed, and they have been described in the following way by Butler and Lewis:

> Ageism can be seen as a process of systematic stereotyping of and discrimination against people because they are old, just as racism and sexism accomplish this with skin color and gender. Old people are categorized as senile, rigid in thought and manner, old-fashioned in morality and skills. . . . Ageism allows the younger generations to see older people as dif-

ferent from themselves; thus they subtly cease to identify with their elders as human beings.[20]

Although attitudes toward the elderly are changing
for the better, they are changing slowly. It is within
this societal context of a prevailingly negative view of
elderly individuals that social workers develop their
values and orientations and the profession of social
work is practiced. Not surprisingly, then, ageism is observable in the general reluctance among professionals
to work with elderly clients, in the limited resources
available for the elderly, and in the distinctions made
in referrals, diagnoses, and treatment on the basis of
the chronological age of clients.

WORKING WITH THE ELDERLY

One explanation offered for prejudice against the elderly among professionals is that work with older clients
may be perceived as representing the antithesis of social
work practice.[21] That is, social workers are dedicated to
and have been trained to effect the improvement or
restoration of their clients' ability to function, but they
may view the elderly individual as being incapable of
responding to treatment. Workers should instead recognize that age and illness may impede improvement of
function and that such improvement may come about
more slowly, less dramatically, and with more difficulty
in the elderly than in younger clients.

Related to this issue is the fact that some social
workers are goal oriented and need to see tangible results from their professional interventions. Others are
inner-directed and can gain satisfaction from less obvious indicators. In general, however, a social worker's
expectations should be adjusted to the characteristics

of the particular client served. In regard to the elderly, these expectations should not include the anticipation of instant and dramatic change but of a modification in behavior, condition, and functioning. Professional practice with the ill, the handicapped, the old, and the dying demands a maturity and a humanism consistent with what the profession values most highly.

Another explanation for the seeming lack of attraction felt by many workers for the elderly client is their perception that the effects of professional intervention with such a client may be short-lived and that work with the elderly is an inefficient use of professional talents and personnel. Crane has reported that many physicians evaluate patients for treatment in terms of the psychosocial aspects of their illness and the possibility of their resuming their former social roles. Moreover, a relatively high percentage of physicians surveyed admitted that they withheld treatment on the basis of such evaluations.[22] Is it possible that social workers make similar decisions regarding the withholding of treatment?

Furthermore, since work with the elderly often involves exposure to serious illness and death, it may be unattractive to many workers because it reminds them of their own mortality. Although the professional literature and the media have begun to emphasize the importance of work in the areas of death and dying, some professionals may dread working with the elderly. It is interesting to note that workers frequently have negative feelings about institutional settings for elderly people but often refer older clients to such settings. While doing so, they may communicate their unfavorable attitudes to clients and their families and to institutional staff. The myth that those living in institutions cannot be helped results in an unfortunate self-fulfilling prophecy. In addition, professionals are influenced by the belief that those working within institutions for the elderly are less competent than their colleagues who work in other settings.

The attitudes of workers toward the elderly may also be influenced by experiential factors. An unfortunate personal experience with an older person in the past may determine an enduring attitude on the part of an individual. In addition, unrecognized idiosyncratic, latent, and unresolved personal problems may be triggered by contact with elderly clients and result in negative attitudes toward them.

Ultimately, if social workers perceive elderly clients negatively, it may be because they come into contact with what is, in a sense, a biased sample. In general, helping professionals come into contact with older individuals who are ill, poor, dependent, or confused. Although recently graduated professionals frequently begin practice with high ideals, a firm commitment to provide care, and positive expectations for clients' improvement, their colleagues may ridicule their "idealism" and instill in them a more "realistic" perception of the ability of elderly clients to be helped. This may especially be true when the clients involved are ill, poor, or minority group members.

To sum up, the origin and persistence of attitudes, both positive and negative, are related to a multiplicity of factors. Differences in attitudes toward the elderly among social work professionals may be traced to personal, professional, and societal sources. Given the premise that all social work professionals who work with the elderly should have positive and appropriate attitudes, what mechanisms can be set in motion to assure that they do? The authors will discuss four such mechanisms that in their opinion warrant the profession's consideration: formal education, short-term training, staff screening, and social change.

FORMAL EDUCATION

All too often, required core courses in the social work curriculum that deal with human growth and development virtually ignore the development of the individual beyond adolescence. The study of adulthood and the years leading to old age is frequently dealt with as secondary in importance to the exploration of the adolescent years and contributes little to the student's understanding of life-cycle changes or the process of maturation.

Moreover, schools of social work vary greatly in regard to the amount of gerontological material covered in their course offerings and the field placements they make available to students. Several schools have course concentrations and specialized centers relating to work with the elderly, but others have attempted to include material concerning the later part of the life cycle in their courses on human development. Too frequently, however, material relating to later adulthood is squeezed in at a course's conclusion.

All schools of social work would therefore do well to institute required courses in social gerontology.[23] Mandatory courses in gerontology or geriatrics would stimulate the interest of future professionals in academic practice, sensitize all students to the characteristics and needs of the elderly, and explore the personal attitudes of students toward older individuals. Such a recommendation is, of course, predicated on the belief that education can change attitudes.

EDUCATION AND ATTITUDES

Can education actually affect attitudes? Cicchetti and his colleagues studied the attitudes of medical students toward the elderly before and after exposure to a course in social medicine that focused on older people.[24] Attitudes remained negative in both the control and experimental groups, and the authors pointed out that their findings were consistent with those of other studies. They drew the following conclusion:

> The results suggest that the negative findings reported in other investigations of attitude change can probably not be understood on the basis of methodological deficiencies alone. Moreover, if the findings of this study are generalizable, then medical schools may have much to accomplish in order to cope with society's ever-increasing geriatric problem.[25]

Other studies of medical students' attitudes, such as that done by Spence and Faigenbaum, found that the students' prejudice regarding the elderly was stronger than their racial prejudice.[26] Would studies conducted with social work students reveal similar findings?

Apparently nursing students may often have prejudiced attitudes toward older people. In a report on long-term care, the American Nurses Association recommended that "basic and graduate educational programs for registered nurses need to emphasize gerontology and geriatric nursing care, not only in the classroom but in clinical facilities." [27] Steinbaum also recognized the need for nursing students to change their stereotypical beliefs about older people and designed a course in which students came in contact with healthy older people.[28] She found that significant positive changes did occur in the attitudes of the students and that an increased number of them indicated a preference for working with the elderly. Although such findings are encouraging, they do not help answer the questions of whether attitudes change and, if so, for how long.

In contrast to the contradictory findings in regard to education's effect on attitudes, Biehler has stated that attempts to teach pupils attitudes and values appear to produce results. He has also suggested that pupils' attitudes are influenced by teachers who have certain qualities but that the pedagogical methods used by teachers have little effect in this regard.[29]

Although some of the findings described challenge Biehler's optimism, the authors nevertheless believe that future social work practitioners, planners, and administrators should at least be exposed to material dealing with gerontology and geriatrics in their courses if they have not taken specialized courses in these areas. Schools should also coordinate students' field work placements with the content of their courses. If students worked with the elderly while they were learning about them, their field placement would reinforce their classwork.

SHORT-TERM TRAINING

Various efforts have focused on changing the attitudes of professional social workers who deal with the elderly. In general, these efforts have attempted to increase the workers' knowledge of and sensitivity to the special needs of elderly individuals, and they have frequently taken place in the form of workshops at the state, regional, and local level. For example, the National Association of Social Workers recently conducted Project Provide, a training program for social workers and their designees working in facilities providing long-term care. The project was funded by the U.S. Department of

Health, Education, and Welfare, and approximately 2,700 persons participated in it.[30] Although the program was considered a success in terms of the number of people who participated and the increase in interest expressed about the elderly, it is not known whether the changes in attitudes that were presumed to take place were real and long lasting. Indeed, as Hickey and his associates have pointed out, "without systematic evaluative data, the possibility exists that programs meant to improve attitudes may in fact be confirming negative attitudes and stereotypes." [31]

Other efforts to influence professional attitudes have taken place within schools of social work, some of which have instituted continuing education programs as well as seminars in working with the elderly. Again, although it is generally assumed that such programs are effective in modifying attitudes, empirical findings regarding them may not be wholeheartedly endorsed by research methodologists who question the value-laden measurements of benefits received from workshops, classes, and seminars.

In addition, in-service training for professional social workers that takes place within their agencies has been an especially popular method of attempting to change attitudes. As is true with other such attempts, research evaluating these efforts has been generally lacking. Nevertheless, a recent study of the impact of in-service training on the attitudes of health care staff concluded that the content and the form of training activities had different effects on participants.[32]

Various other studies have raised doubts about the effectiveness of in-service programs in changing attitudes. For example, when the senior author, Cohen, and Mendlovitz surveyed the attitudes of staff in a home for the elderly in which periodic in-service training programs were held, they encountered negative attitudes among staff members both before and after training.[33] Length of time employed in the facility was found to be unrelated to attitudes, and the researchers concluded that the training had little impact on the attitudes of the staff. When a follow-up study including volunteers and board members of the same institution was carried out, similar findings emerged.[34]

STAFF SCREENING

The negative findings of the studies just described raise certain disturbing questions. If, despite being exposed to in-service training over the years, supervisors and staff who have worked in a facility for some time do not have more positive attitudes than more recent employees, the issue of better screening for new employees becomes much more important than previously realized. As the administrator of the facility studied indicated, "While it is possible to train employees for performance of technical duties, changing attitudes is clearly a more difficult task." [35]

Schools of social work, professional organizations, and agencies have an obligation to assure society that their members possess the appropriate attitudes as well as the appropriate professional credentials for carrying out their responsibilities. A growing body of literature deals with the importance of certain characteristics that professionals should possess, such as empathy, warmth, genuineness, and self-awareness, and the existence of these characteristics in a care-giver is generally thought to be related to the effectiveness of the treatment he or she provides. Positive attitudes toward the elderly are necessary in the professionals who work with them, and the attitudes of these workers should be assessed at some point.

It is too soon to conclude that formal education, in-service training, and staff development efforts are not as effective as had been assumed in changing the attitudes of professionals toward the elderly. Education and training programs should continue, for the profession's understanding of their impact on attitudes will increase over time. However, until more is known, a careful screening process for new employees is certainly needed as an interim safeguard to be used by those responsible for hiring staff or for training professionals who will work with elderly clients.

SOCIAL CHANGE

Schools of social work do not function in isolation from society at large. It may therefore be said that the content of social work curricula and courses dealing with the elderly reflects values and attitudes prevalent in society. There is, then, a need for advocacy efforts that challenge currently widespread ageist values. Although undertaking such a challenge is a lengthy and formidable task, schools of social work and the profession should nevertheless initiate this kind of effort. By alerting as many students as possible to ageism and to myths and stereotypes regarding old age, the profession may assure the sensitization of future professionals to the characteristics, strengths, and needs of the elderly.

Social change can also be effected by the actions of professional social workers. Social policy is, at once, a reflection of general attitudes toward the elderly and the determinant of opportunities for elderly individuals.

The profession can focus on the effects of ageism as evinced in the limited resources and alternatives available to older persons, which preclude their self-determination; the overuse of institutions that deny the possibility of independent living for elderly individuals; the prevalence of adverse conditions within institutions for the elderly, which help deprive them of their individuality and self-respect; and the biased treatment of the elderly by professionals, which affords older persons what is at best second-class citizenship.

The social work profession should also focus on the causes of negative values and practices that perpetuate a dependent role for the elderly. Specifically, older people should be provided with greater opportunities and assistance for the attainment of economic security, with a variety of available vocational and leisure activities, and with more accessible and affordable health care based on the philosophy that care is a right for all and not a privilege of the younger or wealthier members of society. Overall, if the elderly were allowed to be independent, active, involved, and healthy, society's perceptions of them would change.

In summary, both the causes and the effects of ageism must be dealt with, and the social work profession must help usher in these changes. In addition, it is obliged to make certain that those of its members who work with the elderly are, at the very least, offering them the same care and treatment available to younger clients. Social workers have tended to assist older people to accept and adjust to adverse social conditions. As the senior author has pointed out elsewhere,

> We have treated the elderly where we have found them and provided them with traditional casework

and groupwork services. The emphasis has been on helping them adjust to their station in life, rather than attempting to change their situation.[36]

This tendency should be eliminated. Social workers should initiate a greater emphasis on social change at the local level of the agency and at the national level as well through lobbying efforts on Capitol Hill.

Social workers will increasingly be directly or indirectly involved with the elderly, yet the attitudes of professionals toward older people have generally been found to be less than positive. As Maldonado has stated, certain myths about the elderly have "blinded both social scientists who formulate theories and the practitioners who provide social services." [37] It is thus important that the attitudes of professionals be assessed for work with elderly individuals, along with their technical skills and knowledge. In describing the gap that exists between social work training and practice, Brody has indicated that "discrepancies appear in outmoded and inappropriate attitudes towards the aged." [38]

In addition to exploring research findings on professionals' attitudes toward the elderly, this article discussed the role of formal education, short-term training, and social change in altering attitudes. Evaluative studies of the effect of these elements on attitudes have resulted in findings that are, at best, inconclusive. Often, empirical research has not been undertaken at all. Some findings have indicated that formal education and in-service training may not be able to reverse personal and social forces helping to create and sustain negative attitudes toward the elderly. The question then becomes whether careful screening can be initiated to assure that care-givers hold appropriate attitudes. Until further knowledge of effective methodology for changing attitudes is developed, the authors advocate the meticulous screening at the entry level of professionals who will work with the elderly.

This article has not intended to denigrate the importance of formal social work education in gerontology or of in-service training and staff development for those already in the field. It has attempted to point out that such efforts do not *ipso facto* guarantee attitudinal changes along with the development of knowledge and skills. Above all, social work must seek change in societal and professional attitudes toward the elderly. From change should follow more effective and equitable care and treatment.

About the Authors

Jordan I. Kosberg, Ph.D., is Associate Professor, School of Applied Social Sciences, Case Western Reserve University, Cleveland, Ohio. Audrey P. Harris, Ed.D., is Clinical Social Worker, Neuropsychiatric Institute, University of California, Los Angeles. An earlier version of this article was presented at the Annual Scientific Meeting of the Gerontological Society, New York, New York, October 16, 1976.

Notes and References

1. Frederick R. Eisele, ed., *Political Consequences of Aging: The Annals of the American Academy of Political and Social Sciences*, 415 (September 1974), p. iv.

2. Donald G. Fowles, "U.S. 60+ Population May Rise 31% to 41 Million by Year 2000," *Aging,* Nos. 248–249 (June and July 1975), pp. 14–16; and U.S. Bureau of the Census, *Some Demographic Aspects of Aging in the United States,* "Current Population Reports," Series No. 43 (Washington, D.C.: U.S. Government Printing Office, 1973), p. 1.

3. Nora Piore, "Health as a Social Problem: Economic and Social Consequences of Illness," in *Encyclopedia of Social Work,* Vol. 1 (New York: National Association of Social Workers, 1971), p. 498.

4. Milton Wittman, "Social Work Manpower for the Health Services," *American Journal of Public Health,* 64 (April 1974), p. 371.

5. *NASW News,* 20 (March 1975), p. 8.

6. Eva Kahana and Rodney M. Coe, "Self and Staff Conceptions of Institutionalized Aged," *Gerontologist,* 9, Part I (Winter 1969), pp. 264–267.

7. Ibid., p. 267.

8. Robert L. Wolk and Rochelle B. Wolk, "Professional Workers' Attitudes Toward the Aged," *Journal of the American Geriatrics Society,* 19 (July 1971), pp. 624–639.

9. Jordan I. Kosberg, Stephen Z. Cohen, and Al Mendlovitz, "Comparison of Supervisors' Attitudes in a Home for the Aged," *Gerontologist,* 12, Part I (Autumn 1972), pp. 241–245.

10. Jordan I. Kosberg. "The Nursing Home: A Social Work Paradox," *Social Work,* 18 (March 1973), pp. 104–110.

11. Lillian E. Troll and Nancy Schlossberg, "A Preliminary Investigation of 'Age Bias' in the Helping Professions." Paper presented before the 23rd Annual Meeting of the Gerontological Society, Toronto, Ontario, Canada, October 1970. (Mimeographed.)

12. Catherine Cyrus-Lutz and Charles M. Gaitz, "Psychiatrists' Attitudes Toward the Aged and Aging," *Gerontologist,* 12, Part I (Summer 1972), pp. 163–167.

13. Ibid., p. 167.

14. Robert Kastenbaum, "The Reluctant Therapist," *Geriatrics,* 18 (April 1963), pp. 296–301.

15. Arlene B. Ginsburg and Steven G. Goldstein, "Age Bias in Referral for Psychological Consultation," *Journal of Gerontology,* 29 (July 1974), pp. 410–415.

16. H. R. Conte, R. Plutchik, and M. B. Weiner, "Qualities Characteristic of Successful Workers with Aged Persons." Paper presented before the 27th Annual Meeting of the Gerontological Society, Portland, Oregon, October 1974. (Mimeographed.)

17. G. Burger, "Casework Differences in Attitudes Toward the Aged." Paper presented before the 25th Annual Meeting of the Gerontological Society, San Juan, Puerto Rico, December 1972. (Mimeographed.)

18. Louis Lowy et al., "Attitudes of Nurses and Social Workers Toward Aging and Their Relationship to Life Satisfaction of Patients and Clients." Paper presented before the 27th Annual Meeting of the Gerontological Society, Portland, Oregon, October 1974. (Mimeographed.)

19. James A. Thorson, Lynda Whatly and Karen Hancock, "Attitudes Toward the Aged as a Function of Age and Education," *Gerontologist,* 14 (Autumn 1974), pp. 316–318.

20. Robert N. Butler and Myra I. Lewis, *Aging and Mental Health: Positive Psychosocial Approaches* (St. Louis, Mo.: C. V. Mosby, (1973), p. ix.

21. *See* Jordan I. Kosberg, "Social Work with Geriatric Patients and Their Families: Past Neglect and Present Responsibilities," in Elizabeth R. Drichard et al., *The Family and Death: Social Work Perspectives* (New York: Columbia University Press, 1977), pp. 155–168.

22. *See* Diana Crane, "Decisions to Treat Critically Ill Patients: A Comparison of Social Versus the Medical Consideration," *Milbank Memorial Fund Quarterly: Health and Society,* 53 (Winter 1975), pp. 1–33.

23. *See* Jordan I. Kosberg, "A Social Problems Approach to Gerontology in Social Work Education," *Journal of Social Work Education,* 12 (Winter 1976), pp. 78–84.

24. Domenic Cicchetti et al., "Effects of a Social Medicine Course on the Attitudes of Medical Students Toward the Elderly: A Controlled Study," *Journal of Gerontology*, 28 (July 1973), pp. 370–373.

25. Ibid, p. 373.

26. *See*, for example, Donald L. Spence and Elliott M. Faigenbaum, "Medical Students' Attitudes Toward the Geriatric Patient," *Journal of the American Geriatrics Society*, 16 (September 1968), pp. 976–983.

27. *Nursing and Long-Term Care: Toward Quality Care for the Aging* (Kansas City, Mo.: American Nurses Association, 1975), p. xvii.

28. Barbara H. Steinbaum, "Effects of Selected Learning Experiences on the Attitudes of Nursing Students Toward the Aged." Paper presented before the 26th Annual Meeting of the Gerontological Society, Miami Beach, Florida, November 1973. (Mimeographed.)

29. Robert F. Biehler, *Psychology Applied to Teaching* (Boston: Houghton Mifflin Co., 1971).

30. *NASW News*, 21 (October 1975), p. 6.

31. Tom Hickey et al., "Attitudes Toward Aging as a Function of In-Service Training and Practitioner Age," *Journal of Gerontology*, 13 (November 1976), pp. 681–686.

32. Ibid.

33. Kosberg, Cohen, and Mendlovitz, op. cit.

34. Jordan I. Kosberg and Joanna F. Gorman, "Perceptions Toward the Care of Institutionalized Aged," *Gerontologist*, 90 (Winter 1975), pp. 398–403.

35. Kosberg, Cohen, and Mendlovitz op. cit., p. 245.

36. Kosberg, "A Social Problems Approach to Gerontology in Social Work Education," p. 79.

37. David Maldonado, Jr., "The Chicano Aged," *Social Work*, 20 (May 1975), pp. 213–216.

38. Elaine M. Brody, "Serving the Aged: Educational Need as Viewed by Practice," *Social Work*, 15 (October 1970), p. 42.

Strategies are outlined for maximizing medical/social data collection by non-medically trained interviewers and minimizing stress to participants with mental and physical limitations. The problem areas include limitations in hearing, vision, language function, mobility, and balance, and complications related to balance, pain, fatigue, emotionality, and mentation.

Interviewing the Ill Aged

Martin Bloom, PhD[2], Edna Duchon, RN[3], Gertrude Frires, BA[4], Helen Hanson, MSW[5], Georgine Hurd, PhB, MSN[6], and Vivian South, RN, MA[7]

Social research should be conducted in accordance with two fundamentally interrelated values: The continuing search for objectively verified scientific knowledge and the continuing sensitivity to, and responsibility for, the well-being of the participant involved. This paper concerns interviewing ill adults whose problems may be chronic or acute, physical or mental, single or multiple. All of these types of problems present the interviewer with a need for a special sensitivity to the stress which any interviewing process inevitably poses. Each ill person needs to be understood in terms of his particular limitations but also in terms of his available strengths, so that the interviewer can more nearly attain the twin goals of maximizing data collection and minimizing stress for the person involved.

The purpose of this paper is to inform the non-medically trained interviewer about the types of difficulties ill persons face and to provide several methods for dealing effectively yet responsibly with these difficulties in order to obtain scientific information. The amount of information presented here has been strictly limited to whatever is of direct utility to the interviewing process or to the necessary background toward that end. Obviously, for more complete information about medical considerations or general interviewing practice, the reader is directed to standard texts and to easily available popular materials such as the American Heart Association booklets on stroke (see Cannell & Kahn, 1968; Shaffer, Sawyer, McClusky, & Beck, 1967; Taber; 1969; Webb, Campbell, Schwartz, & Sechrest, 1966).

This paper identifies nine general limitations of physical and/or mental functioning commonly found in ill persons. Four sections follow each: (a) the limitations will be described behaviorally as they would appear to an interviewer; (b) the diseases which commonly cause this functional problem will be given; (c) the meaning of the limitation to the ill person will be suggested because this is important in knowing how to

1. The research upon which this paper is based was carried out at the Benjamin Rose Institute, Cleveland, and was supported in part by grants from the A. M. McGregor Home of Cleveland; by Welfare Administration Grant #175, Department of Health, Education, and Welfare; by the National Institute of General Medical Science Grant #GM-12302, Department of Health, Education, and Welfare; and by Health Services and Mental Health Administration Research Grant #CH-00385, Department of Health, Education, and Welfare. This is a shortened version of a paper published by the Benjamin Rose Institute, Jan., 1969 (mimeo).

2. Formerly Senior Research Associate at the Benjamin Rose Institute, now Associate Professor and Director, Center for Social Work/Social Science Interchange, School of Social Work, Indiana University-Purdue University at Indianapolis, 925 W. Michigan St., Indianapolis, 46202.

3. Formerly Research Interviewer at the Benjamin Rose Institute.

4. Formerly Research Interviewer and Interviewing Supervisor at the Benjamin Rose Institute, now Research Assistant, Department of Community Health, Case Western Reserve University, School of Medicine, Cleveland.

5. Formerly Research Interviewer at the Benjamin Rose Institute.

6. Formerly Training Consultant at the Benjamin Rose Institute.

7. Formerly Nursing Associate, Research Department, at the Benjamin Rose Institute, now Director of Nursing Services, Richmond Heights General Hospital, Cleveland.

approach him; (d) a set of *research interviewing strategies* will be presented to overcome the limitations while at the same time lessening stress to the ill person (see also Travis, 1966).

Limitations in Hearing

Behavior.—Hearing limitations may be detected by the presence of a hearing aid or by other behavioral cues, such as the person who seems to be inattentive or who has a strained facial expression particularly when listening. He may lean toward the interviewer with his "good" side, tilt his head, or cup his hands behind his ear. Or he may show none of these behavioral signs but merely answer a question inappropriately or ask the interviewer to repeat the question.

Diseases.—Many generalized diseases affect hearing. There are also many diseases specific to the ear including otosclerosis, Meniere's disease, mastoiditis, ototis media. These often cause hearing loss—especially in the present aged population who did not escape infection or have antibiotics when they were younger. Inner ear nerve damage from trauma, drugs, or infection is not correctable with mechanical devices. There is also hearing loss in some stroke patients (from brain damage) since the person may have lost the meanings for the words his ears hear.

Meaning.—Being limited in any sensory modality presents numerous problems in otherwise routine events. Deafness is socially isolating to some measure, resulting in possible danger and/or humiliation. The deaf person may tire easily or show annoyance because of pain or auditory blurring when the interviewer speaks *too loudly.* It requires a great deal of effort for the hard-of-hearing person to listen and to sort and file sounds into meaningful thoughts, especially when the conversation and the interviewer are both strange to him. Therefore, he may tire and may even give up the effort—especially if it is not in any way rewarding to him. It is not well understood by the non-deaf that wearing a hearing aid is sometimes uncomfortable and presents difficulties in adjusting the equipment. Moreover the sounds heard are not normal sounds in the same sense that eye glasses correct visual problems into normal vision.

Strategy.—In interviewing a person who has a hearing difficulty, the interviewer should speak in a *normal* voice, always talking directly to the person, making sure that the speaker's face is in clear light. This helps the client to read lips. The interviewer should also speak clearly, but should not accentuate words; he should avoid smoking and covering his mouth while speaking. If the older person has glasses, he should wear them since seeing tends to facilitate hearing. If the client is wearing a hearing aid, the interviewer should wait until he adjusts it before speaking. If it is possible to speak slowly without becoming strained or artificial, the interviewer should do so. There may be a lag between the reception of sound by an inadequate ear or nerve and the decoding of the sounds by the brain of the hard-of-hearing person. A hearing aid magnifies all sounds surrounding the client. It is important to minimize extraneous noises such as a TV playing in the next room, other conversations nearby, or the rustling of papers.

The interviewer should give the person a chance to repeat the question to make sure that he has heard it clearly. The clearer, shorter, and simpler the question, the better the chance that it will be successfully communicated. If the older person does not understand what is being said, the interviewer might try alternative ways of expressing the questions, because some words are difficult to "see" in lip reading. Other modalities should be used when possible, like nodding or pointing, to reinforce what has been said. It is likewise useful to have a written form of the questionnaire which a deaf person can read for himself, or at least come prepared with a pencil and paper to be able to write questions if necessary.

Limitations in Vision

Behavior.—Difficulties in vision of the interviewee may be identified by the presence of thick or dark glasses, a cloudy film over the eyes, or other discoloration in the eyes. However, some visual problems have no obvious signs, and the interviewer is left to infer visual limitations by the manner of the client's mobility, balance, etc.

Diseases.—There are three conditions which cause most of the limited vision of the aged: glaucoma (increased interocular pressure), cataracts (opacity of the lens of the eye or of its capsule), and hemianopia (defective vision in half the visual field).

Meaning.—The person with visual loss may be fearful, distrusting, and awkward in movements. He depends upon immediate sounds and tactile sensations to maintain his sense of security. With some types of visual problems, the person may be in pain or nauseated, have visual field deficit, or be subject to visual distortion.

Strategy.—The interviewer should be careful that objects to be seen by the client are held within an area in which he has ability to see—in the center, for the person with glaucoma; at the edge, for the person with cataract; and on the side (the right or the left half of the visual field) which the person with hemianopia sees. The person who is blind, contrary to popular assumption, does not automatically use his other senses more intensely. He must be taught to use his other senses to better advantage.

The interviewer should maximize the use of the other senses by speaking clearly and distinctly in order to announce his presence and credentials. The tone of voice conveys much information usually obtained by seeing someone. A calm, quiet reassuring voice is most effective in establishing rapport.

Shaking hands as a physical contact may be very useful and expressive. However, it is probably upsetting to the older person who cannot see to be touched without being spoken to first. The interviewer should maximize whatever visual acuity is present by keeping out of the glare and by sitting in a place where the client can see the interviewer to the best of his ability.

One form of visual loss may not preclude another form of visual performance. For example, with blurring or tunnel vision, the older person may still be able to discriminate among objects, although he may need gentle encouragement to attempt a visual problem outside of the area where his own deficit exists. In general, a person who always needs glasses should be wearing them; otherwise his other senses will be dulled. Aged persons in particular rely on visual clues to hearing—often more than they realize.

Limitations in Language Function

Behavior.—Difficulties in producing language are immediately evident as the person attempts to speak. Difficulty in understanding language is a separate issue, although it may be associated with difficulty in producing meaningful word patterns. Inconsistency or inappropriate response is the best way to identify the latter aspect of language limitations, although these responses may be caused by other limitations as well. It is important to note that difficulty in producing and understanding language varies in degree and kind. For one person a narrow range of language loss may be evident; for another, almost all may be lost. The aphasic (that is, the person

with interference in the use or understanding of language) may be unable to form words, although he knows what he wants to say. Or he may be unable to comprehend what is said to him, or both. As language is the major vehicle for abstract thinking and judgment, limitations in language or understanding may give an artificially poor picture of the person's intelligence and personality.

Diseases.—Diseases such as amyotropic lateral sclerosis (a disease marked by the hardening of the lateral columns of the spinal cord with muscular atrophy), Huntington's chorea (characterized by chronic occurrence of a wide variety of jerky but well coordinated movements, performed involuntarily), multiple sclerosis (sclerosis occurring in sporadic patches throughout the brain and/or spinal cord), and Parkinson's disease (a neurological disease marked by tremors of resting muscles, slowing of voluntary movements, masklike face, festinating gait) often affect the ability to produce the spoken word due to inadequate muscular functioning. The Parkinsonian, for example, begins speech adequately but loses breath and by the end of the sentence may be inaudible. The person with a stroke, on the other hand, has a loss within his brain. These problems may also involve loss of muscle control if he has paralysis of this nature. There is also the problem of temporary voice loss after laryngectomy. However, these persons often can hear well and write a response.

Meaning.—Persons with aphasia are especially sensitive to the attitude and moods of others and may become irritated over minor incidents. Frustration is often present at the inability to communicate. There may be marked loss of self-confidence and self-worth.

Strategy.—Patience and planned stimulation are the keys to communication with aphasics. A person with language problems will speak better if he initiates the conversation with a listener with whom he feels comfortable in a familiar and unhurried environment. He will understand better if he can see the speaker and if he knows what is expected of him. Most importantly, the interviewer must give him time to understand and to respond, without applying pressure.

Communication will be improved if the aphasic is given visual cues and gestures to accompany the words. Again, the shorter and clearer the words, the more likely the meaning will be communicated. It is also important that the older person be given as many non-spoken cues as are appropriate. For example, the interviewer may pantomime an action being discussed, or hold or touch the object mentioned. It is also helpful to use sounds other than words to give the person clues about meaning. For example, the older person might not understand "pen," but he might understand the little snapping sound a ballpoint pen makes when the point is released.

Understanding the "broken" speech of some aphasics becomes easier as the interviewer listens carefully and builds up an understanding of how the older person communicates. The context of the questions will help. The interviewer should encourage the aphasic to communicate, even though it is slow going and the interviewer may not understand all that is being said, so long as the meaning is communicated. The interviewer should nod when he understands, but be attentive (not discouraging) when he does not. This interest and concern will help the aphasic's recovery without any contamination to the immediate interview. As a double check on the meaning of what the aphasic has said, the interviewer can reword his understanding of the meaning: "In other words, you would say that. . . ."

Limitations in Mobility

Behavior.—Identification of limitations in mobility, or paralysis, is made by noting the lack of movement of an affected limb or body part together with a set of rigid posture or complete lack of muscle function. Possibly physical props like a plaster cast or a pillow under an arm or special equipment like a "walker" may be present.

Diseases.—There are diseases such as Parkinsonianism, arthritis, stroke, fractures, and multiple sclerosis, which cause difficulty in mobility. There is visual information about these diseases whereas there are other diseases which cause no obvious damage that would lead the interviewer to expect limitations in moving about. Emphysema, pernicious anemia, and severe cardiac damage, often leave the person with limited energy for mobility. Sometimes this is so extreme that moving the hands or lifting objects (such as a notebook) exhausts the patient's reserve.

Meaning.—The ability to move about at will and to control one's actions is precious to every human being. When a person has limitations in some aspect of mobility, certain coordinated movements become difficult for the person to perform independently or it becomes difficult for him to predict his own movements. This can be very stressful; such persons may show irritability, defensiveness or fear. They are sensitive to close observation of, or comment about, peculiarities in gait, mannerism, or loss of control. However, some persons may want to treat their problem objectively and frankly. The interviewer should follow the person's lead in this matter. Part of the older person's embarrassment comes from the uncomfortable feelings which the interviewer exhibits.

Reactions to limitations are variable. One person may look upon tremors as "part of the disease" while another person may hold down his trembling limb during the interview out of embarrassment—and hence become overfatigued while apparently sitting in a restful position. Moreover, many simple events may distract the person because even routine things like getting to the toilet now require more time, effort, help, and planning.

Strategies.—The interviewer should be careful about the physical arrangements of the interview—seating, lighting, the availability of a table on which to spread materials if necessary—so as to minimize the need for the older person to move or to perform on his affected side. All this takes but a moment as the interviewer enters the room. For instance, if there is paralysis on the right side, sit on the left so that the left hand can be used for pointing, gesturing, and so forth. The pace of the interview must take into consideration the older person's limitations. He should not be allowed to tire, although he should be encouraged to use whatever level of mobility he has attained.

Problems Related to Balance

Behavior.—Unlike the problems discussed in the previous sections, problems of balance may not be easy to detect, although these problems may impose great difficulties on the older person. Clues include slowness or unsteadiness in any type of behavior, or when things not normally used for support are grasped firmly by the older person.

Diseases.—Some problems of balance are due to a lack of correct input into the brain, as, for example, in tertiary syphilis (late stage of syphilis characterized by a set of peculiar skin affections, bone lesions, and/or extensive disease of internal viscera) or pernicious anemia (non-nutritional anemia with damage to ascending tracts of the spinal cord). These persons have to use a tripod gait (usually with a cane) in order to maintain balance. Persons with Meniere's disease can suddenly without warning have such severe vertigo (the room appears to wheel around) that they cannnot balance or walk. Arteriosclerotic patients are subject to constant or intermittent loss of a feeling of balance or may be dizzy. Parkinsonians have a characteristic leaning forward posture and can lose their balance and fall, or because of their shuffling gait they fall on rugs or small level changes. Arthritics tend to balance their weight on the less painful extremity and have difficulty walking over changing surfaces or on unlevel surfaces. Stroke patients have similar balance problems because of the inequality of weight between the strong and weak sides of their bodies.

Meaning.—Difficulties in balance are very terrifying and produce considerable insecurity. There may also be distortion in the perception of objects. Persons with problems of balance need to move very slowly and to achieve stability *before* and *after* moving.

Strategy.—The pace of the interview will have to be slowed down in order not to upset the person. Most of these persons can take auditory cues, but these should be given in a soft voice. Loud noises or sharp sounds should be avoided. Bright colors or rapid motions and other intense stimuli should be minimized. The interviewer should present objects for the person's examination slowly and quietly—not move them quickly or allow them to reflect light into his eyes. Also, it may be necessary to present objects in such a way that the person can see them without any postural adjustment.

Pain: Severity, Frequency, and Location

Behavior.—There are both cultural and biological determinants to the way pain is felt and expressed. Some bear pain silently, but show a drawn face, beads of perspiration, abnormally rapid breathing, or perhaps an unusual posture which protects or reduces pain. Others express pain verbally as well. Still others may verbalize more pain than the actual situation would seem to necessitate. The longer the pain is present, the less the capacity to tolerate pain. Likewise, different locations involve different levels of tolerance. In general, people vary greatly concerning pain, but it is usually very easy to identify. It is more difficult to determine how to approach the person in pain.

Diseases.—All diseases have some kind of pain or discomfort. Very often, chronic pain regardless of intensity, is remarkably well tolerated, while acute pain and intermittent pain are poorly tolerated.

Meaning.—There are, then, many meanings of pain for the interviewer. Severe pain may be considered reason for stopping an interview; however, for some persons an interview may act to distract the person from his pain. Questions about the validity of the responses of a person in pain should be considered—is he able to give a true picture of his general opinions or of facts, uncolored by the pain? Also questions of reliability—would his opinions and facts be the same if he were interviewed at another time when he was not in pain? Mention should be made of the fact that medications given to reduce pain may have important side effects on the mental clarity and emotional tone of the person. If any of these problems have an adverse effect on the purpose of the interview, it would be better to reschedule it for another time.

Strategy.—A person in pain is susceptible to distraction. This tends to lessen his perception of his pain, provided the pain is not at an intolerable level, in which case attempts at diversion may increase the tension of the person. Because of the individual variation in feeling and expression of pain, the interviewer should openly discuss the problem with the person when appropriate, recognizing that it is difficult to answer questions under these conditions, but trying to motivate the person's interest. The interviewer might ask if the person would like to try some questions to see whether his attention might become concentrated on these rather than on the pain.

The interviewer should be attentive to the person's reactions, but he should not continually remind him of his pain. If the older person gives additional signs of discomfort, the interview might be postponed. The person in pain needs time to answer, but an over-long delay may mean that the task is overtiring him.

The matter of empathy for the person in pain may be a problem for some interviewers, where the empathy interferes with obtaining information. It is preferable that the interviewer admit this problem and limit the interview rather than to collect data that are invalid.

Fatigue

Behavior.—Normal fatigue appears only after strenuous or boring work, and a rest period rapidly restores the person's feeling of well-being as well as his capacity for other activities. In the case of disease-related fatigue, the person frequently arises from a long rest period more fatigued than ever. Fatigue is identifiable in many ways—among them are diffuse physical weariness, low level of energy, postural changes, changes in facial expression, even sighing or grunting sounds, and perhaps sleepiness. There may also be lowered motivation and mental dullness and inattentiveness. Aged persons have a different pattern of fatigue from younger adults; aged persons fatigue more quickly and take longer time to replenish their energies.

Diseases.—Fatigue is part of most illnesses and also may result as a side effect of some drugs. Stressful fatigue is particularly evident in a person's adjusting to sensory deficits, mobility problems, and balance problems. Communicating with others, especially strangers, is likewise fatiguing.

Metabolic disturbances, such as myxedema, (extreme hypothyroidism), may be accompanied by unstressful fatigue on the part of the older person. This type of fatigue and dullness makes interviewing almost impossible. This fatigue is evidenced by the older person's apathy and loss of motivation.

Meaning.—The person who is fatigued may not be aware of this feeling, but it may be evidenced by a lowering of patience, interest, and poor performance or omission of social amenities. More often, the person is aware of fatigue, of feeling tired or without energy, and would appreciate being given the chance to talk at some later time.

Strategies.—The first problem is to identify the source of the fatigue. If there is some substantial reason for fatigue, that is if it is pathologically caused, then it would be best to make another appointment. If the fatigue emerges from having recently performed strenuous exercises or from boredom with the interview itself, then a short break might be sufficient time to allow the person to regain his energies in order to continue the interview.

Timing is an important consideration. The interview should be planned for optimal times during the day, not too early in the morning for some older persons, not too close to meal times, or when other appointments are due (as ill persons get anxious to be ready for the other events), and not after exhausting exercises or treatments. Aged adults may need a period of relaxation after sleep in order to become fully reoriented and able to participate in the interview. This does not leave much time, especially for hospitalized persons.

To recognize and to be considerate of another person's fatigue is a common courtesy and it also helps to build rapport for the follow-up interviews, if there are to be any.

Emotionality

Behavior.—Emotionality covers a very wide range of expressions of behavior. In general, these have in common the fact that the person's feelings are playing a more important part in directing his behavior than are his planned thoughts. Emotions tend to be short-run, hedonic, and self-centered (although other emotions are not excluded such as passionate commitments, self-hatreds). There tends to be a disproportionate expression of feelings as a guide to action. Emotional lability (the sudden change of mood) or a chronic state of fixity of emotion (such as constant depression or flattened affect) may be exhibited.

Emotions are a part of all personality functioning. Greater emotionality may be characteristic of some persons, just as suppression or control of emotions may be characteristics of others. Emotionality connected to illness means even greater presence of feeling than usual, as a reaction to any illness or event. The focus is often directed toward the self. Expression of emotions is culturally and socially influenced, but when illness is present it takes greater energy than the person may have available to control their normal expression.

Diseases.—As in pain, emotionality is a social and cultural expression and is evident in all disease. There is more emotionality expressed in diseases which threaten normal functioning of activities of daily living. For example, loss of bladder control or permanent bowel colostomies require great adaptation and are often socially and psychologically embarrassing to the person. Paralysis or permanent loss of mobility due to severe heart disease are more threatening to the self-image because of the physical drain on the body. A stroke patient or any disease involving brain damage may lead to a physically caused emotionality rather than an emotionality of psychological or social origin.

Meaning.—Some persons are not fully aware of their own emotional style and may not be aware of any changes due to illness. However, in other persons, there may be great awareness of changes in emotional reactions. For instance, the person who cries as part of the physiological reaction in stroke is usually embarrassed, but occasionally a person may say to the interviewer, "Don't mind this crying, it's just part of the illness."

Strategies.—In general, the interviewer must be adaptive in the face of emotionality which is disruptive to the interview. A quiet pause may be sufficient to help the person regain control and to continue on with the questions. A thoughtful word or gesture may also convey the interviewer's feeling that the person's emotional feelings are understandable.

The sick role, especially for the chronically ill, is a difficult role for most persons to play. If, in addition, the illness is characterized by exacerbations and remissions, the patient is required to change roles often. Added to this the special role of participant in an interview situation may impose difficulties which the person is not able to handle without aid. The thought that the older person is contributing to the growth of important information—and the research should be significant enough to warrant interviewing of the ill—may be helpful if clearly presented and if permissible by the research design.

When the older person is very apathetic or disoriented, it is very important to spend the time to make a thorough attempt to communicate. A great deal of patience is needed, in asking a question, in waiting, in responding approvingly when some gesture or word is forthcoming. Such patience is often rewarded, especially in institutional settings where such patience may not be possible from the staff. If the interview fails, nothing but a few minutes is lost in the attempt to respect the dignity of a human being. The successes are all the more meaningful when they occur.

Problems in Mentation

Behavior.—Problems in mentation occur in one, or combinations, of the following areas: orientation, memory, comprehension, judgment, and integration of facts and ideas. Orientation concerns the ability to know one's self in relation to other persons, places, and in time. Problems in orientation are most often revealed as the person talks. Memory involves recall of immediate as well as remote experiences. Forgetfulness and deficiencies in judgment manifest themselves both in verbal and behavioral cues. Comprehension refers to the ability to understand what is said and is evidenced by appropri-

ate answers. Judgment is a more complex process involving evaluation and formulation of opinions and is evidenced by incorrect or inappropriate responses, depending upon the nature of the interviewing tool being used.

Integration of facts and ideas is a higher level of thought which utilizes comprehension and judgment, possibly with contributions from memory. Failure in this area would, again, be evidenced in different ways, depending on the tool used.

Diseases.—The two most common diseases affecting mentation are stroke and cerebral arteriosclerosis. In either disease the mentation problems may be constant or intermittent. Communication with these persons is difficult but answers can be reliable in certain areas. This problem calls for astute judgment on the part of the interviewer. If the mentation problem is intermittent, the time the interviewer chooses to interview is of critical importance.

Meaning.—Deficits in mentation are not an all or nothing affair. Some persons may be aware to some degree of their deficits in one or more areas of mentation. It is also reasonable that this is a matter of great worry and concern to them, a cause for defensive and coping strategies. Denial of the problems may occur more in maximally deficient than in those minimally so. Denial, if present, requires that the interviewer use judgment in recording answers depending on whether straightforward accuracy is desired or whether the exact response to a standard stimulus is desired (Bloom & Blenkner, 1970).

Strategies.—The most useful strategy is patience to allow the older person to understand the question and to gather his thoughts and then to report his decision. While it might be possible for an interviewer to provide various types of orientation or benchmarks, utilizing where possible objective evidence like a calendar, this might accentuate the person's awareness and concern over the deficit. If an orienting statement could occur naturally, this would facilitate the interview. The more questions concern the immediate and the concrete, the easier it will be for a person with some problems in mentation to answer. Questions, as ever, must be constructed for the utmost clarity, simplicity, and brevity. Sometimes, supplying the person with relevant reference points assists their recall. "You said that you were in the hospital in the summer, and now you are at this nursing home. What happened in the fall?"

Summary and Case Illustration

This paper is a working document; it is an attempt to suggest strategies derived from our experiences to both maximize data collection and minimize stress to older interviewees. It is, necessarily, incomplete but it will have succeeded in its purpose if it stimulates the reader to think more clearly about the problems of interviewing the ill aged and to add his experiences to these recorded here.

We have arbitrarily distinguished nine functional problems, but it is rare that only a single problem is present. With multiple problems, one must be sure that the total interviewing strategies complement one another. We would like to present a case study which demands of the interviewer consideration of several groups of strategies. This case, an actual although disguised case, challenges the ingenuity of the interviewer.

Mrs. S. was an 89-year-old widow of 30 years, who lived alone in a single dwelling which she worried about constantly. Her only sister lived out of state and was continually trying to get Mrs. S. to move. Mrs. S. knew she should move but could find no solution to her problem, since she truly needed her familiar surroundings to function independently. She was almost blind from cataracts and very fearful of becoming housebound. If a day passed that she did not get to the corner store, she would worry about ever "getting out" again. She was a person who needed freedom and space. Mrs. S. also had colitis and gall bladder disease, and this in addition to her visual loss had dulled her appetite. She had hypertension, which often affected her sense of balance, and had fallen several times. Her hearing was becoming quite poor and with her visual loss this prevented lip reading or orienting herself visually toward a speaking person. She was becoming quite isolated. She was lean, and had no orthopedic or cardiac problems, so that walking **per se** was not difficult, but walking **somewhere** was. When she walked to the store, she was so tense that her legs became lame for hours after her return home. A stranger seeing her would not be aware of this, but rather would see an angry-looking old lady, so thin that her arms and legs were like pipestems, leading with her chin, staring unseeing straight ahead, not hearing people who greeted her, walking rigidly and determinedly, asking strangers to pilot her across busy intersections.

Mrs. S. might seem to have overwhelming problems which would make interviewing extremely uncomfortable and difficult. However, by considering her problems and adapting to them, interview data can be obtained without undue stress on either Mrs. S. or the interviewer. During the initial period of rapport finding and throughout the interview, Mrs. S.'s hearing problem would be minimized by the interviewer's speaking distinctly in a low-pitched normal voice and by speaking directly to her. Extraneous "chit-chat" should be eliminated. Because of Mrs. S.'s visual problem, the other hearing strategies mentioned above are not pertinent. The interviewer should maximize whatever visual acuity is present by sitting in a good diffused light, if possible avoiding glare and reflections from Mrs. S.'s glasses. It would also help to avoid excessive movements, both personal and of objects such as notebooks. Since Mrs. S. is intelligent and independent by nature, the interviewer could ask her where she could sit to make the interview more comfortable and productive.

If the interview does not involve Mrs. S.'s moving about, her balance problem does not affect the interview, but if the interview requires that she move about she would need to move very slowly and be given time to achieve stability both before and after moving.

The pain associated with colitis and gall bladder disease is of the intermittent type and, therefore, may or may not be present at the time of interview. If pain is present, the interviewer is justified in starting the interview to see whether the client can tolerate it, or whether the interview should be rescheduled. Also, at times the pain may be due to psychological causes which may be alleviated by the social contact of the interviewer and by reassurance.

Thus, even in a complex case with multiple problems, it is possible to select suitable strategies, to minimize stress both for the client and the interviewer, and to obtain valid and reliable information.

References

Bloom, M., & Blenkner, M. Assessing functioning of older persons living in the community. **Gerontologist,** 1970, **10** (No. 1, Pt. 1), 31-37.

Cannell, C. F., & Kahn, R. L. Interviewing. In G. Lindzey and E. Aronson (Eds.), **Handbook of social psychology,** Vol. II. (2nd ed.) Reading, Mass.: Addison-Wesley, 1968.

Shafer, K. N., Sawyer, J. R., McClusky, A. M., & Beck, E. L. **Medical-surgical nursing.** St. Louis: C. V. Mosby, 1967.

Taber, C. W. **Taber's cyclopedic medical dictionary.** Philadelphia: F. A. Davis, 1969.

Travis, G. **Chronic disease and disability: A social worker's guide.** Berkeley: University of California Press, 1966.

Webb, E. J., Campbell, D. T., Schwartz, R. D., & Sechrest, L. **Unobtrusive measures.** Chicago: Rand McNally, 1966.

Elin J. Cormican

Task-centered model for work with the aged

Underlying assumptions are that most elderly clients
can, want, and need to make decisions for themselves
in order to remain functioning in the community

Elin J. Cormican is assistant professor, Human
Services and Psychology, Mohawk Valley Community
College, Utica, New York.

An examination of the recent literature dealing with social work and the aged reveals that practice emphasis seems to be directed toward the institutionalized or severely mentally impaired aged. The practice literature glosses over the 95 percent of the over-65 population who remain in the community[1] but who are also often in need of services. This article describes a model based on task-centered casework that focuses on short-term services to the community-based elderly population.

Assumptions underlying the model are that most clients, although elderly, can make decisions for themselves, want to make those decisions, and need to make those decisions in order to remain functioning in the community. As Esther Twente maintains, "Old people . . . should have the opportunity to assess their own capacities, needs, and interests and make the decisions that affect their well-being."[2] Persons who have the decision-making power taken away from them stagnate, lose touch with themselves and their environment, and often become in-

stitutionalized.[3] Task-centered casework fits this model because it is "based on the assumption that a person who asks for help should be able to choose what he wants help with and what he does not."[4]

William Reid and Laura Epstein posit that social work methods are most effective "if they are concentrated on helping clients achieve specific and limited goals of their own choice within brief, bounded periods of service."[5] The time-limited nature of task-centered work (eight to twelve interviews in two to four months) also makes it applicable to older clients who have "an awareness that future time is scarce."[6] Motivation is increased as the client realizes that change is possible within a brief period of the short time he has left to live.

A model which stresses the client's ability to cope within a limited time framework naturally calls for a worker who has a positive view of the client system. In our society, the elderly are often considered victims because

[1] Elaine M. and Stanley J. Brody, Decade of Decision for the Elderly, Social Work, 19:44-54 (September 1974).

[2] Esther E. Twente, Never Too Old (San Francisco: Jossey-Bass, 1970), p. 14.

[3] Gerald L. Euster, A System of Groups in Institutions for the Aged, SOCIAL CASEWORK, 52: 523-29 (October 1971).

[4] William J. Reid and Laura Epstein, Task-Centered Casework (New York: Columbia University Press, 1972), p. 36.

[5] Ibid., pp. 146-47.

[6] Robert Kastenbaum, The Foreshortened Life Perspective, in Readings in Gerontology, ed. Virginia M. Brantl and Sister Marie Raymond Brown (St. Louis: C.V. Mosby Co., 1973), p. 76.

of their age and cannot, therefore, be helped by a worker who reinforces this attitude and has a negative view of aging. "The self-image and the image of oneself held, or thought to be held, by others [including the worker] always play a vital part in the capacity to use potentials and to be self-directing."[7] The worker's assessment of the older person should likewise focus "on his strengths, in addition to considering his limitations."[8]

Unfortunately, however, social workers frequently spend so much time delineating problems that they lose sight of the client's strengths. "Changes in status and role, retirement from productive work, physical and physiological changes, reduced income, changes in housing arrangements, loss of spouse and friends"[9] are often viewed as negative changes for the elderly. This negativity compounds the tendency to overlook the strengths and potential of the client, and it is often difficult for both the worker and client not to be overwhelmed by the situation. Yet, it is precisely these positive elements that must be employed to work constructively on any problem area.[10]

One method of releasing or rekindling the client's strengths and positive self-image is to allow him to share his past and present achievements.[11] In other words, the beginning interviews, besides being used to explore problems and to select together the one to work on,[12] should provide opportunity for functional reminiscing.[13] Allowing the elderly client to reminisce also individualizes him

and provides insight to his adaptive strategies.

Out of the myriad problems and possible solutions the older client may present, some selection must be made. The assumptions mentioned above imply that the client knows what is troubling him the most or what he wants to work on first. The worker needs to be attuned to the client's priorities.[14] Denying the problem as the client defines it only lowers the client's self-image, reduces his motivation, and, thus, creates additional problems. In work with the aged, especially, an attitude of "the worker knows best" increases dependency in a group which has independence as a primary goal.[15] The worker's role is summarized by William Reid and Laura Epstein: "The practitioner attempts to determine what the client thinks he should do about the problem and tries to formulate task possibilities consonant with the client's own push for change."[16] Their assumption is that "the client's motivation is the most potent factor in problem reduction and, hence, must be utilized to the fullest."[17]

A positive self-image is fostered by achievement of age-related tasks.[18] In assisting the client in task (or goal) selection, the worker should see that "the task is so structured that the chances of its being accomplished, in whole or in part, are high."[19] The elderly client already facing many losses does not need to lose at something else. The task should be explicit and verbalized in such a way that the elderly person, whose language often tends to be conservative,[20] understands. Behavioral terms appear to be best suited to

[7]Twente, *Never Too Old*, p. 16.

[8]Helen Lokshin and Darya Penn, Social Services and the Aging, in *The Field of Social Work*, 6th ed., ed. Arthur E. Fink (New York: Holt, Rinehart and Winston, 1974), p. 226.

[9]Twente, *Never Too Old*, p. 28.

[10]Reid and Epstein, *Task-Centered Casework*, p. 111.

[11]Lokshin and Penn, Social Services and the Aging, in *The Field of Social Work*, p. 232.

[12]Reid and Epstein, *Task-Centered Casework*, p. 21.

[13]Allen Pincus, Reminiscence in Aging and Its Implications for Social Work Practice, *Social Work*, 15:47–53 (July 1970).

[14]Lokshin and Penn, Social Services and the Aging, in *The Field of Social Work*, p. 231.

[15]Twente, *Never Too Old*, p. 23.

[16]Reid and Epstein, *Task-Centered Casework*, p. 106.

[17]Ibid.

[18]Herbert G. Steeger, Understanding the Psychologic Factors in Rehabilitation, *Geriatrics*, 31:68–73 (May 1976).

[19]Reid and Epstein, *Task-Centered Casework*, p. 22.

[20]John D. Comican, Breaking Language Barriers Between the Patient and His Doctor, *Geriatrics*, 30:104–110 (December 1975).

this framework; professional jargon must be avoided. Structuring the task so that primary responsibility or duty for reaching it is the client's and not the worker's, promotes independence. If the task is such that the client must work on it at home, it will ease the feeling experienced by many elderly of having too much time to put to satisfying use.[21]

Interviews following the establishment of tasks focus on the client's activity in relation to the task.[22] In task-centered work with the elderly, the worker's primary roles tend to be ones of encouraging and planning. Encouragement is needed to aid the client in presenting and maintaining a positive self-image to attack the task and cope with the problem; it releases and mobilizes unused potential.[23] Planning centers on what needs to be done by the client and worker before the next interview. It is of special concern when the task involves dealing with the bureaucratic structure with which the aged person may not be familiar.

While this model stresses independence of the client, it is that same quality which often makes termination at the agreed upon time more difficult for the elderly client than for many others. Negative attitudes toward aging are so prevalent in American society that when the elderly do discover someone who views them positively and encourages them to action on their own, they may want to maintain that relationship for as long as possible. The worker who contemplates extending the contract beyond the initial date must seriously consider what the ultimate effect will be on the aged client.

Case illustrations

The two following case summaries illustrate the model. The first one clearly shows the older person's desire for independence, ability to make and follow through on decisions, and adaptability despite advanced years.

---

[21]Kastenbaum, The Foreshortened Life Perspective, in *Readings in Gerontology,* p. 76.

[22]Reid and Epstein, *Task-Centered Casework,* p. 177.

[23]Twente, *Never Too Old,* p. 159.

Mrs. S appeared at first to fit the stereotyped image many have of the elderly. She was eighty-two years of age, a widow, and frail looking. She had recently been hospitalized for a head injury following her fourth fall in two months; her physician had urged her to get live-in help or move to a health-related facility. She had returned to her small apartment to "think it over," but really did not want to give up her independence. She told the worker, "I've managed alone for twenty-five years, and I can keep doing it."

The initial interview revealed that Mrs. S had been in the United States for twenty years and in her current apartment for a year. She had no savings, and her only income was from Supplemental Security Income. Her only son had been paralyzed in an automobile accident three years earlier and was institutionalized. Reminiscing about her decision to leave her homeland at age sixty-two, she talked at considerable length about her teaching English there for five years following her husband's death and about the tutoring she had done in this country up to six years ago. She demonstrated that she could adapt to new situations, could relate to others, and did take pride in being independent. The falls had made her cautious about going out (except for the weekly visits to her son), but she remained alert and informed, read a great deal, and regularly telephoned a local radio talk show.

Although Mrs. S had agreed to talk to the worker, she made it clear that she would not consider a nursing home and that her apartment and income would not permit live-in help. Her fear of falling again and lying helpless for hours or days, however, made her willing to explore other alternatives. The task then was to "accident-proof" Mrs. S's apartment as much as possible and to establish a telephone check-in system for her. She began a list at home outlining what were possible accident-causers; she included any time she stumbled or felt dizzy. She also read whatever she could find that dealt with household safety. Successive interviews focused on her list and what to do about problem areas. For example, she realized that she felt dizzy whenever she bent over to check food in the oven; purchasing a large toaster-oven solved the problem.

The telephone check-in system was initially more difficult for her to adjust to. The worker had arranged for Mrs. S to be called each morning by a volunteer of the Reassurance Hotline. In the successive interviews she complained about "feeling like a child" and hinted that the telephone-in was unnecessary since the apartment was safer and she had not fallen for a month. She would mockingly imitate her volunteer caller in a teacher-to-student voice. "I've had years of practice at that," she added, and that led to the restructuring of the task and to her volunteering to telephone shut-ins rather than being telephoned herself. At the end of two months, Mrs. S was feeling more comfortable about her living arrangements, had maintained her independence, and once again saw herself as being useful to someone else.

The above example illustrates two additional aspects of the model. First, while the initial interview was held at the agency, subsequent interviews were conducted either at Mrs. S's apartment or over the telephone. Transportation is a problem for many elderly, and the provision of services in their home assists in keeping them involved in the casework process.

Second, the willingness of the worker and client to restructure the task once it had been formulated again stresses the client's ability to make decisions. Helen Lokshin and Darya Penn best summarize this reasoning:

Respect for the older individual's right and ability to cope with and make decisions about his life includes our acceptance that he also has the right to test out his thinking and planning and to make other plans should the initial ones fail to meet the purpose.[24]

The second summary illustrates that the elderly do maintain strong family ties and that the worker's assessment should focus on family dynamics[25] and family image.[26] Family support is needed for the older person to function in the community; "when their [the family's] image of him is low, he may revise his self-image and lose confidence in his abilities."[27] For example:

Mrs. H, sixty-seven years of age and a widow, and Miss B, her sixty-five-year-old sister, contacted the worker for help in planning for their seventy-seven-year-old brother. The three had

---

[24]Lokshin and Penn, Social Services and the Aging, in *The Field of Social Work,* p. 231.

[25]Alida G. Silverman, Beatrice H. Kahn, and Gary Anderson, A Model for Working with Multi-generational Families, SOCIAL CASEWORK, 58:131–35 (March 1977).

[26]Twente, *Never Too Old,* p. 72.

[27]Ibid., p. 26.

maintained a household for twelve years, but now the brother, who had recently had a stroke, was partially paralyzed and increasingly disoriented. Mrs. H's children were urging them to place him in a nursing home when he was discharged from the hospital.

As the women talked with the worker, it became increasingly apparent that a nursing home was not *their* solution. They wanted to care for their brother at home as long as they were physically able, and they also knew that he would prefer to be at home. They talked at length about how he and an aunt had raised them after their parents' death sixty years ago and now they wanted to repay him. They had had little doubt about their ability to manage until Mrs. H's children began stressing how much care he needed and how the sisters were not young themselves any more. The sisters wanted to maintain the household, and Mrs. H wanted her children to understand and accept the decision.

Several sub-tasks were undertaken to achieve the above goals. A conference with the family physician, Mrs. H, Miss B, the brother, Mrs. H's son and daughter (both in their forties), and the worker was arranged and held in the brother's hospital room. The sisters verbalized to the group what they had shared with the worker and were pleased that despite objections from Mrs. H's children, the doctor hesitantly agreed that the brother could go home. The sisters set out to prepare the house in readiness for their brother's discharge. With suggestions from the visiting nurse, they converted the downstairs dining room into a bedroom. The worker referred them to agencies for necessary home-health equipment. The physician printed explicit instructions for medications, exercise, and diet. The sisters accompanied their brother to therapy during his remaining two weeks in the hospital.

For a month following the brother's discharge, the worker met weekly with the members of the household. Discussion focused on dividing the work so that the sisters could still maintain outside-the-home activities. They quickly discovered that necessary chores at home got done more quickly and with much less tension once each sister determined her area of responsibility. Returning to usual activities, such as bridge clubs, church circles, and so forth, revitalized the sisters and eased some of the continued pressure from Mrs. H's children.

At the end of three months, the household was being effectively managed, although Mrs. H said her children were still not convinced the sisters had made the right decision. Miss B, Mrs. H, and Mrs. H's son and daughter were present for the worker's final visit. The H children admitted that their mother and aunt seemed pleased with the tasks that had been accomplished, but they were still afraid that care of their uncle was too much of a physical and emotional strain on their mother. The group discussed every person's need for encouragement and trust from those he loves; at the same time the children's fear was acknowledged as a sign of that love rather than a form of rejection. As a compromise, the children agreed to stop asking if the sisters were ready to change their minds if Mrs. H and Miss B would agree to quarterly medical examinations.

As the above cases illustrate, task-centered casework is applicable to elderly clients. Old age need not mean relegation of decision-making or inability to cope. Adapative patterns and family ties formed earlier in life continue into old age and can assist the elderly to remain in the community and out of institutions.

Faye Sander

Aspects of sexual counseling with the aged

Failure to incorporate results of research studies into
practice of the helping professions perpetuates
the denial of sexuality in the older years

Faye Sander is in private practice, New York,
New York. At the time this article was written she
was a caseworker, Jewish Association for Services
for the Aged, New York, New York.

In the past decade there has been an
increased interest in the subject of sexual
patterns, behavior, and attitudes in the population of the elderly. This interest, however,
has mostly been confined to the discipline of
research, conducted, for the most part, in institutionalized settings. Little attempt has
been made to implement and incorporate the
results of these studies into the practice of the
helping professions.

The research findings have impressed upon
the author the importance of the pyschosex-
ual aspects of life in the later years, and the
necessity of dealing with sexual patterns in
counseling the older client. It is conceivable
that denial of sexuality in the older years, by
the professional as well as by the client,
damages the aging person's sex life and has
negative impact on his or her self-image.
Denial also affects and distorts interpersonal
relationships in marriage and remarriage,
and creates antitherapeutic situations in institutions for the aging.

Implications for social work

The social work field with its special social
commitment and dedication has been sadly
remiss in addressing itself to the cluster of

sexual problems in the aging. In the training
of social workers, attention must be paid to
preparing them to give adequate heed to the
sexual needs of older people, as a vital and
legitimate matter affecting the general health
of that particular age group.[1] Those involved
in working with the aged must assume the
responsibility of disseminating full information relating to the sexual proclivities of older
people.

A key element in the treatment of sexual
functioning in the elderly is that older people
need and want information on the sexual
norms of their peers. A considerable proportion of them are inclined to feel shame or guilt
or even to be depressed about having sexual
impulses. They tend to withdraw from social
interaction because they do not know what is
normative for their age group. According to
William H. Masters and Virginia E. Johnson,
ignorance is one of the greatest deterrents to
effective sexual functioning in all ages, but it
has been most damaging to the aging.[2]

As with younger persons, sexual data, past
and present, are an important part of the individual's psychosocial history. Discussing
sex may be alien to many aged clients who
are culture-bound by the turn of the century

[1]Elliot M. Feigenbaum, Viewpoint: Sexual
Attitudes in the Elderly, *Geriatrics,* 22:47
(July 1967).

[2]Fred B. Belliveau and Lin Richter, *Understanding Human Sexual Inadequacy* (New York:
Bantam Books, 1970).

values. People are reasonably open about their sexual behavior, however, when information about it is sought by an objective observer who is himself comfortable with the subject of the inquiry.

Research has revealed a number of facts relating to sexuality in old age and societal attitudes toward the subject. From a practice perspective, the author has found the following points significant:

1. The fact that sexual activity and potency decline in the elderly is no indication that desire is nonexistent. The impact of societal attitudes influences the aging to repress and deny their sexual feelings.

2. As in the younger male, impotence of the elderly man results from fear of failure; however, fear of failure in the older man is often based on misinformation or lack of knowledge as to what is normative in old age.

3. Women are capable of sexual response in later years to a greater extent than men, but are affected by the capacity of their partners.

4. Any distortion of sexual patterns and behaviors continues into old age and is apt to be exacerbated by the aging process.

5. Because older people have suffered many losses, they have the tendency to replace love objects more readily than younger people and seek dependent love relationships with any or all of those around them.

This article will attempt to show through case illustrations how the above considerations were integrated in casework services in a nonresidential community setting. The setting is a senior citizen center in New York City. The agency is the Jewish Association for Services for the Aged. The project, funded by the Department of Human Resources, provides a five-day program which includes hot lunches and cultural, creative, and social activities. Social services, available on a nonfee basis, include marital and individual counseling, crisis intervention, and quick-response casework. The population, predominantly Jewish with some representation of minority and ethnic groups, ranges from age sixty and over. The persons described were mostly retired blue- and white-collar workers.

A question of expectations

In dealing with any sexual complaint raised by older clients, the counselor must consider the expectations of the individual. The male is a more popular subject for studies of sex activities in older people, a situation which probably results from a differential male interest in impotence problems. Masters and Johnson report that most aging marital couples who come for treatment are referred for

correction of male symptoms of sexual dysfunction, such as secondary impotence or premature ejaculation. It is indeed rare that marital units in this age group are referred primarily at the instigation of a female partner wishing correction of her own basic dysfunction, even though they have never been orgasmic in their younger years.[3]

Sexual activity, although decreasing, is still present in 70 percent of males at age seventy, if they are married. From age seventy to seventy-five there seems to be more serious decline — only 50 percent of men are still sexually active. Black men remain active longer than white, poor men longer than the more prosperous.[4] Aging men who have been sexually active for much of their lives may expect to maintain interest and activity even in old age. Men who have commenced activity in late life and indulged infrequently are more likely to discontinue performance in advancing years.[5]

In most sexual relationships of this age group, submits Axel L. Finkle, the male is generally the lifelong aggressor, but the female regulates the frequency of intercourse. Men may feel a sense of failure, however, even when they may actually be quite adequate. An aging man can accept with some grace curtailment of physical prowess, yet he

[3]William H. Masters and Virginia E. Johnson, *Human Sexual Inadequacy* (Boston: Little, Brown and Co., 1970), p. 343.

[4]A. D. Claman, Sexual Difficulties after Fifty, A Panel Discussion, *Canadian Medical Association Journal*, 94:207 (January 1966).

[5]Alfred C. Kinsey, Wardell P. Pomeroy, and Clyde E. Martin, *Sexual Behavior in the Human Male* (Philadelphia: W.B. Saunders Co., 1948).

might believe that he should perform sexually several times a week, even though there is no pressure from his wife.[6]

Mr. R remarried at age seventy-one. His bride was sixty-eight and had never been married. After a few months Mrs. R came into my office requesting an emergency appointment. Weeping copiously she cried that her husband was a "sexual athlete." Upon being asked what she meant, she stated that he demanded sexual intercourse every night, and it was very difficult for her because she didn't have the stamina to cope with his loss of erection. Because of the new marriage, she was afraid to discuss it with her husband. She also refused a joint interview. Because Mr. R had been a client of mine, I contacted him to congratulate him on his marriage and asked him to drop in to see me. A few days later, Mr. R arranged an appointment. During the interview he revealed that his former wife had rejected him sexually. When he met the present Mrs. R, she was sexually responsive, which he found most stimulating, and a major influence toward remarriage. In his eagerness to maintain his restored image, he felt that he should indulge frequently in sexual activity. When her desire seemed to abate, he blamed her for his inability to maintain an erection. Unfortunately, the source of this problem proved to be physiological rather than psychosexual. When Mr. R had his medical checkup, it was discovered that he was suffering from a malignancy.

The treatment goal in this case was to emphasize that sexual intercourse by itself does not convey the whole story of a human condition, that the ultimate ingredients of a marital relationship are love, affection, tenderness, and object relationship. When the initial shock of the diagnosis began to diminish, Mr. R soon appeared to exhibit a measure of relief that he was not expected to "perform," while Mrs. R seemed to blossom in her role of devoted and caring wife, instead of the sex object.

Sex and communication

While the consensus of the experts is that regularity of sexual activity is the essential

factor in maintaining an effective performance, it is important to emphasize that current problems might stem from prior emotional experiences.

In many instances, older men, when confronted with repeated erectile slowdown, are apt to jump to the conclusion that they have become impotent and that impotency is an unavoidable concomitant of the aging process. This self-diagnosis usually results in secondary impotence, which is provoked by the fear of loss of sexual functioning. Sexual functioning may have altered, but this may be an advantage rather than a failure. There is no doubt that sexual responsiveness to sexual stimulus declines with age, that ejaculatory jets decrease in vigor, the frequency and strength of erection diminishes, and a longer period is required to reach climax. Invaluable reassurance can be provided by the professional, who should alert the client to the benefits in lovemaking gained from delayed ejaculation.

In fact, it is the female who has reason to complain about nature's sex arrangement. Whereas the decline in the activity of the male sex gland is so gradual as to be almost imperceptible, in the female it is more abrupt and results in the so-called change of life, or climacteric. Physical changes do occur in the sexual organs of women — loss of estrogen, thinning of the lining of the vagina, shrinking of the vagina and labia majora, diminishing of lubrication; all of these changes may lead to painful intercourse. Fortunately, most of these symptoms can easily be treated by hormonal replacement.

In very old age, women are capable of sexual response to a greater extent than men. Their responses may, however, be affected by the capacity of their spouses. A women is not periodically "in heat." She is receptive, more or less, all the time, in the sense that her receptiveness for intercourse is unaffected by whether or not she is ovulating. An aging woman, however, does need to feel attractive and wanted by her husband; consequently she might interpret her husband's waning interests and energies as a personal rejection. When these two reactions, the man's fear of impotence and the woman's feeling of being rejected, occur and remain unspoken, the relationship is likely to deteriorate drastically.

[6]Axel L. Finkle, Emotional Quality and Physical Quantity of Sexual Activity in Aging Males, *Journal of Geriatric Psychiatry,* 6:70-77 (1973).

Mr. and Mrs. N, both in their late sixties, were experiencing marital difficulties after their retirement. Mrs. N had owned a lingerie store and had "employed" her husband when he had developed back trouble and was unable to work as a machine operator. Mrs. N complained that since their retirement, her husband's behavior had changed dramatically: He would insult her in front of her friends by flirting outrageously; he would disappear and leave her stranded during joint shopping trips and social engagements; and he would commit himself to vacation plans and back out at the last minute. When she attempted to talk to him he would become abjectly apologetic. She cried that she could not cope with his behavior, which vacillated from hostility to cloying endearments.

Mr. N recounted that before they had retired his wife had been so involved in the business that she had had no time for him. During that time, she had avoided sexual and social involvement, claiming that she was exhausted from the responsibilities and efforts of buying trips. He blamed her for his impotence, insisting that he was suffering from atrophy due to sexual disuse. Now that she had time on her hands, he stated, she expected to reverse the situation by demanding positive "input" from him, which he resented. Both said that their marriage, although they had had their differences, had been a good, working one.

It was apparent that previously effective coping mechanisms were rendered ineffective by the change in their lifestyle. Mr. N, feeling that he no longer was so dependent on his wife, seemed to be retaliating for past neglects, and then would become overwhelmed by guilt. His wife, having been relieved of the burden involved in being a breadwinner, was attempting to create a compatible relationship. Many sessions were devoted to ventilation of past and present angers, and to redefining the relationship. When Mr. N was reassured that his wife considered him an attractive and desirable man, he began to regain his male identity. Continued counseling with the couple was aimed at debunking the myth that sexual intercourse is the only vehicle for sexual expression and advocating revision of habitual sexual patterns.

Misuse of sex

It would be remiss not to take into account some of the uses people make of sexual performance. While there might be real affection and interest in sexual activities, the fact that there is sexual activity does not necessarily mean that the pleasure of sex is the goal. Sex can be considered as a need, as a drive, or as a behavior. For most people it means pleasure; for some it might be a means of self-assertion; for others it is used to satisfy a need for companionship or protection; others use it to dominate and to enslave. The latter interactions are the only pleasure some people derive or have derived from sex, and they persist and are reinforced in old age.

Sidney Levin cites that when sexual needs do lead to activity, they may be expressed through aim-inhibited, sublimated, or narcissistic outlets, rather than through clearly erotogenic ones.[7]

Mr. S was a bright seventy-nine-year-old man with manic tendencies. His manner was seductively authoritarian, especially toward women. Under the guise of rendering help, Mr. S manipulated people into becoming involved with him. Mrs. S, a childlike woman of seventy-seven, depended on her husband to manage every facet of her life. She resented his preoccupation with other people's problems but was afraid to express herself openly to him. When her husband would become overinvolved, Mrs. S would resort to passive-aggressive maneuvers, such as taking to her bed when he invited people to her home, refusing to serve meals under the guise of ill health, or sitting withdrawn in a corner. This behavior would infuriate her husband, and he would harass her, verbally and physically. When that failed, he would "rape her," according to Mrs. S "to show her who was boss." While she complained bitterly, she resisted any form of separation. "I cannot live with him or without him," she cried. Mr. S refused to become involved in counseling, loudly proclaiming that he was perfectly capable of handling his wife and that he would not countenance outside interference. He also forbade her to visit the Center without him. Mrs. S would then sneak out early in the morning while he was asleep.

Mrs. S was counseled to tell her husband that she recognizes that he was a very busy

---

[7]Sidney Levin, Some Comments on the Distribution of Narcissistic and Object Libido in the Aged, *International Journal of Psychoanalysis*, 46:200 (December 1965).

man and had many people depending on his services. Because she does not want him to worry about her while he is away for long periods of time, she will become involved in some activities in the Center. Mrs. S displayed a penchant for painting, and would sit for hours engrossed in her work. Mr. S would use her paintings to embellish his self-image, by bragging that his wife was an artist. Gradually Mrs. S learned to be self-assertive without antagonizing her husband. While the marriage remained skewed, Mrs. S was helped to maintain herself in her activities rather than resort to illness when under stress. Mr. S checked on his wife's activities daily, making sure that he directed her life, thus retaining his feeling of the omnipotent man.

Denial of sexual needs

The fact that the aged person shows little sexual activity has been used as a proposition for the argument that the libido becomes markedly weakened in old age. The fallacy in this argument lies in the tendency to measure the strength of an instinct by the quantity of activity it evokes.[8] It is well established that the production of sexual hormones is low in old age; however, this fact has limited significance as a measure of motivation.

Cornelia V. Christenson and Alan B. Johnson, in interviewing a group of older women who never married, found that although they shared a common bond of remaining outside the social-sexual matrix of marriage, they also showed a wide range of individual differences. The sex histories of a third of them gave little evidence of the development of erotic interests; thus the aging factor could not be traced. The remaining two-thirds reported active sexual behavior of varying types and levels. Compared with previously married women, these women showed lower levels of activity.[9] A striking fact that emerges from all the studies is that a person's sexual

patterns of the earlier years have much to do with the potential and reality of sexuality after age sixty-five. The self-image and sexual behavior of elderly people correlate strongly with their sex life in the younger years, and frequency of activity has psychological and social antecedents, as well as being affected by physiological changes.

Miss C, a sixty-seven-year-old woman, was referred to the Center by a psychiatric outpatient clinic. Her psychiatrist thought that she needed to be involved in social activities. Miss C had never married, and she claimed that she had never experienced any sexual interaction. She insisted that she was not normal because she was unmarried, and she blamed her sister who had told her when she was seventeen that she was not marriageable material. Miss C was enuretic up to the time she began to menstruate. Her mother would drag her out of bed while she was asleep and berate her for wetting her bed. She feels that her mother's treatment engendered a pattern of sexual avoidance. She informed me that she had held responsible government jobs despite two mental breakdowns for which she was not hospitalized. In her sessions with the social worker, she focused on her unmarried status, stating that she was abnormal. In her fantasies of marriage for herself, sex played no part. Intellectually she knew that sex is associated with marriage, consequently she had avoided sexual involvement in the past. Convinced that she had reached the age when it was socially acceptable and appropriate to exhibit nonsexual behavior, she felt safe to explore the possibility of marriage.

Because Miss C was in psychotherapy elsewhere, the treatment plan was geared to the current situation rather than exploration of past history. One of her physical complaints was severe pressure in the back of her neck. The author suggested that she participate in the body movement dance program. The program specialist was contacted to arrange that Miss C be placed near a male participant, preferably a sexually nonaggressive man. Casework sessions were devoted to discussions of her experiences in the group, some of which she narrated with a great deal of humor. In her last session she said that the pain in her neck had disappeared and that she had gone to the movies with a member who was a "real gentleman."

[8]Ibid., p. 200

[9]Cornelia V. Christenson and Alan B. Johnson, Sexual Behavior in a Group of Older Never-Married Women, *Journal of Geriatric Psychiatry*, 7:80-98 (1973).

A taboo subject

It seems likely that much of the alleged decline in sexual interest among women is not so much physiologic as defensive and protective. It may well be adaptive in the sense of inhibiting sexual strivings when little opportunity for fulfillment exists. With advancing years, fewer and fewer women have a sexual partner available. Every study of older people, submits Isadore Rubin, has shown that large numbers of them engage in masturbation as an alternative method of gaining release from sexual tension, although some of them are disturbed because they feel that it is wrong for persons of their age to engage in this practice.[10]

Authorities on the subject state that many older people who engage in masturbation require assurances of the counselor that the practice is acceptable as well as necessary. Nevertheless, masturbation seems to be one of the few words that is socially unacceptable to the older client. Any attempt on the author's part to discuss the subject, even though delicately approached, has met with resistance. Older people feel that such attempts are impertinent, interfering, and an invasion of privacy, and refuse to become involved in such discussions. It is possible that counterresistance is hampering further investigation.

Positive use of love transference

When older persons have lost those with whom they had close relationships, they suffer profound emotional deprivation. The resulting anxieties drive them to seek replacements from any or all of those about them. In a helping situation, when working with the opposite sex, the therapist or social worker is in the position where the aged person is likely to select him or her as such a replacement. The experienced caseworker recognizes the sexualized love transference and takes responsibility for fulfilling the love expectations within appropriate limits.[11]

Mr. A came for counseling because he felt depressed and lonely. He was a spry, wiry, eighty-year-old, who looked much younger. He was worldly, well-groomed, and articulate. He appeared to be well-read and informed, but his attitudes were narrow, rigid, and opinionated. He claimed to be superior in intelligence and experience and stated that he despised all seniors because "they are all pigs." He stated that he hated people who exhibited weaknesses, defining weakness as self-indulgence, which includes smoking, drinking, over-eating, and mental illness. In his opinion these people should be put out of their misery because they have no right to live. Mr. A's first marriage took place when he was forty. It lasted thirteen years, during which time he said that his wife was mentally ill. He tried to help her by advising her to get out of bed, but she would not listen to him. He finally had to institutionalize her and then obtained a divorce. At age sixty-two, he remarried, this time to a nurse whom he had met when he was undergoing surgery. The second marriage lasted three years. He said that he had divorced her because she "bled me dry and made a sucker of me." Both wives, he informed the worker, were "beautiful and high class."

During his casework sessions Mr. A talked of his past successes and how he was best at everything: better than other salesmen; a superb restaurateur; a world traveler; a big spender; and a connoisseur of women. When questioned about his current social life, he stated that all his friends were dead and that it was difficult for him to make friends at this stage of life. Nevertheless, during the many contacts, he expressed deep love for the author, claiming that if he were younger he would marry and cherish her.

I accepted his declarations warmly but without sexual response and encouraged him to elaborate on his fantasies, while clarifying the boundaries of the professional relationship. The treatment goal was to use these feelings constructively in order to restore his sense of male identity and to motivate him to seek female companionship within the group. When Mr. A found that his worker was not responding to his blandishments, he began to discuss the type of woman he would like to meet. After six months, Mr. A announced that he had finally met a sixty-two-year-old divorcée, who was attractive, cultured, talented, and well educated.

[10]Isadore Rubin, *Sex after Forty — and after Seventy, An Analysis of Human Response* (Boston: Little, Brown and Co., 1966).

[11]Helen Turner, ed., *Psychological Function* of Older People (New York: National Council on the Aging, 1967), p. 36.

Societal indictment

It is essential to consider the prevalent sociocultural biases against expression of the sexual desires in old age. Rubin writes:

The fullest expression of the sexual needs and interests of men and women over sixty cannot take place in a society which denies or ignores the reality of these needs and interests, or in an atmosphere which prevents full and open inquiry into them. Nor can it take place in a soil which nourishes every kind of myth and misconception about these later years. Sexuality after sixty is not an invention of those who are studying it and discovering its extent and its variety of manifestation.[12]

Yet, the widespread notion persists that old age is a sexless era and, if it is not, it should be. What is deemed virility at twenty-five becomes lechery at sixty-five. An important root for this image of sexless old age stems from the timelessness and persistence of early oedipal reactions. The child clings fiercely to his conviction that his parents do not indulge in sex relations. Because the elderly themselves retain primitive oedipal attitudes, they may retain a negative view of their own sexual desires, feelings, and fantasies. Also, oedipally tinged attitudes of grown children may squelch sexual interaction between aging parents both within new marriages of elderly parents, and between unwed elderly partners. Although only an estimated 5 percent of the elderly population is in long-term facilities, institutional life further reinforces the impression that the elderly are sexless. Most homes for the aged, nursing homes, and mental institutions tend to rigidly segregate the sexes. They make no provisions for privacy and seldom permit visits from the opposite sex. In many residential facilities, couples are separated, with no provision for conjugal visits between spouses. Staff members are apt to react with revulsion when the elderly resort to masturbation.

Physicians, too, are often embarrassed about discussing sex with the aged; they are prone to exchange amusing stories about sex in older patients, almost as if such behavior is bizarre. These attitudes not only influence the cultural value system, but are also the basis for much countertransference on the part of the helping professional.

Taking all these factors into consideration, Martin A. Berezin posits:

A greater understanding of the significance of psychosexual life in old age will undoubtedly enable those who are involved in the treatment and management of the elderly to evaluate and assess more accurately the total personality organization of the elderly individual.[13]

The more we study the elderly the more we realize that sexual drives are not so much diminished as diffused, and the more we realize how important it is to find sexual outlets, including fantasy ones. Nevertheless, the geriatrician must be wary of the impulse to evangelize. He should strive for continuity of lifestyles to the degree possible with some adjustments to reality. In working with the aged, sexual counseling by itself is apt to cause embarrassment and also meet with resistance In the author's experience, that it is only within the context of presenting interpersonal problems that a counselor can explore, support, and encourage sexuality for the aged.

The aged of the future will most surely have different needs and a different image from the elderly of today. Many changes will result from continued and growing advances in technology, medicine, and new attitudes toward sexuality. Cosmetic surgery will become less costly and more socially acceptable. Marriages or relationships between older women and younger men may become more feasible. As the proportion of older persons in the population increases, perhaps the emphasis on youth will diminish. Older lovers may increasingly replace the younger lovers in popular fiction, movies, and television. It is to be hoped that expressions of sexuality in the elderly will no longer evoke negative reactions.

---

[12]Isadore Rubin, *Sexual Life after Sixty* (New York: Basic Books, 1965), p. 231.

[13]Martin A. Berezin, Psychodynamic Consideration of Aging and the Aged, An Overview, *American Journal of Psychiatry*, 128:1485 (June 1972).

Grandparents and Intergenerational Family Therapy*

GERALDINE M. SPARK, ACSW†

---

*Unresolved loyalty conflicts and unsettled accounts between first-
and second-generation family members are often projected onto, or
lived out, in the marital or parental relationship. An intergenerational
treatment focus may yield greater possibilities for constructive and
fundamental change in a family system.*

ONE COULD endlessly debate whether ties with maternal and pa-
ternal grandparents are sources of conflict and competition or
resources of positive support and constructive influence to the nuclear
family. Whether they fall into one or both categories, the reality is that
these relationships do exist and are not peripheral ones that can be
denied or minimized. As the focus of study and treatment moves from
the individual to the family as a unit, logically the therapist must also
include the extended and in-law family system.

The first purpose of this paper is to emphasize and to illustrate that
working clinically on "unfinished business" between a parent and
grandparents, and even siblings, facilitates structural as well as symptomatic changes in the family system. Beatman (2) asserts that "the
therapist's perception of the pervasive quality of these relationships
can direct him, however, to involve the grandparents in sessions with

---

* A portion of this paper was presented at the annual convention of the American
Psychiatric Association, Montreal, Canada, August 31, 1973.

† Family Psychiatry Division, Eastern Pennsylvania Psychiatric Institute, Philadelphia,
Pennsylvania.

the family, to clarify the character of the parent-grandparent relationships, and to deal with its reciprocal and even complementary reinforcement by the parent and grandparent and with its effects on the marital interaction and parent-child relationships."

While a second purpose is to make a brief comparison between different theoretical concepts, the main emphasis is on describing some techniques of intergenerational family therapy. Before focusing on each of these points, it may be helpful to explore and dispel some myths. While today most grandparents and great-grandparents do not share the same domicile with their adult children, there is not as much physical or emotional separation between the generations as is commonly believed. Only a small percentage of the aged population of the United States live in institutions, and even they are not necessarily "abandoned."

While nuclear families are geographically distanced from their families of origin, it does not follow automatically that the generations are emotionally divorced from each other. Invisible loyalties and indebtedness between these root systems may be denied, but these interlocked family relationships remain crucially important forces and must be examined. The inclusion of three generations in therapeutic explorations may yield renewed energy and hope for fundamental change and maturation between the generations.

Theoretical Dimensions

Although family system theoreticians have long been aware of the nature of these interlocking physical, emotional, and existential bonds between nuclear and extended family members, their major treatment focus has been on the marital and/or parental relationships. Bowen (5) focuses on the differentiation of self in the marital, parental, and extended family relationships to get out of the amorphous "we-ness" of the intense, undifferentiated, family ego-mass. Ackerman, Lidz, Wynne, and Jackson, pioneer family therapists, have also discussed generational issues in family systems. Boszormenyi-Nagy (3) has consistently attempted to push his theoretical and clinical understanding beyond the known psychodynamics of the individual and the observable characteristics of his relationships with important others. Now Boszormenyi-Nagy and Spark (4) in their current conceptualizations introduce a dialectical perspective on family theory and therapy that revolves around the concepts of loyalty, justice, and the balance of merits. In other words, two of the major and basic unifying tenets of intergenerational family system theory are those of loyalty and obligation. These concepts include but go beyond the individual and his unmet dependency needs. For multiple reasons, some parents consciously try to give more both emotionally and materially to their children than they received from their own parents. They may do so at their own expense while at the same time neglecting the grandparents. The underlying anger, resentment, and guilt feelings toward their families of origin may remain untouched. Yet these experiences of exploitation and injustice may be important long-term motivational determinants.

In other words, whether the quality and quantity of the caring has been minimal or maximal, loyalty ties exist and indebtedness occurs. A family member may be caught in a denied or otherwise invisible loyalty bind and so may find himself inevitably in a guilt-laden position that may interfere with his involvement and commitment in his marital and parental relationships.

By helping all family members face their invisible loyalties and obligations, a rebalancing of time, effort, interest, or concrete services may begin to take place. The therapist may help dispel disappointment, anger, and lack of trust, thus relieving guilt feelings and improving the functions of all family members. The scapegoated older person, marital partner, or child may be relieved of these negative roles.

Many spouses often give the impression that there is little or no direct involvement with their families of origin or that repayment of emotional indebtedness is not expected of them. Such statements must be explored carefully and fully to determine the nature and extent of the involvements. Often it is the spouse or young children who make the most accurate comments regarding current relationships between the parents and their families of origin. The children carry the wishes and hope for reconnection and reconciliation. Since they are also less disappointed and guilt-ridden, it often will be the children who directly reveal the intensity of the current involvements with both sets of grandparents.

Family members who continue actively to appropriately balance their obligations as they pass through, and into, new phases of family life can then tolerate and support individual and family growth process. For example, in the illustration that follows, as Mrs. P.'s relationship with her husband and her parents improves, her individual symptoms disappeared.

Intergenerational Family Therapy Techniques

In the course of family treatment, when it has become evident to the young adults that the relationship with one or both families of origin needs exploration and improvement, the practice is to suggest that the grandparents become actively and directly a part of the treatment process whether physically present or not. The choice as to whether the grandparents do or do not attend sessions is left up to the parent and grandparent. Bowen seems to bring this issue up much earlier with patients and family therapy trainees. He "coaches" the persons about their visits to their families of origin and other important extended family members. (See also "Toward the Differentiation of a Self in One's Own Family," Anonymous [1]).

After working through much anxiety, fear, and other resistances, some families do eventually bring grandparents into the sessions, while others refuse even to extend an invitation. It requires much discussion of purpose and aims before there is some relief of anxiety and fear about the grandparents attending sessions.

While the direct inclusion in sessions provides *in vivo* learning for the family members, as well as for the therapist, improvement has occurred even when the grandparents refused to come. In some instances, the grandparents live far away, yet changes in the relationship are reported verbally and confirmed from the telephone exchanges, holiday visits, and letters that are shared with the therapist.

The family therapist must help the parents convey to the grandparents that the purpose is not to use either generation as a destructive target for the other's hurt, disappointed, angry feelings. Fears must be dispelled regarding verbal or physical loss of control because of parents' underlying, angry feelings about past injustices committed by the grandparents. The tentative *aims* are steadily clarified: more adult-to-adult understanding and improved overall relationships. This can only develop as old feelings and accounts are faced and reworked. The parents must rectify also their hopelessness about change ensuing between the generations—the more symbiotic the family, the more "certainty" about "unchangeability" between the generations.

It should always be made clear that the family is free to arrive for any session in any combination of persons. There is no way of predicting who will have courage for the explorations or at what point a grandparent or sibling will arrive. However, if the husband chooses to include his mother-in-law and father-in-law in a session, the therapist should emphasize that the focus will not be on the in-law relationship but that they will be placed in the observer's role. Some families are able to talk openly and freely in the presence of their in-laws, while others will be frozen. A parent may also decide not to include the children when the grandparents attend the sessions. These choices and decisions should fundamentally be left with the person who is bringing in the older generation.

In an initial parent-grandparent session, at first there is usually a polite, but tense, phase. The grandparent must be helped by the family member and not by the therapist alone by openly stating the hope and purpose of the session. Invariably there may be some degree of disappointment; bitter recriminations about past injustices and a seeming impasse may ensue. In other cases a defensive protectiveness blocks meaningful exchanges. The hope is to move out of the "blame syndrome" to a deeper level of reciprocal discussion between the generations.

The therapist may then encourage the grandparents to share information about their lives. Frequently, in the telling, painful affect is attached to the events, and this often is a very moving experience for both generations.

This therapeutic process enables a new phase of identification to begin between the generations and may replace the old, deprived, or distorted aspects of their relationship. It does not develop merely as a result of confrontation or abreaction between the generations. It can only evolve in a process that brings about a rebalancing of indebtedness and reciprocal repayment between the generations. Each family member in all three generations becomes acutely aware of the complementary, relational positions of being a parent or a child, as well as of changing phases and needs, both individually and as a family. The inclusion of adult siblings from one's family of origin also facilitates the process of change.

Clinical Illustration

A young couple in their late twenties were referred for marital therapy. They had a daughter, Sandra, age one-and-a-half. Mr. and Mrs. P. were the oldest siblings in their families of origin. Each had one younger sibling of the opposite sex. Mr. P.'s sister liver on the West coast, and Mrs. P.'s brother lived in the mid-West.

They were considering separating because of incompatability in the sexual, personal, and social areas of their living. Each one described various individual symptoms and complaints. Mrs. P. said she suffered from spastic colitis and, after the birth of their daughter, severe headaches. Mr. P. was unhappy and restless over the lack of progress in his career and was constantly frustrated sexually by his wife's frigidity. As a parent he felt left out because his wife and child were "closed off" to him.

Mr. P. was the more open and verbal of the two, although he tended to be highly intellectual about himself, his wife, his child, and his parents. Mrs. P., although pursuing a creative art form, was the one least in touch with her feelings. She described herself as often feeling isolated and detached, withdrawing into silence when hurt or angry. She was chronically depressed except when she was with her daughter, Sandra, yet, three mornings a week, she left the child with a neighbor because of a need to have time for herself. She expressed resentment toward her husband because she felt he was not sufficiently involved with Sandra either emotionally or physically.

There were frequent trips to see both sets of parents, who lived in other cities, and frequent long-distance phone calls. Yet Mr. P. alleged that he wrote off his parents as hopeless. He stated that he had been left with housekeepers from the age of three. Later this picture was greatly modified when he described his mother's seductiveness toward him even up to the time of his marriage. In his adolescence he was also his mother's confidant regarding her intense loneliness and poor relationship with his father. His parents had been against his marriage and refused to have any contact with their son's in-laws. On the other hand, Mr. P. felt "adopted" by his wife's family and had long, personal conversations with his mother-in-law. In addition to concentrating on the individual dynamics within the marital relationship, the focus was kept continuously on the couple's relationship with their families of origin.

Mr. P. was open and direct about loving his wife and child and said that he was committed to them. Mrs. P. did not even like the term "wife" applied to herself. Often she stated the marriage was a mistake and the solution was for Sandra and her to leave. While she felt burdened and drained by Sandra and her needs, she could also at times be patient and lovingly affectionate with her. Sandra attended several sessions and thus far appeared to be a happy, bubbling, and affectionate child.

Technical Considerations

After several months of marital therapy, with some improvement, the therapist again brought up the idea of having each set of parents attend separate sessions. The response again was that it was impossible and purposeless. The basic reaction was, "My parents will never change, and I've given up trying." Fear and anxiety and feelings of over-protectiveness toward the parents and themselves had to be worked on before such a meeting could take place. Even though there was mutual reluctance and resistance, competition developed over who had more courage to take such a step. Although Mrs. P. seemed the more troubled, it was she who was the first to bring her mother to a session. Mr. P.'s parents were seen twice toward the end of the second year of therapy, since they, in collusion with their son, refused to come earlier.

The therapist had to establish sufficient trust to allay fears of being "scapegoated" and to stimulate hope that eventually something constructive could result from such meetings, i.e. that new avenues of reciprocity in the relationship would be explored.

In the therapeutic interview that follows, the decision to include the husband was left with the family. When Mr. P. arrived with his wife and mother-in-law, the therapist deliberately requested that he remain as an observer until the last few minutes of the session, when he could make comments. This was important in this family because Mr. P. tended to speak for his wife and thus reinforce her use of silence as a distancing safety mechanism. Since the major focus was the mother-daughter relationship, the son-in-law was silenced to afford the fullest opportunity for mutual dialogue.

First Session with Maternal Grandmother

Mrs. A. (maternal grandmother) and Mr. and Mrs. P. were present. It was reported that Mrs. A. had arrived at their home the night before and a long conversation had ensued between Mr. P. and his mother-in-law. Mrs. P. had spent the entire time stretched out on the sofa in a "paralyzed state." She had been silent and having one of her severe headaches.

Mrs. A. said she had not known about her daughter's and son-in-law's problems. She described her own current difficulties working in an office and taking care of her seriously ill and invalided husband. Mr. A. had had two severe heart attacks with many complications and was unable to travel to this city.

The therapist suggested that Mrs. P. and her mother try to talk to each other instead of telling the therapist about each other. Mrs. P. took the initiative:

Mrs. P.: I always felt that I had to succeed or excel in whatever I did—

everything was always for your sake because it seemed your happiness depended on me—there was nothing between you and Dad. Yet no matter what or how much I did, I never felt I did enough, and inside I never knew who or what I was.

Mrs. A.: I never knew any of this—or that my daughter cried in her bedroom. Yet I guess I heard her cry, and I cried too.

Mrs. P.: I felt guilty because you gave me so much attention—much more than my father or brother received. You gave up your whole life for me.

Mrs. A.: I don't agree with my daughter that I gave up my whole life for her and her brother, or that I only lived for and through my children.

The initial angry accusation in the daughter's confrontation was followed by the start of clarification of their different perceptions of the relationship. The therapist then asked Mrs. A. how this compared with her family of origin? This introduced the generational loyalty and indebtedness aspects of the relationship and helped them to begin to try to move out of the scapegoating-blame level that had existed between them. By showing a personal interest in the grandmother, the therapist stimulated her to seek help in understanding how her own problems were connected and interlocked with her daughter's. It could open the way for a more positive relationship to develop.

Mrs. A.: My mother was very domineering and controlling. I never felt close to her. My father was placid, quiet, and weak—but I always knew where I stood with him. As a child I always felt I could never please my mother so I became the family rebel. My mother's demands were insatiable, and it always appeared as if I were bad or selfish. In later years after I became a parent, I reversed my position with them, since I learned to give in, to placate, and compromise. There was little or no affection in my parents' home. My main effort was always to be completely self-reliant and self-sufficient. I worked very hard to cover up my feelings so that no one would know he had hurt me or made me angry.

I tried to be completely different with my children—read books and went to classes (sobs). I never really knew whether I was right or wrong, but I tried. I do believe that my children know that I love them very much.

As if in self defense, Mrs. A. pointed out the elements of her deprived childhood that resembled her daughter's accusatory statements. Yet her daughter was not ready to exonerate her mother.

Mrs. P.: But I needed you so badly after the birth of Sandra. I was overwhelmed and felt you abandoned me. When I tried to tell you how I felt, you gave me a trite answer, "It will pass; your baby is so beautiful you should be completely happy."

Mrs. A.: I didn't know what you really wanted. You had a nurse, and you knew I could not just pick up and go down there.

Mrs. P.: I needed mothering! I don't want to blame you.

Both agreed that in the past they were both so busy protecting each other and themselves that they essentially had been unavailable to each other. When Mrs. A. used to hear her daughter crying, instead of comforting her she would go into her own room and cry too. Rarely had there been any direct expression of tenderness or comforting between them. Yet Mrs. P. was constantly left feeling guilty about all she had received from her mother, while having no opportunity for repayment. As a result of trying to be an extension of her mother's wishes, she did not know internally who or what she was. First they needed to spell out the intergenerational disappointment before they could begin to rebalance their relationship.

Mrs. P.: I always tried to make up or do for my mother all that had been denied to her in her childhood—and also because my mother was in such a miserable marriage. I could never understand why you stayed with my father—he has been such a horrible person.

Therapist: Mrs. A., were you aware that your daughter felt this way?

The therapist used what Boszormenyi-Nagy calls, "multidirectional partiality" in being directly available to Mrs. A. as well as to Mrs. P. Having listened to Mrs. A. recount her past family life, the therapist inquired about her current marital relationship.

Mrs. A.: I never heard her say these things. I don't know if I was trying to live my life through my children. I never wanted my daughter to martyr herself.

Therapist: What about your marital relationship—is it the entire picture? Did the children know what you had seen in your husband that had attracted you? Was the marriage always as stormy as your daughter has described it?

Mrs. A.: My husband was a very difficult person—and maybe I was difficult too. I'm shocked that my daughter sees things this way. After the children left home, my husband and I had a much better period than before—until he became seriously ill. Then Mr. A. became disturbed, overly demanding, and very difficult. I went to work because I could not be locked up in the apartment with him day and night. Mr. A.'s sister stayed with him during the day.

Therapist: You spoke with great pride about being a very independent individual—which is an asset or strength—but had you ever considered that it could in turn, shut out the other person?

Mrs. A.: I never considered that it might have this effect. As a matter of fact, I always thought I was very sensitive to other people's feelings. I never wanted to hurt anyone and so at times this kept me from saying openly what I thought or felt.

Therapist.: Do you both want to try to overcome this lifetime pattern—to become more open and direct with each other, to share and be affectionate? What you could give to each other is so tightly locked within yourselves.

The therapist suggested to all of them that they might wish to arrange other sessions to include Mrs. A., but it was their decision to make.

Therapist: (*to Mr. P.*) You have been silent throughout—are you willing to share your reactions?

Mr. P.: I was astonished. Last night when the three of us talked, everything was addressed to and through me. My wife was silent then. I am very pleased that she brought this much out into the open with her mother—a good beginning!

Interlocking Individual and Familial Dynamics

As an individual, Mrs. P. could be described as dependent, repressed, anxious, isolated, detached from her internal world. Although married, she was not available emotionally or sexually to her husband. Her child was a playmate who could be tolerated in a loving way only for several hours a day; the child's needs were experienced as a burden. Mrs. P. also suffered from headaches and colitis. These issues could make valid areas of exploration in individual therapy—or the couple's complaints could constitute a basis for marital therapy.

Yet, in this session with her mother, it was clear that she had remained in a hostile, overtly detached but dependent relationship with her parents. As her mother described her relationship with her own family of origin, it also became evident that she, too, had been bound in a guilt-laden, exploited way and, in turn, had martyred herself for her children. Both were pseudo-adequate, deprived, sexually and emotionally frozen women. Out of loyalty and indebtedness they both performed a similar function within their nuclear families. As a result of their unrequited primary indebtedness and loyalty ties, neither one was really available to the other or able to commit herself either emotionally or sexually to her marital partner or children.

Viewed in an intergenerational perspective, Mr. and Mrs. P. both came from families in which children were exploited and parentified. Mr. P.'s parents, who had also been parentified children in their own nuclear families, were alternately rejecting, distancing, and seductive with their son. Mr. P.'s father, who worked a fifty-hour week, had limited time available for parenting. Mrs. P.'s parents, while being over-available, were controlling, manipulative, and demanding of too high performance.

Mr. P.'s parents were unwilling to come to sessions until the end of the second year of therapy. Their direct participation at that time facilitated the major changes that ensued. It must be stressed again, however, that much was accomplished as a result of the emphasis placed on both sets of grandparents and siblings regardless of whether they attended the sessions.

Some Therapeutic Improvements

The young couple, their daughter, infant son, and both sets of parents were treated for two years on a once-a-week basis. When requested, individual and extra sessions were provided.

By focusing on and changing the behavior in the marital relationship as well as in the relationships with each one's family of origin, the following improvements occurred:

1. Mrs. P. became sexually orgastic, and the emotional quality of the marital relationship was greatly improved.
2. The first baby had been unwanted and unplanned, and the pregnancy a very difficult one. During therapy they mutually decided that they now felt differently about parenthood. Mrs. P. gave birth to a son six months before treatment was terminated.
3. Toward the end of treatment, Mr. P. stated, "I know now that my wife is the best friend I've ever had in my entire life!"
4. Mrs. P.'s brother and her husband's sister, who lived hundreds of miles away and initially had seemed "out" of the family, moved in to share equally the responsibility for their aging and ill par-

ents. Phone calls, letters, and special visits were encouraged, including family reunions.

5. More positive exchanges developed between the families of origin and the in-law system. Initially a "cold war" had existed.

CONCLUSIONS

Some of the negative, guilt-producing aspects of the family system that are often unconsciously lived out or projected onto the marital partner or onto the children may be rebalanced in constructive action between the generations. The goal is to help produce fundamental and lasting changes between nuclear and extended family members.

In order to work through, or rebalance, relationships so that such change can take place, there must first be open recognition of the injustices and loyalty present in all three generations. However, abreaction, while necessary, is a superficial dimension compared with the time and effort required to reconstruct family relationships. Mere confrontation has the quality of human "exploitation" rather than the kind of mutual gain or growth process that family therapists are trying to promote. What is essential is a gain in basic trust and an attitude of helping every family member regardless of age or phase in life. As a matter of fact, it has been found in some instances, that grandparents may be less rigid and fixated than younger family members.

In intergenerational therapy, grandparents are invited to become active participants in ongoing sessions. Rather than being "used" as a target for the frustrations of the marital couple, they become "patients" in their own right. The grandparents together with all family members are provided equal opportunity to face and mutually rebalance the unrequited loyalty ties and denied indebtedness.

REFERENCES

1. Anonymous, "Toward the Differentiation of a Self in One's Own Family," in Framo, J., (Ed.), *Family Interaction*, New York, Springer Publishing Company, 1972, pp. 111–166.
2. BEATMAN, F. L., "Intergenerational Aspects of Family Therapy," in N. W. Ackerman (Ed.)., *Expanding Theory and Practice in Family Therapy*, New York, Family Service Association of America, 1967, pp. 29–38.
3. BOSZORMENYI-NAGY, I., "A Theory of Relationships: Experiences and Transaction," in Boszormenyi-Nagy, I and Framo, J. L., (Eds.) *Intensive Family Therapy*, New York, Harper and Row, 1965, pp. 33–86.

4. BOSZORMENYI-NAGY, I. and SPARK, G. M., *"Invisible Loyalties: Reciprocity in Intergenerational Family Therapy,* (see especially chapt. 1-7), New York, Harper and Row, 1973.

5. BOWEN, M., "The Use of Family Theory in Clinical Practice," *Compr. Psychiat.,* 7: 345-374, 1966.

Reprint requests may be addressed to Geraldine M. Spark, Family Psychiatry Division, Eastern Pennsylvania Psychiatric Institute, Henry Avenue and Abbottsford Road, Philadelphia, Pennsylvania, 19129.

Anne O. Freed

The family agency and the kinship system of the elderly

The experience of many social workers with the aged is
one-sided in those situations when the personal
support systems of the clients disintegrate

Anne O. Freed is director of professional services,
Family Service Association of Greater Boston,
Boston, Massachusetts.

When social workers are asked to discuss the aging, they inevitably conjure up dramatic case vignettes:

An elderly lady keeping everyone at bay, upsetting the family, and accusing relatives of mean acts.

An alcoholic old man living alone and ill, forgotten by his family, having abandoned them years ago.

An eighty-year-old man recently married to a twenty-year-old psychotic girl, to the distress of his grown children.

A sixty-five-year-old woman asking about divorce from her eighty-year-old husband because he plans to be buried next to the grave of his first wife who died thirty-five years ago.

A son or daughter, struggling with mixed feelings, asking about placing a mother in a nursing home.

An elderly man reviling his children for having put him in a home.

Unfortunately, it is natural for many social workers to think initially of family breakdowns, unresolved problems, and a malfunctioning service system as they view the final phase of the life cycle. The experience of many of them as professionals is one-sided, since the problems with the elderly arise from the disintegration of personal support systems of those who come for help. Being involved with problem-ridden and pathology-focused situations, these professionals understandably overlook the numerous instances in which the natural kinship system is working to support the elderly. Instead they develop an image of themselves as surrogate kin, in contrast with their actual practice.

Margaret Blenkner is unduly harsh on contemporary social work when she asserts, in her article *Social Work and Family Relationships in Later Life*,[1] that its emphasis has been on helping people to separate from the family, thereby concentrating too much on the isolated nuclear family instead of supporting and encouraging the kinship system. If family casework with the aged as actually practiced is a valid criterion this is not true. When an elderly person approaches a family agency, the first casework step is to see if a family is in the client's picture. Unfortunately, a considerable number of the elderly referred to a family agency simply have no family ties. In some instances, however, children or siblings of aged clients do come in to request help for their relatives. They are as-

_____

[1]Margaret Blenkner, Social Work and Family Relationships in Later Life With Some Thoughts on Filial Maturity, in *Social Structure and the Family*, ed. Ethel Shanes and Gordon E. Streib (Englewood Cliffs, N.J.: Prentice Hall, 1965).

suming responsibility, and the agency tries to support them in that role. Generally, they want help for the elderly by specific services, such as homemaker service, transportation, financial assistance, medical care, handling of mental illness, nursing home information, replacing lost Supplemental Security Income checks, housing problems and so forth. The agency uses these services to build upon the supports offered by available kin.

Actual experience with the aged demonstrates that a primary casework goal is to help them and their families find their own linkages with the various support systems in the community. Relatives often do not know the resources available and turn to the agency for guidance. Asked their role, the staff of Service for Older People unit of Family Service Association of Greater Boston comment along these lines: "We are information givers and coordinators. We help the family and the aged client connect with the community resources. We assemble a whole array of supports for them. If there is no natural family, we become its substitute." In light of the complexity of society and the multiplying needs of the elderly, who are living longer, it is not only the aged person himself, but also his relatives who need help in identifying and obtaining resources. Frequently, the relatives assume responsibility once they receive the necessary information. Unfortunately, both they and their elderly relatives need help in maneuvering within and among the several governmental systems they encounter, a task that requires great sophistication.

In assessing Blenkner's observations, it is essential to employ the perspective on society provided by Eugene Litwak, in his analysis of the extended kinship system.[2] His is a refreshing reminder that we function in a broad society that is not merely a web of insoluble difficulties, and that many of the elderly manage to maintain themselves in the community independently, relying on the emotional and social support of relatives—spouses, children, siblings, nieces, and nephews—who provide a network of mutual aid. Similarly, Simone de Beauvoir, in her comprehensive study on aging, quotes many studies in numerous countries, including the United States, showing that the largest number of elderly persons are closely tied to their kin.[3] Erik H. Erikson, in his discussion of the cycle of generations, sees:

Man's psychosocial survival [as] safeguarded only by vital virtues which develop in the interplay of successive and overlapping generations, living together in organized settings. Here, living together means more than incidental proximity. It means that the individual's life stages are 'interliving,' cogwheeling with the stages of others which move him along as he moves them[4]

He defines this as the concept of mutuality—the generations need each other.

In addition to traditional kinship supports, the elderly receive an expanding array of governmental and other aids, including Social Security, Supplemental Security Income, Medicare, Medicaid, Medex, homemaker services, home care corporation services, Meals-on-Wheels, day centers, telephone reassurance programs, nutrition centers, and residences for elderly. In this way, governmental and private social services increasingly share the support functions with the family. Litwak refers to this as "The Shared Function Theory." While many of these resources are inadequate or poorly distributed, especially when compared with those in Scandinavian countries whose variety of services is enviable, nevertheless our own list is growing steadily.

It is illuminating to examine Mr. Litwak's observations on the various kinds of

[2]Eugene Litwak, Extended Kin Relations in an Industrial Democratic Society, in *Social Structure and the Family*, ed. Shanes and Streib (Englewood Cliffs, N.J.: Prentice Hall, 1965), pp. 290-323.

[3]Simone de Beauvoir, *The Coming of Age* (New York: G. P. Putnam's Sons, 1972), p. 248.

[4]Erik H. Erikson, Human Strength and the Cycle of Generations, in *Insight & Responsibility* (New York: W. W. Norton, 1964).

family systems in an industrial democratic society. He describes four generic family structures as they relate to kinship systems: the extended family, the dissolving family, the isolated nuclear family, and the modified extended family. The first is found in traditional old societies where the family is a complete economic and political unit composed of nuclear subfamilies living in the same house or nearby. The other extreme is the dissolving family structure, in which practically all functions are performed by formal organizations, leaving only the husband and wife relationship. In the third, the isolated nuclear family is composed solely of husband, wife, and children, and the essential functions are performed by the single family. Between the extended and nuclear system is the one, he suggests, that is most common in our society, the modified extended family consisting of a "coalition of nuclear families in a state of partial dependence," where members "exchange significant services with each other," yet retain autonomy and are not "bound economically or geographically."[5]

In a typical large family agency, Family Service Association of Greater Boston, for example, most of the families served fall into the modified extended family system, although the aged are increasingly in dissolving families. Confronted with the dissolving family among the aged, the agency is called upon by the elderly clients, their families, or the community to offer protective services, to assemble and coordinate community resources if the elderly person is to be maintained in his home, or to make the serious decisions that most families must make themselves regarding relocation or institutionalization. Where the family support system is not available, or is too weak, indecisive, or conflicted, the family agency virtually becomes the surrogate family.

While in many cases modified extended families may be adept at using the fairly complex community systems and re-sources, frequently they are ill-prepared to handle the interpersonal relationships arising in the role reversal involved when adult children help their parents. Often they do not want to talk about their own feelings with regard to their parents. As Clara Rosenthal states: ". . . we have not been too successful in involving the middle generation—adult and child—in a case-work relationship around his feeling about aging parents and how these affect and often hinder planning."[6] These two generations usually are seen by agencies during a crisis that brings them together. The social worker is brought into the midst of a shift in family equilibrium and the conflict that ensues. Elias Stavitsky and Harold Sharkey, in a speech before the Boston Society for Gerontologic Psychiatry (1970), point out why it is so difficult to work with these families. During a crisis, they observe:

The adult children's capacity to tolerate being a person depended upon by the parents is tested, as is the aged person's capacity to handle dependency feelings upon the children. Since such feelings are often fraught with disturbances dating from earlier life experience, we may note a reactivation of prior psychopathologic patterns.[7]

Family service clients and their kinship systems

In an analysis of the clients of the nonsectarian family agency cited in terms of Mr. Litwak's schema, the distribution among the several groups he identifies, including one for the already dissolved family, is noteworthy:

1. The isolated, impoverished, and physically disabled elderly, usually friend-

[5]Litwak, Extended Kin Relations in an Industrial Democratic Society, p. 291.

[6]Clara Rosenthal, Casework With the Aging—An Intergenerational Approach, unpublished paper, presented at F.S.A.A. Biennial Conference, San Francisco, Calif., November 15, 1963.

[7]Elias Savitsky and Harold Sharkey, Study of Family Interaction in the Aged, *Journal of Geriatric Psychiatry*, 5:3-19 (1972).

less, with few, if any, close family ties, comprise what is probably the largest group. They are unable to obtain alone the available life-sustaining services; some need protective services. With the present pressure to maintain people in their own homes or rooming houses much longer than in the past, an increasing number of these people are seen by the agency. They are from truly dissolved families. They form the lonely fourth of the elderly about whom Simone de Beauvoir reported. Most live in rooming houses or in public housing. It sometimes is suggested that insufficient efforts are made to reach their families. But the seventy-five-and eighty-year-olds in the caseloads (there being very few "young" elderly) frequently have no families whatsoever, or no remaining ties because of a long history of serious personal problems resulting in insuperable ruptures.

A number of these clients are schizoids or former alcoholics, whose relationships to their spouses and children are at best tenuous, if they are not totally estranged from them; they are distancing and isolating people. The community turns them over to agencies for help. Generally, their difficult personalities make them unattractive to most people. At best, the agency tries to help them use such resources as nutrition programs, medical facilities, day centers, and homemaker services, if needed.

Two case examples should help illustrate these kinds of very unhappy people:

Mr. K, age 78, was brought to the agency's attention by his neighbors because of illness and personal neglect. Having deserted his family in his thirties, he had not been in contact with them for decades. In fact, he did not even know where they lived, whether his children were married or single, if he had grandchildren, or if his wife was alive. A schizoid, isolated old man, he had no one to turn to. Only a neighbor and landlord were aware of his existence.

Mrs. P became psychotic early in her marriage, and was hospitalized for a number of years. Her two children were placed in foster homes; one was retarded and later institutionalized. She visited that child occasionally. Her other child was a "drifter" whom she had not seen in years. When she became ill, impoverished, and unable to manage, she turned to an old family friend, who in turn called in the agency.

Serving these clients entails many hours of telephone calls in contacting welfare departments, visiting nurses, Meals-on-Wheels, homemakers, clinics, councils of the elderly, home care corporations, and so forth. Frequently, the clients in this group are referred during a life-threatening crisis, and the agency is called upon to assess the situation, track down any available relatives, make a diagnostic evaluation, and finally assemble the variety of necessary services. All support functions are taken over by governmental and private institutions; none is retained by the family.

2. The next largest group includes the aged from dissolving families. Some relatives, but very few, remain in the picture. The aged person, once independent and relating well to kin, now is widowed and either childless or with his children scattered; he is depressed, grieving the loss of spouse and friends. Such a person does not necessarily have a long history of pathology and disastrous interpersonal relationships.

Mr. J was just such a man in his late 70's. Still grieving the loss of his wife, he was sick, suffering from malnutrition, and ignoring his personal care. He had been emotionally dependent on his wife and could not function without her. He had two siblings, a physically disabled sister, whom he rarely visited, and a brother who appeared only in emergencies, an angry man who avoided involvement. Mr. J had brought up these siblings. He came to the agency seeking money when his Supplemental Security Insurance check had not arrived. In addition to providing a series of supportive services, the worker worked to help Mr. J, as he grieved the loss of his wife. No concrete services could be truly meaningful or helpful so long as he continued to mourn her.

3. As in most agencies, very few nuclear elderly families come for counseling. Caseworkers see mostly individuals and kin. However, as with clients in other

stages of life, they do get some requests for marital counseling. Recently, two social-work students organized a group of six elderly couples experiencing marital problems. The managers of two housing projects brought them to the agency's attention. Formerly living in large homes in old neighborhoods, they had recently relocated to small apartments in low-income housing for the elderly. In an unfamiliar locale and a tiny apartment with no space between them, their marital disharmony, long under control, broke out. As neighbors complained of their bickering and the spouses complained about each other, the project directors soon became involved. These people agreed to meet to talk about their move, their loneliness for old quarters and neighbors, their fears and depression, their dislike of small cramped quarters, and finally their resentment toward each other. When interviewing them, the student social workers observed their smoldering hostility and ambivalence, their conflict regarding dependence and independence, their games at distancing, and their talk of how their children had kept them together all these years. Their old defenses and old feelings were crumbling.

4. Finally, small groups of aging clients come from modified extended families. In such cases, the workers are happily able to offer casework service to both the client and the family. Caseworkers like these situations primarily because the clients generally do not require protective services from the agency which would force the workers to assume the family role.

A good example is Mr. C, whose sister called upon the agency to help her formerly alcoholic, aged brother, a man who had had difficulty for years in relating to his children. Now in his 70's, he was ashamed of his general failure and avoided his family. Although he insisted that he wanted to be "independent," it was evident to the caseworker and his sister that he no longer could live alone. A married younger son was contacted. After considerable discussion, he invited his father to live with him. Like an adolescent, Mr. C literally ran away. The worker's primary task was to help Mr. C face reality. Accepting his feelings, she helped him examine his alternatives, which were either living with his son or in a group home. The latter he dreaded. Working with the son, the caseworker focused on the normal problems of a three-generation family, exacerbated here by the father's history of poor interpersonal relations. Interestingly, in this case, once the elderly father accepted his situation realistically and the son sympathized with the father's dilemma, Mr. C settled in "like a lamb," the worker reported. "He knew it was the end of the line and he could adapt."

Unfortunately, some modified extended families' relationships do not lend themselves to successful resolution. Such was the case of Mr. and Mrs. R.

A former chemical engineer sales manager, Mr. R traveled a good deal and was away from home frequently. He was a quarrelsome, domineering man, narcissistic and demanding. His wife and two sons tolerated him because of his frequent absences. Although Mrs. R thought of divorce on many occasions, she decided to keep the family together. The sons, as soon as they went off to college, resolved never to return home to live. Each married upon graduation, and one moved to Florida. The younger son lived nearby, visiting his mother when his father was away. Trouble started in earnest when Mr. R retired. Neighbors reported fierce, loud battles between the couple. The mental health clinic they applied to after a series of institutional placements for Mr. R became concerned with Mrs. R's pattern of withdrawing her husband from treatment when he seemed to improve. Mr. R's hearing was poor, he had numerous neurological problems, and at times he was disoriented. In addition, his demands and quarrelsome behavior increased in his old age. When Mr. and Mrs. R were seen together, he pathetically pictured himself as a loving man, proud of his sons, suffering from old age, and living with a wife who did not understand him. He clung to the fantasy that his sons loved him and would care for him. As he talked in a very loud voice, Mrs. R, aware of his deafness, maintained a parallel conversation, giving a contrary account. The sons confirmed their mother's tales and acknowledged that she did not want to see him improved, yet could not live without him. When the worker tried to engage them in planning, they turned a deaf ear, claiming that they could not change their mother, and hated their father. They felt that she should have left him years ago. With that, they vowed to do nothing until a "real crisis arises, like the death of Father and the need to decide what to do with Mother." This is an example of a case in which the emotional support system of kinship simply breaks down even though the kin are actively involved in the situation. Such families turn to the agency only at times of crises but refuse to prevent the crises from occurring and cannot face their own conflicting feelings.

Casework problems in work with the elderly and their kin

There are a number of particular casework problems in working with the elderly and their kin. Regretfully, the case of Mr. and Mrs. R is not atypical of the type of negative kinship system that presents a serious challenge to caseworkers. However, if the extended modified family has even a spark of relationship left, the caseworkers try to build on it in order to help the client. At times, this attempt can be successful. Unfortunately, when the elderly person is the primary client, families are not normally encountered as readily and as early as would be preferred. In contrast, geriatric institutions frequently meet the families at the point of application. In family agency involvements, elderly clients often do not want to let their children or relatives know of their plight. At times, they claim that their children live far away, that they have no relatives, or that they do not want to bother them. Similarly, they state that their children have their own worries and problems and should not be burdened further, which frequently is true. Caseworkers then try to help them understand that they will share the burdens with the relatives.

Mrs. P, referred to us by a nursing home for purposes of relocation back to the community, denied knowing the whereabouts of her son. When he found her and contacted us, she admitted that she felt sorry for him because he had many problems. He acted as if he wanted to help her until the worker asked about finances, whereupon he disappeared. When located and assured that the Department of Public Welfare and the agency were not expecting his financial support, he became an asset by helping his mother move to an apartment and visiting her occasionally.

When the nuclear family itself is the primary client, there is a risk that the aged member of the family will be overlooked by the agency. A family-centered casework approach, however, should draw the elderly into family interviews, recognizing their roles in the family, which are usually dynamically important. This casework orientation is essential to bring forth otherwise hidden, unidentified clients whose influences in the family are strong.

One of the most trying types of cases involving the elderly encountered by family agencies is the mother and unwed adult child dyad. These situations involve the middle-aged children, who, dutifully or otherwise, are caring for the aging mother and are resenting it. Unable to assert themselves emotionally, they struggle with many unresolved feelings about being the unfavored, the less loved, or the neglected children. They see themselves as making major sacrifices to help the parent. They resent living with or caring for the mother, but cannot live without her. Ambivalence and guilt are characteristic. Like sado-masochistic marriages, hostile, dependent, and antagonistically symbiotic issues are constantly acted out. They have not attained the stage of "filial maturity" which Margaret Blenkner considers essential for the middle-aged child. Theirs is a filial immaturity fixated on earlier life stages. The mother's demands, manipulations, and dependency control the relationship in an infantilizing way. As this kind of parent grows older, the conflict sharpens because the middle-aged child still wants parenting from the mother who now needs to be parented. Role confusion, role conflict, and communication difficulties magnify the problems.

Emotional stresses in role reversal

Role reversal of the type just discussed is a pervasive factor in working with the elderly. Casework with the aged and their families takes place at the painful moment when the formerly strong supports for the elderly are dissolving and the sources of new supports have not yet been formulated. The homeostasis is disintegrating. Siblings and spouse are ailing or dead and the kin the aged depended upon in past life-crises are unavailable. The children find it painful to recognize that their parents' capabilities and productivity are declining and that not only are they no longer a source of strength for them but have even become dependent upon them and their grandchildren. This dependency has a special impact on middle-aged children, drained on all sides by financial burdens. At the same time that they are called on to help their aging parents, they have to meet the expanding needs of their own growing families; simultaneously, society, through the tax structure, demands that those middle-aged children provide funds for governmental operations. The financial toll is enormous. For some, these accumulated pressures are intolerable, especially when their own needs appear to be ignored. They cannot easily reject their children; they cannot refuse to pay their taxes. The only outlet for their frustrations is to try to defend themselves against the demands of their aging parents.

A particularly serious stress in role reversal of the families of aged parents arises when painful action must be taken to help them relocate, accept their physical or mental disabilities, or, at the extreme, to place them in an institution. Stanley Cath describes this poignantly:

As they [the adult children] confront each other, facing the compelling and intense necessity for deciding the fate of a parent, many new and old conflicts arise. A reservoir of conscious and unconscious affect-laden memories, experiences and traumatic upsets become a family resource to be called upon under stress. The decision that amounts in effect to the final annihilation of a parental image and way of life requires long working through. Its finality activates deeply buried unresolved conflicts that include realization of unconscious oedipal and sadistic-ridden wishes with the reactivation of early fears of retaliation for aggression, greed, and sibling rivalry. Each member of the family now faces within himself the realization of all-too-human death wishes coped with from our younger years.[8]

[8]Stanley Cath, The Institutionalization of a Parent: A Nadir of Life, *Journal of Geriatric Psychiatry*, 5:25-46 (1972).

A substitute kinship system

Since kin provide an important measure of support to the elderly, their absence leaves a serious vacuum. Caseworkers and friendly visitors fill the gap when called upon. A number of valuable supplementary systems can be developed by enterprising professionals. For example, it might be feasible to develop a new system of foster kin for those without natural kin. The foster-grandparents program is directed toward helping needy children, and, incidentally, bringing satisfaction to elderly people. It seems advisable to reverse that model with an "adopt-a-grandparent" program. Although such a program must be organized on a neighborhood basis, many types of neighborhoods are fertile ground. Young families without grandparents might be interested in joining such a program. The clients who live in housing projects and rooming houses are extremely lonesome. For those whose personalities permit, a new foster-family relationship could be most welcome. Certainly around the times of the year that can be depressive, such as holidays and special days, substitute family relationships could help make those ordinarily painful times actually enjoyable. This approach seems to provide a means for supplying much needed emotional support as well as sheer sociability. It is hoped that this relatively simple example might suggest a number of other approaches by which existing serious deficiencies in the normal kinship system can be overcome.

Conclusion

In summary, when the kinship system is working successfully in the extended modified family, "acts of filial and kin responsibility are performed voluntarily without law and compulsion."[9] But when the system breaks down and there is need

[9]Marvin Sussman and Lee Burchinal, Kin Family Network: Unheralded Structure in Current Conceptualizations of Family Functioning, in *Middle Age and Aging*, ed. Bernice Neugarten (Chicago: University of Chicago Press, 1968), p. 252.

for help either by the kin or the elderly themselves, then the family agency is called upon either to share the functions with the kin or to act in lieu of them. Essentially, the agency tries to rely on the kinship system to enable it to perform its role. The family agency participates more fully only when supplemental help or protective services are needed to help the elderly and their families cope with the problems of aging. The agency assumes responsibility when the elderly or the kin no longer can perform.

A theoretical analysis of selected problems related to aging in contemporary society and their
implication for professional services to the aged are presented. Expansion of social work
curricula to include gerontological content, the use of group process, and the application of
videotape techniques are suggested as possible means of alleviating these problems.

Group Work with the Aging

An Issue for Social Work Education

Nazneen S. Mayadas, DSW,[2] and Douglas L. Hink, PhD[3]

The ideas presented herein stem from the experiences of the two authors in practice with the aged, group therapy, and the use of audiovisual techniques in education and social work practice. The result is intended to suggest teaching and practice possibilities in applying knowledge of group dynamics and visual aids as a means of providing service to the aged. Both theoretical and empirical literature related to groups suggests that man's sense of alienation is reduced and his social functioning enhanced when he interacts with others within the context of a group (Lieberman, Yalom, & Miles, 1973). Based on this thinking, the authors suggest that the aged, who perhaps are one of the most alienated and neglected members of society, could benefit by this method of service to adjust to an entire range of life style changes regardless of whether intervention is instituted at the time of a particular crisis, or when the individual feels a vague discontent with the prospect of growing old.

The material to follow concentrates on the concept of educating potential social workers to provide group services for elderly individuals who are physically able to function adequately, but whose social life may vary considerably. Since the definition of "aged" is as nebulous in professional terminology as in one's own self-appraisal or estimation of others, the question of what constitutes "old" becomes crucial. However, for the purpose of this paper, aged will include all those persons who consider themselves to be in the latter part of life for whatever reason.

Group Work and Aging

A review of selected literature in the area of group work with the aged indicates few attempts to involve the functioning, noninstitutionalized older adult. The limited number of controlled studies in this area are with institutionalized older adults in nursing homes, age-segregated housing, and hospitals (Burnside, 1970). The elderly who do not fall into any of the above-mentioned categories often get overlooked in their struggle to adapt to a number of social changes inherent in the transition from an active life to a qualitatively different life style. These are the persons who are obscurely hidden away in independent lodgings and manage to function at a minimal level of adequacy. Their isolation increases their sense of alienation, perpetuating the problem of loneliness, loss, and a gradual degeneration into a prolonged period of relative inactivity. Since hardly any empirical knowledge exists about the adaptation patterns of this category of the aged, it is suggested that the knowledge from the field of small group research may be one way to study the non-institutionalized adult, develop intervention techniques, and improve the methods of service delivery to this segment of the population.

Studies in small group research abound in attempts to empirically investigate concepts such as role-identity, cohesiveness, norms, cooperation versus competitiveness, expectations

1. Based on a paper originally presented at the annual meeting of the Council on Social Work Education, San Francisco, Feb., 1973.
2. Associate Professor, Graduate School of Social Work, Univ. of Texas at Arlington, Arlington, Texas 76010.
3. Formerly Visiting Associate Professor, Graduate School of Social Work, Univ. of Texas at Arlington, Arlington, Texas 76010.

and performance, leadership, social acceptance, and reference groups, to name but a few, as partial explanations of interpersonal behaviors. Through the group process the individual meets his social needs and learns to cope with his environmental demands. Hence the use of this knowledge and the applied strategies of group work are perhaps two of the most relevant and efficient methods of intervention with an age group whose major concern is preservation of identity and a need for acceptance as persons in a society which strives to foster a youth culture and relegates age to a virtually ignominious position in the social structure.

Use of groups in social work has been a major form of service delivery since the early stages of the profession's development (Wilson & Ryland, 1948). As such the application of the principles and techniques of group work to services for and by the senior citizen population is not entirely a novel notion. The literature in this area focuses on activity groups as a means of providing the elderly with the opportunity for social exchange and purposive behavior (Kaplan, 1953; Shore, 1964). Implicit in this approach is the assumption that through structured creative activities such as clubs, camps, service projects, etc., the aged's sense of futility is reduced and his dignity as a worthwhile human being is enhanced. The authors concur with this position and suggest that along with activity-oriented groups the elderly should also be exposed to group encounters in order to enhance their interpersonal awareness for mutuality of support in adjusting to their changing life styles. Hence, selected aspects of teaching the practice of group work with the aged are presented from two perspectives: (1) where the target of service delivery is the individual in terms of his personal and social gains, and (2) where the target of intervention is the community in terms of improved social conditions for a specific group.

Three major assumptions underlie this discussion of specifics in educating students for the practice of group work with the aged. First, society has the responsibility to make service delivery economically and physically accessible to the elderly. Second, social work as a profession has an obligation to the aged since the discipline assumes responsibility for serving all human beings. Third, while some form of structured help should be available, it should be on the basis of choice and not coercion. Individuals often voluntarily select that life style which best suits their psychosocial needs and results

in optimal adjustment with reference to their physical health, financial status, and general environment (Havighurst, Neugarten, & Tobin, 1968; Riesman, 1954; Vickery, 1972). The elderly should be permitted the same right to independence as other members of society to participate in structured group activities, according to their preference.

Some Considerations in Serving the Aged Through Groups

A basic question that arises is related to how does the professional learn to differentiate between those senior adults who have an active interest in joining groups and those who are relatively satisfied with their isolation? First of all, the social worker must be clear as to the purpose he intends to achieve through the group and the outcome goals he has in mind for the members. Second, studies in interpersonal attraction and group cohesion suggest that compatibility of members is perhaps the key variable to a successful group experience (Goldstein, 1971). Prior to deciding whether a person should be in a group, the worker must determine the level of attraction of the person for groups *per se* and specifically for the group (in terms of interpersonal relationships and group goals) he is being invited to join. Another area to consider is the expectation the individual has of himself, the worker, and the group. Since expectations are related to performance outcomes (Mayadas, 1972), it is important that individuals, too, should have clearly formulated goals for what they wish to accomplish through group membership. The individual's past experiences with groups, together with his current social life style, are additional variables to be taken into account in determining the individual's capacity for joining (Vickery, 1972). Perhaps the most important variable is the management of the interpersonal control the worker exercises in imparting to the senior adult his own conviction that the potential group experience will have positive outcomes for the members.

Techniques of working with the elderly can include group discussion and/or recreation as reinforcers of self-worth and role identity. Empirical studies found reminiscing to be a viable tool in helping the elderly cope with current stress by revitalizing their past sense of self-esteem (Pincus, 1970). This technique of reminiscing can be combined with reality testing in the "here and now" to facilitate interpersonal awareness among group members and to provide them with a meaningful sense of direction and purpose. The following are some areas of concern which the authors suggest may be manifested with advanced age and which can be resolved meaningfully within the context of a well-formulated group experience.

Reestablishing or Reaffirming a Sense of Personal Identity

Through the loss of a person, or an object, older individuals may find it difficult to redefine their status in realistic terms. Some people may feel themselves relegated to the nebulous position of simply being "old" by society's definition without any other role that is meaningful. This problem is dramatic when identity has been based primarily on being a worker or a wife. However, there can also exist more subtle problems in self-definition such as a general feeling of lack of direction or purpose. The social worker must be alert to the behavioral cues which suggest role ambiguity and help the individual establish a new sense of identity through group experiences that provide alternative purposive role behaviors (for example, foster grandparent, volunteer worker, craftsman, friendly visitor, or whatever area best fits the individual's needs). These roles can be created for older individuals in the community through organized service groups to which the individual can belong and draw his sustenance in the same manner as he may have done previous to his retirement from membership in a union, club, or civic organization. The organized service groups can serve not only as a liaison between the senior citizen and the community, but also provide the opportunity for intimate discussions where the senior volunteer can share his experience with others in similar situations and benefit from the therapeutic aspects of the group process.

However, the need for new activities for status identity requires more consideration than a simple listing of alternatives as above. Such alternatives require the consideration of three primary situational questions. First, what are the psychosocial needs of the individual? The social worker should be familiarized with the various personality theories concerning the elderly and be sensitized to the wide variation in degree of involvement desired by older persons. An interesting anecdote illustrates this point well. Two old ladies living in the same house made daily entries in their diaries. The

two entries read respectively: "Nobody came to see me today," and "Nobody came to see me today, thank God!" (Field, 1968). Second, what new roles are possible given currently available possibilities or what roles can be offered through the instigation of the social worker? As suggested above, foster grandparents, senior advisor to small businessmen, volunteer advisor in the church and educational field, and VISTA are examples of currently established programs designed to involve older people. However, the social worker may well find certain capabilities in individuals that cannot be utilized in organized group programs. It is then his responsibility to investigate the development of new programs in which role expression can take place. Finally, the worker must take into cognizance whether the role activity is accessible to the person. Too often concrete problems such as the location of the program are overlooked by workers in suggesting or developing new role behaviors for the senior individual. The time factor is another consideration in program planning. Agencies providing structured program activities for the elderly have seldom thought it necessary to replicate a workday situation. However, note should be taken of one experience where participation in a group center increased among men when hours were changed from the evening to normal working hours, i.e., 9 am to 5 pm. For retirees it may be important to make leisure activities structurally similar to a work situation.

Maintenance of the Sex Role

It seems worthwhile to single out the sex role for special emphasis since it has been so often neglected in work with the elderly. Research in sexual activity of the elderly also has suffered from a tendency to avoid this "taboo" subject (Rubin, 1967; Vickery, 1972). The stereotype of the aged as a physically unattractive and sexless society is well illustrated by the following extract from the memoirs of the aging Maise:

> Curiosity, yes, she couldn't let go of wanting to know, but the connotation was innocent because she was sexless, neither male nor female (DeGrazia, 1961).

To counteract the social stigma associated with the physical aspect of aging, the use of videotape feedback along with peer feedback in groups is strongly suggested as a method of enabling the elderly to maintain their sex identity. One of the major functions of group encounter is to provide mutual feedback. This potential for seeing one's self from the other's vantage point is greatly enhanced with the instant replay capability of videotapes, which provides an excellent opportunity for self-viewing and checking out the congruence between one's socially projected image, one's own self-perception, and the actual recorded image. The instant, direct feedback of the videotape also acts as a self-corrective device in reducing perceptual distortions about one's self-image (Mayadas & O'Brien, 1973; Stoller, 1968). For the elderly whose self-concept may be undergoing a change due to their changing physical appearance and loss of role identity, viewing themselves on tape in the presence of interacting others may lead to a greater self-awareness and self-acceptance as a sexual being. A positive image of one's body is an integral part of maintaining the sex role and general attractiveness. Therefore, areas of concern such as body carriage, appropriateness of dress, interpersonal postures, speech patterns, nonverbal gestures, mannerisms, and general social skills are to be taken into consideration in utilizing this technique.

In conjunction with identity and role behaviors of the elderly in groups, three attendant needs of the elderly should be considered:

(1) *A sense of belonging.*—While some older persons do disengage from interaction and seem most content in a solitary existence, others may desire social interaction. For these individuals the sharing and cohesion experienced in a group is a meaningful experience. Such persons may actually find isolation painful and anxiety-producing. Carp (1966) describes two interviews with an elderly woman, 14 months apart. In the first she was disheveled, ailing, and the epitome of loneliness. In the second, she was an active, well-groomed, and out-going individual, enjoying a meaningful heterosexual relationship. The miracle of change occurred after she joined a group of her contemporaries and once again experienced herself as a worthwhile person, earning among her new contacts the nickname of "cricket!" In this regard it is, of course, important to make those older people who wish to engage in interaction aware that help is available. The use of television may be more effective than newspaper announcements in communicating the existence of group programs to the elderly. The American Association of Retired People's television campaign is a good example of the use of this medium in reaching people over 60.

(2) *Cooperation among the elderly.*—The social worker needs to develop skills in avoiding the pitfalls involved in highly competitive situations in working with older persons. While a normal part of the rest of the life-span, competition may be extremely threatening and potentially damaging in the later years. Field's study suggests that to guard against failures to achieve, the elderly may overplay their failing strength as a face-saving device and virtually sink into invalidism to avoid competitive situations (Field, 1968). The worker should be exposed to methods of promoting cooperation. Group projects which foster interdependence and sharing can bring satisfactions through cooperative behaviors and achievement of common goals.

(3) *Task achievement.*—Finally, in working with older people in groups social workers should be urged to strive to provide the elderly with a feeling of achievement. Studies in the area of task achievement suggest that probability of successful outcomes leads to higher aspiration levels (Zander, 1968). For the aged, whose sense of self-worth may be at a low ebb, gratification from task accomplishment is important and the worker must help them select realistic goals where gratification is immediate and perceptible. When the activities provide no apparent result, the relative impotence of the elderly can get reinforced and result in a despondent belief that they are no longer capable of contributing to society.

Group techniques with the elderly need not only be supportive in terms of maintenance of personal identity and self-worth but can be used also to implement societal change. A recent newspaper article (Jan., 1973) described the "Gray Panther" movement, an activist group of senior adults in Philadelphia, who organized to implement social and institutional changes with regard to the social position of the elderly. Another article describes how a senior citizens group in Dallas has drawn up its own Bill of Rights demanding individuality, self-help, rehabilitation, and sexuality (Feb., 1974). Questions such as the impact of such groups on the community come to mind. Must the societal image of the elderly change before such groups can be influential in securing the rights they are fighting for, or can groups such as these change the societal image and status of the elderly? The above illustrations at least suggest an attempt toward the second conjecture. Social work researchers, educators, and students of gerontology can contribute a great deal in areas such as these through developing practice principles and putting them to empirical tests in actual organization of groups manned by the elderly for service delivery and system change.

Educating Social Workers in Gerontology: A General Statement

Aging is conceptualized as part of the continuum of human growth—as a process which starts with birth and eventually terminates with death at the end of a life-span. However, there are problems of adjustment and transition which are peculiar to the aged and need special attention. It is suggested here that students be familiarized with the existing theoretical and empirical knowledge available regarding the behavior modes of the aging (Blenkner, 1964, 1965; Cumming & Henry, 1961; Neugarten, 1964; Peck, 1956; Rose, 1965). However, substantive knowledge is not sufficient. In order to acquire some ability to adequately transpose theory to actual practice situations, the student must also be sensitized to individual differences in life styles which negate the stereotypic image of the older individual as dependent, losing command of his physical faculties, and relatively inferior to the more privileged younger adult. Wolk and Wolk (1971) found that younger professionals perceived the aged to function below their realistic ability. Landau's (1962) experience with training social work students supported these findings. She observed a marked absence of empathy in the young students toward the elderly and attributed it to the age differential. She further suggested that this stereotyping of the aged can adversely affect the choice of interventive strategies in work with the aged.

Based on these findings, the burden falls on social work education to create in the students an awareness of the psychology of aging along with an understanding of the crucial events, philosophies, and welfare policies which had a critical impact on the pre-1930-depression generation.

Another area which must be explicitly brought to the awareness of the social work student is the indices he should use in determining the social class of his elderly client. It is suggested that in determining social status, factors such as highest income relative to today's inflated dollar, furniture and art objects in the dwelling, the average years of schooling, etc., should be taken into account. Immediate cues, such as housing, physical appearance, current level of income, etc., are not necessarily appropriate indicators of social class and hence should not bias the interpersonal postures to be assumed by professionals in establishing contact with the elderly.

A factor to be taken into consideration when preparing the practitioner for work with the elderly is the possible disparity between the professional's orientation of offering psychological relief and the elderly person's need for very specific, pragmatic help. Often focus has to be on concrete help rather than on an abstract discussion concerning adjustment to existing social reality. The goal in working with the elderly should be to enable them to make adaptive changes in their current environment while taking into consideration their past social position and class affiliation. The more congruent the perception of the elderly is made with their social reality, the greater will be their self-acceptance—which hopefully would enhance their social acceptance . . . "not just add years to their lives, but life to their years" . . . (Weiss, 1971).

Summary

This paper has discussed the phenomenon of aging in a changing society, with its implications for social work education and practice. A survey of both theoretical and empirical social work literature reveals a relative lack in content areas related to aging. In the light of today's trend toward increasing longevity, this appears to be a growing area of concern which falls within the purview of the helping professions. Social work, with its dual emphasis on the individual and his environment, is in a unique position to make a contribution to this area. It is the contention of the authors that principles of group dynamics can be applied to understand and help provide continuing satisfactions to the aging populations through planned manipulation of their interpersonal environment.

An equal emphasis on aging along with other stages of development in the general content of the core curricula is urged. Group work techniques are suggested as one method of creating a social milieu to meet a range of interpersonal needs from recreation to indepth awareness and also, if necessary, to organize groups for community intervention and social change for the elderly.

The directional changes suggested in the content in social work core curricula would tend to produce practitioners better equipped for work with the senior adult and provide the student with a broader understanding of the total field of aging. It is further suggested that, with a growing emphasis on aging, more social work empirical knowledge will be generated in this area and that research efforts would develop to test out some of the postulates and hypotheses that are implicit in this theoretical discussion.

References

Blenkner, M. Developmental considerations and the older client. In J. E. Birren (Ed.), **Relations of development and aging.** Springfield, IL: Charles C Thomas, 1964.

Blenkner, M. Social work and family relationships in later life, with some thoughts on filial maturity. In E. Shanas & G. Streib (Eds.), **Social structures and the family.** Englewood Cliffs, NJ: Prentice Hall, 1965.

Braceland, F. J. Psychological aspects of aging. In C. Vedder & A. Lefkowitz (Eds.), **Problems of the aged.** Springfield, IL: Charles C Thomas, 1965.

Burnside, I. M. Group work with the aged: Selected literature. **Gerontologist,** 1970, **10,** 241-246.

Carp, F. M. **A future for the aged.** Austin: Univ. of Texas, 1966.

Cowgill, D. O. The demography of aging. In A. M. Hoffman (Ed.), **The daily needs and interests of older people.** Springfield, IL: Charles C Thomas, 1970.

Cumming, E., & Henry, W. E. **Growing old.** New York: Basic Books, 1961.

DeGrazia, S. The use of time. In R. W. Kleemeier (Ed.), **Aging and Leisure.** New York: Oxford Univ. Press, 1961.

Field, M. **Aging with honor and dignity.** Springfield, IL: Charles C Thomas, 1968.

Goldstein, A. P. **Psychotherapeutic attraction.** New York: Pergamon Press, 1971.

Havighurst, R. J., Neugarten, B. L., & Tobin, S. S. Personality and patterns of aging. In B. L. Neugarten (Ed.), **Middle age and aging.** Chicago: Univ. of Chicago Press, 1968.

Kaplan, J. **A social program for older people.** Minneapolis: Lund Press, 1953.

Laudau, G. The role of day centers in changing attitudes of personnel toward the aging. In J. Kaplan & G. Aldridge (Eds.), **Social welfare of the aging.** New York: Columbia Univ. Press, 1962.

Lieberman, M. A., Yalom, I. D., & Miles, M. B. **Encounter groups: First facts.** New York: Basic Books, 1973.

Mayadas, N. S. Role expectations and performance of blind children: Practice and implications. **Education of the Visually Handicapped,** 1972, **4,** 45-52.

Mayadas, N. S., & O'Brien, D. E. The use of videotapes in group psychotherapy. **Group Psychotherapy & Psychodrama, 26,** 107-119, 1973.

Neugarten, B. L. **Personality in middle and late life.** New York: Atherton Press, 1964.

Peck, R. Psychological development in the second half of life. In J. E. Anderson (Ed.), **Psychological aspects of aging.** Washington: American Psychological Assn., 1956.

Pincus, A. Reminiscence in aging and its implications for social work practice. **Social Work,** 1970, **15,** 47-53.

Riesman, D. Some clinical and cultural aspects of aging. **American Journal of Sociology,** 1954, **59,** 379-383.

Rose, A. M., & Peterson, W. A. **Older people and their social world.** Philadelphia: F. A. Davis, 1965.

Rubin, I. **Sexual life after sixty.** New York: New American Library, Signet, 1967.

Shore, H. Group work and recreation. In M. Leeds & H. Shore (Eds.), **Geriatric institutional management.** New York: Putnam's Sons, 1964.

Stoller, F. Focused feedback with videotape: Extending the group's function. In G. Gazda (Ed.), **Innovations to group psychotherapy.** Springfield, IL: Charles C Thomas, 1968.

Vickery, F. E. **Creative programming for older adults: A leadership training guide.** New York: Association Press, 1972.

Weiss, C. E. Communication needs of the geriatric population. **Journal of the American Geriatrics Society,** 1971, **19,** 640-645.

Wilson, C., & Ryland, C. **Social group work practice.** Boston: Houghton-Mifflin, 1948.

Wolk, R. L., & Wolk, R. B. Professional worker's attitude toward the aging. **Journal of the American Geriatrics Society,** 1971, **19,** 624-639.

Zander, A. Group aspirations. In D. Cartwright & A. Zander (Eds.), **Group dynamics: Research and theory.** New York: Harper & Row, 1968.

Behavioral group work in a home for the aged

N. Linsk,
Michael W. Howe,
and Elsie M. Pinkston

Elderly people in institutions frequently become isolated and noncommunicative. By using behavioral measurements of group workers and group members, the authors have formulated ways of treatment that encourage members to participate more actively.

N. Linsk, MA, is Director of Social Rehabilitation, Drexel Home for the Aged, Chicago, Illinois. Michael W. Howe, Ph.D., is Assistant Professor, University of Minnesota, School of Social Work, Minneapolis. Elsie M. Pinkston, Ph.D., is Assistant Professor, University of Chicago School of Social Service Administration. The authors express appreciation to Al Mendlevitz, Executive Director of Drexel Home; Arthur Schwartz, Susan Katz, Stephen P. Rook, and Donald Blackman, who consulted about design and data analysis; and Angela Corkey, social group worker for the study.

SOCIAL GROUP WORKERS have used behavior modification to develop group work processes as well as to suggest specific approaches to treatment. A number of writers have discussed techniques for classroom and laboratory research and have speculated on how these can be applied to social work, using specific examples of practice and evaluations of outcome.[1] Similarly, behavioral group work processes that emphasize specific goals and techniques have also been described.[2] In addition to offering concrete behavioral goals and suggesting interventions based on empirically validated principles, the techniques of applied behavior analysis specify a research methodology and ways of recording behaviors that are useful in evaluating the changes in clients and the relationship of those changes to worker intervention.[3]

Although theorists have noted the need for precise behavioral measures of group behavior and interaction, few group work studies have attained this precision.[4] Wodarski, Feldman, and Flax have discussed the development of behavioral social group work and noted a need for complex systems to record multiperson interaction as a basis for behavioral group work technology.[5] A number of investigators have developed techniques of recording behaviors of more than one person simultaneously, but these techniques of measurement have not generally been applied to group work.[6]

Group activities with elderly persons have been described and evaluated nonbehaviorally with nonquantitative measures. The goals and justification of such activities include "revitalizing social drives," "sharing, support, and understanding of psychological and physiological changes," "providing identity," and "replacing roles lost by retirement."[7] These concepts are difficult to measure, particularly in groups that include confused, disoriented, or "senile" members. Because of this, much of the literature describing group activities for the aged has been descriptive or has relied on case histories.[8]

Several writers suggest that the worker's approach be directive and structured; that he take more initiative in planning and providing activities and provide more stimulus to group participation than he might with other adult populations.[9] Specified procedures for intervention with empirically researched evaluation are lacking for deteriorated, institutionalized old people. In this research, group participation as evidenced by appropriate verbalizing reflects the effects that group activities have on individual group members and on the group as a whole.

A few writers have indicated that socialization, participation in activities, and general interaction with the environment constitute appropriate therapy for the aged.[10] The evidence presented from a number of activity programs suggests that the elderly can increase their verbal and active participation in a variety of activities.[11] McClannahan discusses "the importance of engagement with the environment" and lists the consequences of the lack of activity, such as a slowing down of bodily processes, muscular atrophy, and the permanent loss of social relationships.[12]

The approach of applied behavior analysis to therapeutic and prosthetic environments for the aged suggests that more precise techniques be applied to social group work with the elderly. Lindsley writes that the aged individual, having experienced sensory or cognitive loss, may need highly specified stimuli to elicit an appropriate response. He also recommends amplified, intensified, or multisense stimuli to clarify for the patient when it is appropriate to respond. Similarly, external information sources—such as conversation, announcements, or television—may need to be made louder or slower to insure understanding and response. Response feedback systems in which information is repeated by receivers may be in order. The positive or reinforcing qualities of groups for the elderly may need behavioral evaluation regarding immediacy, individualization, and pace.[13] McClannahan notes that the differing attention spans of older people need special consideration.[14]

Current tasks in developing research-based models of behavioral group work include developing appropriate observational technologies, developing new procedures, and applying to group work the procedures used in classroom or individual treatment settings. All these procedures must be evaluated empirically with regard to the specific behavioral goals appropriate to given populations. The study reported in this article evaluated the specific procedure of directing task-related questions to individual members of a group. This procedure was developed from a behavior analysis of the group meetings and from a review of the behavioral literature concerning living arrangements for the elderly.

The research had four major purposes: (1) to devise social work intervention that would increase the group member's participation in the activity, (2) to conduct data-based intervention that would be experimentally controlled and evaluated, (3) to develop observational technology that would contribute useful data for planning and evaluating the intervention, and (4) to contribute research methodology and treatment procedures that would be valuable to social group workers.

SETTING

The study was conducted at the Drexel Home for the Aged, Chicago, Illinois —the specific site being restricted to a 33-bed unit on a nursing floor. The home, which is oriented toward rehabilitation, makes use of a variety of professional workers in a team approach. Residents living on the floor have minimal self-care abilities and are attended by a higher ratio of nursing staff than are residents elsewhere in the home. Staff members assigned to the floor during the data-collection period included a charge nurse, three nurses' aides, housekeeping and dietary staff members, an orderly, and a fluctuating number of volunteers. A full-time social worker with extensive geriatric experience was assigned to the unit. When the study began, she had worked on the unit for three months, during which time she had conducted group activities even though she had had no formal group work training.

There were 31 female residents in the unit who ranged in age from 68 to 96, with a mean age of 85. The subjects had a variety of physical and mental impairments. Nine of the women were able to leave the floor independently for meals; the rest were confined to the floor unless directly supervised because of physical disability or confusion. Several of the residents were so severely confused that they did not know the city they were in, their age, the year, or where their family was. More alert residents were able to take part in off-floor activities such as meals, home committees, and adult education classes. Thirteen of the residents were assigned to scheduled therapeutic activities, which included such activities as occupational therapy, religious services, current events discussions, cocktail hours, remotivation classes, reality orientation classes, and sheltered workshop activities.

Three ongoing group activities were chosen for the study—a newspaper activity, a folktale activity, and a residents' meeting. These were selected because they were conducted at the same time in early afternoon on different days of the week and observations showed that they were similar in format and levels of participation. In the newspaper and folktale activities, the worker read short stories to the residents, pausing occasionally for comments or questions. During residents' meetings, a series of announcements were read by the worker who again allowed time for questions and discussion.

All residents on the floor were invited to participate in these activities, and although less than half of the patients actually came, those who did represented a cross-section of the alert and confused residents on the floor. A small, centrally located poster announced group meetings on the days they were held. Before each meeting, the social worker spent time inviting, encouraging, and requesting residents to attend, as well as wheeling several of them into the room.

A number of definitions were developed for the behaviors of both group worker and residents. Behavior

of the worker included both verbal (speech directed at one or more of the group members) and nonverbal behaviors. Behaviors of residents were also classified as verbal or nonverbal and as appropriate or inappropriate. Behaviors observed, together with recording symbols, are defined in Figure 1.

Two observers, using a stopwatch, clipboard, and recording sheet, were seated adjacent to the group so that they did not interact with members. The recording sheet consisted of a grid on which group worker behaviors were recorded and a series of configurations in which each group member was identified by number. Each configuration represented a one-minute time interval. Figure 2 presents this recording form and illustrates procedures of data collection. Before each session, the names and seating arrangements of residents were recorded on the sheet. Using a stopwatch, the observer recorded one-minute time samples for each resident and half-minute time samples for the worker. The observers spent five seconds per minute observing and recording the behavior of each group member. The numbers on the recording configuration corresponded to the numbers assigned to the residents and the numbers on the clock face, with L representing those intervals in which the worker's behavior was recorded.

Two observers were used to accommodate more than ten residents in the recording periods. Interobserver reliability was provided by arranging that each day the two observations overlapped on some of the residents. To insure that reliability for individual residents was assessed for all residents regularly, each day the seating location of the resident designated as Number One was rotated around the room. The group worker's behavior was recorded simultaneously by both observers so that reliability between the observers could always be assessed.

Agreement or disagreement between the two observers' recording sheets was compared to determine reliability of observation. Reliability for the worker's behavior was recorded in every session; in sessions at which

FIG. I. BEHAVIORAL DEFINITIONS AND SYMBOLS USED TO RECORD DATA

Social Group Worker Behaviors

Behavior	Recording Symbols	Definition
Questions	G, I	a verbal behavior which demands or suggests a response from one or more group members, indicated by words which suggest a question (i.e. why, how) or a direct request or demand for a response
Statements	G, I	a verbal behavior which gives information and does not call for a response from group members and is not a direct consequence of a previous behavior of individual or group of residents. Includes reading to residents.
Positive Comments	G, I	verbal behavior which followed the behavior of one or more group members and relates to this behavior to encourage similar responses. Suggests recognition, approval, or praise.
Negative Comments	G, I	verbal behavior which followed the behavior of one or more group members and relates to this behavior to discourage similar responses, Suggests disapproval or displeasure.
Listening	√	Silence on the part of the worker either while a group member verbalizes or while waiting for resident response in the absence of other worker behavior.
Demonstration/ Participation	√	Demonstrating equipment or activity or participating in activity.
Attending to External events	√	Watching, listening to or talking to a stimulus outside of the activity.

Note: Questions, Statements, and comments were judged as to whether the behavior was directed to an individual (I) or to the group (G).

Group Member Behaviors

Behavior	Recording Symbols	Definition
Appropriate Verbal	◯	Verbal behavior related to current group task (subject under discussion, activity, or relating to activity stimuli, e.g., phonograph recording.)
Verbal Behavior Related to Environment	◯	Verbal behavior related to another person present at activity or related to the room or other aspects of the environment, but not related to the current group task.
Inappropriate Verbal Behavior	⊘	Verbal behavior which does not relate to group task or other residents or staff present or the environment. Verbalizations not audible to the entire group or observers.
Appropriate Attention	△	Visual or apparent listening attention indicated by head orientation or other observable response, which is directed toward social worker, a resident who is making or has just made an appropriate verbal response, or activity stimulus.
Appropriate Activity	▢	Manipulating equipment related to activity as worker has demonstrated or similar appropriate use, helping another resident to do so, nodding or head-shaking appropriately, raising hand for recognition.
Inappropriate Activity	/	Repetitive actions, aggressive actions, manipulating materials not related to group task or activity stimuli, leaving activity, sleeping, talking to oneself, any attention directed away from worker, group task, activity stimuli or a resident making a verbal response.

there were fifteen or fewer residents present, reliability was recorded for five residents. Occurrence reliability was computed by dividing the number of agreements by the sum of the number of agreements and disagreements and multiplying by 100 percent.

In addition to behavioral observations, videotapes were made of at least one session in each experimental condition. These were used as descriptive data for making the measurement of behavior more specific, for analysis with the social group worker, and for the training of observers.

PROCEDURES

The study used a reversal design with the following conditions and procedures:

Baseline The social group worker was asked to conduct the group in her normal manner. She was informed that the experimenters were developing and testing some measures of behavior for the group and that the findings would be discussed with her at a later date. Code development continued throughout the first three sessions of baseline, during which reliability, definitions, and time base were stabilized.

Treatment Following baseline observations and prior to the first treatment session, the experimenter arranged an interview with the group worker at which they could discuss the objectives of the group and view a videotape of a recent session. The group worker and experimenter agreed that increased resident participation should be a major goal of the meetings. The experimenter showed the group worker current data on the

FIG. 2. SAMPLE OBSERVATION FORM USED DURING THREE-MINUTE OBSERVATION PERIODS AT GROUP MEETINGS

Group Activity Study--Observation Form--Observer I   Date_____ Page_____
                                                       Observer_____

Leader Behavior:

	1	2	3	4	5
Questions	G				
Statement		G	G	G	
Comment +		I			
Comment -					
Listening			✓		
Demo/Part					
Att/Ext					

Residents Present:
1._____   6._____
2._____   7._____
3._____   8._____
4._____   9._____
5._____   10._____

Resident Behavior:

(1) ... (2) ... (3) ... (4) ... (5)

behaviors of both worker and residents, and discussed alternatives for increasing resident participation. The experimenter and the group worker decided that frequent questions concerning the material being discussed should be used as a procedure for treatment. The group worker directed these questions to individual members of the group, and as many residents as possible were asked questions.

After this meeting, the treatment intervention was implemented. A written contract between group worker and experimenter was developed that detailed specifically the activities of the group worker and experimenter. The group worker and experimenter met prior to each session to review the directions for the condition and the data from previous sessions.

Baseline After twelve sessions, a reversal procedure was implemented. The worker and experimenter met, and the experimenter presented supporting data to confirm that participation had increased. To ascertain that this increase was the result of the worker's questions, the worker agreed to ask fewer questions of individual group members in the next group sessions and to conduct the meeting as it had been conducted before treatment began. This procedure was written into a contract with the worker. The pregroup meetings between experimenter and social worker to discuss data and review procedure directions were continued during the reversal condition.

Treatment After ten sessions, the worker and experimenter met and determined that the relationship between the worker's questions and increased appropriate verbal participation on the part of residents had been established and that the worker could now return to the question-asking procedure. This was stated in the contract, and the worker implemented this treatment in ensuing sessions. Pregroup meetings were also continued during this condition.

Termination and Follow-up After thirteen treatment sessions, the worker and experimenter decided that for the

purposes of the current research sufficient data had been collected. The progress of the group was discussed generally as well as specifically and substantiated by the data. Individualized data were made available to the worker for her use in the agency, and copies of the graphs designed for the group were given to her. The worker agreed to continue conducting group meetings for several weeks until follow-up data were recorded. No treatment contract was in effect during these meetings.

After five weeks and fifteen additional group sessions, observers returned to record follow-up data. No pregroup interview was held with the worker before this group meeting, and the worker agreed to conduct the meeting as she had in the weeks following the termination of the contract.

RESULTS

Interobserver reliability measures were computed for the group worker's behavior, group members' behavior, and a variety of other behavioral categories. The mean percentage of interobserver agreement for the group worker's total behavior was 88 percent. Mean scores showed the following percentages of agreement:

Total verbal behavior directed to group	90 percent
Total verbal behavior directed to individual group members	61 percent
Questions directed to individual group members	60 percent
Total questions	75 percent
Statements	90 percent
Listening	69 percent

Mean percentage of interobserver agreement for all resident behaviors was 85 percent. Mean reliability scores showing percentages of agreement for specific categories of behavior were as follows:

Total verbal behavior	69 percent
Appropriate verbal behavior	60 percent
Attention	83 percent
Inappropriate activity	72 percent

Figure 3 illustrates the measurement of the group worker's behavior.

The data shown represent percentages of the group worker's behavior as a whole for specific behavioral categories. Fig. 3-A shows the percentage of questions to individual residents for each session. This was the independent variable for the study. The percentage of questions to individual residents was substantially higher during the treatment conditions than during the baseline and reversal conditions. During treatment conditions the mean percentage of group worker questions was 16.1 percent; during the previous baseline conditions this percentage was 3.8. Follow-up measurement indicated that worker-asked questions constituted 20 percent of her behaviors, which was slightly higher than the mean of treatment conditions. Similar patterns of behavior were found for total worker-asked questions, the means of which are shown in Fig. 3-B.

Other behaviors of the group worker that were not part of the treatment contract changed in relation to changes in questioning. Fig. 3-B presents these changes as means for each condition. Listening behavior, which increased in a positive relationship to questions asked, indicated that an increase in questions was accompanied by a decreased number of statements and increased listening behavior on the part of the group worker. Follow-up observations showed that the treatment levels of worker behavior had been maintained on these three behaviors.

Figure 4 shows changes in two measurements of the verbal behavior of residents. Fig. 4-A shows the rate of appropriate verbal behavior for the entire group per minute. The mean rate of appropriate verbalization for the group during the baseline and reversal conditions was .19 behaviors per minute. The mean rate of behavior during treatment conditions was .44 appropriate verbalizations per minute —more than double the rate during nontreatment conditions. Rates during follow-up were considerably higher than they had been in any previous condition (.57), suggesting that the rate of verbalization continued to increase following treatment. Further analysis demonstrated an increase in the number of residents who verbalized appropriately in each session. These results, which are illustrated by Fig. 4-B, indicate the percentage of the total number of residents present in each session who verbalized appropriately during that session. Baseline measures ranged between 8 percent and 36 percent of residents present who verbalized appropriately, with a mean of 21 percent of the residents.

When treatment was first implemented, the range of verbal participation increased to between 27 percent and 64 percent of the residents present, with a mean of 46 percent. This shows that the proportion of group members who participated verbally during the treatment condition was twice that of the baseline condition. During the second baseline condition, the range was 7 percent to 40 percent of the group members present, with a mean of 13 percent.

Reinstatement of treatment returned levels of verbal participation to previous treatment levels, with an average of 44 percent and a range of 26 percent to 67 percent of residents present. This indicates that the number of residents participating in meetings increased from about one-fifth of the residents present during average baseline meetings to almost one-half of residents present during treatment conditions. Follow-up data showed that the higher levels of participation were maintained.

As a further test of the relationship between the worker's questions and appropriate verbalization on the part of residents, the mean rates were compared, exhibiting a strong relationship between these variables. Analysis showed that when the worker's questions increased to .60 questions per minute, appropriate verbalization on the part of group members also increased to .40 responses per minute.

This contrasts with baseline levels of behavior, which showed a lower rate of worker's questions (average of .18 per minute) correlated with an average rate of .23 appropriate verbalizations by residents.

An individual analysis of the twelve residents most frequently present was completed as a further test of the relationship between worker and member behaviors and to determine whether the recording procedures developed in this study could be used to organize individual treatment plans in other group meetings. Three examples of the graphs generated from such individualized analysis are presented in Fig. 5 and demonstrate that individual data not only reflect treatment conditions, but day-to-day changes in participation as well. The individual analysis also showed that 67 percent of the residents increased the rate of appropriate verbalizations during question-asking conditions, as

FIG. 3. RECORD OF WORKER BEHAVIOR

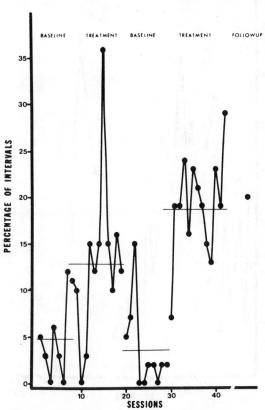

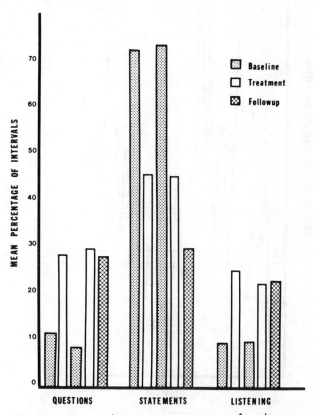

FIG. 3-A shows worker's questions as a percentage of total worker behavior.

FIG. 3-B compares the average percentage of worker questions, statements, and listening behaviors for each condition.

83

compared with baseline and reversal conditions.

DISCUSSION

The study demonstrated a strong relationship between the social worker's use of task-related questions directed at group members and increased levels of appropriate verbalization on the part of the elderly residents in activity groups. The data reflected increases during question-asking conditions both in the number of appropriate verbalizations and in the percentage of residents present who verbalized appropriately. In pretreatment discussions the worker specified increased participation as a major goal for the activity.

Although this research did not directly assess the benefits of such increased participation, benefits may include a more active group experience for residents, more opportunities for residents to become socially engaged with one another, the use of meetings as an improved source of information about both upcoming events and other residents' reactions to previous events, and the use of meetings as a setting that provides opportunities to express opinions and get recognition for such participation.

Elderly people often become isolated and noncommunicative in institutions. Techniques for increased participation provide them with opportunities for communication and

general engagement with the environment. The increased time that the worker spent listening during treatment conditions indicated that residents had more opportunities to contribute in these sessions.

Further analysis of the data showed that, as the study continued, attendance at meetings increased and that the length of meetings was considerably greater during treatment conditions than in nontreatment conditions. During later treatment conditions, meetings were attended by residents who had previously never participated in a group activity, and residents spoke appropriately who had previously remained silent. Although these aspects of the group meetings

FIG. 4. RESIDENT BEHAVIOR

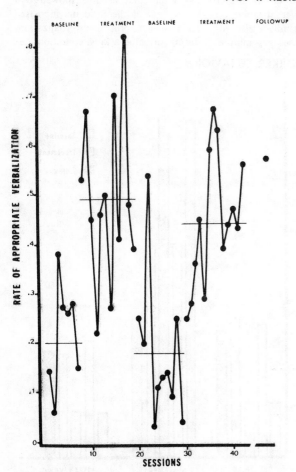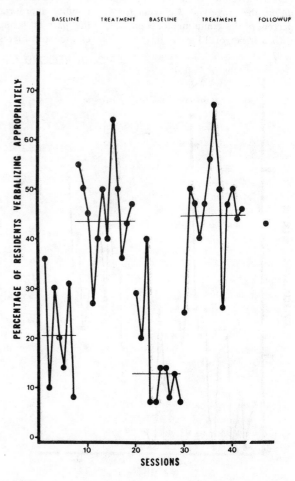

FIG. 4-A shows rates per minute of appropriate verbalization by all residents per session.

FIG 4-B shows the percentage of residents who verbalized appropriately in each session.

84

were not directly measured in the experimental design, the absence of other changes in procedures for notifying residents of meetings or changes in the format of the activity shows that the increased length and size of group activities may have been due to increased levels of participation.

The asking of questions is a behavior that is common in social group work. In this study systematic question-asking was shown to be effective in increasing rates of verbalization with an elderly population. The use of questions as a treatment procedure was indicated by observational data and by the knowledge that older people need decelerated and specific stimuli to help them make appropriate responses. Significantly, this procedure was simple for the worker to learn and control. When the worker increased the number of questions, systematic differences were noted in her other behaviors. This suggests that specific behavioral instructions used in training inexperienced workers may have substantial effects on their behavior as a whole. Behaviors on the part of the worker in turn affect the behaviors of group members. The follow-up data showed that the technique of asking individual questions and the level of resident participation remained at levels similar to those during the treatment condition. This suggests that the technique and its effects are of lasting duration.

An initial goal of this research was the development of an observational technology that could be applied to social group work. This study reports the use of a technology that measures behaviors of both group members and group worker. The data were used to develop and evaluate interventions for the entire group; individualized evaluation and treatment might also be possible, and these should be explored and evaluated in future research. Analysis of verbal participation for individuals as well as for entire groups may be useful with an elderly population, especially when the low frequency of responses makes it difficult for the worker to account for changes without specific data.

FIG. 5. SELECTED INDIVIDUAL RESIDENT BEHAVIORS

VERBAL BEHAVIOR

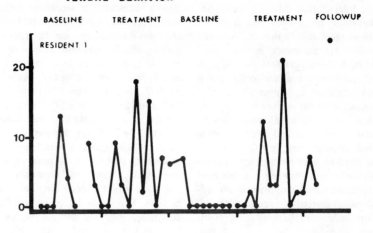

FIG. 5-A shows graphs for two residents, presenting verbal behavior expressed as a percentage of total intervals of behavior.

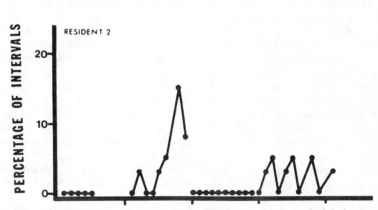

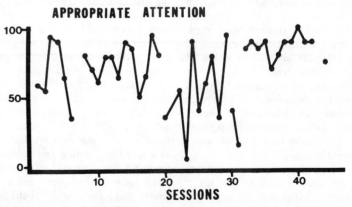

FIG. 5-B shows a graph of appropriate attention as a percentage of total intervals of behavior for an individual resident.

85

In this study, the group worker was able to make use of behavioral data in formulating and implementing treatment intervention. She regulated her behavior by using daily data examinations as feedback. In this, she received considerable assistance in data analysis from the experimenter—a system that may be useful in social group work evaluation, supervision, and training. A social worker with specific training in behavioral approaches to social group work and direct observational research may be able to collect and analyze data independently. This approach works toward a data-based practice of social group work, but additional research is necessary to develop techniques of analyzing treatment procedures. An important task for researchers in social group work is the development of more economical methods of recording—use of counters, tallies, and audio or video recording would enable the worker to record data while conducting group meetings. An alternative approach in which one worker implements treatment intervention while the other records the data could be applied in agencies when co-worker systems are used for group work.[15]

To move the technology beyond the initial stage, future studies should continue to work on time-sampling and on ascertaining the reliability of the methodology. In this study, behavior was observed every thirty seconds for the group worker and every minute for the group members. This procedure allows each group member to be observed regularly throughout each session to assess behavioral trends. In future research, experimenters may consider using samples of more extended intervals in which all behaviors that occur during an observation period are recorded, instead of the one behavior that occurs at the moment of observation. However, whether such a system is manageable in a multiperson recording scheme is still questionable.

Although interobserver reliability was not notably high in this study, considering the nature of behaviors recorded and the continuous change in observation subjects, the scores indicate substantial accuracy. Difficulties in achieving reliability can be attributed to the briefness of the time-sample necessary for recording eleven people simultaneously, the complexity of group interactions, and the task of making all the decisions necessary to observe and evaluate two sets of behavior categories. Accuracy was substantially higher when observers had had considerable practice, and observers trained later in the study achieved reliability more easily than those trained early. Specific training procedures making use of practice sessions or videotapes are necessary before this method of recording data can be used. The methodology used offers acceptable accuracy in recording multiperson behavior and is substantially more specific than the descriptive data often used to describe and evaluate social group work. The technique may be well suited to smaller, more stable groups with a more constant number of members present.

Future interventions could include the following elements:

- Worker verbalizations and tangible reinforcement for specified behavior on either an individual or a group basis.
- Individualization of treatments based on data collected on individual residents.
- Variation of the amount of listening and repetition on the part of the worker.
- Use of amplification equipment for worker or residents.
- Systematic variation in the seating arrangement of residents.[16]

The present study contributes a basis for establishing and validating both an observational technology and a treatment procedure that may prove useful to social group workers. Applications to other settings with other client groups would necessitate different defined and observed behaviors, as well as different treatment interventions. The use of empirical data as a tool for planning and evaluating treatment has several advantages for social group work—increasing accountability, measuring behavioral changes of group members, comparing individual behavior at different stages of treatment, and analyzing social work training and supervision. Each of these advantages became evident in this study.

NOTES AND REFERENCES

1. *See* Harry Lawrence and Martin Sundel, "Behavior Modification in Adult Groups," *Social Work,* 17 (March 1972), pp. 34–43; Sheldon Rose et al., "The Hartwig Project: A Behavioral Approach to the Treatment of Juvenile Offenders," in Roger Ulrich, Thomas Stachnik, and John Mabry, eds., *Control of Human Behavior,* Vol. 2 (Glenview, Ill.: Scott Foresman & Co., 1970), pp. 220–230; Sheldon Rose, *Treating Children in Groups* (San Francisco: Jossey Bass, 1973); John S. Wodarski, Ronald A. Feldman, and Norman Flax, "Social Learning Theory and Group Work Practice with Antisocial Children," *Clinical Social Work Journal,* 1 (Summer 1973), pp. 78–94.

2. Arthur J. Frankel and Paul H. Glasser, "Behavioral Approaches to Group Work," *Social Work,* 19 (March 1974), pp. 163–176; Lawrence and Sundel, op. cit.; Wodarski, Feldman, and Flax, op. cit.; Rose, op. cit.

3. Donald M. Baer, Montrose M. Wolf, and Todd R. Risley, "Some Current Dimensions of Applied Behavior Analysis," *Journal of Applied Behavior Analysis,* 1 (Spring 1968), pp. 91–97; Robert Liberman, "Behavior Methods in Group and Family Therapy," *Seminars in Psychiatry,* 4 (May 1972), p. 145; and Michael W. Howe, "Casework Self-Evaluation: A Single-Subject Approach," *Social Service Review,* 48 (March 1974), pp. 1–23.

4. Joseph E. McGrath and Irwin Altman, *Small Group Research* (New York: Holt, Rinehart & Winston, 1966).

5. Wodarski, Feldman, and Flax, op. cit., p. 89.

6. *See* Donald Bushell, Patricia Wrobel, and Mary Louise Michaelis, "Applying Group Contingencies to the Classroom Study Behavior of Preschool Children," *Journal of Applied Behavior Analysis,* 1 (Spring 1968), pp. 55–61; D. Ferritor et al., "The Effects of Contingent Reinforcement for Attending Behavior on Work Accomplished," *Journal of Applied Behavior Analysis,* 5 (Spring 1972), pp. 7–17; Peter M. Lewinsohn, Malcolm S. Weinstein, and Ted Alper, "A Behavioral Approach to Group Treatment of Depressed Pa-

tients: A Methodological Contribution," *Journal of Clinical Psychology*, 26 (October 1970), pp. 525–532; Michael H. Ward and Bruce L. Baker, "Reinforcement Therapy in the Classroom," *Journal of Applied Behavior Analysis*, 1 (Winter 1968), pp. 323–328.

7. *See* Irene Hulicka, "Participation in Group Conferences by Geriatric Patients," *Gerontologist*, 3 (March 1963), pp. 10–14; Herbert Ackley, "Group Meetings with Men on Old Age Security," in Norman Fenton and Kermit Wiltse, eds., *Group Methods in the Public Welfare Program* (Palo Alto, Calif.: Pacific Books, 1963), pp. 149–151; Jean Maxwell, "Helping Older People Through Social Group Work," in *Potentials for Service Through Group Work in Public Welfare* (Chicago, Ill.: American Public Welfare Association, 1962); Eugenia Shere, "Group Therapy with the Very Old," in Robert Kastenbaum, ed., *New Thoughts on Old Age* (New York: Springer Publishing Co., 1964), pp. 146–160; Joyce Unger and Elaine Kramer, "Applying Frames of Reference in Group Work with the Aged," *Gerontologist*, 8 (1968), pp. 51–53.

8. *See* Susan Kubie and Gertrude Landau, *Group Work with the Aged* (New York: International Universities Press, 1953); Herbert Ackley, op. cit.; Velma Ackley, "Group Meetings in a Home for the Aged," in Fenton and Wiltse, op. cit., pp. 143–147; Maurice Linden, "Group Psychotherapy with Institutionalized Senile Women: Study in Gerontologic Human Relations," *International Journal of Group Psychotherapy*, 3 (January 1953), pp. 150–170; Shere, op. cit.

9. Velma Ackley, op. cit.; Herbert Ackley, op. cit.; Hulicka, op. cit.; Unger and Kramer, op. cit.

10. William J. Hoyer et al., "Reinstatement of Verbal Behavior in Elderly Mental Patients Using Operant Procedures," *Gerontologist*, 14 (April 1974), pp. 149–152; Lynn E. McClannahan, "Therapeutic and Prosthetic Living Environments for Nursing Home Residents," *Gerontologist*, 13 (Winter 1973), p. 425.

11. Hoyer et al., op. cit.; Lynn E. McClannahan and Todd R. Risley, "Design of Living Environments for Nursing Home Residents: Recruiting Attendance at Activities," *Gerontologist*, 14 (June 1974), pp. 236–240; Lynn E. McClannahan and Todd R. Risley, "Design for Living Environments for Nursing Home Residents: Additional Strategies for Increasing Attendance and Participation in Group Activities," unpublished manuscript, University of Kansas, 1973.

12. McClannahan, op. cit., p. 425; Lynne E. McClannahan, "Recreation Programs for Nursing Home Residents: The Importance of Patient Characteristics and Environmental Arrangements," *Therapeutic Recreation Journal* (Second Quarter 1973), pp. 26–31.

13. Ogden Lindsley, "Geriatric Behavioral Prosthetics," in Kastenbaum, op. cit., pp. 41–61.

14. McClannahan, "Recreation Programs for Nursing Home Residents."

15. Michael W. Howe, op. cit.

16. McClannahan, "Recreation Programs for Nursing Home Residents." ◀

A detailed presentation is made of the techniques used in four community-based support groups for elderly persons experiencing moderate stress as a result of the aging process. The support groups were structured as informal workshops which were presented over ten 2-hour sessions. Group leaders provided objective information about normal changes in the later years and helped clients develop more effective interpersonal skills to cope with these changes. Pre- and posttest results indicated that the majority of clients experienced decreased anxiety about the aging process, became more effective in problem solving, and began to make use of community resources.

Support Groups for Elderly Persons in the Community[1]

Beryl J. Petty, MSW, Tamerra P. Moeller, PhD, and Ruth Z. Campbell, MSW[2]

Multidisciplinary interest in the use of group processes with elderly persons has basically developed during the last 20 years. Treatment plans (Burnside, 1970) as well as theoretical and methodological issues (Toepfer, Bicknell, & Shaw, 1974; Unger & Kramer, 1968) have been reported. Group treatment programs have been practiced in institutional and community settings and with clients who differed greatly in their capacity for rational discussion (Brudno & Seltzer, 1968; Burnside, 1973; Klein, Shan, & Furman, 1965; Mayadas & Hink, 1974; Saul & Saul, 1974). In these programs, efforts have been concentrated on helping older persons to become less agitated and more communicative, to increase their independence and feelings of self-worth, and to utilize problem-solving skills in making new adjustments.

In the present paper, a description is given of a therapeutic program designed for older persons living in the community and experiencing moderate stress due to the normal aging process. Specifically, group techniques were used to work with the concerns expressed by older individuals in the areas of health, sensory changes, mobility, and family relationships; these techniques were practiced in small group settings and with clients representing diverse socioeconomic backgrounds. The primary goals of the support groups included presentation of objective information about normal changes in old age and, second, individual development of more effective interpersonal skills to cope with these changes.

Group Members

Participants were 30 persons (26 females, 4 males) in four support groups, which varied in size from 6 to 9 members. The members ranged in age from 62 to 85 years and had been recruited from the patient population screened through a pilot geriatric arthritis program. One group was composed of residents of a small farming community; members in the other three groups came from a university town. In all groups, the members were heterogeneous in educational background and economic status. In three groups, all members were white, and in one, 4 members were black, 3 white. All of the groups met in community sites.

Most of the members were experiencing mild to moderate depression in their adjustment to the aging process; however, they were reluctant to inquire about community mental health programs. These individuals did not view themselves as having problems serious enough to require counseling services; inherent in their attitude was an acceptance of feelings of unhappiness as part of aging.

[1]The authors wish to acknowledge the cooperation of the staff and patients of the Pilot Geriatric Arthritis Program at University Hospital, Univ. of Michigan.
[2]3 Washington Square Village, #F-1, New York 10012. For reprints: TPM.

Consequently, support groups were developed for clients who were encountering moderate difficulties in adjustment and who had no experience in reaching out to obtain supportive services.

Outreach and Recruitment

In the present project, it rapidly became apparent that implementation of outreach strategies would be central to the successful involvement of clients in supportive groups (Tine, 1963). Potential group members were sent letters explaining both the rationale and possible content of the group sessions; for some individuals, particularly those who were isolated and depressed, home visits and a prior relationship with a staff member were needed to facilitate entry into a group setting.

Group Structure

The groups were structured as informal workshops to provide a nonthreatening atmosphere in which clients could respond to the content on varying levels; the open-ended design of the sessions allowed for personal counseling when appropriate. The program included ten 2-hour sessions; each was composed of two 45-minute discussion periods separated by a refreshment break to promote informal socialization among members.

Group Processes

The content of the sessions varied according to the particular needs and objectives of the members in each group; yet, in all four groups, depression, social isolation, and adjustment to sensory and health losses emerged as shared themes. The following description is a summary of the content and organization of sessions that were of primary concern to the members.

Orientation

Content. — The purpose of orientation was to create a comfortable group climate, define group goals, clarify expectations, and explore common bonds. The importance of regular attendance, confidentiality, and individual participation was also stressed.

Group techniques. — Brainstorming became a useful technique for accomplishing the multiple objectives of the orientation stage. Instructions were given: "Free your mind and throw out phrases and ideas reflecting concerns you have about aging." It was usually necessary for the group leader to start the list, checking out suggestions with the group before writing them down in large print on sheets of newsprint. One group's effort at brainstorming resulted in identification of the following problems: missing old family traditions, being a widow, having trouble remembering names and birthdates, not being able to do what I used to do, dealing with other people's hearing problems, handling tension, and being afraid of asking "dumb" questions. The leader categorized the various suggestions, and the group members set priorities for program content. Through this process, a model was established for individual participation and shared leadership.

Memory

Content. — The most significant problems seemed to be remembering dates, medical instructions, and new names, as well as forgetting the names of long-time friends and, consequently, having difficulty introducing friends to each other. Members frequently interpreted memory impairments as a sign of "losing one's mind"; however, group discussion of the relevant research on memory changes (Meyers, 1974) greatly helped to diminish this fear. Significantly, group interaction provided further relief as members began to recognize that everyone was experiencing these changes to some degree.

Group techniques. — Aids suggested by group members and the leaders included writing down information, such as doctor's instructions, associating the name of a new acquaintance with her face, clothes, hobbies, and friends, repeating new names out loud as well as writing them down, and using large, visible calendars for recording appointments.

In addition, attention was drawn to practices that might facilitate retention. For example, one game was devised to demonstrate the benefit and importance of allowing sufficient time to absorb new information. Ten objects were placed on a table. The group was first given 5 minutes to observe the objects, after which they were covered and each person had to write down the items he remembered. The members were then given 2 minutes to memorize another set of ten objects. All the members were able to recall more objects the first time. Another exercise illustrated the importance of associating pieces of information. Each person, after drawing the name of another group member, was assigned to concentrate on what that person said when she introduced herself. Next, each member introduced herself by taking three items from her wallet and briefly describing why they were important to her. After this first round of introductions, each person then introduced the woman whose name she had drawn and told what articles this woman had chosen. The success rate in this exercise was also high, and members were pleased to know someone had been carefully listening to what they had said.

Since memory lapses were frequently accompanied by feelings of embarrassment and inadequacy, members practiced how to handle difficult situations involving memory loss. One situation concerned meeting an old friend and not being able to remember her name. Group members suggested responses which were then practiced in role-playing sequences. Also emphasized was the importance of not apologizing or degrading one's own intelligence with comments such as, "I'm so stupid," or "My mind must be going."

Finally, the strategy of making assignments was adopted in all sessions to promote the generalization of problem-solving skills from the group setting to the home environment. Initial assignments were based on the subject material of group sessions; later, assignments were designed to relate to specific individual problem areas. Assignments in the memory sessions included writing appointments on large calendars, carrying around a pen and pad of paper, and directly asking others for help in remembering a name or some other item of information. At the following session, each member discussed how she had carried out the assignment.

Vision and Hearing

Content. — Members reported difficulty in reading the telephone book and newspaper, in distinguishing objects in bright sunlight, and in adjusting to the dark. Information was presented on visual aids, such as magnifying glasses, large print books, improved lighting, the use of easily distinguishable colors (reds and yellows), and ways of decreasing glare.

With respect to normal changes in hearing, members had questions about where to obtain hearing tests and hearing aid evaluation. The stigma attached to wearing a hearing aid and the problems in adjusting to it were best handled by a group session with an audiologist who was sympathetic about complaints and who encouraged people to persist in finding the best hearing device possible. A list was compiled of adaptations for hearing loss. These included lip reading, increasing one's proximity to the source of the sound, asking people to repeat or to speak more slowly, decreasing background noise, and requesting a quiet place in a restaurant.

Group techniques. — A forced choice situation was created: "You are hard-of-hearing, and you are late to a meeting. You must decide whether to sit at the back or to walk up to the front of the room. You will hear better in front." The group's own meeting room was divided in half. Those members who would go to the front when late were told to walk to one side of the room; those who would choose to sit at the back when late went to the other side of the room. Each person had to give reasons for her decision. The participants thoroughly enjoyed this and other forced choice situations.

Also, role-playing was used to practice ways of telling a friend, relative, or business colleague that she had a hearing deficit and should have an examination. Role-playing was again used in telling someone, "I can't hear you," or "Could you repeat what you said," and members were asked to practice these techniques at home.

Interpersonal Relationships

Content. — The manner and ease with which older persons were able to ask others to meet their needs constituted an increasingly important issue as these individuals became more dependent on the actions of others. Members reported difficulty asking for favors and handling demands from adult children, relatives, and friends. When help was needed, one frequent source of conflict centered on the idea that adult children should call and help their aging parents out of a sense of duty.

Unsatisfactory personal relationships, often of a long-standing nature, were also discussed. Members had the opportunity to reach new insights and to develop new patterns of interactions. In working through these conflicts, the older person occasionally needed individual counseling outside the group setting.

Filling the "void of touch" was another interpersonal problem expressed by the members. The need for intimacy and companionship aroused intense discussion, and some members felt the development of male/female relationships was hindered by neighborhood gossip and the disapproval of adult children. Also, although several people said they thought sexual contact was important, members universally stressed that their strongest need was for a close companion of either sex.

Group techniques. — In an appreciation exercise, members were asked to think of someone with whom they had a difficult relationship and to list things they appreciated about the person. In another exercise, members closed their eyes and held hands with each other, imagining themselves in a pleasant, restful place. They were then encouraged to become aware of differences in the two hands they were holding. After this relaxing exercise, members were divided into pairs, and each person was told to ask her partner for a "gift of touching" (Genevay, 1975). One woman wanted her hair combed; another asked for a backrub. Embarrassment was soon overcome, and the resulting warmth and pleasure were very moving. However, it was necessary for the leaders to be firm in their instructions and not be dissuaded by the initial hesitation.

Members were also divided into pairs to practice simple assertiveness techniques, such as saying, "No," when asked to babysit, for example. Those who brought up real situations were encouraged to role-play them with another member.

Health Management

Content. — One health-related issue that was of concern to the clients was their relationship with their physician; in particular, many of the members had difficulty asking their doctors questions about diseases and medication. Another issue that was discussed by group members was loss in functioning. This concern was frequently echoed in the complaint, "I can't do what I used to do." Emphasizing, instead, what each client could do was an effective way of helping the members to deal with decreasing capacity. A final health-related concern that was often mentioned was the control of tension. Several people complained about insomnia, saying they could not make their minds "shut off" at night.

Group techniques. — The doctor-patient relationship was very effectively role-played by members who demonstrated why they were successful in getting information from their physicians. Those individuals who were timid about asking their doctors for information then practiced the techniques demonstrated by the others.

Contracts were made with some individuals in order to encourage them to increase their level of independent functioning at home. Each member determined her own goals and received encouragement through individual progress and group reinforcement.

Concepts of deep-muscle relaxation were presented during one meeting and were readily accepted by group members. If relaxation exercises were taught in the very first session and used at the beginning of each subsequent session, this practice might motivate those who were experiencing insomnia and tension to try the exercises at home (Berger & Berger, 1972). Also, such relaxation techniques could enhance feelings of cohesiveness and enjoyment among group members.

Death and Loss

Content. — This topic did not come up spontaneously from the group; the leaders felt it was an important area and they received each group's consent to include it. Discussion centered on stages of grief, problems faced by widows, and society's attitude toward death. Although some members thought it was important to express feelings about death and grief, the more prevalent response was to maintain the necessity of keeping a "stiff upper lip." Often, participation was much lower than it had been in previous sessions, and members apparently wanted to talk about something else. However, in the group evaluations, this session was rated more highly than any other by the members in all four groups. Furthermore, in earlier sessions, when issues related to death had arisen spontaneously, the members had talked freely and intensely about others' deaths, about their own reactions while grieving, and about the type of death they wanted for themselves. It is possible, therefore, that the topic of dying and grief should be discussed when it arises rather than in one particular session. Another suggestion is to expand the topic to include other areas of loss, such as health, occupation, and family roles (mother, wife, etc.).

Group techniques. — One way to illustrate loss involved having two persons hold a long board, one person representing the wife, the other the husband. Other group members representing the house, children, a job, and good health were added to help hold the board. A heavy weight was placed on top of the board. One by one, each person was asked to let go of the board as the leader made statements about losses in the later years, "You have left your job; you have moved from your house; you have lost your good health." As individuals let go of the board, the full burden of what had been lost was vividly seen and felt.

Many of the members mentioned they could easily remember negative events in their lives but wished they had written down some of their more positive experiences. Out of these statements came the idea of having members keep journals of positive events, which could help lift morale during times of loss.

Session on Housing and Relocation

Content. — This topic was of immediate concern to many members who were in the process of deciding whether to sell their homes in order to move to smaller quarters, retirement centers, or nursing homes. For many of these individuals, this move would be their last. The most useful sessions on this topic focused on the difficult decision-making process members were facing. Each person had to consider which needs were most important in choosing new living quarters at this stage in life. Conflicts were inherent in this situation; some of these included disagreements between husbands and wives over where to relocate, pressures from adult children to move from a large family home into more manageable quarters, and the painful process of deciding which possessions could be kept and which had to be relinquished.

Group techniques. — A list of questions to be considered before moving was presented to the members, who then added their own suggestions to this list (Hunter, 1973). Each person was asked to rank the items on the list in order of her own priorities. Some of the fac-

tors included proximity to shopping centers, relatives, and health facilities, as well as type of climate, opportunities to make new friends, financial responsibilities, etc. As each person explained her own priorities, the decisions to be made were more carefully delineated than they had been previously. The support and active interest of group members in each other's predicaments were felt by many to be of value.

Closing Session

Each group planned a special session when terminating, such as a luncheon or pot-luck. Members organized these events and they brought all the food. Afterwards, the members discussed their feelings toward the group, what it had meant to them, and their future plans.

Critique of the Support Groups

Information from Tests

Both pretests and posttests were administered to group members. The pretests were designed to evaluate individual attitudes toward old age, satisfaction with daily activities, psychological and physical concerns, and beliefs about the similarity of one's own concerns and those of other older persons. The posttests were designed to evaluate individual changes in attitudes and behaviors as well as satisfaction with various aspects of the support groups.

The pretests demonstrated that a majority (80%) of the participants were either discontent or only moderately content with their later years; and of these individuals, nearly 80%, again, considered old age to be worse than they had expected it to be. However, also within the groups were members who were very content with their later years and who judged old age to be better than they had expected.

Psychological and physical concerns as well as a lack of meaningful activities may have contributed heavily to the feelings of unhappiness expressed during the pretesting. More specifically, on these pretest measures, most members (93%) checked three or more categories indicating areas of personal change; these categories included vision, hearing, and health, memory functioning, communication with family members, and mobility. To many of the members, such changes may have resulted in isolation, declining morale, and feelings of resignation and uselessness. In addition, of those individuals who had expressed dissatisfaction with their old age, nearly two-thirds stated that they wanted to be involved in more activities; they indicated that they enjoyed the activities in which they participated but that these alone were not sufficient.

The final measure on the pretest concerned members' attitudes about the uniqueness of their concerns. Most of the participants (86%) indicated that their frustrations were *probably* similar to those of other older persons; however, on the posttests, these individuals expressed *certainty* that others not only experienced the same concerns but could also make helpful suggestions about the management of such problems. This finding was further confirmed in the group sessions; repeatedly, clients expressed both amazement and relief that they were not alone in experiencing a number of physical and psychological changes. Over-all, this discovery appeared to lessen anxiety and to increase the ease with which the members developed effective problem-solving behaviors.

In addition to attitude changes about the uniqueness of problems in old age, members also demonstrated behavioral changes. On the posttests, every individual mentioned new behaviors in which she had engaged. For example, members had improved the visual and safety conditions in their homes, obtained hearing tests, visited possible sites for their next move, or started the process of communicating their own needs more clearly to adult children. In general, the members had become more adept at both analyzing sources of physical and psychological discomfort and adopting new behaviors to cope with these concerns.

Observations

Some changes were not measured by the tests but were instead observed by the group leaders. Two of these changes involved the development of new friendships and the use of community resources. Through group processes, members were encouraged to reach out first to each other and, later, to people on the outside. These practices were particularly beneficial to individuals who had no previous model for developing close friendships and for others whose opportunities for friendships

had diminished in recent years. Participants also were told about the services of several community agencies; by the end of the workshops, a majority of individuals in each group had begun to make use of resources such as information and referral services, programs utilizing older volunteers, community college courses, health clinics, senior citizen clubs, homemaker services, and "talking book" libraries.

Future Applications

Although this program was used in a community health setting, its success with heterogeneous groups suggests its applicability in a wide range of settings—nursing homes, senior centers, even community colleges. The groups might also be offered by community counseling agencies so that the older person could receive individual counseling, if necessary, without leaving the original agency.

Another adaptation in design concerns group size. For example, a program that was an outgrowth of one of the four groups attracted 30 to 40 participants weekly. This program was held in a large senior housing complex, and in the workshops, a greater emphasis was placed on informational content than on small group techniques designed to develop problem-solving skills.

Finally, it should be emphasized that group members do not need to possess highly similar backgrounds. As mentioned previously, one group in the present project was mixed in terms of race as well as educational background and economic level. This group was led by two social workers, one black, one white. In comparison to the other groups, the members in this group took longer to respond in a cohesive manner, but the final outcome was rewarding for these participants. In the last few sessions, people spontaneously paired off—not along racial lines—but with individuals who shared common problems. This situation may have special implications for groups in cities where some elderly people find themselves relatively alone in racially mixed neighborhoods. Too often older people are thought to need protection from potentially challenging situations. In the present project, the elderly were able to broaden their experiences and ideas and to taste the excitement that comes with growth and change.

References

Berger, M. M., & Berger, L. F. Psychogeriatric group approaches. In C. J. Lager & H. S. Kaplan (Eds.), *Progress in group and family therapy*. Brunner-Mazel, New York, 1972.

Brudno, T. T., & Seltzer, H. Re-socialization therapy through group process with senile patients in a geriatric hospital. *Gerontologist*, 1968, *8,* 211-214.

Burnside, I. M. Group work with the aged: Selected literature. *Gerontologist*, 1970, *10,* 241-246.

Burnside, I. M. Touching is talking. *American Journal of Nursing*, 1973, *73,* 2060-2063.

Genevay, B. Age is killing us softly . . . When we deny the part of us which is sexual. In I. M. Burnside (Ed.), *Sexuality and aging*. Andrus Gerontol. Ctr., USC, Los Angeles, 1975.

Hunter, W. W. *Preparation for retirement*. Inst. Gerontol., Univ. Michigan—Wayne State Univ., Ann Arbor, 1973.

Klein, W. H., Shan, E. J., & Furman, S. S. *Promoting mental health of older people through group methods*. Manhattan Society for Mental Health, New York, 1965.

Mayadas, N. S., & Hink, D. L. Group work with the aging: An issue for social work education. *Gerontologist*, 1974, *14,* 440-445.

Meyers, R. *Is my mind slipping?* Los Angeles, California: Andrus Gerontol. Ctr., USC, 1974.

Saul, S. R., & Saul, S. Group psychotherapy in a proprietary nursing home. *Gerontologist*, 1974, *14,* 446-450.

Tine, S. Process and criteria for grouping. *Social Group Work with Older People*. National Assn. of Social Workers, New York, 1963.

Toepfer, C. T., Bicknell, A. T., & Shaw, D. O. Remotivation as behavior therapy. *Gerontologist*, 1974, *14,* 451-453.

Unger, J., & Kramer, E. Applying frames of reference in group work with the aged. *Gerontologist*, 1968, *8,* 51-53.

GROUP THERAPY FOR HIGH UTILIZERS
OF CLINIC FACILITIES

Julianne Maienknecht Morrison

The Question of a Group

It is my opinion that group therapy, now a vogue in treatment modalities, is often used indiscriminately. In order to make the decision to treat a person in a group setting, it is necessary to fully assess his mental status and personality, and to evaluate his need and motivation for treatment, whether it be individual or group treatment. In addition, in forming a group, one should consider: (1) the treatment goals, (2) the number of patients that can be handled effectively, (3) the duration of time allotted for therapy, and (4) the limitations of the therapist. Several questions need to be proposed and resolved before the decision to initiate a group is made. The most significant, in my opinion, are: (1) Why should the individuals be considered for a group? (2) Are they compatible for effective group function? (3) What are their particular needs? (4) How might a group meet these needs? (5) Are there any other alternatives that would better meet the patients' needs?

I identified eight patients utilizing the Comprehensive Clinic of the University of California in San Francisco who experienced difficulty in effectively coping with their life situations. All the patients selected were widows who had multiple functional or psychosomatic disorders. I asked myself whether these patients would benefit from involvement in a community activity such as a senior citizen group offers, involvement in individual therapy, or participation in a therapeutic group. Which of these alternatives would be most appropriate and most likely to improve their ability to cope? This paper is about the data and rationale which led to the decisions I made in response to the above questions.

Choosing the Patients

The high utilizer of clinic facilities presents a problem in management to the medical profession. The Comprehensive Care Clinic of the University of

California in San Francisco carries a large proportion of patients who make more than ten clinic visits per year; in the case of such patients, it is necessary to clarify the medical condition for which care is received, and to assess the degree to which care is supportive.

Densen's criterion for a high clinic utilizer states that the patient requires predominately supportive care in more than ten clinic visits per year.[1] I utilized this criterion to identify eight high utilizers of clinic facilities in my caseload, all of whom were widows. Silverman[2] has identified the population of people widowed and over sixty years of age as having a high risk of developing mental illness. The mean age of the identified patients was 64.3 years, with a range from 54 to 72, and a mode of 65. The statistical prognosis, frequency of unscheduled visits to the clinic, and rescheduling of appointments indicated that nursing intervention beyond attention to physical symptoms was needed.

Psychodynamics

The psychodynamic patterns observed in these patients were very similar. Most of the patients presented multiple complaints, and many of these were functional and lacking in etiology. Headache, backache, nerves, lightheadedness, and fluttering in the heart were common symptoms. Moreover, the patients had few interpersonal relationships and little involvement in activities. Each individual expressed feelings of depression, and suffered from one or more realistic stresses caused by organic damage or focus on an object loss. I observed also that these patients demonstrated remarkably similar modes of interacting with staff at the clinic. The predominate characteristics of their interpersonal relations were: (1) demanding behavior, (2) use of psychosomatic symptoms, (3) anxiety, and (4) some evidence of cognitive disturbance—e.g., memory loss, or preoccupation with the past. Both loneliness and the utilization of an illness to obtain gratification could be inferred from my observations and interviews.

Use of Symptoms

The symptoms presented appeared to give the patients a channel for communication and attention, and to provide reasons for them not to initiate activity. For example, one sixty-five-year-old patient consistently stated, "I can't possibly go to Senior Citizens. I might have another chest attack." The anxiety in most of these individuals took the form of concern about their physical symptoms—"I'm nervous because I can't sleep," "I keep having headaches; do you think it's a tumor?" *This somatization seemed to bind up their anxiety and give it a focus*; as a result, a lesser degree of free-floating anxiety was manifest. Also, I found that, as the use of somatic complaints decreased, feelings of depression were recognized.

Gramlich states that chronic grief and depression are often manifested in chronic physical complaints. This was found to be particularly true in the elderly individual.[3] *Thus, chronic physical complaints may mask an underlying emotional* conflict and deny its resolution.[4] With the exception of one fifty-four-year-old woman who had problems with an adolescent son at home, the patients did not seem to be aware of the relationship between their anxiety, their somatic complaints, and their intrapersonal or interpersonal relationships.

Interpersonal Relationships

Interestingly enough, the patients denied a large segment of their dependent behavior. All of them spoke of themselves as independent, even though each received financial assistance and utilized one or more community resource. Perhaps they were independent when dealing with peers, but in the clinic they preferred or demanded authority and leadership, giving dictates on what they needed to handle their discomfort and their daily problems in living.

In a comparative study of psychologically oriented and somatically oriented individuals, Rickles et al.[5] found the somatically oriented were more dependent on authority, demonstrated lower self-ideals and goals, and had greater autonomic awareness than the psychologically oriented. The authors of this study inferred that the somatizing was used as a means of binding anxiety and minimizing the distortion of external reality. Anxiety was reduced by internalizing conflict and developing somatic complaints. *It appears that such patients develop discomfort as a way of generating a personally acceptable explanation of their environmental situation and focusing their anxiety.*

Zigler and Phillips found somatizing to be linked with reduced social competence. In addition, they found patients in the Low social competence group ". . . have both a longer period of institutionalization and a greater likelihood of rehospitalization than patients in the High group."[6] If lack of personal and social resources is used as a prognostic tool, one may suspect that symptomatic relief from medication is likely to be short-term in individuals expressing psychological conflict through somatic complaints.

Summary of Patient Characteristics

In summary, these eight women appeared to be a homogeneous group regarding: (1) age, (2) sex, (3) marital status, (4) ego strength, and (5) use of clinic facilities. Their social history was similar; four of them came to the United States as young adults, and these four foreign-born patients reported backgrounds similar to those of the native-born Americans; only one patient was from a large family; all reported rigid parental controls. Their past family size differed, but all had relatively similar life situations at the time I worked with them.

Preliminary Considerations in Establishing the Group

The literature indicates that although differences in race, religion, intellectual capacity, and cultural background may initially be a problem in a group, this is rapidly overcome, and within a short time patients align themselves according to previous emotional experiences and problems rather than to similar backgrounds.[7,8,9]

One clinic patient was diagnosed as schizophrenic. Her behavior was appropriate for group membership; she was not disturbed by hallucinatory activity, and was able to socialize with others. She was seen as a potentially valuable catalyst to group function on the basis of her ability to accurately perceive and comment on the feelings and the nonverbal behavior of other group members. For these reasons, she was retained in the group.

Each patient was initially seen individually; a strong reaction toward the therapist was noted in six of the eight patients during the first encounter. However, the patients trusted the therapist implicitly and completely relinquished decision-making power after the initial interview. As a group, the patients were homogeneous because of: (1) psychosomatic illnesses, (2) high dependency needs, and (3) what appeared to be a strong transference toward the therapist. These factors are considered to be good indications for group therapy.[10]

Identifying Patient Needs

The need to learn skills in interpersonal relationships and to make new role adjustments was identified in these individuals. Bowlby[11] sees bereavement as occurring in three stages: (1) the impact stage where the system is focused on the original object, (2) the recoil stage where disorganization of the person is accompanied by pain and despair, and (3) the recovery stage in which a reorganization and redefinition of role takes place. There is abundant literature concerning normal and pathological grief, but less about the problems resulting from the social redefinition of a woman as she moves from the status of a married to a widowed person. It was my hypothesis that these particular patients had not made a successful transition in the recovery phase. The following factors formed the basis for this hypothesis: (1) activities were directed to the past rather than the future ("as he would have wanted me to do . . ."), (2) attempts were being made to recapture the deceased in spirit, and (3) irrational feelings about life, loneliness, and worthlessness were in evidence.

The tasks confronting these patients were: (1) to learn to live successfully without their marital partner, (2) to find a meaningful emotional life, (3) to find a meaningful social life, and (4) to deal realistically with stress.

There are indications that senior citizens' groups and other social community groups are utilized only by people who are motivated and eager for such activity. Readiness for interpersonal contact occurs only after the individual begins to feel alive again, and is aware of his loneliness and sense of separation. It is of note that our society often does not permit an individual to vent feelings of bereavement and to deal with those feelings. The patients I described needed to examine and to share their grief. They were poorly motivated to resume social activity. This is illustrated by the following case report:

A sixty-five-year-old Caucasian widow was seen in the clinic six months after the unexpected death of her husband. She complained of pain originating in the abdomen and radiating to her back. This pain was accompanied by a burning sensation along her spinal column. She had no appetite and slept poorly. She was told by her relatives that she must be brave, and that her husband would not have wanted her to cry. She had, in effect, been told to stop grieving. She expressed feelings of worthlessness. She saw no purpose to her life now, as "all I ever did was work with my husband and care for his needs."

Widows reportedly need personal, unstructured, human encounters. Therefore, the structure of traditional individual therapy, its lack of personal involvement, and the often impersonal neutral environment of an office setting make it potentially dysfunctional to the widow.[12] In addition, seeing a therapist individually defines a psychological problem rather than a difficult life situation. The patients I studied did not recognize psychological conflicts as a difficulty or as a cause of their symptoms. The results of Silverman's study[13] indicate that a widow is the most effective caregiver for another widow, and that the relationship often results in a mutual assistance that makes possible a movement toward health.

Because of the similar life situations of the patients selected, their lack of insight, and their lack of motivation for involvement in a community activity, group therapy was decided upon as the most appropriate treatment modality.

Structure of the Group

The group was planned to consist of eight members, but to remain open-ended. It was to be a short-term group, and to meet weekly for four months. Because of the short duration of the group, and the participants' obvious lack of interpersonal skills and lack of motivation to look beyond symptoms, the group required a directive therapist. The degree of direction to be given remained flexible, and was contingent on the functioning of the group. The group was conceived as verbal, directive, and dealing with the here and now. Historically, this technique has been successful in assisting individuals to find an interest in life and to focus on the present and future. Moreover, the technique reportedly results in decreased symptoms and decreased use of clinic facilities, and has been found to be particularly useful in the treatment of psychosomatic patients.[14]

The nature of this short-term group requires an emphasis on the commitment to work when the members did meet. In order to increase the effectiveness of this short-term group, we made a specific, concrete contract for each member.

Resistance to Group Involvement

Most patients tend to resist being in a group. The major source of resistance to this particular group, and an obstacle to group functioning, was the feeling of being "dumped" into a group and deprived of individual attention by an authority figure. This problem was handled by encouraging regular medical appointments, and by setting aside time before or after a group session to check distressing symptoms or medication problems.

Pretherapeutic transference was another obstacle to the group. The assumption seemed implicit that the therapist had all the answers and explanations concerning how to live more successfully. This attitude may have been due to the group members' long association with the medical model; it may also have resulted from their dependence on authority and demand for leadership.

Therapeutic Goals

The goal for this group was conceptualized as: "How do you let go of the past and form new relationships?" With these patients, the realization of this goal involved developing a new "I," or self-concept. The needs of these patients to be met by group therapy were identified as: (1) attention to urgent problems in living, e.g., welfare, (2) improvement of self-image and raising of self-esteem, (3) increased ability to share with others, and (4) reduction in the use of physical symptoms of illness.

The group therapy was not intended to change basic personality trends, but rather to encourage a reorientation of attitudes. A group can facilitate such reorientation by:

1 Providing an opportunity to develop a group identity.
2 Giving an appointment, even when the client complains of no symptoms.
3 Providing an opportunity to analyze resistance as a means of avoiding working in the group, e.g., the use of physical complaints allows the individual to avoid dealing with his feelings.
4 Encouraging outside contacts for social and supportive encounters, with the possibility of later movement into community social groups.
5 Learning reality testing—a chance to recognize distortions of reality and test new insights.

The Group Experience

Individuals respond expressively, and in a group they manifest all the significant roles and feelings experienced in their lives.[15] The group therefore is a laboratory to assess, modify, and test new behavior by trial and error. Several of these patients observed the similarity between the physical complaints of others and their own, and recognized the compulsive nature of these complaints. These patients had been engaged in long-standing struggles with doctors to prove their symptoms were not psychosomatic or imaginary. Such a stance became increasingly less necessary in the group setting, because other patients were in the same position. With the obstacle of somatization reduced, the relationship between expression of feelings and relief of symptoms was gradually explored. The therapist interpreted somatic complaints as a resistance to dealing with underlying feelings. Rationalization for such feelings as failure, guilt, worthlessness, and loneliness may have been another reason for physical complaints. Several individuals demonstrated movement to the point of asking for help directly and by recognizing that they were welcome in the clinic with or without symptoms.

There were no meetings in which every member was present. One patient became delusional, experienced hallucinatory activity, and was later hospitalized for congestive heart failure. Her treatment was followed up on an individual basis. A second patient stated that she realized she was afraid to try to live without her husband. She was encouraged to cry during a meeting, and did so for almost an hour. After this session her physical complaints decreased and she was eventually able to enroll in an adult education course. This patient was seen individually once after she left the group. She no longer had physical complaints, was actively participating in her adult education course, and had resumed social contact with friends. She felt that she could now talk honestly with her doctor and receive support from him.

A third patient joined a senior citizens group and chose not to attend the clinic group. A fourth, aged seventy-two, came to the clinic for one hour every two weeks and met with the clinic aide, whom she found supportive. This patient stated that she was lonely and wanted to meet some new people. A fifth patient, who identified feelings of guilt about her husband's death as the cause of her anxiety, was seen on an individual basis by the therapist. She no longer mentioned physical complaints. Two patients failed to come to the group at all, stating that they only wanted to visit their doctor. The eighth patient, a fifty-four-year-old widow, was eventually able to verbalize her grief; she began going out socially and found a boyfriend. She had not been back to the clinic for three months.

Although the group was smaller, and its duration shorter than I had anticipated, group therapy appeared to be a catalyst for several patients to begin to identify their feelings, evaluate their behavior patterns, and share their feelings with others. These patients were able to resume social contacts and engage in outside activities. The consistent emphasis of *"physical symptoms are real and distressing, but often represent an expression of how you feel emotionally"* was successful. The use of physical complaints decreased, and the patients were able to talk directly about the feelings they were experiencing. Referral agencies, families, and the attending physician were contacted as needed to establish channels of communication, obtain information, and provide data. This resulted in improved continuity of care.

Therapist Techniques

The therapist for such a group needs to maintain a patient, noncritical, and consistent attitude. The principle techniques of the therapist should include:

1 Emphasizing ego strengths.
2 Utilizing group members as auxiliary egos.
3 Focusing on reality.
4 Dealing with dreams and fantasy on a reality basis.
5 Engaging interrelatedness.
6 Encouraging relationships outside the group.

7 Utilizing outside people as needed for reality problems (e.g., social workers or medical consultants).
8 Recognizing transference as it occurs, and, when appropriate, identifying the behavior to the group. Such identification helps the group to deal with the behavior in the new context of understanding. It is not necessary to delve into the patient's past to find the origin of the transference.

Summary

A directive-verbal type of group dealing with the here and now was the treatment chosen for eight widows who were identified as high utilizers of clinic facilities. The group was short-term for a selected number. The patients were a relatively homogeneous group with: (1) psychosomatic complaints, (2) high dependency needs, (3) strong initial transferences to the therapist, and (4) reduced social skills. The lack of successful transition in the recovery phase of bereavement was identified as a source of anxiety requiring a possible redefinition of the individual. It was hypothesized that, through group therapy, the group members would gain increased awareness of their feelings and a decreased need to use psychosomatic complaints as their primary mode of communication and means of dealing with stress.

This experience with eight elderly widows indicated to me that short-term informal group therapy might be valuable in the outpatient clinic to assist patients in coping with difficult life situations. Perhaps more professionals should try this group approach.

REFERENCES

1 Bernard Schoenberg and Robert Senescu, "Group Psychotherapy for Patients with Chronic Multiple Somatic Complaints," *Journal of Chronic Disease*, vol. 13, no. 6, p. 655, 1966.
2 Phyllis Rolfe Silverman, "Services to the Widowed: First Steps in a Program of Preventive Intervention," *Community Mental Health Journal*, vol. 3, no. 1, pp. 37-44, Spring 1967.
3 Edwin P. Gramlich, "Recognition and Management of Grief in Elderly Patients," *Geriatrics*, vol. 23, pp. 87-92, July 1968.
4 Ibid., p. 89.
5 Karl Rickles, Robert W. Downing, and Mildred H. Downing, "Personality Differences Between Somatically and Psychologically Oriented, Neurotic Patients," *Journal of Nervous and Mental Disease*, vol. 142, pp. 10-18, 1966.
6 Edward Zigler and Leslie Phillips, "Social Competence and Outcome in Psychiatric Disorders, *Journal of Abnormal and Social Psychology*, vol. 63, no. 2, p. 270, 1961.
7 Irene Burnside, "Group Work Among the Aged," *Nursing Outlook*, vol. 17, no. 6, pp. 68-71, June 1967.
8 Paul Leiderman and Veronica R. Leiderman, "Group Therapy: An Approach to Problems of Geriatric Outpatients," in Jules H. Masserman (ed.), *Current Psychiatric Therapies*, vol. 7, Grune and Stratton, New York, 1967, pp. 179-185.

9 Schoenberg and Senescu, op. cit., p. 651.
10 Asya L. Kadis et al., *A Practicum of Group Psychotherapy*, Harper and Row, New York, 1963.
11 John Bowlby, "Process of Mourning," *The International Journal of Psychoanalysis*, vol. 42, pp. 317–340, July–October 1961.
12 Silverman, op. cit., p. 43.
13 Ibid., p. 44.
14 Schoenberg, op. cit., p. 656.

SOCIAL WORK IN THE
NURSING HOME:

A NEED AND AN OPPORTUNITY

Lou Ann B. Jorgensen, MSW, ACSW
Robert L. Kane, MD

ABSTRACT. *Working on a Nursing Home Demonstration Project seeking alternative forms of care for this "abandoned" population, and testing the cost-effectiveness of these forms, is the vantage point from which the social worker involved assessed how her professional skills meshed with patient needs. How patients' levels of functioning and behavior were improved through the exercise of administrative, educational and practice skills is defined.*

The aged in institutions are perhaps the most power-less, voiceless, invisible, and uncared for group in this country. For the most part, the conditions under which they live tend toward dehuman-ization, loneliness, and dependency. Nader[1] and his colleagues are not exaggerating when they describe these people as "an aggregation of poverty, sickness, loneliness, and powerlessness." The few homes that are humane, competent, and mindful of their residents' need for activity and meaning in their day highlight the staggering gap between what should be attainable in an affluent society and what is too frequently the reality for nursing home residents.

The knowledge and skills to help fulfill the human needs of the aged in our nation's nursing homes exist in many professions, one of which is social work. Social workers have a commitment to serve the disad-vantaged, regardless of age and health, in whatever settings they are found. 'though many social workers now give their personal and professional selves to promoting proper care of the institutionalized aged, the professional social worker has a responsibility to go into facilities that heretofore he has been reluctant to enter. As Brody[2] states: "Past neglect of the elderly indicates that there is still a need for special advocacy for the aging population as a whole and particularly

Ms. Jorgensen is Assistant Professor, Graduate School of Social Work, Social Work Building, University of Utah, Salt Lake City, Utah 84112. Dr. Kane is Associate Professor and Project Director of the Nursing Home Demonstra-tion Project, Department of Community and Family Medicine, College of Medicine, University of Utah. The research referred to was supported by the Intermountain Regional Medical Program and a contract from the Health Resources Administra-tion, Department of Health Education, and Welfare, and ASM-110-73410.

disadvantaged subgroups." The institutionalized aged in nursing homes constitute such a subgroup.

Some advocates of the elderly suggest that an attitudinal change in the educational process may be necessary. While many graduate schools of social work have field placements in agencies dealing with the elderly, and 14 of the 69 schools accredited by the Council on Social Work Education have student units in such settings, few schools have included the aged in their curricula.[3] On a practical level, there must be changes in curriculum, training, and research if the elderly are to be given a proportionate share of attention.

In social work education, there is evidence of a growing emphasis on developing working skills with the geriatric client; nonetheless, the graduate social work students typically indicate that while they are doing some of their training in a nursing home setting, they do not plan to practice in such an institution. Ther plans for geriatric practice focus on the elderly functioning outside of institutionalized settings. Thus the interest of social workers in meeting the needs of the elderly has not had an impact on the nursing home population. Kosberg[4] points out that professional social workers have negative attitudes toward (a) private practice, (b) proprietary facilities, (c) institutions, and (d) the elderly as a client group. This fourfold bias has conspired to make social work practice in nursing homes unattractive to many social workers.

The belief that practice with the elderly in proprietary institutions is certain to be discouraging and unrewarding and that methods of intervention are inadequate to the overwhelming task becomes a self-fulfilling prophecy and is reinforced by the fact that the kinds of consultation offered by social work in nursing homes have for the most part been insufficient.

NATURE OF THE NURSING HOME DEMONSTRATION PROJECT

In connection with a Nursing Home Demonstration Project developed by the Department of Community and Family Medicine of the University of Utah College of Medicine, an intensive effort was made to intervene on behalf of nursing home patients. The social worker found herself using the full range of her skills and knowledge in what proved to be a challenging and rewarding enterprise. We have tried to articulate the substantive nature of that experience which offered a rare, if not unique, exposure to this voiceless, invisible group.

Although the project was established to test the cost-effectiveness of the nurse clinician in the primary care role, the planners recognized that much of the care needed by the elderly consists of emotional support and assistance in coping with the degenerative processes associated with the aging phase of their lives. Such care might be rendered equally and perhaps more efficiently by a social work practitioner. Therefore, it seemed appropriate to look at these two modalities of care as they would function separately and together. The design of the study took cognizance of this by dividing randomly into three equal groups the 13 participating intermediate care nursing homes with their approximately 300 patients. One-third of the homes received the services of a nurse practitioner supervised by a physician. One-third continued with whatever traditional medical services they had had before the study began and in addition received the services of a social worker. The final third received the services of the entire nurse-practitioner-physician-social worker team. Thus, social services at the practice level were active in two-thirds of the homes.

Recognizing the tremendous burden of daily care that falls on nursing home staff, the project sought to involve personnel actively in a meaningful training program that could provide them with new tools and skills for understanding the people for whom they care. The major focus of the educational efforts has been around the development of skills in patient observation and recording.

Special scales of patient function and behavior have been developed. The functional scale (Appendix A) indicates the highest level of physical and social functioning achieved by the patient each day and is summarized over a 2-week period. The behavioral scale (Appendix B) looks at 15 items of normal and abnormal behavior once every 2 weeks. These data, along with other information on the use of drugs, the use of other health care facilities, the use of community outpatient activity programs, and the total cost of health-related expenditures, are maintained on each patient in each of the homes in the study population. The scope of the demonstration model is described more fully elsewhere.[5]

The problem-oriented record system has been introduced into all the homes in the project. A recent article indicated that just as the problem-oriented record forces all physicians who use it to relate any orders for drugs and tests to a specific problem, so all social workers are expected to associate plans, referrals, or requests for consultation to a numbered problem. In institutional settings where other personnel help carry out plans, the problem-oriented record has the effect of helping everyone to understand why certain actions are taken. It seems axiomatic that persons perform better when they understand the reason for what they are doing.[6]

The problem-oriented record system format in the nursing home setting has been adapted for utilization by nursing aides with minimal communication skills. A manual has been developed that outlines a set of observations for each of a series of problems common to the nursing home population. The manual goes on to specify the frequency with which these observations should be made and the acceptable range of variation. When a preset limit has been reached, a course of action is indicated for the nursing home staff. Generally this indicates that the project staff should be notified of the deviation. The observation requirements have been set up in such a way as to make minimal demands on the writing skills of the nursing home aides. The material is entered into a flowchart format designed to utilize abbreviations for each of the recordings of observations.

SOCIAL WORKER'S RESPONSIBILITIES

The role and functions of the social worker in the Nursing Home Demonstration Project are threefold: project administrator, educator, and social work practitioner. Work with families, staff, and patients in the nursing homes is geared to increased understanding of the patients' needs and the devising of realistic interactions to meet these needs. In this role the social worker collaborates with other disciplines, the nurse practitioner, physician, and clinic pharmacist, where a team is in operation and works individually in homes traditionally staffed.

As project administrator, the social worker represents the project in the community as well as within the university medical center where it is housed. Working closely with the nursing home owners and administrators and the Utah Nursing Home Association, effort is made to integrate knowledge gained from the project into the health care system. Close contact with the State Division of Health, Medical Review Unit and Standard and Licenser Departments, related the project to the departments' established standards as well as introducing to them areas for possible change and improvement.

Individual councils were formed at the beginning of the project where the people who are involved in the nursing home business would have the opportunity to meet together to exchange ideas, make suggestions to the Nursing Home Demonstration Project team, and develop relationships that would enable the project team to become an accepted and effective extension of the nursing home staffs. These councils have met every 3 months. They have been invaluable in the area of keeping everyone informed as to project direction, the Nursing Home Demonstration Project's expectations, and clarifying mutual expectations of project staff and the nursing home owners, administrators, and staffs.

EDUCATION

Education takes a large part of the social worker's time; this role encompasses counseling, consultation, and teaching the nursing home staffs as well as being involved in the project research.

Too often a demonstration project comes into a setting for a period of time and then leaves, making the desired impact only when the project members are present. Staff education has, therefore, received heavy emphasis in the Nursing Home Demonstration Project. From the outset of the project, it was determined that help must be given to nursing home staffs in developing permanent skills to be used regularly with the patients.

Relationships had to be built on an individual basis with each staff member in the nursing home before he was able or willing to risk himself in helping to make needed changes. These relationships were built by project staff responsiveness to any need the nursing home staffs considered important, no matter how minute. Planned contact was maintained with the nursing home staff members on a regular basis during the early stages of the project. Often the principal value of these contacts was demonstration to the nursing home staff members that their needs were important to the project. Many hours were spent counseling the nursing home staff members with personal problems. Literature was provided and resources sought where they could get information and help. The result of these efforts was that staff persons were able to function at a higher level themselves. They also became more responsive to the goals of the project.

Development of an education curriculum took into account that nursing home staff members generally do not have a great deal of education and often have few successful experiences in their own lives. Commonly those caring for elderly patients do not understand the needs of these persons. They may feel that the only way to get a patient to do something for himself is to raise their voice to him. The social worker developed programs that have helped the staff members to a greater understanding of themselves and their own needs and how to relate this awareness to the needs of other people. Sessions have included exercises in communication skills with the nursing home patient, how to make the patients feel secure in the nursing home setting, understanding the need for activity and enrichment programs, opportunities for the patient to get out of the nursing home for short periods of time, and how to help the nursing home patients relate to each other. Throughout, the emphasis has been on how to achieve a higher level of functioning for the patient.

The social worker role has included teaching the nursing home staffs the use of outside resources and the value of these resources to them. Help was given to them in developing referral files to record any volunteers available as well as the date the volunteers last had contact with the nursing home and the talents they offered (e.g., making cookies, chauffering residents to the doctor, securing tickets for theater productions, providing entertainment in the nursing home setting). For nursing home personnel, dealing with community resources is not easy. They have now been exposed to the basic organization and management skills that will help in this area. In the homes where there is a social worker and those where a team is present, an Activities Director position has been developed. This person plans on a weekly basis for each individual patient. After each patient's capabilities are evaluated and medical and physical problems are taken into account, a weekly plan is made whereby the patient becomes involved in many activity areas outside the nursing home as well as within the institution.

Through coordination with other agencies in the community, nursing home patients are able to go out of their homes to a Multiple Handicapped Center or Senior Citizen Center, work in sheltered workshops, and attend socialization groups at the mental health centers. Many patients have volunteers working with them on a one-to-one basis, and this affords them the opportunity to get out of the nursing home setting, if only for a shopping excursion or a short walk. It has been found that those who are able to leave the nursing home occasionally function more independently and with a higher level of self-esteem.

DIRECT PRACTICE

Eighty-two percent of the patients had at least one social problem, and almost every patient had multiple problems. Moreover, most medical problems in the nursing home setting can be diminished when there is a good activity program where patients have something to look forward to and find a purpose for living.

In counseling with patients on individual problems, we discovered that most patients are able to accept nursing home placement if they can continue some links to the life-style they previously knew. For example, a patient who played the piano well was never asked to play the piano in the nursing home because no one knew of his skill. Because of his depressed state, he could not initiate or perform on his own. Looking at the total patient facilitates the maintenance of existing skills and in some cases even the development of new ones. The problem-oriented record used in the team homes is particularly valuable because it includes not only physical problems but social and psychological problems as well. Through the social assessment, historical facts are pulled together about the patient, helping to achieve a profile of the total person. Planning with this information is a much more thorough process than most nursing home patients have had before this time.

Individual projects for nursing home patients have been tried as another means of raising the patients' functioning and making them feel a part of the nursing home setting. The patients' satisfaction with these projects enhances their sense of individual worth. The social worker has directed the nursing home patient and staff into planning sessions where the needs of the home, patients, and staff are examined, plans made, constructive changes agreed upon by all parties involved, and an evaluation process for these changes established by the group. These planning sessions for both patients and staff have been most effective in areas where patients feel desolate, lonely, and believe that nothing can be done to change the feelings they are experiencing. Involvement does much to change attitudes, and in the nursing home setting this is a new and innovative idea.

The social worker has sought to involve the families of the nursing home patient, where families are residing in the area. The social worker has had family groups meet, where families have had the opportunity to discuss, understand, and test their ideas regarding nursing home placement for a family member. Families participating in these groups are more supportive of the nursing home staffs and have a better understanding of the coordination needed in the care of the patient.

The families participating in the groups found it difficult to understand the need for rehabilitation programs for the nursing home patient. Historically a nursing home is viewed by families as a last resort, a warehouse. One patient who had been placed in a nursing home because of brain deterioration after an accident had been very hostile toward his wife during her daily visits. He said she came to visit when the patients were having planned activities, causing him to miss these activities. His wife felt her visits were important, and she could not understand his behavior. When she presented this in the group, discussion around the needs of the patient emphasized the importance to the patient of the activities in the nursing home as well as those outside. After this, the wife accepted her husband's behavior and scheduled her visits less frequently and coordinated them with the patient's other activities. The group discussion also helped the patient's wife to understand her husband's capabilities and not to expect him to relate to her as he did prior to entering the nursing home.

IMPLICATIONS

The Nursing Home Demonstration Project revealed many untouched areas where social work knowledge could be applied. During this demonstration phase, definite responsibilities and goals had to be set because of the time limits involved. It is anticipated that many other areas can be tapped during the operational stage, but the setting of priorities will remain crucial because of the many needs.

The preliminary response of the nursing home participants to the project has encouraged the transition to an operational stage that will utilize the full team concept in all homes. Although the ultimate evaluation of the project awaits the analysis of all data, it is already clear that social work involvement in this project has contributed measurably to its success. It is evident that the aged population, in the nursing home setting, needs more contact with professional social workers.

Until 1966 there were few legislative or administrative requirements (national, state, or local) that made social work mandatory for nursing homes to be licensed or receive governmental reimbursement. Although the original Medicare regulations stipulated that nursing homes had to provide social services in order to be reimbursed by the government for the care of eligible patients, the recently enacted Social Security amendments of 1973 rescinded that requirement on the grounds that professional resources to meet staffing and consultant requirements are scarce or unavailable in many areas. Consultants in the area of social services, activity programming, and meal services have been eliminated.[7]

Social work in nursing homes has become, at best, optional. Hiring professional social workers or any other additional staff would of course increase operating expenses and reduce profits in these facilities, which are mainly proprietary. It seems improbable that nursing homes, for whom minimum requirements too often become maximum performance standards, will raise their standards in this voluntarily. Only the most enlightened owners or administrators can be expected to see the strong need for social workers and voluntarily hire them.

The financial dilemma posed by nursing homes reflects a more fundamental question: the need for rehabilitation of the aged. A study of 2,000 public welfare patients of New York nursing homes concluded that extensive rehabilitation of aged residents in nursing homes is neither practical nor socially productive.[8] The basic technique of rehabilitation—keeping the patient active—has been systematically precluded by the way such homes are filled and financed. Bedridden patients receive a higher welfare payment, require less attention, and have less turnover.

Government has grudgingly acknowledged its responsibility for providing at least minimum care for this segment of the population. Efforts to establish better standards grew out of the Title 18 and Title 19 amendments to the Social Security Act. The approach taken was one of regulation and utilization review. Major efforts were devoted to means by which the growing costs of such chronic care could be constrained. It would appear that the government, at both federal and local levels, is disinclined to view with favor any programs that would require increased allocations of funds. The challenge, then, is to make visible the needs of this group, to validate the relevance and effectiveness of social work to those needs, and to demonstrate a credible sense of cost-effectiveness.

Society's collective value system is the final determinant in quality life issues for those who cannot force their demands. That value system can, however, be influenced. The presentation of sensible, compassionate plans that are fiscally possible must come from the expertise and imagination of those who have assumed caretaker roles.

While the formal outcome findings of this project are still being developed, the "soft data" assessment of need and opportunity has compelling implications.

REFERENCES

1. Nader, Ralph. Introduction to *Old Age: The Last Segregation*, by Claire Townsend. New York: Grossman Publishers, 1971.
2. Brody, Elaine M. "Aging." *Encyclopedia of Social Work*. New York: National Association of Social Workers, 1971.
3. Brody, Elaine M. "Serving the Aged: Educational Needs as Viewed by Practice." *Social Work*, October 1970, p. 49.
4. Kosberg, Jordan J. "The Nursing Home: A Social Work Paradox." *Social Work*, March 1973, p. 106.
5. Kane, Robert L.; Jorgensen, Lou Ann B.; and Pepper, Ginette A. "Can Nursing Home Care Be Cost Effective." *Journal of American Geriatrics Society* 22 (1974).
6. Kane, Rosalie A. "Look to the Record!" *Social Work* 19 (1974):412.
7. Department of Health, Education, and Welfare, Social Rehabilitation Service, Medical Association Program, January 17, 1974, Washington, D.C., vol. 39, no. 12, pt. 2.
8. Burger, Robert E. "Who Cares for the Aged?" In *The Coming of Age*, app. 2. New York: Warner Books, 1973.

APPENDIX A

Functional Scale

The statements below describing the activity level of patients are placed in order of increasing activity. Thus, each statement shows an increased level of activity over the statement before it. Choose the number of the statement that describes the highest level of activity of a patient for today and place it in the box beside his name.

1. Hospitalized	In another institution.
2. Completely bedfast	In bed at all times.
3. Bedfast with bathroom privileges	Got out of bed only to use bathroom.
4. Stays in room	Left room only for bathroom privileges but was out of bed in chair or ambulatory.
5. Stays in home	Did not leave building or house.
6. Remains on grounds or property	Sat or walked outside of building in yard or on porch.
7. In and out of nursing home, supervised	Any visit away from home grounds except overnight or trips to doctor,

dentist, or clinic, with staff member, family member, or someone else supervising.

8. In and out of nursing home, unsupervised

Any visit away from home grounds (for patients not requiring supervision) except overnight or trips to doctor, dentist, or clinic.

9. Living away from the nursing home

Anytime the patient leaves the home overnight except if hospitalized.

APPENDIX B

Behavioral Scale

Instructions: In using this rating form, observers should adhere to the following guidelines:

1. Circle the one statement that most accurately describes the individual as you have usually observed him.

2. Focus on what you have seen the individual do in the last week. Several examples have been provided to indicate the kinds of activity that constitute each category. In selecting the most accurate descriptive statement, base your decision, whenever possible, on such indices as the frequency with which the activity occurs, its intensity, or its duration.

3. Rate all individuals on each item before moving on to the next item.

4. Be objective and don't let personal feelings bias your ratings.

5. An individual may have both favorable and unfavorable ratings in different areas. Judge each category independently of all others.

Behavior Category

1. *Complains* of physical problems
   a. More than once a day
   b. At least once a day
   c. Less than once a day
   d. Almost never

2. *Eats* all of prepared meals
   a. Almost never
   b. At least once a day
   c. More than once a day
   d. Nearly always

3. *Sleeps* well
   a. Less than once a week
   b. About four times a week
   c. Almost every night

4. Is *pleasant* in dealings with others
   a. Usually very grouchy
   b. Most often grouchy
   c. Most frequently pleasant
   d. Almost always pleasant

5. Is *sullen* or *depressed*
   a. Always sullen
   b. Most frequently sullen
   c. Rarely sullen
   d. Most often cheerful

Signs

Spontaneously or upon inquiry complains of such problems as pain, sleeping problems, fatigue, or restlessness.

Consumes all of the prepared meal except for occasional food dislikes.

Sleeps uninterrupted throughout the night.

Gives friendly answers when spoken to; gets along with others; is neither irritable nor grouchy.

Nonresponsive to others; preoccupied with gloomy thoughts; talks or moves sluggishly.

6. Is *hostile* or *irritable*
   a. Always hostile
   b. Usually hostile
   c. Rarely hostile
   d. Usually friendly

Gives abrupt or unfriendly answers when spoken to; is demanding or complaining.

7. Is *excited*
   a. Always very excited
   b. Usually excited
   c. Rarely excited
   d. Almost never excited

Talks quickly and frequently, changes the subject; flighty; unable to sit still for longer than a few minutes.

8. Is *suspicious*
   a. Very frequently suspicious
   b. Often suspicious
   c. Rarely suspicious
   d. Almost never suspicious

States that others are out to get him or pick on him, or have prevented him from attaining certain goals; reacts strongly to slight and unintended injury.

9. Is *disoriented* or *confused*
   a. Always very disoriented
   b. Usually disoriented
   c. Rarely disoriented
   d. Signs of disorientation not observed

Makes inaccurate statements about happenings in the home; cannot perform routine tasks without becoming "lost"; cannot participate in back and forth conversation; does not know his name.

10. Shows signs of *poor memory*
    a. Always very forgetful
    b. Usually forgetful
    c. Rarely forgetful
    d. Poor memory not observed

Forgets to carry out routine assignemtns as well as names of patients and staff around him; requires frequent reminding.

11. Shows signs of *impaired thinking*
    a. Never really understands
    b. Understands some of the time
    c. Usually understands
    d. Immediately grasps what he is told

Requires repeated explanation before grasping things that are told to him. (Exclude difficulty attributable to hearing loss.)

12. Is *withdrawn* socially
    a. Very withdrawn—will not speak
    b. Moderately withdrawn—interacts only when encouraged by others
    c. Frequently talks with others and initiates functional activity on his own

Sits alone most of the time; rarely talks or moves around.

13. *Appearance* is
    a. Almost always disorderly
    b. Frequently disorderly
    c. Rarely disorderly
    d. Almost never disorderly

Appearance includes dress, hair, and beard for males.

14. Shows *independent action*
    a. Almost always dependent on others
    b. Usually dependent on others
    c. Occasionally dependent on others
    d. Usually behaves independently of others

Does things that are *expected of him* without having to be told how and when to do it; does not rely on others to perform tasks he could do himself.

15. Engages in *activities*
    a. Almost never
    b. Infrequently
    c. Sometimes
    d. Regularly

Has hobbies, plays games, watches TV, reads, attends functions away from the nursing home, etc.

INDIVIDUAL PSYCHOTHERAPY WITH THE INSTITUTIONALIZED AGED

Judah L. Ronch, Ph.D., and Jan S. Maizler, M.S.W.

Contrary to the predisposition of many mental health professionals, this paper contends that insight-oriented, dynamically-based, individual psychotherapy is an effective treatment modality with the institutionalized elderly. Issues such as dependency, transference and countertransference, contrasts to psychotherapy with younger patients, and methodological modifications are discussed, and clinical examples are offered.

This article will consider some of the problems inherent in doing psychotherapy on an individual basis with elderly persons in long-term care institutions. Our experience has been with patients aged 65 to 96 at the Miami Jewish Home and Hospital for the Aged, where the average age of a resident is 86. In this article, we will use age 65 and over to delineate the group we call elderly. This age delineation is not meant to imply there is any magical process that occurs on an individual's 65th birthday to render him "old" or "elderly." (In the outpatient mental health program at Douglas Gardens Outpatient Mental Health Center, affiliated with Miami Jewish Home and Hospital for the Aged, we have been successfully using an age of 50 or 55, depending on catchment area demography, to establish eligibility for service in a program specializing in treating the "elderly" and providing "primary prevention" services.)

We shall carefully avoid pretending to prescribe the long and short of how to do psychotherapy with this population, since each of us practices this art with a unique blend of our own personality, training, and philosophical approach to the human condition. We

Submitted to the Journal in November 1976. Based in part on a 1976 presentation to the American Psychiatric Association, in Miami, Fla.

Authors are at: Douglas Gardens Outpatient Mental Health Center, Miami, Fla. (Ronch); and Miami Jewish Home and Hospital for the Aged (Maizler).

hope, rather, to shed some light on heretofore under-scrutinized issues in this field.

For our purposes, and as a true reflection of how we tend to categorize our approaches, we shall initially use Wolberg's [22] definition, that:

Psychotherapy is a form of treatment for problems of an emotional nature in which a trained person deliberately establishes a professional relationship with a patient with the object of removing, modifying, or retarding existing symptoms, or mediating disturbed patterns of behavior, and promoting positive personality growth and development.

In recognition of the generic quality of the foregoing definition, we also hold that "psychotherapy proper" is a viable treatment modality with institutionalized elderly, and we adhere to Blank's [2] more specific definition that psychotherapy is

. . . a mutual agreement between patient and therapist that the therapist will undertake a formal, disciplined method in order to help the patient resolve mental distress.

We are, therefore, speaking of methods that counter the widespread belief that non-insight-oriented techniques are the only fertile therapeutic ground for the institutionalized aged. As Blank [2] pointed out, we must distinguish between that which is therapeutic, and psychotherapy.

Historically, the elderly have been excluded from the psychotherapeutic services which have been available to other age groups. Freud [6] felt that psychoanalysis would not be of benefit to the elderly for a number of reasons, most notably because they were "no longer educable" and because the treatment would take too long. A recent survey by Weintraub and Aronson [21] indicated that this pessimistic view is still prevalent; of a sample of 30 psychoanalytically-oriented psychotherapists in private practice, none was treating any patients over 60 years of age. (We are currently exploring this phenomenon among other mental health professionals as well.) Furthermore, persons 65 and over have typically constituted only 2.4% of all patients seen in outpatient psychiatric clinics, while private psychiatrists have been found to allocate approximately 2% of their time to these elderly persons.

These statistics are most telling when juxtaposed to the data issued by NIMH which indicate that the evidence of new cases of psychopathology was 236.1 per 100,000 population in persons 65 and over, while at age 35 to 54 the incidence was 93.0 per 100,000.[3] With more than one million persons over the age of 65 in institutions, primarily nursing homes, and in view of the fact that over 50% of these people have evidence of some psychiatric problem or mental impairment, it becomes imperative that the need for psychotherapy in the elderly be attended to. In particular, it has become crucial for those who practice psychotherapy to look at the need for such services in our institutionalized elderly population.

These data, we think, eloquently endorse the need for psychotherapy with the elderly, and we invite a discussion of some of the issues that make individual psychotherapy with the institutionalized elderly a qualitatively different endeavor. One method of clarifying the nature of this process is to compare psychotherapy with the elderly to therapy with younger persons, with particular emphasis on the elderly in long-term care institutions.

Unlike the child, adolescent, or younger adult, our treatment of the older adult is aided by neither biology (as in the developmental progression in children) or society. We cannot hope that the institutionalized aged will outgrow the problem, receive increased familial or educational support, or find satisfaction in different vocational choices, living arrangements, peer group changes, or life-style adjustments. Unfortunately, but realistically, most of our institutionalized elderly will most likely not experience any radical biosocial changes of a progressive or an enhancing nature. Rather, the elderly will continue to experience decrements in biological and, to some extent, psychological functioning as they age. Our direction and perspective in individual psychotherapy must therefore be adjusted to meet the needs of these patients. A case which illustrates this point is a recent admission to our home for the aged.

Patient A. is a white male is his mid-eighties. Physical problems which necessitated his admission were hypertension, increasing blindness, a stroke, the recent installation of a cardiac pacemaker, and recurrent depression. Patient A.'s wife has been in a mental institution for the last thirty years and neither of his two children were able or equipped to take in their father, because of their own tasks and problems.

While Patient A. tries to be optimistic, and struggles to regain as much of his ability to master the environment as he formerly had, his progressive physical deterioration frustrates both patient and therapist in their attempts to recapture previous levels of functioning. Our direction, goals, and perspective in individual psychotherapy must therefore be adjusted to meet the needs of this aged patient.

One method that proved moderately successful with Patient A. is based on the "life review" theory proposed by Lewis and Butler.[13] In this approach, the older person brings into consciousness his past experiences, frequently focusing on his unresolved conflicts. Some common themes include the wish to undo some previous life patterns, the desire for new starts and second chances, the need for help in recognizing the source of anxieties and fears concerning death, and reaching some degree of accommodation with the inevitable.[4]

In this vein, Kubler-Ross [12] has pioneered the exploration of the psychodynamics of death and dying, as they relate to both patient and therapist, and has shed significant light on the dynamics of all forms of loss. Consonant with the idea of "life review," Kubler-Ross's work gives the therapist a basis upon which to help the institutionalized elderly come to terms with their "keen awareness of time, grief and restitution for the loss of loved ones, and fear of physical illness and disability." [13] Much of this method is congruent with Jung's [11] realization of the importance of reassessment of values and introspection derived from his work with older persons. Erikson's [5] stage-appropriate task for old age is the development and maintenance of a sense of ego-integrity, as opposed to despair. A basic assumption of these efficacious treatment modalities is the finding that reminiscense, far from being an inevitable and ominous symptom of senile dementia, has much adaptive and therapeutic significance.

Another contrast between individual psychotherapy with older and younger persons suggests itself. With children, Freud said, the task of psychoanalysis was to replace id processes with those of the ego for more effective adaptation. With the elderly now in therapy, we all too often find that, on the contrary, we must replace the dominating supergo processes with ego,* a task most clearly required by the dynamics of depression. It is these supergo processes, very often punitive and harsh, which do not allow for the free expression of feelings in the elderly we are currently treating. Our task with the elderly, therefore (and this more easily said than done), is to replace the strict parental prohibitions against feelings, particularly against the ambivalent feelings surrounding lost objects, with more realistic, more adaptive, less unyielding defenses.

Another consideration in doing psychotherapy with the elderly relates to the specific social conditions of their childhood and youth.[5] If one were to postulate a "generational psyche" for today's elderly, it would be seen that the effects of war, emigration, poverty, and a "boot-straps mentality" all played into the supression and repression of disturbing and distracting feelings, particularly those of anger.

Patient B. told us, "My father died when I was two. Because of the war and the Depression, mother was too busy trying to earn money for five children by mending and sewing, so she couldn't give us individual attention. If I ever talked about my needs, she would tell me to stop the foolishness, and work on bringing in money for my poor family. I was very young at the time."

A crucial and often neglected area of consideration in psychotherapy with the institutionalized aged is the heightened resurgence of dependency conflicts because of the institutionalization itself. One must deal with increased manifestations of ambivalence and anger towards the providers of dependency gratification (institutional staff), and the correlated fear of abandonment. In working with younger patients, we are often cautioned to avoid or prohibit the development of a dependency relationship. Goldfarb[9] argued that, in the elderly, independence will never be achieved, and that psychotherapy should instead aim simply at making the person less dependent. Attempts to deter dependency in the individual therapy situation will, he felt, lead to a patient-therapist struggle that could increase the patient's feelings of helplessness and inadequacy. Rather progress in therapy is made when the therapist accepts the role of surrogate parent, and thus allows the patient to grow more independent in a secure relationship. To equate independence with cure in psychotherapy with the institutionalized elderly belies the issues and undermines the patient, who knows that there has been deterioration in his ability to function independently, which is why he is in an institution.

Whether or not one agrees with Goldfarb's viewpoint, we believe he raises the most important of the many countertransference issues that arise in our work with the elderly. The depressed, dependent elderly patient can, and usually does, arouse many feelings in the therapist about his or her own

---

* We are indebted to Christopher Corrie, Ph.D. for this formulation.

unmet dependency needs, and about the therapist's relationship with his or her aging parents, as well as fears about the therapist's own aging. In addition, there are other conscious and unconscious reactions we have toward old, sick people that differ significantly from our response to younger patients. An ominous example of the attitude called "ageism" is offered in a study [19] which reported that first-year and fourth-year medical students accepted the myths about aging, and indicated a definite preference for younger patients.

While depression is common among elderly persons with psychiatric disorders, it is often a by-product of the aging process itself, especially in relation to the commonly-occurring losses the elderly encounter with each passing year. Therefore, individual psychotherapy may be needed for those institutionalized elderly with reactive depression who, after treatment, may be able to function normally should no further psychiatric problems (*e.g.,* organic brain disease) set in. In fact, entering a nursing home is a frequent precipitant for some degree of depression in most cases, since the person must abruptly alter a familiar way of life. The need to determine the etiology of psychiatric symptomatology and behavior inevitably demands the attention of the psychiatric practitioner working with an institutionalized geriatric population. One may have to ask, "What is masking what?"

Patient C., a white male, aged 70, was admitted to the Home following a short psychiatric hospitalization for a suicide attempt. Upon admission, he was diagnosed as having a psychotic depressive reaction and Alzheimer's Disease, a pre-senile dementia. For the first few days, he was placed in the locked psychiatric facility, because much of the behavior deriving from the depression was of a paranoid, combative nature.

For the next eleven months, the mental health staff at the Home, by concentrating therapeutic efforts upon the functional illness—the depression—made much progress with the patient. He is now residing on the second highest area of self-care of the eleven levels of progressive care at the institution. The staff also does therapy related to the manifestations of the patient's organic brain disease, using a corrective feedback technique, called reality orientation, to solidify any gains in judgement, memory, intellect, and orientation.

The issue of transference in psychotherapy with this population is quite deceptive. A very generic definition of transference by Greenson,[10] which has gained clinical acceptance, holds that

. . . transference is the experiencing of feelings, drives, attitudes, fantasies, and defenses towards the person in the present which are inappropriate to that person and are a repetition, a displacement of reactions originating in regard to significant persons in early childhood.

While we expect the patients to project onto us their attitudes toward their adult children, we have experienced cases where the transference has been in the nature of the therapist as the patient's mother, father, and all siblings. All of these are not unusual distortions in younger patients, and should be seen as potential projections onto the therapist by the older patient, as well as opportunities for achieving insight in the therapy.

During psychotherapy with the institutionalized aged, there occasionally occurs "an intense demand for gratification and productive . . . work ceases; serious psychopathology is thought to be present." [17] As Rappaport noted, "the patients are not embarrassed or ashamed by such wishes." [15] It is frequently indicated that such patients, who overplay the erotic component in the transference, want the analyst (or therapist) to behave towards them as a parent. They express their anger only when the therapist does not comply with their demands. Rappaport [15] correlated such intensely sexual demanding reactions ". . . with the severity of the patients' pathology. . . These patients try to convert every significant person into a parent."

Patient D., a 69-year-old white woman, was recently admitted to the Home following spinal surgery, this being the major physical problem. The worker was referred to see the patient because of problems created by her attempting to monopolize the time of all the professional staff by anxious demands that, "I be first amongst others and get what I want right away." Patient D. complained of no energy, or "get-up and go," since the onset of her spinal problems, well before the operation. She stated that she had no appetite at all and had to force herself to eat. Frequently, she would awaken in the middle of the night with "disturbing thoughts," and be unable to get back to sleep. She said that she was unable to concentrate on anything because of "the pain," and upcoming tasks of the day made her feel overwhelmed. The patient complained of being "frightened" of everything and appeared very tremulous. She stated that she had a "short fuse" and couldn't wait for anything, that she would have to be first, because she "was in the greatest pain," and no one had the pain that she did. She felt that the spinal operation was a failure (which it wasn't), and continually requested, on a daily basis, rediagnosis from staff because, "I know I'll be this way for the rest of my life."

After seeing Patient D. for an evaluation, it was the worker's impression that a nosological diagnosis of agitated depression with multiple somatic delusions was in order; the patient's basic personality seemed to be of a primitive narcissistic type. The patient's descriptive developmental level was on the oral level of psychosexual development, with very poor drive mastery. Her object relations were on a pure need-gratification level, and her anxiety was of an object-loss type, with identity formation regressed predominantly on a symbiotic level. Patient D. wholeheartedly accepted the therapeutic contract, initially perceiving it as a magical rescue; the worker, in continually struggling with the patient's dependency needs, reclarified the alliance to be one in which the work would proceed toward diminishing the massively unrealistic expectations, increasing frustration tolerance, and allowing the timed ventilation of rage, while structuring the defenses against the drives she barely held at bay, frequently turning the rage against the self.

The early sessions, which were basically visits to her room, were conducted while the patient was lying down on her bed "because of her back." The next few sessions were pivotal in their significance because of a number of actions. While Patient D. was interviewed lying down, she frequently made allusions to her sexual organs; this was followed by highly inappropriate body posturing and sexual displays. Through case conferences and supervision, it was decided that not only was it rehabilitative for the patient's back not to lie down, but it was psychotherapeutically not indicated, because of the massively eroticized transference.

The next interview began with an insistence by the worker that therapy would only be done sitting up, preferably in the dayroom, garden, etc. This proved to be indeed beneficial for the patient, in that the focus of efforts now more clearly told her that she would be helped mastering her drives; this was not only reassuring, but aided in the patient's efforts at physical rehabilitation through walking and sitting because of an appropriate model gained in therapy. Future investigations were then aimed at the interpretation of the wishes, such as attempts to gain physical love as manifestations of symbiotic longings. This has met with considerable success, in that Patient D.'s defenses have consolidated so that she is now able to function more independently, and is less needy.

Though this is a rather unusual case for an institutional geriatric population, it points out in rich detail, and in contrast to some therapists' ageist prejudices, that the psychic life of many geriatric patients is far from flat and "burnt out."

Many argue [18] that transference takes place outside the analytic or psychotherapeutic situation as well. Thus, given the nature of the institutional environment, it is not unexpected that the helping figure will be seen as the giving mother or denying father (or vice versa), and that other residents may be seen as rival siblings for the ward clerks, orderlies, psychotherapists, nurses, or administrator's (parental) attention. In early-phase treatment with the institutionalized aged, the therapist spends much time dealing with the patient's expressed conflicts about these figures, duly noting the transference implications. Whether these are ultimately interpreted back to the patient will depend upon the given variables of the specific situation. But it is most frequently the physician or psychiatrist who is invested by the resident with (hoped for) omniscient, omnipotent, even shamanistic powers.

Due to the previously mentioned considerations, it is often necessary to modify our usual techniques of individual psychotherapy when working with the aged in long-term care facilities. On the most general level, the establishment of a warm relationship with elderly patients can be enhanced by a simple touch, a warm smile, and other departures from the position of neutrality we have been taught to establish with young patients. Since personality restructuring is rarely, if ever, attempted with the elderly, goals can be more limited; as Pfeiffer [14] pointed out, some sort of symbolic giving can be undertaken by the therapist to help replace, on a symbolic level, some of the many losses the person has suffered. Along with physical "giving," allowing the elderly person to know us as people, by sharing a bit of ourselves and our lives, goes a long way in establishing a therapeutic relationship.

While the issue of touching has received treatment by differing schools of thought, as yet the issue has been far from resolved and standardized for an institutionalized geriatric population. Blanck and Blanck [1] maintained that

. . . the psychotherapist follows the same rule as the psychoanalyst that the patient is not to be touched. The exception is that one shakes hands when the form of physical contact is appropriate. Otherwise, the patients' corporeal intactness is not to be intruded upon.

On the other hand, workers such as Fuchs [8] hold that,

Nevertheless, anything that aids in reaching the goal of increasing emotional honesty and forthrightness may be desirable. Touching is one way. Perhaps what is missing from the current emphasis in psychotherapy is an awareness of its differential significance for individual patients at different junctures in the treatment relationship.

In terms of specific methodological modifications, Weinberg [20] suggested that therapy may be done over a shorter period of time with increased frequency of sessions. Goldfarb,[9] recognizing the problem of insecurity and dependency in the elderly, suggested brief sessions of from five to fifteen minutes, irregularly scheduled, and as far apart as possible. He found the casual, almost accidental meeting to be best suited to his purposes. By remaining reality-oriented, and avoiding in-depth probing, that type of meeting can be productive in giving the patient the feeling that he has succeeded in getting the attention of the therapist, and thus his protection and aid. The objectives of this approach are limited to the reduction of tension and the alteration of the pattern of social adaptation, and this seems to have been effective in 50%–75% of mild to moderately deteriorated patients.

Rechtschaffen [16] summarized other modifications in technique, among which are: greater activity on the part of the therapist, since the aged adult may not be able to assume as much responsibility for the conduct of the session as younger patients do; employment of some environmental manipulations to facilitate adjustment, a technique particularly helpful and valuable in institutional settings; the use of educational techniques; the gentle and careful interpretation of resistance and transference; and the gradual tapering off of therapy, rather than its termination. The kind of relationship that is built up with these patients many times demands that they be seen on an intermittent basis, with long intervals between sessions, instead of concluding treatment altogether.

Another major modification of technique in individual therapy is necessary with the hard-of-hearing or visually-impaired aged, since the facial cues or intonational variations we may use with younger or nonimpaired patients are rendered ineffective. In working with the hearing-impaired, we are left with the problem of separating our reassuring messages from their usual intonation, resulting in a paradoxical (to observers) and dissonant (to us) therapeutic communication; yet this frequently is necessary. (Imagine trying to offer gentle reassurance to a hearing-impaired patient in a tone reserved for hailing a taxicab.) We must, therefore, be alert when dealing with these patients so as to convey our message clearly and unambiguously, and take care not to reinforce any existing tendencies toward psychopathology, such as paranoia in the hard-of-hearing elderly.

Patient E., a white female in her eighties, was transferred to our Hospital because of a severe cold. Her comprehension of the situation was minimized, and her anxiety raised, by her total deafness and inability to read lips. When the caseworker was able to devise a means of communicating with her by printing on paper, which she was able to see and understand, the patient's anxiety diminished, since she now felt in touch with the worker and with her own situation.

We are aware (and, in fact, are hopeful) that some of the observations we have made in this discussion may be seen as provocative, and we hope that some may be reassuring. The paucity of literature in the field of psychotherapy with the elderly, whether in institutions or living in the community, requires development of a body of literature on the theory and practice of psychotherapy with the aged. As a developmental theory of aging emerges from discussion (at times heated) held at various professional forums, gerontological mental health institutions can then be encouraged to try to learn and refine the art of psychotherapy with the institutionalized elderly.

We must reiterate that this paper is not meant as a comprehensive prescription for this field, but aims merely to raise some issues which our work has shown to be demanding of consideration. In practice, we have developed some methods by which to improve psychotherapeutic efforts on behalf of the elderly in our institutional settings. As a result, we are able now to take issue with Freud's statement that cure with elderly patients would be reached at a time of life when "much importance is no longer attached to nervous health." [6] The question today is not whether "older people are no longer educable," [7] but whether we, the mental health professionals, are.

REFERENCES

1. BLANCK, G. AND BLANCK, R. 1974. Ego Psychology: Theory and Practice. Columbia University Press, New York.
2. BLANK, M. 1974. Raising the age barrier to psychotherapy. Geriatrics 29:141–148.
3. BUTLER, R. 1974. Mental health and aging. Geriatrics 29:59–60.
4. BUTLER, R. AND LEWIS, M. 1973. Aging and Mental Health: Positive Psychosocial Approaches. C.V. Mosby, St. Louis.
5. ERIKSON, E. 1959. Identity and the life cycle. Psychol. Issues 1:101–164.
6. FREUD, S. 1959. Sexuality in the aetiology of the neuroses. In Collected Papers 1: 220–248. Basic Books, New York.
7. FREUD, S. 1959. On psychotherapy. In Collected Papers 1:249–263. Basic Books, New York.
8. FUCHS, L. 1975. Reflections on touching and transference in psychotherapy. Clin. Soc. Wk J. 3:167–176.
9. GOLDFARB, A. 1969. The Psychodynamics of Dependency and the Search for Aid in the Dependencies of Old People. Institute of Gerontology, University of Michigan, Ann Arbor, Mich.
10. GREENSON, R. 1965. The working alliance and the transference neurosis. Psychoanal. Quart. 34(2).
11. JUNG, C. 1933. Modern Man in Search of a Soul. Harcourt, Brace, New York.
12. KUBLER-ROSS, E. 1969. On Death and Dying. Macmillan, New York.
13. LEWIS, M. AND BUTLER, R. 1974. Life review therapy. Geriatrics 29:165–173.
14. PFEIFFER, E. 1971. Psychotherapy with elderly patients. Postgrad. Med. 50(5): 254–258.
15. RAPPAPORT, E. 1956. The management of an eroticized transference. Psychoanal. Quart. 25:515–529.
16. RECHTSCHAFFEN, A. 1959. Psychotherapy with geriatric patients: a review of the literature. Gerontology 14:73–84.
17. SANDLER, J., DARE, D. AND HOLDER, A. Basic Psychoanalytic Concepts: Special Forms of Transference. Institute of Psychiatry, London. (undated)
18. SANDLER, J. ET AL. Some Theoretical and Clinical Aspects of Transference. The Hampstead Child Therapy Clinic, London. (undated)
19. SPENCE, D., FEIGENBAUM, E. AND FITZGERALD F. 1968. Medical student attitudes towards the geriatric patient. J. Amer. Geriat. Soc. 16:967–983.
20. WEINBERG, J. 1957. Psychotherapy of the aged. In Progress in Psychotherapy: Anxiety and Therapy, J. Masserman and J. Moreno, eds, Grune and Stratton, New York.
21. WEINTRAUB, W. AND ARONSON, J. 1968. A survey of patients in classical psychoanalysis: some vital statistics. J. Nerv. Ment. Dis. 146:98–102.
22. WOLBERG, L. 1954. The Techniques of Psychotherapy. Grune and Stratton, New York.

Elaine M. Brody, Charlotte Cole, and Miriam Moss

Individualizing therapy for the mentally impaired aged

The existence of disabilities accessible to therapy
signifies that the label of chronic brain syndrome
should indicate intervention, not benign neglect

Elaine M. Brody is director, Department of Social
Work, Philadelphia Geriatric Center, Philadelphia,
Pennsylvania, and principal investigator of the
research study, Individualized Treatment of
Mentally Impaired Aged. Charlotte Cole is a social
worker, Philadelphia Geriatric Center. Miriam
Moss is project coordinator of the research study,
Philadelphia Geriatric Center. This article is based
on a paper presented at the annual meeting of
the Gerontological Society, San Juan, Puerto Rico,
December 19, 1972.

Until the past few years, therapeutic pessimism characterized the attitudes of the public and most professionals toward older people suffering from senility or chronic brain syndrome. Services and programs designed to help this group are notoriously underdeveloped, despite the fact that the behavioral symptoms (confusion, disorientation, memory loss, deficits in intellectual functioning, and poor judgment) make it one of the most personally and socially disruptive of all ailments.

The situation of these mentally impaired people has gained visibility as the number and proportion of the elderly have increased. It is estimated that about 20 percent of the 20 million people sixty-five or over in this country have some degree of this form of impairment—about four million individuals. During the decade between 1960 and 1970, the number of people seventy-five and over increased at three times the rate of the group between sixty-five and seventy-four.[1] Be-

cause there is the highest incidence of chronic brain syndrome among these very old, it is clear that the problem is increasing.

Most impaired old people reside in the community, and the burden of their care is borne by their families. However, many are concentrated in nursing homes, voluntary homes for the aged, psychiatric hospitals, and other institutions. Experts agree that more than half of the 5 percent of older people who are in institutions (about a million individuals) are mentally impaired. It is, therefore, important to develop knowledge and treatment methodologies for them. In the past decade, work by gerontologists regarding the potential for improvement has encouraged the testing of various social therapies that aim to improve the functioning levels of this group.

This article describes the clinical aspects of a research study of a highly individualized interdisciplinary treatment program of elderly women in the Philadelphia Geriatric Center's (PGC) institutional facility, the Home for the Jewish Aged (HJA).[2] In addition to the 340-bed home, the geriatric center includes two apartment buildings for the elderly ac-

---

[1] Herman B. Brotman, The Older Population
Revisited, *Facts and Figures on Older Americans*
No. 2 (Washington, D.C.: Administration on Aging,
Social Rehabilitation Services, U.S. Department of
Health, Education, and Welfare, 1971).

[2] This study was financed in part by National
Institute of Mental Health grant no. 15047.

commodating a total of 500 people, a fully accredited hospital, and the Gerontological Research Institute. The major research findings support the hypothesis that the behavior and functioning of the mentally impaired residents with moderate to severe chronic brain syndrome could be improved.[3] Predictors of improvement[4] and predictors of mortality[5] that were identified have been reported elsewhere. The focus here will be on the treatment procedures developed and tested in the project, and on the incorporation of the approach into the day-by-day institutional program.

How did the actual clinical approach operate? What were the specific procedures? How did the members of the treatment team function in relation to each other and to the older people who were the subjects? What techniques were used to coordinate staff activities and to assure control of the recommended treatments? What are the similarities and differences between this approach and that of the traditional interdisciplinary team?

Background of program

The clinical program was given its shape and direction by the three underlying principles on which the project rested: individualization, multiplicity of disabilities, and realistic goals. The highly individualized approach stemmed from accumulated knowledge regarding the

[3]Elaine M. Brody, Morton H. Kleban, M. Powell Lawton, and H. A. Silverman, Excess Disabilities of Mentally-Impaired Aged: Impact of Individualized Treatment, *The Gerontologist*, 11:124–33 (Summer 1971).

[4]Morton H. Kleban, Elaine M. Brody, and M. Powell Lawton, Personality Traits in the Mentally-Impaired Aged and their Relationship to Improvements in Current Functioning, *The Gerontologist*, 11:134–40 (Summer 1971); Morton H. Kleban and Elaine M. Brody, Prediction of Improvement in Mentally-Impaired Aged: Personality Ratings by Social Workers, *Journal of Gerontology*, 27:69–76 (January 1972).

[5]Elaine M. Brody, Morton H. Kleban, M. Powell Lawton, Richard Levy, and Asher Woldow, Prediction of Mortality in the Mentally-Impaired Institutionalized Aged, *Journal of Chronic Diseases*, 25:611–20 (November 1972).

heterogeneity of older people. Despite the homogeneity of the subjects—all suffered moderate to severe brain damage and all were institutionalized women with an average age of eighty-two and a common ethnic origin—they inevitably would vary in degrees of physical and mental impairment, as well as in specific socioeconomic background, personal life experiences, personality, adaptive capacities, family relationships, interests, and life-styles. This high degree of human differentiation was the rationale for a unique treatment program tailored to each individual.

It is recognized that this group is characterized by a multiplicity of disabilities that often cluster and interact so as to mask and exacerbate each other. For this reason an interdisciplinary approach was indicated, with treatment in each sphere specific and clear, yet integrated to focus on the whole person.

It was also necessary to set goals that were realistic in terms of the limitations and potential of the subjects. The more global goals often set for younger populations, such as discharge from hospital to community and resumption of paid employment or household management, were inappropriate for this population. For these clients, goals might be movement from wheelchair to a walker or from apathy to some degree of social participation.

Clinical procedures

The treatment program for each elderly woman had four phases: baseline evaluation, diagnosis and planning of treatment, treatment, and final evaluation.

Baseline evaluation

The baseline evaluation consisted of two parts: the gathering of clinical information about the subject's past and present and the detailed rating of her present functioning along the specified dimensions of self-care, interpersonal relations, physical health, mental status, and personality characteristics. Each member of the multidisciplinary team (physician, psychiatrist, social worker, occupational and recreational therapist, psychologist, physical therapist, and nurse) reviewed all available past information and history on the subject; evaluated her by direct examination; discussed her with regular personnel of the Home for the Jewish Aged; wrote a detailed narrative report of his findings; and summarized findings on the examination protocols and rating scales developed for the project.[6]

Intensive review and evaluation of the individual subjects were fundamental to defining the problems and deciding upon the appropriate treatment. Therefore, a great deal of preliminary work went into the development of a social history, protocols for recording clinical data, and scales to rate the subject along medical, psychological, social, and detailed behavioral dimensions.

The clinical protocols consisted of medical and psychiatric history and examination forms and narrative psychological and social evaluations. The social history and evaluation gathered data about the subject's personal and familial background and current social functioning. It inquired about the elderly woman's performance and competence in past roles, her characteristic responses to stress, her premorbid personality, and the underlying continuity of her personal and social functioning. The history was taken when possible from the subject herself, but was generally augmented to a considerable degree by interviews with one or more close relatives. Family sessions were used when possible to minimize retrospective distortions of memory and to provide an in vivo picture of family relationships. Informants for the evaluation of current functioning were family members and all levels of HJA staff who were in contact with the subject.

Diagnosis and planning of treatment

The tasks just described were preparatory to the team meeting at which an integrated diagnosis and formulation of treatment plan took place. Personnel present included the interdisciplinary project staff. However, direct-care personnel, with their intimate

minute-to-minute contact with residents, not only were in a position to contribute relevant information but were necessary to implement treatment programs. Therefore, the nurse and practical nurse serving that particular resident invariably were present, and other personnel were invited when indicated, no matter what department they represented.

Each staff member gave an oral summary of his findings and impressions, followed by general discussion and interchange of ideas. At that point, one of the most critical features of the program took place: Each disability of the resident in every sphere of functioning was reviewed to determine whether it was "excess," that is, whether it was accessible and amenable to therapeutic intervention. An excess disability was defined as the gap between actual and potential functioning in any sphere. The accessibility to treatment of the disabilities pinpointed were considered in the light of the subject's strengths or assets as well as her deficits or liabilities. Particular attention was given to the social history of each subject, since the clues to appropriate treatment goals often were to be found in her past functioning and interests. For example, if a woman with good vision historically had shown no interest in reading, reading would not automatically be an area of focus for treatment. However, if during her lifetime she had evidenced an interest in reading about politics, the team would attempt to encourage resumption of this activity.

Disabilities identified as excess by consensus of the staff were noted as such on the master chart that had been developed by the project staff, and the excess disabilities became the focal points for the treatment plan. The staff was free to develop new treatments, to select treatment elements from among existing programs at the Home for the Jewish Aged, and to utilize specialists and consultants when indicated in order to effect positive change in an excess disability.

A master chart was made up to spell out in a concise manner: (1) the excess disabilities to be treated, grouped categorically as activities of daily living, behavioral, interpersonal, and environmental social disabilities, occupational and recreational therapy, psychiatric and medical concerns; (2) the potential for

---

[6]Protocols and rating scales are available from the authors on request.

changing the disability or prognosis, stressing that a disability becomes excess only if the clinical team decides that there is potential for positive change; (3) the specific objectives for treatment or goals, all required to be realistic in terms of the capacities and potential capacities of the residents; (4) the specific therapeutic steps to be taken; and (5) the responsibilities of each team member in implementing the recommendations.

Each team member whose skill was appropriate to treatment of the denoted disability was given specific tasks relative to the condition, and disciplinary lines were often crossed when indicated. It was intended that the separate activities of the team would reinforce each other in the planned treatment program. Any given excess disability might require participation by one or all of the staff. Thus, to enable a resident, for example, to increase the emotional gratification and the range of her social relationships required involvement by the social worker, the worker in occupational and recreational therapy, and the physical therapy staff.

Treatment

During the ensuing year, the interval between baseline and final evaluations, the experimental subjects received intensive treatment from the project staff. Team meetings were scheduled halfway through the treatment period, that is, six months following the initiation of treatment, to review progress and to reformulate treatment plans if necessary. If a major significant event such as catastrophic illness of the subject or death of a close relative occurred in the life of a subject, the team convened for the same purpose. These meetings helped to keep treatment coordinated, contemporary, and flexible with respect to the subject's response. The coordination of the team's activities and follow-through to ensure implementation was the responsibility of the project social worker.

Final evaluation

At the end of the year of treatment, the total baseline evaluation was repeated and the resident was studied by the entire staff once again. At the final evaluation meeting, the overall status of the resident was discussed, each originally noted excess disability was reviewed, and the final column of the master chart was filled in with results in terms of specific functional change in the disability.

Differences from traditional team approaches

The program, of course, bears many similarities to the traditional team approach to diagnosis and treatment. There were also some significant differences. These were:

The involvement of all "significant others" at every step: family and direct care personnel (aides, food-service personnel, housekeepers, as well as the professional team of physician, psychiatrist, occupational and recreational therapist, social worker, psychologist, and nurse);

The attention addressed to modification of such environmental factors as institutional routines and programs, room furnishings and decorations, and staff attitudes;

Identification of excess disabilities as the points of departure for diagnostic and treatment procedures;

The use of a master schedule to control, coordinate, and integrate diagnosis and treatment;

The specificity of goals and tasks outlined for treatment personnel;

The insistence on detailed, meticulous follow-through via implementation of treatment plan; and

The focus of the reevaluation on the fate of the excess disabilities and the resultant feedback to staff.

The excess disabilities and treatment responsibilities

There were seven professional groups who could potentially be assigned responsibility to implement treatment: social worker, administrators (including director of social service, director of nursing, project coordinator), occupational and recreational therapist, psychiatrist, physician, physical therapist, and nurse.

Although the most frequent disabilities were in the medical area, these were not equated with the functional excess disabilities. Medical disabilities generally represented a need for evaluation or treatment of chronic conditions or for consultation. Although the physician was assigned diagnostic and treatment tasks which related primarily to these physical disabilities, he was also assigned to work collaboratively with other team members on a number (14 percent) of the nonmedical or functional disabilities. Here the physician may have reassured the patient in order to alleviate anxieties or encouraged the subjects to comply with special treatment needs to facilitate improved physical or social functioning. The medical disabilities were not, however, solely in the sphere of the physician; 29 percent of the treatment assignments for these disabilities were to other team members, particularly the social worker and the physical therapist.

For the thirty-two experimental subjects there were a total of 113 nonmedical excess disabilities enumerated for treatment; their distribution (see table) demonstrates the wide range of areas and the frequency with which the subjects had excess disabilities designated in these areas.

The largest proportion of subjects (78 percent) had excess disabilities in the category of group activities. They included specific reference to minimal or no participation in certain occupational or recreational therapy activities, a lack of opportunity to express a special interest, or an unmet wish by the subject to extend her activities. Although twenty-five of the thirty-four assignments (74 percent) for these twenty-eight excess disabilities were to the occupational and recreational worker, about one-fourth were to such other team members as social worker and physician.

Excess disabilities in the social sphere involved isolation from peers, roommate problems, problems in perception of staff, or need for supportive casework during recurrent hospitalizations. Personal self-care excess disabilities included care of possessions, appearance, and self-feeding. Family excess disabilities focused on quality of relationships with relatives, frequency of visiting, and individual problems of relatives that impinged upon the

Categories of nonmedical excess disabilities and staff assignments for treatment

Total *excess disabilities* in category (N=113)	Number	Percent
Group activities	28	25
Social interaction	27	24
Personal self-care	19	17
Family interaction	14	12
Psychiatric	11	10
Locomotion	8	7
Individual activities	6	5
Total *subjects* with one or more excess disabilities in category (N=32)		
Group activities	25	78
Social interaction	19	59
Personal self-care	14	44
Family interaction	13	40
Psychiatric	9	28
Locomotion	8	25
Individual activities	6	19
Total *staff assignments* for excess disability treatment (N=146)		
Group activities	34	23
Social interaction	34	23
Personal self-care	23	16
Family interaction	14	10
Psychiatric	19	13
Locomotion	15	10
Individual activities	7	5

resident. Psychiatric excess disabilities centered around depression, anxiety (often about health), disorientation, and need for psychiatric evaluation. Locomotion excess disabilities were in the specific area of difficulties in ambulation. Excess disabilities relating to individual activities generally identified activities unique for that particular person independent of her group occupational and recreational therapy participation.

Excess disabilities in each category were assigned to more than one discipline on the treatment team. Team members were able to function so as to complement and sensitize each other. The largest number of nonmedical excess disabilities were assigned to the social worker (57 percent) and the occupational and recreation therapist (36 percent), followed by the physician (14 percent). The categories of excess disabilities assigned to each varied considerably. Social workers were assigned responsibility for implementation of treatment for social disabilities, as well as for those in areas of self-care, family problems, medical problems, and psychological problems. The occupational and recreational therapist was given responsibility for implementing treatment in group activities and also with respect to social and psychological disabilities. The physician was assigned problems of locomotion and personal self-care in addition to medical problems.

One of the explicit treatment procedures was to seek consultation where it was deemed potentially helpful for diagnosis and treatment. Of the thirty-two experimental subjects, nineteen had one or more conditions which the clinical team felt warranted a total of thirty consultations. Consultations were primarily in the medical area (twenty-five)—most frequently in relation to vision (eight), hearing (five), orthopedic problems (three), and arthritis (two). Other consultations included speech, rehabilitation, dental problems, and family therapy.

Case illustration

The project research data indicated that residents characterized as aggressive (that is, bossy, with management problems, complainers within control of their aggression) im-

proved the most.[7] These are the people who traditionally are difficult residents and who elicit negative reactions from staff. Yet within the framework of project treatment, it was possible to capitalize on the constructive aspects of their behavior. The case of Mrs. R is presented to illustrate how the program worked.

Mrs. R, aged seventy-seven, had been a resident of the Home for Jewish Aged for six years when selected as a project subject. She was born in Russia, and her childhood can be described as economically and emotionally austere—loss of her father when she was a small child, economic deprivation, and the frequent real physical danger of pogroms. She was apprenticed to a dressmaker to learn a trade and was given private tutoring. Throughout her life, Mrs. R stressed the importance of education both for herself and her children. She continued at night school when she came to the United States at the age of nineteen, and she was still taking evening courses at the age of sixty-eight.

Mrs. R's husband was a gambler, an alcoholic, and a poor provider who often left the family. Mrs. R acted as buffer in the conflicts between him and their two children. The children hated their father who insisted they seek employment as soon as possible, but Mrs. R's insistence that they have a high-school education won out.

Although unable to display affection, Mrs. R gave her children the necessary physical care and what material things she could afford. When the children were in their teens, Mr. R left home for the last time. Intrafamilial tensions were reduced, but a greater responsibility was placed on Mrs. R who was employed. She sometimes beat the children with a cat-o'-nine-tails if they refused to eat.

Mrs. R remained independent and active in the community in her old age. She took pride in being able to manage her household alone, but when her health began to fail and it became increasingly difficult for her to maintain her own home, she finally required institutional care.

Prior to admission, Mrs. R made her wants known, specifying her choice of room, number of roommates, and so forth. Once admitted, she manipulated the environment to gain her own ends. She had an insatiable desire for attention

---

[7] Kleban et al., Personality Traits.

and an aggressive, irritating method of obtaining it. Mrs. R continued to follow her lifetime pattern of being critical and complaining, generally about somatic problems. She fell on numerous occasions, resulting in several fractures and many minor injuries.

Mrs. R's main excess disabilities were lack of proficiency in using her walker, absence of emotionally gratifying relationships, dissatisfaction with her room, lack of activities, depression, and pain in leg and wrist.

The narrative case record and project staff notes indicate that during the year of treatment the social worker visited regularly and allowed Mrs. R to express her complaints about family, staff, and other residents. The social worker also kept in close touch with Mrs. R's children, although Mrs. R continued to use them, as she did the staff, to complain. They began to visit more frequently and to show more interest in her. Mrs. R also was visited several times a week by an undergraduate student in human relations at a local college. The recreation worker involved Mrs. R daily in both group and individual activities. Mrs. R functioned at her best in the occupational therapy room.

Despite Mrs. R's complaints that it was difficult to manipulate her walker, she managed the long distance to the institution's adjoining hospital to speak to the project physician on the average of four times a week. These visits became so time-consuming for the medical staff that although Mrs. R required physical therapy only twice a week, orders were given that she be given treatments any time she felt the need.

Mrs. R thrived. Her physical condition stabilized and her morale rose. The frequency of her falls was reduced dramatically: She suffered only two falls during the entire year of treatment. The sense of humor she began to show made her constant complaints bearable to staff, so that at the end of the treatment period a twinge of regret was felt on the part of staff—even the project physician. Despite the means used to attain her ends, staff agreed that her attitude was healthier than simply giving up.

Incorporation of approach

A frequently voiced complaint in the field of human services is that research findings are not utilized in practice. The host agency at which the project took place, the Philadelphia Geriatric Center, undertook to incorporate the positive findings in its everyday procedures.

There was an educational process during which the senior project staff described and explained the study, its findings, and its procedures to all department heads. A specific area of the institution was selected to initiate the program, and an administrative liaison committee was appointed to provide feedback to administration. Subsequently, the educational process was repeated with all staff serving the selected area. From the large number of instruments used for the research, the project staff selected a small group of the protocols and evaluation measures that would be most useful and manageable for an ongoing institutional program. The master chart was, of course, to be utilized.

The program became the responsibility of the floor team. The project staff withdrew from direct involvement but remained available when requested to consult about procedures or use of forms. The unit manager of the area acted as coordinator of the team which consisted of physician, social worker, registered nurse, aide, recreational therapist, physical therapist, and other staff as indicated. The floor team chose to include the physical therapist as a regular member because of the high incidence and importance of ambulation disabilities in this particular area of the institution.

Residents selected for the program were those who presented severe management difficulties (because the floor team noted that their problems affected staff and other residents on the floor) and those who showed marked changes in behavior or overall functioning. The plan and its purpose were invariably shared with resident and family.

The floor team selected a six-week interval from baseline to reevaluation. A specific place on the resident's medical chart was designated for recording notes related to the tasks outlined on the master schedule. The team ruled that each of its members make biweekly entries and that nursing staff from each of the three shifts make weekly notes.

After the implementation had been underway for seven months, the following case was presented in reporting progress to date.

Mr. W and his wife, aged eighty-five and eighty-three, had been admitted to the Home for Jewish Aged four years prior to his selection for implementation of the mental impairment project. He had previously suffered a cardiovascular accident with residual right hemiparesis and he used a folding walker on wheels. He was oriented and alert, but his hearing was impaired and he was moderately aphasic, making communication difficult. Mrs. W showed mild confusion. Shortly after admission, she busied herself in assisting other men with their personal needs. Mr. W's response was to be verbally and physically abusive to her. The psychiatric evaluation noted: "He is abusive and hostile to the staff as well as his wife. The frustrations of his present situation have aggravated a preexisting irritability."

Intrafamilial relationships had always been poor. The sons felt only resentment toward their father because of the years of abuse they and their mother had suffered at his hands. His favorite name for his older son was "idiot." His temper had always been volatile when his own needs were not immediately satisfied, and this pattern of behavior continued under institutionalization.

It became obvious to staff that if Mr. W's demands were not satisfied immediately, his wrath would be incurred. Through the years there had been repeated unsuccessful attempts to motivate him to participate in physical and occupational therapy.

Because Mrs. W became extremely impaired mentally, it was soon necessary to move her to another area within the Home. At first, Mr. W visited her occasionally, but stopped when she became unable to recognize him. The sons ineffectually threatened not to visit him at all if he did not visit their mother daily. Then Mr. W fractured his ankle, withdrew to his room, refused to dress or participate in any activities, and sometimes refused to eat.

The floor team selected Mr. W to work with because of the problems he presented both to roommates and staff. The excess disabilities identified were volatility of temper with outbursts directed at roommate and staff, lack of ambulatory movement, inability to function in terms of activities of daily living (he was not dressing, washing, or grooming himself), and no participation in occupational or recreational therapy activities. It was felt that the potential for change was good in all spheres. Nursing, social service, and occupational therapy departments were assigned to implement specific recommended treatments. All levels of staff resolved on a kind, consistent, but firm approach. After six weeks, Mr. W was reevaluated by the floor team. During this short period of time, the treatment plan had proved dramatically successful. Mr. W had become ambulatory with a walker; his temper tantrums had subsided, and he behaved much more agreeably to staff and residents. He had become able to dress himself partially, wash himself, and comb his hair; and he had begun to be active in the sheltered workshop.

A second case presented by the unit manager demonstrated that treatment had been interrupted when hospitalization was necessary for the resident. Administrative staff thereupon began to formulate plans to ensure continuity of treatment when a resident is transferred to another area of the institution.

Implications for practitioners

The major findings generated by the research data have been reported and discussed elsewhere. The major findings that have implications for practitioners are summarized below.

The existence of excess disabilities that are accessible to treatment intervention signifies that the diagnostic label of chronic brain syndrome should indicate treatment intervention, not benign neglect. Improvement occurred in the family relationships of various project clients. The fact that it is possible at such a late stage in the family life cycle encourages therapeutic optimism. The importance of the individual's social history in selecting appropriate program elements and improving social relationships was supported by the responsiveness of the clients to that approach.

Those who benefited most from the project treatment were the aggressive, difficult-to-manage people, who often are excluded by institutional admission criteria and who are likely to be problems when they are admitted. The treatments developed for these "fighters" were congruent with their inclinations and previous personality patterns and capitalized on the constructive aspects of their aggression. The time and energy usually spent by institutional staff in dealing with the crises occasioned by this group were channeled more profitably by the project approach. Payoff, in addition to gains for the individuals concerned, was also in the coin of positive effects on family, staff, and other residents. Such people, who often fall between the slats in relation to admission criteria of various institutions, can be contained if treated appropriately.

A major issue concerns the functioning of the older people after experimental treatment is withdrawn. In this study, as in all other previous experimental programs addressed to mentally impaired older people, the gains made dissipated when treatment terminated.[8]

This fact is not to be interpreted as failure and as a rationale for nontreatment. On the contrary, it reinforces the basic knowledge concerning chronicity: By its very nature, chronic illness, mental or physical for young or old, demands sustained treatment. This statement is not consonant with the present inappropriate crisis-and-cure orientation of the health systems and underlines the need for major renovations of therapeutic philosophy, approaches, and organization.

[8]Elaine M. Brody, Morton H. Kleban, M. Powell Lawton, and Miriam Moss, A Longitudinal Look at Excess Disabilities in the Mentally-Impaired Aged (*Journal of Gerontology*, in press).

Social Service
Programming
in Nursing Homes

MICHAEL J. AUSTIN
JORDAN I. KOSBERG

What can be done to improve the care being given the growing population of elderly citizens in nursing homes? The authors propose a comprehensive social service model that would help fill the need these residents have for socialization and therapy.

THE NUMBER OF AGED persons in the United States is growing. It is anticipated that there will be about 24 million of them by 1980 and over 28 million by the year 2000.[1] In Florida alone, over 20 percent of the population is over 60, and the figure is projected to increase drastically within a decade.[2]

Somehow, in keeping people alive longer, advancements in the social sciences have failed to keep pace with progress in the physical and technological areas. Although we are faced with a growing population of aged persons, we are only just beginning to understand their needs, aspirations, and strengths. Accordingly, social policies, programs, and services have been viewed

HEALTH AND SOCIAL WORK, *Vol. 1, No. 3, August 1976*

as focusing on problems but not causes—as being well intentioned but ineffective. As a target population for services and programs, the elderly have historically been accorded low priority. Only recently has society become aware of and concerned about the plight of the aged person in our country.

As a function of age, health problems increase. Three-fourths of all persons over 65 have some chronic health condition, a figure twice that for the total population.[3] It has been estimated that the elderly have hospitalization rates and stays in hospitals that are twice the national average.[4] For all first admissions to mental hospitals, 25 percent are 65 years of age and older, and between 30 and 65 percent of the patients in state hospitals are elderly.[5] Because hospital care for the elderly is expensive, beds scarce, and convalescence lengthy, elderly populations must be discharged to different settings. Mental hospitals are discharging their geriatric patients. Where do these people go? And where do the elderly go who can no longer care for themselves independently or whose families can no longer care for them? The chances are it will be to a nursing home.

WHAT INSTITUTIONALIZATION PROVIDES

Although about 5 percent of the elderly are institutionalized, it has been estimated that 20 percent of this population will be institutionalized at some future time.[6] Even the figure of 5 percent amounts to over one million elderly persons living in institutional settings. Nursing homes (alternatively known as convalescent hospitals or extended care facilities) play a significant role in caring for the ill and elderly person. Yet these institutions for the aged have been the object of an abun-

> **As a function of age, health problems increase. Three-fourths of all persons over 65 have some chronic health condition, a figure twice that of the total population. Where do people go? The chances are good it will be a nursing home.**

dance of criticism that has pointed to maltreatment, routinization of care, emphasis on custodial control as opposed to rehabilitative and therapeutic treatment, and isolation from the outside community. Because almost 90 percent of all nursing homes are privately owned, many attribute the scarcity of resources, the meager care, and the poorly trained staff to the need for these facilities to accumulate profits.

Given the use—or overuse—of nursing homes in the care of the ill and dependent elderly population, what has been the role of social workers? As Kosberg pointed out, the impact of social workers on nursing-home care has been limited.[7] Research and practice, however, have demonstrated that great advantages are to be gained from social work involvement in nursing homes. Giordano and Giordano have described the importance of social workers in recreational programs and as change agents in nursing homes.[8] Shore has discussed the effectiveness of group work in providing institutionalized persons with a feeling of status and worth and in increasing their activity.[9] Farrar and her colleagues have indicated that casework skills can be extremely beneficial to the resident during preplacement, at the time of admission, and at other stages in institutional life.[10] Furthermore, studies have found that changes in the social involvement of the elderly, which can be aided and encouraged by social workers, are accompanied by changes in statisfaction and morale.[11]

By publishing guidelines and monographs, government agencies have recently encouraged an increase in social work involvement in nursing homes.[12] The National Association of Social Workers (NASW) has become active not only in assisting those social workers employed by nursing homes, but also in advocating increased social services in these facilities. Through its sponsorship, a training program has been instituted for social service providers in long-term care facilities in ten regions of the country.[13]

WHY SOCIAL SERVICES?

At present there are virtually no requirements for social services in nursing homes. Although Medicare had originally mandated social work involvement, this requirement was rescinded in 1972. Accordingly, it has been only "the most enlightened owners or administrators [who] would see the strong need for social workers and voluntarily hire them." [14] The Joint Commission on Accreditation of Hospitals accredits nursing homes that meet requirements above the minimum standards set by state licensing bodies.[15] The specificity of social service standards has been kept to a minimum and ways of implementing them are optional.

A pilot study of nursing home administrators and directors of nursing in twenty-seven Florida nursing homes revealed a limited understanding of what constituted a comprehensive social service program and a wide range of viewpoints on the definition of the social components of patient care.[16] The study included an analysis of the resources and practices needed to im-

FIG. I. SELECTED RESPONSES OF ADMINISTRATORS AND DIRECTORS IN A PILOT STUDY OF NURSING HOMES (IN PERCENTAGE)

	Yes	No
Is there an orientation program for new patients?	56	44
Are most patients expected to participate in cleaning their rooms and making their beds?	8	92
Do patients occasionally prepare their meals or a favorite dish in a special kitchen reserved for their use?	4	96
Do you have a counseling program staffed by a trained mental health professional for patients during times of personal difficulty?	21	79
Do patients participate directly in the planning of recreational activities?	27	73
Are patients allowed to have pets other than those prohibited by law?	27	73

(Figure continued)

plement a comprehensive social service program. The social components that were assessed included provisions for the individualization of services to the aged, the care and treatment provided, and the attempts to meet the social needs of the institutionalized population.[17] Selected findings from the pilot study are presented in Figure 1.

Although many of the nursing home administrators and directors of nursing claimed that their services met the social needs of patients, the responses indicate that only limited efforts were made to implement these

FIG. I. (Continued)

	Yes	No
Are adult education classes available for patients in your facility?	27	73
Is there a governing council for patients in your facility?	17	83
Could social workers assist administrators with public relations responsibilities and improving staff communication?	85	15
Are recreational programs developed for nonambulatory, bedfast patients?	46	54
Has the staff received training during the past year in the support of dying patients?	48	52
Do the majority of patients have opportunities at least once a month to go out into the community?	44	56
Should your nursing home have a designated member of the staff responsible for formulating treatment plans related to the social-emotional needs of patients?	85	15

social improvements. The majority of respondents indicated that if sufficient funds were available, a social worker would be employed to assist both in the primary care of patients and in the administration of the nursing home. For example, if a part-time social worker were loaned to their nursing home, administrators identified personal counseling, admission interviews, and development of a recreational program as constituting his primary responsibilities. However, despite the administrators' receptiveness to social work involvement, it was apparent that creating a balance between the medical component of care and the social components of care requires a better understanding of what a comprehensive social service program might consist of.

The limited awareness that administrators and directors of nursing have shown about the nature of a social service program is not surprising. Most textbooks on nursing home administration include little information on social services.[18] Inasmuch as administrators and directors of nursing are the key decision-makers in the development of a social service program, their understanding of the social components of medical care and the need for social services is important. If social work consultants are to assist them in providing the social components of nursing home care, a comprehensive social service program needs to be defined.

A COMPREHENSIVE PROGRAM

A wide range of objectives for social services in nursing homes has been itemized in the social work literature. Putting these objectives into operation has been a challenge to the proefssion. Figure 2 shows graphically the components of the program that are related to social service objectives. These range from an intake service, which constitutes the minimum requirement for a social service program, to interagency program coordination and development. The components are ordered in a series of steps to allow a nursing home to build a social service program by starting with the first component and progressing toward an increasingly more comprehensive program. Such a program could be staffed by social workers, although other human service professionals and paraprofessionals might also be involved. As a result, the proposed definition of a comprehensive so-

FIG. 2. A COMPREHENSIVE SOCIAL SERVICE PROGRAM FOR A NURSING HOME

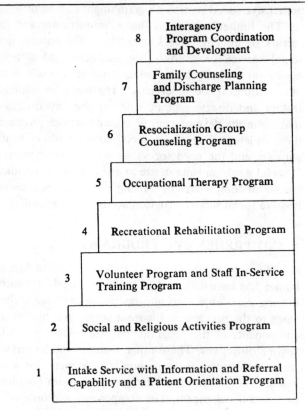

8 — Interagency Program Coordination and Development

7 — Family Counseling and Discharge Planning Program

6 — Resocialization Group Counseling Program

5 — Occupational Therapy Program

4 — Recreational Rehabilitation Program

3 — Volunteer Program and Staff In-Service Training Program

2 — Social and Religious Activities Program

1 — Intake Service with Information and Referral Capability and a Patient Orientation Program

cial service program emphasizes the service and not the personal requirements.

Intake services

The first component of a comprehensive social service program is an intake service that provides information and can make referrals when necessary. The intake

> Nursing homes vary in size and organizational structure, and therefore the development of a comprehensive social service program should be based on an assessment of the existing resources for meeting patient needs.

process, in which a social service worker helps the family and the elderly person make the best possible decision for short- or long-term care begins even before the elderly person applies to the nursing home. Alternatives to care should be presented that are based on up-to-date information. Such alternatives to which the patient could be referred include community-based services, such as Meals on Wheels and Homemaker Services. These might be utilized instead of admission to a nursing home or after short-term treatment. A joint decision on a treatment plan by the patient and his family not only can help the elderly person regain some sense of self-determination, but can help members of his family deal with their sense of guilt. The decision to admit a patient to a nursing home involves the assessment of physical, mental, functional, and social resources of the older person and his family, and the availability of community resources. Upon admission, a complete social history is necessary to assess and evaluate an individual's psychosocial characteristics, economic situation, educational and cultural background, adaptive behavior patterns and potentials for adjustment, and occupational and recreational interests. Only then can individualized treatment goals be formulated.

When the patient is admitted to the home, he must be given a tour of the facility to orient him, be introduced by name to other patients and staff members, and be made familiar with daily schedules and routines. Particular attention should be given to the normal tensions of adjustment to strange people and surroundings that may require supportive counseling. Feelings of abandonment, lack of self-worth, loss of identity may cause rapid regression and increasingly dependent behavior. The orientation period may last as long as several months, but can be made easier by the enlistment of volunteers and other residents to act as guides or "buddies." An important advantage of the buddy system is the feeling of self-worth gained by the established residents who help the newcomer.

Program activities

The second component of a comprehensive social service program includes a wide variety of activities that are designed to involve the patient in routines typically found in a family situation. Although social and religious activities are traditionally available to nursing home residents, in many homes these activities are limited. For example, religious activities may include only Sunday morning or Friday night services without any religious discussions planned for other times during the week. The same is true for social activities. Bingo on Thursday nights and an outdoor picnic once a year are not sufficient; a complete social program would include activities both inside and outside the home. For example, senior citizens' clubs rarely include nursing home residents and hold their meetings in the home only infrequently. High school students can provide entertainment on a regular basis, but such social activities require more planning and consultation with residents than is found in most homes.

Volunteers and staff training

The third component for social service programming involves both a program for volunteers and an in-service training program for staff members. These two programs are linked for several reasons. Involving volunteers in nursing homes is an important means of involving residents with the outside community. If the elderly resident still lived in his or her own home or with relatives, neighbors and friends would provide a source of companionship. Through the effective use of volunteers, these important relationships can be reconstructed. Specialists in music, drama, and crafts may also volunteer their time for planning and directing educational or therapeutic programs.

The presence of volunteers in the institution sometimes presents problems for staff members. New ideas and suggestions from volunteers are often viewed as interference, and staff members may resent the fact that volunteers are held in high regard by the residents. Accordingly, the use of volunteers can provide a unique opportunity to initiate and develop in-service training for all staff members including volunteers.

Recreation

The fourth component of a comprehensive social service program is the design and implementation of a recreational rehabilitation program. Examples might include the development of a resident's advisory council that can contribute to the development of a recreational program. The program might combine the therapeutic goals of physical therapy with games designed to increase muscle coordination. Similarly, a music program utilizing the goals of music therapy would encourage withdrawn residents to participate either by singing or by playing an instrument. The planning of recreational programs—from shuffleboard to dramatics or gardening—can have both a social and therapeutic orientation. Educational activities conducted by local adult education teachers might also be included in a recreational program.

Occupational therapy

Closely related to recreational programming is occupational therapy, which constitutes the fifth component of a comprehensive program. With the guidance and consultation of a trained occupational therapist, residents can engage in a wide variety of activities that also meet such rehabilitative goals as improved manual dexterity. Similarly, planned cooking sessions and work activities can contribute to the resident's sense of self-importance. A comprehensive occupational therapy program seeks to evaluate the capabilities of residents and to help them regain such skills necessary for daily living and, ultimately, for self-sufficiency as bed-making, dressing, shopping, or do-it-yourself repairs.

Group counseling

The sixth component of a social service program is designed to meet the psychological needs of residents through the use of group counseling. A trained mental health therapist can assist the staff in meeting the emotional needs of residents through planned discussion sessions. Group sessions such as these are also important in helping individuals regain skills in socializing and in expressing feelings and problems.

Resocialization groups can be a component of a therapeutic milieu in which the entire staff acts as supportive counselors. This approach to therapeutic care requires the examination of the total environment to assess its effect on the functioning of residents. A major goal would be to insure that the treatment and care provided are personalized. Different techniques of resocialization or remotivation include reality orientation, attitude therapy, remotivation therapy, reinforcement therapy, and sensitivity training.

Family counseling

The seventh component of a comprehensive program—family counseling and discharge planning—is an area that seldom receives enough attention from nursing home staff. Families should be involved throughout the resident's stay at the nursing home, and their needs should receive the same attention given those of the resident. Ideally, the family should be closely involved in the resident's care from the time the application is first made. Instead of being ignored, families should be included as a part of the treatment team and can be encouraged to share recreational activities, trips, holidays, and religious celebrations. Group meetings for relatives at which feelings of guilt, discontent, and complaints are aired should form a part of the social service program. Feelings about old age can be dealt with constructively, so that the family can learn to be supportive of the resident who is facing death.

Most nursing home patients need permanent care. For the patients who do not, however, discharge planning with the family should begin at the first contact and include discussion of the options open to the patient and his family. In this way, both parties are prepared psychologically for the change. The patient and his family frequently have mixed and conflicting emotions about leaving the nursing home. The resident may be afraid to leave the security of the institution or feel guilty about being a burden to his family. On the other hand, the family may be concerned about how they will care for the patient and be reluctant to assume the responsibility. Before the final decision regarding discharge is made, many feelings and alternatives need to be explored. All available community resources should be mobilized to help the family care for the elderly relative.

Administration

The eighth and last component of a comprehensive social service program concerns the nursing home's administrator and its relation to the community. Too often, nursing home facilities have been considered "closed" institutions that offer their residents total care but that rarely make use of community resources to supplement their services. Social service staff should be actively involved in helping community agencies and citizen groups evaluate the programs and resources for the aging population both inside and outside nursing homes. Community agencies have the responsibility for the welfare of the institutionalized aged and should be encouraged to remain in direct contact with residents and be familiar with their needs. Public welfare agencies have a continued obligation to assess the needs of indigent elderly patients in nursing homes.

The social service worker must be a change agent who will open the doors of nursing homes to the community and establish a link between the services of community agencies and the needs of the aged in nursing homes. Serving on interagency committees to coordinate services and develop new ones represents a first step in the process of integrating the services of the nursing home with the services of community agencies on the outside.

CONCLUSIONS

In this article the authors have proposed a model for developing a comprehensive social service program. Because specific administrative structure has purposely been omitted, the proposal deserves careful review and evaluation by nursing home administrators and directors of nursing, as well as by the social work profession. Nursing homes vary in size and organizational structure, and therefore the development of a comprehensive social service program should be based on an assessment of the existing resources for meeting patient needs.

Many nursing homes have employed social work consultants in the past, but the results of the consultation process have not yet received careful documentation. There is some indication that the consultation has been less effective than it should have been. If the social component of care in nursing homes is to improve, the nursing home industry and the social work profession will need to embark on a more cooperative process of discussion and collaboration. Only then can patients be assured of humane treatment that is geared toward rehabilitation and, in some cases, a successful return to community life.

About the Authors

Michael J. Austin, Ph.D., is Associate Professor, School of Social Work, Florida State University, Tallahassee; and Jordan I. Kosberg, Ph.D., is Associate Professor and Assistant Director, Human Services Design Laboratory, School of Applied Social Sciences, Case Western Reserve University, Cleveland, Ohio. A version of this article was presented at the 28th Annual Meeting of the Gerontological Society, Louisville, Kentucky, October 1975.

Notes and References

1. Bernice L. Neugarten, "The Aged in American Society," in Howard S. Becker, ed., *Social Problems: A Modern Approach* (New York: John Wiley & Sons, 1967), pp. 167–196.

2. *Profile of Florida's Elderly and Needed Supportive Services* (Jacksonville, Fla.; Department of Health and Rehabilitative Services, Division of Family Services, Bureau on Aging, February 1973), p. 1. Mimeographed.

3. Neugarten, op. cit., p. 177.

4. *New Facts about Older Americans,* Pamphlet No. 73-20006 (Washington, D.C: U. S. Department of Health, Education & Welfare, 1973).

5. *See* M. Kramer, C. Taube, and S. Star, "Patterns of Use of Psychiatric Facilities by the Aged: Current Status, Trends, and Implications," in Alexander Simon and Leon J. Ipsteing, eds., *Aging in Modern Society—Psychiatric Research Report No. 23.* (Washington, D.C.: American Psychiatric Association, 1968); and Stanley L. Englebardt, "Your Mother Died Three Years Ago," *Today's Health* (March 1971), pp. 18–25.

6. Robert Kastenbaum and Sandra Candy, "The 4 Percent Fallacy: A Methodological and Empirical Critique of Extended Care Facility Population Statistics," *International Journal of Aging and Human Development*, 4 (Winter 1973), pp. 15–21.

7. Jordan I. Kosberg, "The Nursing Home: A Social Work Paradox," *Social Work*, 18 (March 1973), pp. 104–110.

8. Joseph L. Giordano and Grace Giordano. "An Activities Program in a Home for the Aged in the Virgin Islands," *Social Work*, 14 (April 1969), pp. 61–66.

9. Herbert Shore, "Group Work Program Development," in Morton Leeds and Herbert Shore, eds., *Geriatric Institutional Management* (New York: G. P. Putnam's Sons, 1964), pp. 166–205.

10. Marcella Farrar, Margaret B. Ryder, and Margaret Blenkner, "Social Work Responsibility in Nursing Home Care," *Social Casework* 45 (November 1964), pp. 527–533.

11. J. H. Britton, "Living in a Rural Pennsylvania Community in Old Age," in Frances M. Carp and William M. Burnett, eds., *Patterns of Living and Housing in Middle-Aged and Older People*, Public Health Service Publication No. 1496 (Washington, D.C.: U. S. Department of Health, Education & Welfare, 1966), pp. 99–105; see also George H. Maddox, "Activity and Morale: A Longitudinal Study of Selected Elderly Subjects," *Social Forces*, 42 (October 1963), pp. 195–204; Erdman P. Palmore, "The Effects of Aging Activities and Attitudes," *Gerontologist*, 8 (Winter 1968), pp. 259–263.

12. *See* B. C. Harper, ed., *Social Services in Extended Care Facilities: A Blueprint for Action* (Washington, D.C.: U.S. Department of Health, Education & Welfare, 1970); *A Guide for Social Service in Nursing Homes and Related Facilities*, Public Health Service, Publication No. 1878 (Washington, D.C.: U. S. Department of Health, Education & Welfare); Elaine M. Brody, *A Social Work Guide for Group-Term Care Facilities* (Rockville, Md.: National Institute of Mental Health, 1974).

13. Helen Gossett, "A Curriculum for Social Work Personnel in Long-Term Health Care Facilities." (Mimeographed report prepared for National Association of Social Workers, undated.)

14. Kosberg, op. cit., p. 105.

15. *Standards for Accreditation of Extended Care Facilities, Nursing Care Facilities, and Resident Care Facilities* (Chicago, Ill.: Joint Commission on Accreditation of Hospitals, 1968), p. 38.

16. Michael J. Austin and Jordan I. Kosberg. "Nursing Home Decision-Makers and the Social Service Needs of Residents. Unpublished manuscript, Tallahassee, Florida, 1976.

17. For an enumeration of these components, *see* S. Hans Falck and Mary K. Kane, *Social and Emotional Aspects of Residential Care* (Washington, D.C.: U. S. Department of Health, Education & Welfare, 1971).

18. A review of the texts used in a community college program for nursing home administrators tends to reflect a job description of social workers rather than a description of a social service program. *See,* for example, Harold Baumgarten, Jr., *Concepts of Nursing Home Administration* (New York: Macmillan Co., 1965); Lee J. Jacobs and Woodrow W. Morris, *Nursing and Retirement Home Administration* (Ames: Iowa State University Press, 1966); Florence L. McQuillian, *Fundamentals of Nursing Home Administration* (Philadelphia: W. B. Saunders Co., 1967); Dulcy B. Miller, *The Extended Care Facility: A Guide to Organization and Operation* (New York: McGraw-Hill Book Co., 1969).

An Integrated Service Delivery Program For the Elderly: Implementing a Community Plan

RONALD WEISMEHL

Executive Director

and

DANIEL SILVERSTEIN

Director, Evaluation-Service Center, Council for Jewish Elderly, Chicago, Illinois

I. Background

THE programs of the Council for Jewish Elderly were developed in accordance with guidelines established by a long range planning study. This planning effort was initiated by the Jewish Federation of Metropolitan Chicago in 1968, and was carried out by the Jewish Federation's Gerontological Council. The study and final report was published in the Spring of 1970 under the title: *A Jewish Community Plan for the Elderly.*[1]

The Jewish Federation of Chicago, and its affiliated agencies, organized a community gerontological council as a means of confronting some basic problems. The affiliated agencies wanted to develop new programs and construct new facilities. The Federation was faced with mounting costs, multiple requests for capital funds for new facilities, and no way of measuring priorities. The Federation was operating three long-term care facilities (625 beds), and each of these homes for aged had produced a "long range plan" which took little account of the plans of the others.

Within a few months following publication of the Plan, the Gerontological Council Report was ratified unanimously by the governing boards of the agencies and the board of the parent group, the Jewish Federation. In taking this action, this community committed itself to a single plan, to the implementa-

tion of a new service delivery system, and to a *new* schedule of priorities.

The significance of the community gerontological council emerged only as the "Planning Contract" was developed. The Federation agreed to fund a community program for elderly which was developed jointly by the affiliated agencies. The only condition was that a *single* community plan be developed and that this plan be endorsed by all of the agencies.

The agencies agreed and the Federation demonstrated its good faith by funding the planning group and committing its top leadership to serve on the council alongside the leadership from the agencies.

II. An Integrated Service Delivery System for the Elderly

"There is general agreement that the present system of providing service and care for the aged can be conceptualized as a straight line leading from the home environment, through a referral system of independent and largely uncoordinated agencies, directly to the nursing home or home for the aged."[2] Such were the conclusions of the planning study. As a remedy, the planning group called for the creation of a new service delivery system which would be flexible and, by design, compatible with individual needs.

---

[1] Samuel Spiegler, "Fact and Opinion," *Journal of Jewish Communal Services*, Vol. XLVII, No. 2 (1970), p. 171.

[2] "A Jewish Community Plan for the Elderly." An unpublished report of the Gerontological Council of the Jewish Federation of Metropolitan Chicago, Spring 1970, p. 9.

In implementing the community plan, the Council for Jewish Elderly of Chicago has made the determination that it would provide a highly diversified service inventory and systems of control which would insure the availability of needed services, the evaluation of need, the development of highly individualized service plans, the speedy and effective delivery of services, and the effective monitoring and follow up on service plans.

The Service Inventory

The services provided by the Council for Jewish Elderly are not in themselves unique. What is unusual is that the broad spectrum of services are delivered under the direction of a single agency.

It is also important to note that the complete service inventory was mobilized simultaneously.

The planners were concerned that, if services were developed in accordance with a so-called "practical" priority schedule, one could not adequately test the impact of the new system, since one or more services were surely to be on the drawing board, marked for future delivery. The planning group stated:

> We must take care that we do not initially offer to the community a product which is overdesigned, but we must also be concerned that, in our desire to reduce risk, we do not underdesign the presentation of our product.[3]

Therefore, it was recommended that the totally conceived program be implemented as a unit. The service inventory was conceived as "Interlocking Service Resources." The notion that these services had to be implemented simultaneously was in keeping with this concept.

In a period of one year, the following services were developed and made operational:

---

[3] *Ibid.*, p. 37.

Casework services
A medical evaluation unit
A home health service team
A housekeeping service
Home delivered meals
A transportation program
A Group Living Residence (Intermediate Housing)
Two housing facilities (Independent Housing)
A comprehensive outreach program
Two drop-in centers ("Coffee Houses")
A "Senior Service Corps" (Employment for the Elderly)
A legal counseling service
A data bank service
Liaisons with long-term care facilities

The implementation of the total network in such a short period of time was made possible by:

A. The availability of a comprehensive plan and the community support generated through the planning process;

B. The early availability of a skilled management team;

C. The effective utilization of knowledgeable consultants in systems;

D. A commitment by the Jewish Federation to fund the program in a flexible manner.

The implementation task was also realizable since the model was to be developed in a defined geographical area which was limited in size and densely populated.

The implementation plan called for the development of a program consisting of all the proposed program elements, but the program was to be realistically scaled in size. The miniaturization of the total program would enable the delivery of enough service to test the program design, while allowing for flexibility to expand or change the emphasis of the program, when this was appropriate and feasible.

The Target Community

The target community covers a relatively small geographical area. The area is mainly residential with a low and middle class mixed population totaling approximately 61,000. As of 1970, 13,300 or 22 percent of the total population were 60 years of age and older. Of the total elderly population in this community, approximately 7,000 are Jewish.

Organization of Services Around a Number of System Models

Although systems specialists can provide a definition of what differentiates an integrated system from a non-integrated system, a practical and meaningful explanation of this concept, as it relates to the pilot program, is that all programs and services are organized in such a way as to make these resources readily available to the elderly. This means the system is organized around a concept of how best to meet a variety of needs.

Since the Council's service system relies heavily on outreach and reaching the elderly, rather than the adult children or relatives, an intake system needed to be devised which was easily maneuvered by the elderly. This meant that intake *could not* be restricted to a central location. Secondly, if one seeks to be highly responsive to needs, changes in needs, and new problems as they arise in the community, one must develop a means by which those staff workers, who are closest to the elderly and the community, can communicate information to the policy makers and the more centralized service staff. Under these circumstances, policies and supporting systems must be strong enough to counterbalance the sometimes overwhelming influence of the centralized staff, which tends to be the highly trained professionals. The focus is not on castrating the professional, but rather in equalizing the influence of various staff groups on program development.

Thirdly, provision must be made so that the older person is not overwhelmed by the availability of a variety of services. The older person must be buffered from the natural tendency of staff to sell a specific service.

The older person must be given the opportunity to secure a highly individualized service plan.

The older person must be given assurances that he will not be lost or mislaid after he has received a service. Follow up provision must be structured.

And finally, the older person must be given the opportunity to pull out when service is no longer required or when service needs have been reduced.

Agency policy has provided a flexible framework within which the older person can request and receive services. Systems have been applied to guide practice. Requests for service may be made through a number of entry points. The broad spectrum of services are available to the older person no matter at what point he enters the system (i.e. via the outreach worker, via the Area Service Center, via the Transportation Program, or via the Central Intake Service). Service delivery may be provided at the same location or setting in which the service is requested. Service delivery may be provided by the same staff worker, or staff team, which received the request for service. All of this is achieved, while still maintaining control over service resources.

Maintaining the Older Person in the Community

The Planning Study concluded that the new program should focus on maintaining the older person in the community, as a *functioning* and *participating* member of that community, for as long as possible. The issue of maintaining an older person in the community is intrinsically bound to the concept of service through selective intervention. A mechanism must be developed which allows for the development of highly individualized service plans. If the agency, by policy, seeks to support independent functioning, a checks and balance system must be developed which insures that *only that service which is required is delivered*.

In the case of the CJE program, this is accomplished through an operation which relies on the assessment of the request for service by a multi-disciplinary team, and a procedure which demands that final authorization of the service plan must be made by the older person himself.

The Interlocking of Outreach With the Delivery of Concrete Services

Outreach, as a program function, has assumed an increasingly important role in the delivery of services to the elderly.

If outreach is to be an effective element of the service delivery system, it must become a part of that system and must have the capacity and the authority to initiate the delivery of a service.

In order to achieve this type of program, a number of steps must be taken:

1. Operational policies must link outreach to the intake system;

2. Outreach staff must be assigned the responsibility and given the authority to initiate a service directly;

3. Outreach staff must be integrated into the service delivery team so as to insure their involvement in the evaluation process, the delivery of the service, and the follow up.

Outreach is not an end in itself. In the integrated service delivery system, outreach is a pathway for service, an entry point.

By making sure that the elderly know of the various services offered in the community, and by providing easy access to the needed services, the outreach program seeks to offer ongoing support to the older person so as to prevent serious crises from occurring. This is accomplished, in part, through the operation of "Drop-In" Centers.

Area Service Center facilities serve as "Drop-In" Centers or "Coffee Houses" for the elderly. The openness of the "Coffee House," plus its visibility in the neighborhood, allows it to function most successfully as a visible entry point to the service system. Elderly can drop in and use the facility and the unstructured programs on their own terms.

As already noted, outreach workers may act as intake workers. Outreach workers can initiate the service by reporting directly to the service team, contributing to the preliminary evaluation, and making recommendations regarding the nature of the service to be delivered.

A concrete service may be given by the outreach worker as part of the outreach effort. Letter writing, friendly visiting, assistance in filling out forms, advocacy and a host of other basic services may be provided by the outreach worker as part of the outreach function.

Application of the Selective Intervention Concept

"If we assume that it is possible to take any individual and, through a process of evaluation, place him at a precise point in terms of his particular medical, social and psychological dependency needs, and if we can assume that we have the wisdom to put together whatever is necessary to meet those needs precisely, then we have the basis for *selective intervention*. It is possible, and indeed essential, to determine precisely the social needs and environmental needs of individuals as well as their medical or psychiatric needs. If we can do so then we must conclude that for each individual in need there is a 'treatment of choice.' We can determine what that treatment of choice is that will best meet those individual needs. In addition, we must take a prospective view of the person and seek a prognosis against which we can formulate goals and measure effectiveness of any prescribed program of treatment."[4]

We assume that people who have lived as part of a community for at least 65 years want to maintain themselves as individuals in that community for as long as possible. Our service is aimed at intervening in their lives with the kind of help that will be just enough to best support this continuance of a decent independent life as defined jointly by the agency and the client. This means providing service that will produce a dependency of the clients on the agency — put another way — to provide service to enhance their independence. This also means that the agency must enter into a contract that allows for the client to be involved in assessing and determining his own needs.

It has been observed that elderly tend to request concrete services first. The agency will provide the requested service even though that service, by our assessment, may serve a minimum of the person's total needs. We know that in the course of an elderly person's life any and all of our services could be appropriate to some degree. The issue is to provide appropriate service when it is most needed. Who could argue that transportation is a problem for most elderly, or nutrition, or loneliness, or decent housing at a reasonable cost, etc. Our goal is to provide the transportation, or any other service, where and when it helps each individual person to achieve on his own.

[4] Elias S. Cohen, "Selective Intervention: An Approach to Serving the Aging." Presented at the Annual Meeting of the Illinois Association of Homes For The Aged in Chicago, Illinois, May 1, 1970.

Our newness has the advantage of not categorizing service into fixed definitions. We encourage and support new ways if the traditional model does not fit. Since this includes many different aspects of service and crosses professions, we have developed, as a core unit, multi-discipline teams that make these decisions. This kind of team concept in community social service agencies is relatively unique, but is necessary if we are to provide appropriate service.

Each case comes to the team, and an individual client plan is devised. The client plan is the key to the coordination of the work as it asks what services are to be provided, for how long; by whom, and why. It assigns specific tasks to certain team members who, by their presence in the discussion, know the needs of the person to be served. It further asks the team when it thinks these services should be re-evaluated. Each client is assigned a principal worker, although several staff may be providing service. The principal worker is usually the worker who has the most effective relationship with the older person and, again, may be any team member. By re-evaluating on a planned basis, we can determine when to decrease, increase, or add additional service, as a person's problems develop or diminish. An additional function of the team is to provide some degree of training. A medical, social work, and psychiatric consultant sit in on appropriate case presentations and point out in the discussion some general principles relating to client's need. This is done in addition to a formal in-service training program. This is an important function as the newness of the agency and its staff requires a conscious effort in staff development.

Utilization of Staff in New Roles

Let me describe briefly how the staff structure is organized as this is a critical

157

factor in how service is delivered. The Community Service Task Force is made up of paraprofessionals and some volunteers who may perform multi-functional activities including friendly visiting, shopping assistance, housekeeping, or basic nursing activities. These geriatric community aides can, therefore, help in providing a tailor-made service to an individual. This staff function is a new one, and provides much flexibility in meeting basic needs of people in a tailor-made, individual fashion. The Medical Department provides basic evaluations and is prepared to offer a wide range of medical service in the home as part of a Home Health Team by training others or by working with the older person's own doctor or hospital. The Social Service Unit may provide basic evaluations, case diagnosis, counseling service and outreach. Its staff consists of MSW's and some BA level people with experience.

The Area Service Staff provides drop-in center activities, plus a major outreach effort and basic answers to concerns that need minimal followup. The Area Service Center also employs elderly to participate in the outreach efforts, to staff the "Drop-In Centers," and at times to provide friendly visiting.

The Volunteer Service has utilized a variety of people, many of whom have a professional background, and may perform tasks with a client as assigned by the Team.

A mention needs also to be made of Housing Services. Apartment buildings within the community are being renovated to provide a housing resource. Placements in the apartments are based on a Team determination of the need for the service by the client. When the older person has a problem related to housing, the agency can intervene and provide: 1) apartment in CJE facilities; 2) help in locating apartments in the community; 3) counseling and assistance in working out problems related to existing housing

conditions; and 4) a Group Living Home which is a communal living situation for people assessed to be not able to live totally independently, but not ill enough to be in a conventional institutional setting. Residents share in cooking and eat together. They carry other responsibilities that are aimed at capitalizing on their resources.

The hallmark of providing needed service effectively is to integrate every service so that the service package is designed or tailor-made to meet the individual's special needs. The interdisciplinary team is the means of achieving this goal, and does this by providing evaluation, control, interaction, planning, and coordination.

Finally, staff performs as advocate for the elderly in the community. Legal service is provided directly to clients. Broader issues of a legal nature (i.e., housing violations) are raised and examined and pursued. The CJE is a community agency, and is responsive to community problems.

One of the results of the team approach has been the development of an attitude among staff that whatever needs to be done to help a person will be done. Traditional roles are shifted or dropped if they are inappropriate in providing a service. The character of intervention is determined in relation to need and staff assignments are related to which staff person can do the best job. Roles and function of workers are defined on the basis of client need. This is a modification of the more traditional approach which tends to provide service in relation to clearly defined professional roles. Although this sounds elementary, it often is not when you consider the wide range of service interventions possible. A client came to our attention because of her inability to get to a doctor for an arm injury. Although it appears logical that a nurse should see the client, which she did, it is a departure from traditional routine to not have this first visit done by a social worker.

A final point on role development is in the area of inter-agency coordination. The charge to the agency is to become an umbrella on aging services which crosses the lines of other Jewish Federation agencies who have been serving elderly for many years. We have the task of developing models of cooperative service that will lead ultimately to a coordinated comprehensive effort. This effort which is a staff-to-staff and lay board-to-lay board understanding is a subject for another paper. Suffice it to say that working on an inter-agency level is, at times, much more difficult than developing an approach to direct service.

III. Conclusions

The program of the Council for Jewish Elderly of Chicago was established upon a firm planning base.

The Council for Jewish Elderly has concluded that one cannot adequately test the effectiveness of a comprehensive service program unless all services are implemented as a unit.

The availability of multiple services does not in itself produce an effective program. The older person must be able to utilize the services. This means that systems must be developed that insure the availability of the service, the application of service resources towards meeting highly individualized needs, the monitoring of service delivery so that services match changing needs.

It is possible for one agency to direct all services for the elderly while still preserving the individual's right to receive a tailor-made service.

And finally, it is possible to tie an outreach program effectively to a service delivery system so as to produce a decentralized intake program, and a continuity in service from the point of intake through the actual delivery of the needed service.

Delivery of service is a complex operation involving a recipient and a provider; milieu factors also influence the outcome. Obstacles arise out of ignorance of the interactions of the participants in this process and because faulty assumptions are made about them. Overriding the obstacles and obtaining better service for elderly persons depend on a better understanding of the dynamic interactions of caregiver, recipient, and the milieu in which a service is offered.

Barriers to the Delivery of Psychiatric Services to the Elderly

Charles M. Gaitz, MD[2]

Planners and providers of health services make many assumptions about the people they intend to serve. Basing their programs on stereotypes, they often fail to take into account such obvious differences as age, ethnicity, and social class, and they neglect the recipients' own perceptions of what is needed and acceptable. Intent on their own roles, the caregivers and planners tend to ignore the inherent implications of the work involved in reaching their objective—which, stated simply, is to deliver a health service to a person in need.

In practice, achieving this objective is no simple matter. Some of the complicating factors will be highlighted in this discussion. Attention will be focused to some extent on the delivery of psychiatric services to elderly persons, but much of what follows is relevant to all types of social and medical services.

Ignorance of the implications of service delivery and faulty assumptions about the beneficiaries-to-be are the foundation of the barriers in the delivery of service. We assume, for example, that the needy person recognizes his need and is quite ready to accept a service if and when it is provided, implying thereby that the need for the service is known, that it is possible to provide it, and that a provider is available. That the service will benefit the recipent and that other persons, significantly re-

lated to him, agree with, understand, and will cooperate in whatever ways are advantageous or beneficial to the needy individual is accepted without question or reservation.

One could add to this list of wishful fancies with little effort or imagination. When one reviews the list, however, it becomes apparent how many obstacles can arise to break the continuity of what began as a simple and well-intentioned matter of delivering a service.

First, obviously, one must determine who is to receive attention. Presumably the primary focus of attention is on the person in need. But even this is not always as clear as it may first appear. A planner's perspective should include the needs of several persons: the spouse, a child, and even the caregiver may need equal consideration.

In a typical model for delivery of service, one person is designated "patient," the other "therapist," but the individual designated as the patient is not always the one in greatest need nor is he always the one upon whom attention should be concentrated. We know from family studies, for example, that family dynamics often force one member into the limelight, and that this person then manifests symptoms that become the ticket of admission to a treatment center. A more reasonable approach may be to involve all members of the family, not only the one who became the family's target of hostility or rejection.

So what appears as a rather simple design, to deliver a service to a person in need, must be viewed as a complex process often involving several persons. Uncertain what service is

1. Paper presented at the Joint Symposium. Breaking the Barriers to Better Health Care and Delivery Services for the Aging, 26th annual meeting of Gerontological Society, Miami Beach, Nov. 8, 1973.

2. Texas Research Institute of Mental Sciences, 1300 Moursund Ave., Houston 77025.

needed, who is to provide it, and who is to receive it, we sometimes do not know with certainty whether the target problem has been properly defined. Barriers may arise, therefore, in a variety of circumstances.

Consequently, an examination of the process of delivery of services will reveal more about potential barriers than would a study of the details involved in providing a specific service. To study the process, we should recognize that a dynamic relationship exists between the recipient and the provider, and, equally important, the milieu in which the transactions occur. Factors influencing the delivery of service can thus be divided into at least three categories—those related to the recipient, the provider, and the milieu. The delivery or nondelivery of a service is contingent on the interaction of many factors which can be divided arbitrarily into categories. None of these is discrete, but for the sake of clarifying the impact they have on the delivery of service, let us examine some of the factors that influence the delivery of psychiatric services in terms of the three categories mentioned.

The Recipient

Possibly the single most important factor in delivering a service is the potential recipient's awareness of his need for assistance. We sometimes call this insight. If the beneficiary-to-be has insight, if he admits that a problem exists and that he needs help, the process of providing a service may begin. A caregiver offering help to someone who does not agree that he needs help is not likely to encounter a kind reception. Concurrently the potential therapist considers the situation and evolves a treatment plan that is dependent on his own perceptions. Recommendations vary. Manifestations of organic brain syndrome, an emotional disorder, a continuation of mental illness of long standing, or an illness related to problems associated with aging are treated differently. In any case, the treatment plan selected is more likely to be successful when the recipient and the provider agree that a problem exists and when they agree on the nature of the problem and its possible solution.

How much effort will be required of the recipient to obtain a service? How resourceful must he be? These also are important factors. If a service is easy to obtain, an elderly person with impaired mobility, physical weakness, and reduced financial resources is much more likely

to use it. Having to search out a provider in a nonsystem of health services is an insuperable barrier to many elderly persons, even when a need is acknowledged. Such persons are likely to have impediments—physical, communicative, intellectual, financial—that seriously interfere in their search for an appropriate caregiver.

Let us turn to some of the social and cultural factors that influence the individual to acknowledge a need for and to either accept or reject a service. The present generation of aged persons is still very reluctant to acknowledge a need for psychiatric and mental health services. Their resistance is often fostered, perhaps unwittingly, by family members who have similar attitudes. To admit the existence of emotional disorder in a family member may be as difficult for a spouse or a child as for the patient. The dynamics are likely to be complex. A spouse, for example, may feel threatened by the realization that his mate is ill and that the mate will require more attention than he is willing or capable of providing; possibly even more important, he himself loses a source of sustained emotional support. The result is an impasse. The family avoids facing the situation realistically and the need for help goes unrecognized or is deliberately denied. Help which might have been forthcoming is not obtained.

There are other ramifications one could explore in understanding the recipient's role as a positive or negative force in the delivery of a service. For the sake of brevity, let it suffice to emphasize that the provision of a service largely depends on the willingness of a potential recipient to acknowledge the need for it, on his capability to cooperate with the caregiver, and on his condition being one for which a known service or treatment exists.

The Provider

The provision of a service ultimately becomes the responsibility of an individual, but just as we must consider the recipient of a service as belonging to a group or a family, we must understand that a provider also is part of a network or system. The provider's attitudes and activities can be better understood when one conceives of him in this broader perspective. A particular practitioner's interests, capabilities, attitudes, and resources are ultimately critical in determining if and how a service will be provided; but even if he is quite capable and strongly motivated to care for the aged, he will encounter many obstacles unless his agency has a strong commitment to the elderly. Other aspects of this interaction will be discussed later as factors related specifically to milieu. For the present, let us return to the individual caregiver and examine his participation in the health delivery system.

The recognition by a provider of an elderly person's acknowledged need sets the process of delivering a service in motion. His perception or diagnosis, however, are influenced by his training and experience. His own ability and willingness to give a service will influence his perception of what is needed. He is more likely to formulate a problem as being capable of solution when he has a full armamentarium of techniques and secondary support, is personally competent to cope with the need, and can do it at reasonable financial and emotional cost and with a reasonable expenditure of time and energy. Failure to meet these self-imposed tests leads to a sense of futility, and blame may be projected to the potential recipient.

Mental health workers, like the providers of other services to the elderly, are strongly influenced by their own attitudes. Those with limited experience and training often are convinced that the problems of older people are insoluble and that aging inevitably is associated with decline in functional capacity and poor prognosis. They have not learned that impairment cannot always be equated with disability, that illnesses in the aged often are reversible, and that psychological symptomatology manifested by old people is not inevitably and inherently related to organic brain conditions for which there is no treatment. If these negative attitudes are not dispelled by teaching and experience, therapeutic nihilism becomes a strong barrier to the delivery of service.

Another potential source of difficulty is the failure of practitioners to realize that each stage in the life cycle has some unique features. This frame of reference offers a meaningful approach to treatment; it applies to middle and old age as it does to infancy and childhood. The failure to recognize the dynamic aspects of personality development late in life leads some practitioners to believe that problems of the aged can be prevented only by giving enough attention to children and young adults. This presupposes that the process of personality development ends in early adulthood, if not in early childhood, and that few significant, personality-molding life events occur in middle and old age. The shortcomings of such a theoretical

framework are evident to anyone who views even casually the impact of children leaving home, retirement, role reversal, and other phenomena associated with middle and late life.

It has been suggested that resistance to recognizing changes and dynamic factors in these periods of the life cycle may relate to a practitioner's refusal to consider the implications of aging as they relate to himself. The changes he identifies in his client or patient become alarming because he sees them as similar to the difficulties he will himself encounter. Viewing the later stages of the life cycle as characterized by inevitable decline leads younger therapists to pessimism, if not overt rejection of elderly persons.

The principle that an individual's adjustment at a particular stage in the life cycle depends largely on his experiences at earlier stages is widely accepted. Yet one should not assume that giving enough attention to children and young adults will guarantee the sparing of a generation from the problems of old age. While it is true that coping successfully with the problems characteristic of each life-cycle stage prepares one for the next stage, one should not conclude from this that old people cannot be treated. The belief that attempts to do so come too late in their lives can be a dangerous barrier, possibly resulting in practitioners turning away from older persons who have remediable problems.

The tendency to respond to negative stereotypes of aged persons can be overcome only by education, training, and experience. Practitioners must become aware of the relationship between their personal attitudes, the types of patients they will accept for treatment, and the kind of treatment they are likely to prescribe or administer. If one assumes mistakenly that psychiatric disorders in the aged are beyond treatment, then neglect of elderly persons who may have remediable conditions is an understandable approach. A regimen filled with dehumanizing procedures becomes acceptable only if one assumes that an elderly person is only waiting for death to relieve him, his family, and his caregiver of a burden. A practitioner may become the unwitting instrument of implementing inadequate and often negative treatment plans when he believes that a patient, his family, or society is unwilling to invest the time, energy, and money to obtain the best treatment available for his patient.

These are intolerable approaches, none of

them based on feasible, realistic modes of therapy already available. We must learn and we must teach that old age is not synonymous with hopeless, irreversible illness.

The Milieu

The preceding discussion has dealt with characteristics of the recipient and provider as potential barriers to the delivery of service. We turn now to the milieu in which the delivery of service will occur. Consideration of the milieu should include the usual environmental factors, but I believe that socio-cultural factors also need to be considered under this heading. Such aspects of the immediate environment as proximity of recipient and provider, availability of transportation, and the setting in which a service is being provided are important, but the broader sociological aspects—society's attitudes toward age and ethnic groups, for example—also affect the delivery of service. Society's attitudes often are expressed in the policies of government agencies that strongly influence the availability and patterns of services to the aged.

I shall mention only briefly some of the environmental and socio-cultural factors that facilitate or interfere with the delivery of service, but I believe these influences must be included along with the consideration of the characteristics of the recipients and providers. Proximity of recipient and provider is a critical factor. Elderly persons are unlikely to benefit from even the most sophisticated and comprehensive service if it is provided only at a site which the elderly person cannot reach. Public transportation in many areas is inadequate, and elderly persons with physical handicaps or limited financial resources find it difficult to take advantage of many services. Community organizers and planners may give low priority and scant attention to satisfying the needs of the elderly. A housing project, for example, may be located in one section of the city and be quite adequate for most of its residents, but when social and health services are not close by, elderly residents will be deprived of some services they need. Similarly, a large urban community hospital and clinic may be near a medical school for a variety of good reasons, but it may be far removed from the low-income elderly who have no other clinical service. One should also examine how the organization of such medical facilities affects services to the elderly who need psychiatric treatment. Dividing services into several medical specialties has its advantages, but it results in multiple appointments—one day in the medical clinic, another day in the psychiatric service. An elderly person, lacking the energy and resources to keep multiple appointments, then is forced to decide whether his appointment in the diabetes clinic is more important than the one in the psychiatric service. This situation is aggravated when the system also requires all patients to come for clinic appointments at the same time, to wait perhaps several hours before seeing a physician, and then another hour or two for a prescription from the pharmacy.

In metropolitan areas where psychiatric facilities are available, interest in serving the elderly is usually low. In rural areas, where few or no psychiatric services exist for anyone, aged persons have even more difficulty.

The attitudes of our society to the aged strongly influence the availability and development of agencies providing psychiatric treatment. The distaste for aging, for disease and disability, the fear of lost virility, the dread of dying and death are paradoxically intertwined with the commandment to "honor thy father and mother." A similar ambivalence is expressed in the insistence on high standards in treatment of animals used in research and experimentation, while a much lower level of service is tolerated for residents in long-term care facilities. Regulations governing the safety of the physical plants of nursing homes and hospitals are helpful, but little has been done to satisfy the aged person's social and psychiatric needs.

The persistence with which governmental regulations form barriers to service cannot be excused with the assumption that officials do not know better. The unwillingness to fully apply —and pay for—services that have proved beneficial must be attributed to other factors. For example, current Medicare regulations are discriminatory. They limit payment for psychiatric services compared with other medical services. Not only is there a restriction in the number of days of treatment covered, but reimbursement for outpatient services is inadequate. Usually, Medicare covers 80% of the "reasonable medical fee." For psychiatric services this allowance is further reduced and permits payment of only $62\frac{1}{2}\%$ of the 80% of "reasonable fee allowance." Furthermore, services provided by a nurse or social worker, even if under supervision of a psychiatrist, are not reimbursable as a professional service.

Regulations regarding welfare services also

do not allow for payment of adequate tees to encourage, or facilitate, the delivery of psychiatric services. Certainly, by now, persons in positions of authority in government know that elderly persons need many services and that a combined effort of health and social service personnel achieves a higher quality of care than that available in the present fragmented, often chaotic, system. The point was made earlier that the potential recipients of care fail to receive it if the service is difficult to obtain. Many practitioners are similarly handicapped because they do not understand the complex process by which a provider of service might be compensated. This factor alone may discourage a provider who may have overcome some of the other barriers mentioned.

Aged persons with psychiatric disorders are in double jeopardy, and the full effect of negative attitudes and social discrimination result in inferior and inadequate service for them. This will not change until education, training, experience—and persistence—convince practitioners and government officials that treatment is possible, practical, and that our society is ready to pay the bill.

Conclusion

The paucity of health services and lack of interest in the elderly are compounded when the dynamic interactions of caregiver, recipient, and the milieu in which a service is offered are ignored or misunderstood. This paper examines service delivery from the perspective of the three components, stressing the view that each must be examined as it impinges on the others.

Ruth G. Cohen

Outreach and advocacy in the treatment of the aged

Three projects with different structural designs
demonstrate the value of maintaining older
persons in the mainstream of community life

Ruth G. Cohen is district director, Services
for Older Persons Unit, Jewish Family Service
of Philadelphia, Philadelphia, Pennsylvania.
This article is based on a paper presented at
the Twenty-fifth Annual Scientific Meeting of
the Gerontological Society, December 18, 1972,
San Juan, Puerto Rico.

Hanns Sacks once wrote, "Life is like a spiral staircase; the end is as the beginning but on a higher level."[1] Today, there is a concerted movement toward outreach programs and advocacy, and it was these techniques that characterized the beginnings of the whole social work movement, with Jane Addams, Grace Abbott, Graham Taylor, and others who were then labeled do-gooders. Much has happened in the intervening decades, with a full sweep of the pendulum from one extreme to the other. Now we are striving for the happy medium—the "higher level" about which Dr. Sacks wrote; this is true of our current efforts to use techniques of outreach and advocacy as effective strategies in the treatment of the aged. The difference is that those of us who are engaged in these practices are now labeled "with it," rather than being criticized as were our courageous predecessors, some of whom were maligned and actually jailed. For this generation of trained social workers, engaging in outreach

programs and serving as advocate for the disadvantaged were part of professional training.

Social work moved from its concern with the everyday, pressing problems of unemployment and poverty resulting from the Depression of the 1930s and early 1940s into the affluence following World War II and the 1950s. It was not until the 1960s that our attention again became focused on what Franklin D. Roosevelt called "the ill-fed, the ill-clad and the ill-housed." Today these persons exist in greater numbers and are much more visible. The climate of the times, the efforts of those who have been oppressed, and our social conscience, too, have moved us to pay more serious attention to those who are disadvantaged and deprived, both materially and psychologically; these disadvantaged include the majority of our older adult population.

In this article, the writer describes several aggressive approaches to reach out to the elderly and the methods by which Jewish Family Service of Philadelphia (JFS) was able to bring services to them. The Services for Older Persons Unit of this agency has been a specialized department for the elderly since 1953. In 1973 the unit provided a variety of services to more than 2,800 older persons, their families, and their adult children.

The mandate of this unit is to maintain the older person in his own home in the community as long as he is physically and mentally able to remain. The operational directive

[1] Hanns Sacks, *Masks of Love and Life*
(Cambridge, Mass.: Sci-Art Publishers, 1948).

of the agency is that anything that will help to accomplish this purpose will be undertaken, within the agency's fiscal capabilities. Any agency program is only as good as the help it offers to the people it serves, the emphasis being on the value as seen by the client who is both the dictator and the evaluator of the service. Therefore, the designing of services has begun to shift from the professional to the client or the consumer, but it is still the professional's responsibility to design the service so that it operates at optimum effectiveness.

Although numerous efforts to reach out to those in need had been made consistently throughout the 104 years of the agency's existence, the agency began to pay increasing attention to an area in Philadelphia popularly known as Strawberry Mansion. Throughout the greater part of this century, Strawberry Mansion had been the site of an active, thriving Jewish community. Adjacent to the park from which it took its name, the area provided recreational facilities, fresh air, and even, for some, a lovely view, all combined with excellent and easy transportation to the center of the city. The class composition ranged from professional and business to working class, with some poor among them. The average population of Strawberry Mansion had felt the effect of the Depression of the 1930s and 1940s. Yet it continued through the war years as a self-sustaining, viable community. Changes began to be felt by the elderly in the early 1960s.

In a 1969 study commissioned by the Federation of Jewish Agencies of Greater Metropolitan Philadelphia, and carried out by the research division of the Philadelphia Geriatric Center under the direction of Dr. Powell Lawton, there is a clear analysis of Strawberry Mansion's population shift and its effects. In summary, as the younger generation of Jewish families began to move to newer neighborhoods, some black families moved in—the unfortunate, but familiar phenomenon of a white exodus. The 1969 study found approximately 250 Jewish residents left in Strawberry Mansion, of whom roughly three-fourths were at least sixty years old, many of them suffering from the financial and health problems likely to attend advanced age and

decreased income. At the same time, all the many social ills affecting the rest of the nation had struck with increasing intensity in Strawberry Mansion, until it was classified a high-risk area, one of the worst in the city. As a result, JFS, which was already serving some clients in this area, was charged by the Jewish community through the Federation of Jewish Agencies (FJA) with the central responsibility for setting up and carrying through a concentrated service project for the benefit of this area's older Jewish population.

A neighborhood service project

The purposes of the project were (1) to help each older resident to determine for himself whether he wished to move or to stay; (2) to give him all assistance possible, according to his own needs and wishes, in either direction and in coping with other problems not necessarily related to the locality per se; and (3) to gather additional data to identify and define unmet needs, in order to make provision for these within the agency's program of services for the elderly, with commensurate funding by the parent body, the Federation of Jewish Agencies.

The charge was clear: Jewish Family Service was assigned the responsibility of reaching out to the older Jewish community of Strawberry Mansion, thus expressing the Jewish community's concern and readiness to help. Every Jewish man and woman, aged sixty and over, was offered the opportunity to use help in thinking through what he wanted and needed most, in defining the obstacles, if any, and, to the extent possible, in coping with those obstacles. Although with a research component which resulted in a clearer picture of the community and pinpointed its unmet needs, this project was service-oriented, enriched by specific concrete services whose needs were uncovered in this outreach effort.

Letters of invitation were sent to every known resident of the area to attend a neighborhood meeting. These letters were followed up by telephone calls, and arrangements were made to transport those who wished to attend the meeting but could not travel alone or were too fearful. At the meeting an explanation of the program was given and individual home visits were arranged. For those who did not attend, additional outreach efforts were made by telephone, door-to-door visiting, and so forth.

During the outreach program, which was concentrated into a three-month period, 549 in-person interviews were held, 394 with the older person himself and 155 with collaterals (adult children or other relatives). In addition, 739 telephone interviews were held, 355 with the clients and 384 with collaterals.

Whenever possible, the family counselor completed a four-page form during or after each first interview. The form focused primarily on problems or difficulties evidenced by each household, with specific emphasis on living arrangements, finances, mobility, social relations, and health (both physical and mental). Space does not permit a description of the drama of door-to-door canvassing of the many streets in the area, preceded by either a letter or telephone call or both, explaining the agency's interest and wish to be helpful; the disbelief on the part of the residents that a community cared; the suspicious peering through the window or opening the door on a chain lock; the responsiveness on the part of the majority; the promise that the agency would follow through and provide needed services whenever possible; and the helpful participation by many of the residents to direct the staff to other isolated, unlisted residents of the community. In all, 136 households, numbering 172 persons, were reached.

Briefly, what were the major results of these efforts? It was learned, contrary to the community's original belief, that many of the elderly residents wished to remain in the neighborhood. For those who wished to move, FJA responded with the creation of a new agency, Federation Housing, Inc., which is currently serving the low-cost housing needs of the elderly through (1) the construction of a 304-unit apartment house for the elderly, with numerous supportive services, to be completed by July 1974; (2) the conversion of two two-story buildings into ten apartment units, which gave priority to residents from this area who are receiving services from FJA; and (3) a limited rent subsidy program. Similarly, FJA responded to the needs of these people by helping them to locate other housing, by assisting them with moving expenses and with the purchase of small items of furniture or necessary appliances, and by offering whatever additional services were needed to help them find a new place for themselves in the area to which they moved.

Despite the serious reality-based problems of the neighborhood, many residents wished to remain in Strawberry Mansion. For these residents, several new services were developed in response to their expressed needs and supplementary to the established program of services. Of these, the shopping service has proved to be the most popular and widely used. About fifty residents are taken every other week to a shopping center about twenty minutes away, where they can do their marketing, as well as utilize many other stores such as a pharmacy where low-cost drugs can be purchased, a five-and-ten-cent store, a hardware store, and so forth. One group is taken in the morning and another in the afternoon, so there is ample time for shopping. The driver, a grandmother fifty-three years old, helps with the packages and escorts many of the clients into their dwellings. Not only does this service meet an important sustenance need but its concomitant value of socialization is almost as important. The group interaction, such as arguing about who sits where, provides an inestimable energizing and vitalizing effect. Many residents have become quite friendly, telephoning and visiting each other frequently and performing services for each other.

A foot care service initiated by one of the social work staff has also been developed through a podiatrist, who provides free treatment, usually on a monthly basis. Here, too, the agency provides the transportation in its minibus.

Numerous opportunities for socialization have been planned throughout the year, usually in cooperation with such other social agencies as the Jewish Y's and centers and other service organizations like B'nai B'rith and Golden Slipper.

Sustaining these other services is the agency's traditional counseling service, with continuing supportive help to enable the residents to cope with the problems of day-to-day living. A number of critical situations of mentally impaired or severely physically incapacitated elderly persons living in extreme neglect and under the most unsanitary conditions have come to light. In these cases, the staff has assumed an aggressive advocacy role in an effort to obtain for the elderly those services to which they were entitled from the department of public welfare, community mental health centers, hospitals, and other appropriate agencies, often incurring criticism of colleagues in these agencies. Too often, clients penalized by the bureaucratic procedures of many community resources had neither the courage and the energy, nor the capacity, to fight their own battles.

Services ranged from obtaining legal aid to enlisting the help of the police department in order to gain entry into the homes of recluses who were seriously ill and in need of medical care. In offering services, the agency attempted to recognize the strengths of people who needed little help as well as the deficits of those who needed a great deal. Although the range of services required might well differ in kind and degree from those required in other neighborhoods, the people were much like people anywhere, varied in personality, yet much alike in needing to know that they were still living in a caring community. Perhaps the most valued result of this outreach effort has been that the residents of the area are now convinced of their "hot line" to JFS, a comforting awareness that the community does care.

The model of the project is currently being applied to another neighborhood. In this geographical area, however, the stimulus for the outreach program came from several civic groups. The manpower being used consists largely of volunteers from these groups, under the professional supervision of the agency. Although this survey is not yet completed, the findings are already indicating that the problems of residents are similar and the services needed are the same.

A joint project

A second program, of a different nature, is a project sponsored jointly by the JFS and the Jewish Y's and centers to reach out to a group of elderly men who daily frequented Cedarbrook Mall, a large shopping center. Clusters of older men and women habitually sat around with apparently no socialization, observing the passing scene. The object of this program was to develop family life education and treatment services in order to enrich the lives of these individuals and to spark some interest in their caring and doing more for themselves. This group was somewhat more affluent than the residents of Strawberry Mansion, although many of them were also living in a changing area with its accompanying problems. These elderly seemed to be coping better because they had somewhat higher incomes and more adequate shopping facilities, and some still had their automobiles and were, therefore, more accessible to medical facilities and to their relatives, but their opportunities for socialization were limited. Their paramount problem seemed to be that they had too much time on their hands, with a resultant feeling of inertia and uselessness.

A part-time worker was hired to approach these people, to let them know of the agencies' interest in being helpful to them, and to ask them what kinds of services they might need and were interested in. The interviews were conducted on both an individual and group basis, the former being a structured interview which provided a profile of the person interviewed, the problems encountered, and the services needed. The group interviews related more to programs that might be of interest to them.

At the first meeting, only five rather reluctant men responded to the invitation of both agencies to meet with them. "What do you want from us?" they asked, and when, after an explanation of the agencies' interest, the question was turned around and asked of them, they looked rather stupefied. "Someone cares about us?" an elderly gentleman ventured to remark. When it was explained that this was precisely the reason for this outreach effort on the part of the Jewish community, they became more willing to engage in a dialogue.

Interestingly enough, men eventually responded much more positively than women, expressing considerable interest in forming a club where they could play cards, hold discussions of current events and political issues, plan social activities, and have a drop-in lounge where coffee and conversation would be available. Because of this response, it was decided, for the first year, to concentrate on the group needs of the men because funds were limited and there were insufficient staff to engage in a more encompassing program. At first, this group was suspicious that the interest in them was a kind of fund-raising "gimmick." Many of these men, who had busily engaged for forty or more years in working and providing for their families, had had little time to think of the problems that retirement might create, and they were ill-prepared for the empty hours that resulted. Thus, they had gravitated to that bench in Cedarbrook Mall—the hallmark of boredom —in search of a more meaningful existence.

In one year, the group grew to forty-five men who gradually began to take an interest in more purposeful roles for themselves. In addition to their card-playing, which was of paramount importance to only a small nucleus, other programs were developed that involved them in community-action programs. They became quite vocal as advocates for improved social legislation to meet the needs of the elderly. In addition, following several sessions of group counseling, they began to discuss some of their individual problems, and more than half have received counseling help from the JFS staff. Through weekly sessions, they also became more knowledgeable of their rights as elderly citizens—participation in food stamp plans, Medicare and Medicaid benefits, the Rentwatch program, and so forth. They became a source of recruitment for the agency's volunteer and friendly visitor programs, and a number have begun to take part in the Retired Senior Volunteer Program.

Later this group was invited to send representation to the Senior Adult Council of the Jewish Y's, and their president is now an officer of this council. Given sufficient staff time and money, similar outreach efforts could be utilized in other concentrated areas, such as high-rise apartment houses where large numbers of elderly reside.

Friendly visitor project

A third program undertaken by JFS utilizes older persons as paid friendly visitors to provide services to other older persons who are partially or entirely homebound. This program developed out of an increasing conviction that one of the most effective ways of maintaining or improving the mental health of an older person is to engage him in useful and productive activity. Many older people in the agency's caseload were suffering from the debilitating effects of lack of socialization, isolation, and loneliness. As professionals, the staff were experiencing the frustration of having insufficient contact with these older persons to alleviate their pain of rejection, feelings of uselessness and overwhelming loneliness. Yet, because of its responsibility for spending the community dollar as judiciously as possible, the agency could be subjected to considerable criticism if it utilized additional professional time and skill in order to increase the contacts with these older people. The volunteer program did not meet this need. Although the volunteers were willing to accept one-time assignments of a varied nature, there was a reluctance to visit elderly clients on a regular, sustained basis. On the other hand, there were elderly clients in the agency's caseload who, because of their warmth and particular interests, had much to offer others in the way of socialization and combating the problem of loneliness. These elderly persons were living on limited incomes and unable to afford the niceties of living—and in some cases the sheer necessities. To meet the needs of these two groups— those who could serve a useful role and profit from some remuneration for their services and those who needed attention and socialization and even some small services performed for them—the agency developed the paid friendly visitor program. In the month of November 1972, thirty-eight friendly visitors gave 542 hours of service to eighty-one clients. The friendly visitor and the family counselor work as a team, the roles of each being clearly defined by the professional worker and understood by the friendly visitor and the client.

A valuable aspect of this service is its flexibility and its vast potential for services to clients. In addition to special arrangements made with the agreement of the client, the friendly visitor, and the family counselor, the following guidelines enumerate the primary functions the friendly visitor carries.

1. To provide companionship in the form of conversation, games of cards, chess, or checkers, or shared activities when feasible.

2. To listen with understanding to client's problems without becoming too deeply involved or offering specific advice.

3. To adhere to the case plan as devised by the family counselor in terms of frequency and duration of visits and nature of activities and to modify the plan only with the approval of the counselor.

4. To act always as a staff member representing the agency, with the understanding that any contact with a client represents an agency activity and not a personal one.

5. To perform small personal tasks of a nonmedical and nontechnical nature that the client requests and the counselor agrees would be helpful. These might include shopping, helping with the dishes, helping to prepare an occasional meal, assisting a client to shampoo her hair, and so forth.

6. To accompany the client on such outings as visits to a doctor or clinic, shopping trips, and visits to a barber or beauty shop, when the client is unable to go alone.

7. To encourage the client to renew old interests or undertake new ones, such as crocheting, knitting, reading, chess, or card-playing.

8. To provide, insofar as possible, the invaluable benefits of being a friend, with the added dimension of being there for the client.

Once a client expresses an interest in the service, an effort is made to match the personality and attributes of the friendly visitor with the needs of the client. The family counselor meets with the friendly visitor, charts the plan, and shares any information about the family that will be helpful to the friendly visitor in carrying out his function. Then the counselor and friendly visitor visit the client together, a three-way discussion of the plan is held, and then the counselor leaves the two together. From this point on, the friendly visitor is supervised by the family counselor, by telephone or in person, as often as necessary and the family counselor maintains a contact with the client.

In addition to the individual supervision that the friendly visitor receives, there is an ongoing in-service training program through monthly group meetings. These meetings serve two main purposes: (1) They provide an opportunity to discuss mutual concerns and ways in which the service can function at optimum effectiveness; and (2) they also provide an additional form of socialization for the friendly visitors, many of whom have formed meaningful friendships and have found a new support system in dealing with their own lives.

The dynamism of this triangular relationship—client, worker, and friendly visitor—is difficult to convey. Elderly clients come to life in a way that is hard to describe, and this process is as true for the friendly visitor as it is for the client.

Case illustrations

A case in point is that of Lillian C, a mentally retarded spinster in her early seventies who was completely devastated by the death of her mother with whom she had lived all her life. Such details as keeping house, preparing meals, paying her bills, and writing checks overwhelmed her, and for a while it seemed as if the best plan for Lillian C would be institutionalization; she had been institutionalized during her earlier years. Although she did not want to go into a nursing or boarding home, she found the responsibilities of everyday living difficult, even though she had taken some responsibility for performing these tasks while her mother was alive. It was decided to try service by the team of friendly visitor and family counselor in order to reteach Lillian C the management tasks of daily living.

The friendly visitor, Mrs. S, a widow of sixty-eight, was a client of JFS and had herself been helped, through counseling, to recover from a severe depression following the death of her spouse. Rather reluctantly, Mrs. S agreed to take on the assignment. Little by little, under the supervision of the counselor, Mrs. S began to teach Miss C to take on the tasks of day-to-day living. Gradually, trips were made to the supermarket, menus were discussed and written down, lessons were given in how to write checks and pay bills. Trips were made to the bank to cash checks and to make deposits. The day of "graduation" came when Mrs. S took Miss C downtown to shop for some much-needed clothes and shoes. This trip was highlighted by lunch at a restaurant. For months afterward, Miss C talked about this trip, and another was planned. With the help of a volunteer driver, Miss C and Mrs. S attended a matinee performance at a summer playhouse. It was a great event in the lives of both women.

This service has had inestimable value for both Miss C and Mrs. S. For Miss C, it has meant being able, with help, to remain in her own home and to take increasing responsibility for her own life management. For Mrs. S, it has meant added purpose and meaning in her daily existence as well as supplementing her meager Social Security grant and thus enabling her to take a long weekend vacation during the summer.

One of the friendly visitors is Mr. Z, a sweet, gentle, and aristocratic man of eighty-two. Mr. Z was a self-educated man and has an indefinable air of culture and refinement. One of his clients was a widower, Mr. B, in his early seventies who had been blind for two years, was extremely melancholy, and brooded all day. His children did not know what to do with him; their sincere efforts to draw him into their lives had met with constant rebuff. One day, out of sheer desperation, they called the agency for counseling. After the family counselor had established a good working relationship with Mr. B and his children, she suggested the possibility of a friendly visitor as part of the service plan. At first, Mr. B rejected the idea, but then he said he would be willing to try it "only to please the children." When Mr. Z, the friendly visitor, was introduced to the client it was instant companionship. Mr. Z was able to succeed in some areas where both the counselor and Mr. B's children had failed. He interested Mr. B in attending the senior citizens' group at the Y where Mr. Z was very active and then interested him in joining a group of blind adults to which Mr. B had formerly objected violently. After a few months, Mr. Z introduced Mr. B to a blind widow in her middle sixties and eventually Mr. Z was best man at their wedding.

Not all the cases end this romantically, but in most of them there is the romance of companionship, of conversation, and of caring, which is often as beneficial to the friendly visitor as it is to the client. For the friendly visitor, in addition to a renewed purpose in life is the sense of earning money again, of supplementing a meager income to help make possible the shift from existing to living.

Elderly men as well as elderly women relate well to this service, both as friendly visitors and as consumers. Sometimes the only cooked meal an elderly widower enjoys is one prepared by a friendly visitor, and the psychological value of sharing lunch with another person is more nutritious than the meal itself.

Although the three projects described in this article have different structural designs, each has the goal of dealing with the problems of rejection and withdrawal and the experiences of isolation, loneliness, and desocialization that many elderly persons suffer in today's society. They demonstrate dynamically the utilitarian value of maintaining older persons in the mainstream of community life.

Outreach Services in "God's Waiting Room"

JEFFREY R. SOLOMON

Miami Beach—or "God's Waiting Room" as some have flippantly named it—has an overwhelming number of elderly people living on low incomes. This article describes the community-based programs instituted by one long-term care facility that not only provide a viable alternative to institutionalization, but are cost effective as well.

DURING THE 1970s, the planning of gerontological services has been beset with problems. The theme of "too little–too late" is found in all areas of service to the elderly population in this country. The continued numerical and proportionate growth of the geriatric population has left us with inadequate human service systems to care for their many needs. From income maintenance to health care, from social services to transportation, the elderly person has consistently been denied adequate and equitable services.

In recognition of the desperate need for increased services to the elderly, Callendar, former director of long-term care of the U. S. Department of Health, Education, and Welfare, stated:

> We see [homes for the aged] as a part of an inevitable trend toward a long term system which will offer a range of services under one central management, ranging from skilled nursing care and intermediate care on an inpatient basis to outpatient day care and home health and homemaker services without moving the patient from one overall management of care to another.[1]

The purpose of this article is to describe the efforts of one community and one home and hospital to catch up with the needs of the elderly. However endemic the problem is to the country as a whole, certain peculiarities exist because of the nature of the city. Historically, Miami is a relatively new town. Its development as an urban center, which began only in the early 1900s, has accelerated quickly since the development of home air conditioning some twenty-five years ago. Consequently, the social institutions and welfare agencies seen in other major communities throughout the country simply do not exist. At the same time that the Charity Organization Society in New York and Hull House in Chicago were beginning to lay the foundations for modern social work, alligators were practically the sole inhabitants of the swampland that is now Miami.

Despite the fact that many residents of Dade County think of the Miami area as "New York City's sixth borough," this county represents an anachronism even among poor southern communities. One study undertaken several years ago by the U.S. Department of Health, Education and Welfare compared states on the basis of what proportion of personal income was spent on health and welfare programs. Florida ranked forty-ninth of the fifty-one jurisdictions. To complicate the horrendous picture of funding for health and welfare services in the state as a whole, Dade County has been seriously shortchanged in part because it represents the strange version of urban blight that has descended upon the South.

MEDICARE BY THE SEA

Dade County residents sometimes refer to Miami Beach as "Medicare by the Sea" and "God's Waiting Room," for of the 90,000 residents of the city, the median age is 64 compared to age 28 in the nation as a whole. Moreover, in Miami, as in the United States as a whole, societal prejudices are at work that constantly merge and reinforce each other. Ralph Nader called old age "the last segregation." [2] By isolating our elderly and our poor, whether on the southern tip of Miami Beach or on the fringes of business districts in virtually every city in this country, we hope to ignore their plight.

The Miami Jewish Home and Hospital for the Aged (MJHHA, or Douglas Gardens, as it is sometimes known) was founded thirty-five years ago as an institution intended to serve the elderly in need of long-term care. The philosophy of MJHHA has always been to serve the needs of the community and the individual. In this they express the philosophy of the National Association for Jewish Homes for the Aged, which stated:

> NAJHA affirms the conviction that older people have the inherent right to alternatives, choices appropriate to their life style and functional capacities; therefore, there is an obligation to assure provision of quality solutions. These rights and needs should give impetus

to the fullest exploration and expansion of services and the development of new systems of delivery, staffing and financing. Jewish Homes should become the "center" from which services for the aged emanate. Homes must become a geriatric agency rather than an institutional service.[3]

Although 65 percent of the MJHHA residents are indigent and receive public assistance, no distinction in the quality of care is made for any resident. In fact, financial information regarding residents remains confidential and is known only to staff members in the social service and accounting departments.

INSTITUTIONAL CARE

Since its inception, MJHHA has become a pioneering institution in the use of progressive concepts of nursing, social services, medical care, and rehabilitative therapy. At present, MJHHA offers field training in a variety of professions, among them nursing, undergraduate and graduate social work, occupational therapy, physical therapy, psychology, and research.

Along with several other institutions in the United States, MJHHA has been accredited by the Joint Commission on the Accreditation of Hospitals as both a nursing home and a specialty geriatrics hospital. The hospital provides more than simple custodial care. An interdisciplinary team of physicians, nurses, social workers, physical and occupational therapists, group workers, and critical support staff provides the resident in need of inpatient care with services that emphasize his individual needs and are primarily aimed at treatment and rehabilitation.

In the constant tug-of-war between individual needs

> **The theme of 'too little–too late' is found in all areas of service to the elderly in this country . . . with inadequate human service systems to care for their many needs.**

and institutional needs, those of the individual consistently win. For example, there are eleven levels of care in Douglas Gardens Hospital. These range from pavilions, which offer the ambulatory aged person a semi-independent life-style, to floors that provide intensive medical or psychiatric care not unlike that found in the most advanced hospitals. The professional staff at MJHHA have developed what is known as the Douglas Gardens Scale. Using this computer-based scale that evaluates a collection of data, they are better able to determine the level of care required by the individual patient.

With increased demand for institutional care from the Miami community, the active waiting list for admission to the home exceeds 600 names. This means that an applicant must frequently wait up to five years from the time he applies until his application is accepted. Clearly, the concepts of care must be extended to offer alternatives to institutionalization.

OUTREACH

The social service department of a hospital has a responsibility to reach out to the community and to make its expertise available to persons in need. This requires that the institution attain a level of strength that exceeds the demands placed on it by its residents. When

177

this has been accomplished, when competent personnel in all areas of care have been recruited, the institution can face outward and offer the community a package of services that is both effective and cost efficient.

The history of Douglas Gardens' involvement with the community goes back many years. Since its beginning, the social services department has provided a counseling service to the general community, but especially to older persons and their families.

The Douglas Gardens Outpatient Mental Health Center was opened in 1974. As the first gerontological mental health center sponsored by an institution offering long-term care, this center already had proved its value to the community. Serving persons from ages 50 to 90, with the median age of 67.2, the program is designed to meet the mental health needs of the many residents who have no other place to go.

Although the diagnosis of patients is varied, the five most common complaints are the depressive disorders, organic brain syndrome, schizophrenia, personality disorders, and anxiety neuroses. Additional medical evaluation frequently uncovers a large number of cases indicating serious geriatric drug abuse, and alcohol problems are also frequent. These patients, whose median income as a group falls below $4,000, are given psychiatric and pyschological evaluation, individual and group therapy, medication, occupational therapy, and other necessary services in a manner that respects their individual dignity.

STOREFRONT CLINIC

Notwithstanding education and discussion to the contrary, society continues to view mental illness in terms

Dade County residents sometimes refer to Miami Beach as 'Medicare by the Sea' and 'God's Waiting Room,' for of the 90,000 residents of the city, the median age is 64 compared to age 28 in the nation as a whole.

of insane asylums, strait jackets, and gross derangement. This is especially true of the older population. As one patient so eloquently put it, "I almost didn't call you. I can't think of myself as being 'mental.' But then I decided that anybody else who could help me would be providing the same service. They just wouldn't use 'mental' in their name." The establishment of a gerontological community mental health program had to override these prejudices. By locating a storefront satellite on the main shopping street in South Beach, MJHHA was better able to serve that population. Frequently an elderly person would saunter in saying, "Nu, what do you do here?" After listening to the services described in either English or Yiddish, he might reply in an off-hand manner, "So it shouldn't be a total loss, as long as I'm here let me talk to someone about my troubles."

Even with the storefront in South Beach, it became clear that the outreach program was not extensive enough. An outreach worker was needed to provide individual psychotherapy in the individual's home, particularly the ones who were unable to come to either of the two existing mental health offices. In addition, the home's own case-finding program was begun. The outreach worker visited many of the myriad of retirement hotels in Miami Beach and sought out the residents who required mental health services. In this way, numerous people became aware of the hospital's services who had previously been totally isolated. The support provided by this mental health service helps to keep these elderly people out of institutions. In this endeavor, the hospital is assisted by supportive programs offered by other voluntary and municipal agencies, among them the programs of the South Beach Activity Center and the Jewish Vocational Service Nutritional program. In addition, the outpatient mental health program opened a "Lucy" booth for senior citizens in a heavily trafficked area. Based on the Charles Schulz "Peanuts" cartoon in which Lucy offers psychiatric consultation on demand, this booth offers information and referral as well as psychiatric outreach to elderly residents who might be reluctant to seek mental health services.

OUTPATIENT SERVICES

In realization of the importance of outpatient services, the home and hospital also operates the senior adult day center. Funded through revenue-sharing moneys from the city of Miami, the home and hospital provides the administrative and technical management to insure a well-run program. Although most of the hundred or so elderly persons are able to maintain themselves by living with their families in the community, they do require day care as a meaningful diversion from their lonely existence. Fourteen of the first twenty-five participants in this program came directly from the waiting lists of nursing homes. Had they been admitted to the home, these fourteen alone would have cost the community $100,800 annually—an amount exceeding the full cost of the day care program.

The viability of day care as an important alternative to institutionalization is clear. In recognition of this, the author has previously commented:

> The obvious concentration of planning efforts must be for the 95 percent of the elderly population that does not require institutionalization. These persons must be able to receive services aimed at assuring their personal self fulfillment. . . . Opportunities for personal counseling must be available. One often forgets the severity of personal and family problems faced by the elderly. Grief from numerous losses of spouse, siblings, and often children tends to facilitate degenerating processes. Often these emotional factors begin a final downward whirlpool in which the physical and the psychological synergistically interact toward severe pathology.[4]

Other community efforts currently administered by the home include a Meals on Wheels program in which the home prepares hot kosher meals for homebound persons. A drug program operated through the home's pharmacy provides indigent residents of the county with necessary prescriptions free of charge.

As a new and innovative program, the home recently began a series of television commercials as a public service to elderly citizens and their families. Known as "Senior Citizens' Update," these commercials are aimed at providing the senior citizen with important information not readily accessible through the public media. The first two commercials produced in July 1975 were directed at the areas of concern that a family should consider when considering a nursing home and important new benefits that are available through Social Security and Medicare.

The critical theme that runs through all gerontologi-

> The outpatient mental health program opened a 'Lucy' booth for senior citizens. . . . based on the Charles Schulz 'Peanuts' cartoon, in which Lucy offers psychiatric consultation on demand.

cal planning and services is the necessity of the home's using its own resources in conjunction with other public and voluntary resources to develop effective and efficient services. Essentially, the departments of a well-managed institution can be readily adapted for community services without significant additional management systems that would result in excessive costs. For example, in developing a home health service, the nursing department of a home provides the obvious base from which to grow. The food service department now serves both the Meals on Wheels and the Legion Park Day Care programs. As the home develops additional residential and community programs, this department will play a critical role in administering them. The housekeeping and maintenance departments have key responsibilities in all the alternative programs offered to the community.

FUTURE PLANS

In the future, MJHHA is planning further expansion into the community. Staff is now engaged in a variety of research studies and planning efforts in conjunction with both public and charitable sources. Among these potential projects is the development of congregate housing for healthy and aged residents, which would utilize the institutional base of the home in an independent community environment. Other plans include the expansion of the Outpatient Mental Health Clinic to a comprehensive Community Mental Health Center to provide the full array of mental health services from information and referral to acute psychiatric care on an inpatient basis. Further development of home health services will be necessary to extend the period of time that a person can function successfully in the community. Research and demonstration projects are being developed in a variety of areas, among the recently recognized problem of drug abuse among the elderly. In addition, MJHHA has not neglected the crying need for institutional resources. An expansion program has been undertaken and construction on a 120-bed wing has begun. Additional staff training for other geriatric programs is being offered. Recently, the hospital held a two-day institute to teach clergymen how to work with the elderly.

As the institutional nucleus expands, the potential for the institution to serve as a catalyst and service provider in the community geometrically expands with it. The goal of MJHHA is to help fulfill the demands expressed by the section on planning of the 1971 White House Conference on Aging:

> In the final analysis, planning in behalf of aging stems from the basic values of society. Those values are translated into goals, objectives, and priorities. As agency planning for aging proceeds, it will be necessary to address these values on priorities. . . . This should be accomplished through a re-ordering of priorities at all levels to increase the commitment of national resources to meet human needs.[5]

About the Author

Jeffrey R. Solomon, Ph.D., is Director of Community Services, Miami Jewish Home and Hospital for the Aged, Miami, Florida. A version of this article was presented at the NASW Professional Symposium, Hollywood, Florida, October 1975.

Notes and References

1. Marie Callendar, "The Future of Long Term Care." Paper presented at a seminar sponsored by the U. S. Department of Health, Education & Welfare and the American Medical Association, Seattle, Washington, March 14, 1973.

2. Claire Townsend, *Old Age, The Last Segregation: The Report on Nursing Homes,* "Ralph Nader Study Group Reports" (New York: Grossman Publishers, 1971).

3. *Position Statement* (Dallas, Texas: National Association for Jewish Homes for the Aged) p. 2. (Mimeographed.)

4. Jeffrey R. Solomon, "Considerations in Planning Services for the Elderly," *Journal of Jewish Communal Services,* 51 (September 1974), p. 92.

5. *Toward a National Policy on Aging: Final Report.* Vol. 2 (Washington, D.C.: U. S. Government Printing Office, 1972), p. 90.

Housing for the Well Aged:
A Conceptual Framework for Planning[*]

Ephraim F. Goldstein

Federation Housing, Inc., Philadelphia, Pennsylvania

Housing Choices for Older Adults

IN considering the shelter needs of older adults, it would appear to be axiomatic that a variety of housing options should be available to this age group, as is true of other segments of the population, to meet their different life styles; i.e., their economic status, social, and cultural patterns of behavior in society.

While the commercial housing market does make a number of choices available, they cater to the more affluent among the elderly. However, almost a third of the elderly live below the poverty line. To cite one example, data prepared by The Special Committee on Aging of the United States Senate indicates that 59.3 percent or 2.1 million of the 3.6 million aged women in the United States in 1966 were living on incomes below the poverty line of $1,565.00 per year or approximately 6 out of 10 were classified as poor.[1] While incomes have generally increased since then, the disparity between income and the cost of living has widened, especially for the aged. Public housing has made a dent in the shortage of apartment units for poor elderly with special legislation aimed at relieving this problem. However, most housing of this kind is located in neighborhoods which Jewish elderly poor do not find in keeping with their needs and desires.

Non-profit sponsors, taking advantage of direct government loan and low-interest loan programs, have stepped in to help fill the gap in housing for middle, and to some extent low, income-level elderly. For the most part, because the need for housing is so evident for this age group and because of the traditional conceptualization of specific sponsors' orientation to the aged, the creation of such housing is accomplished with little consideration for community planning of long range housing needs of elderly, for their changing needs as time passes. The integrity of the sponsor's intent and the value of its contribution to the community may have merit. However, the scope of its contribution might be enhanced by enlarging the frame of reference from that of meeting a specific and immediate housing need to that of creating a broad communal plan for housing this rapidly increasing population group. (There are approximately 20 million older adults today with 27 million projected by 1990 over the age of 65.)

A Fundamental Premise

In Philadelphia the Federation of Jewish Agencies created a new agency, Federation Housing, Inc., to develop housing for the well, independent aged. There exists within Federation a highly sophisticated agency, the Geriatric Center of Greater Philadelphia, which comprises a home and hospital for the infirm aged, a research center, two apartment buildings and several recently acquired

---

*Presented at the Annual Meeting of the National Conference of Jewish Communal Service, Grossinger, New York, June 9, 1971.

[1] Herman B. Brotman, *Who Are the Aged: A Demographic View* (Detroit: Wayne State University, 1968).

row houses being reconverted into efficiency units with common living room to house elderly in semi-independent settings (meals, major housekeeping and some health services are included in the rent-service contract). All evidence in the community points to the need for more shelter facilities of this kind for elderly who cannot sustain themselves in a more independent setting. At the time these housing facilities were opened in Philadelphia their tenant population was younger, mobile and physically able to care for their apartments. With time, the added years and inevitable infirmities and the continuing presence of "house" services, these elderly have become increasingly dependent, calling for even more supportive services from the agency. The agency, in response to these changing needs, had initiated additional services including a special floor catering to the more dependent. Those who reach the point where a degree of self-care is no longer possible are required to relocate to other facilities; the Center's Home, when beds are available.

Are there other housing alternatives which might contribute to sustaining the older adults' ability to function independently in society for a longer period of time?

Can the housing needs of the aged be charted systematically to facilitate a community plan to accommodate the elderly at the several periods in their lives when different kinds of facilities and services are required?

It is the purpose of this paper to set forth a conceptual plan to create and to sustain housing appropriately designed for the elderly at various stages of their lives. An underlying and fundamental premise is that elderly people who are active and generally in good health should be encouraged and assisted to live in their own dwellings for as long a period of time as they are able to do so.

While the uneven and changing quality of their physical, mental, emotional, and financial status modifies the degree of their independence, such changes in this independence—dependence continuum have a direct effect on the efficiency with which elderly can function.[2] Ultimately, therefore, the types of housing which can most suitably meet their needs must be related to this continuum.

Independence—A Need

There are many factors which contribute to prolonging the period of self-reliance, of independence as an older adult in our society. His health, emotional state, relationships with family and friends and any physical handicaps which may impair normal activities are vital factors related to his ability to care for himself.

The majority of aged people do and are able to sustain independent lives when suitable, low cost, appropriate facilities enable them to keep their social and community ties and to live within their income. A Cornell University study[3] (in which a national sampling was made) reported that more than 80 percent were living in their own households, preferred to live that way, and limited evidence showed that they lived longer and "happier" lives than the smaller percentage living in households headed by others or living in institutional settings.

Environmental factors such as the condition and location of their present housing, the neighborhood and its available facilities and services can play suppor-

[2] Margaret Blenkner, "The Normal Dependencies of Aging," *Occasional Papers in Gerontology*. (Ann Arbor: Institute of Gerontology, 1969).

[3] Glenn H. Beyer and Sylvia G. Wohl, *The Elderly and Their Housing*. (Ithaca: New York State College of Home Economics, 1963).

tive or inhibiting roles to the older adult resident. Finally, a vital factor enabling the older adult to maintain his dignity as well as his sense of independence and security, is an assured adequate income. For most people retirement is normally accompanied by a drop in income and brings about a significant change in their budgeting process. While there are some reduced expenses attributable to retirement living (tax benefits, relief of insurance premiums, reduced family financial responsibilities, an abatement of occupation-related transportation, meal and clothing costs), housing takes a proportionately larger share of available income. Health and food costs are also proportionately larger.

Supportive Services Aid Independence

Increased social security benefits, improved health services under medicare, greater use of private supplementary pension programs, tax relief benefits, transportation and other economic concessions and ultimately a guaranteed annual income will enhance the older adult's ability to sustain himself independently. Moreover, the availability of a variety of social welfare services to meet emergencies and to extend appropriate help to the elderly in instances of reduced physical capability go a long way to supporting their ability to remain relatively independent. Meals on wheels, homemaker services, counseling, home health aides, leisure-time services, information and referral service are typical resources essential to keep the aged in the community and out of expensive institutional care. Costly protective care is reduced by providing appropriate social and convenience services as well as temporary health services, when needed, during periods of illness and disability to those in independent housing.[4]

---

[4] *Aging*, Nov.–Dec. 1970. pp. 10 and 12.

Their social outlook and their relationships with friends and family significantly effect their self-image and ultimately their ability to function independently. Recent studies [5] of older adults and their housing environment have pointed out that "independence" serves to enhance personal self-esteem and to promote physical and social health, as contrasted with the passivity, disengagement and preoccupation with self which often characterizes those elderly within institutional settings. Too often, older adults are placed in Homes for the Aged or resigned to live independently almost irrespective of their potential and real capabilities. They often face unnecessary confinement, discomfort, isolation, and loss of a realistic image of self due to inadequate appraisals of their shelter needs or their inability to find suitable housing alternatives.

Comprehensive Community Planning

Community planning for older adult housing should provide a variety of alternatives and the opportunity for older adults to move from one facility to another, in keeping with their needs at the time. This would require a planned, cooperative approach by those agencies directly involved in providing housing for the elderly. It also requires the creation of sufficient units of each type of facility (within the community) to meet the needs of this expanding age group. Unfortunately, the disparity between the cost of adequate commercial housing and the ability of older adults on limited, fixed incomes to pay for such housing, is growing. Moreover, the shortage of appropriate facilities to house Jewish older

---

[5] Leopold Rosenmayr and Eva Kockeis, *Housing Conditions and Family Relations of the Elderly*. (Washington, D.C.: U.S. Public Health Service, 1965).

adults is acute at every level; independent housing, boarding facilities, intermediate or semi-dependent settings, beds in Homes for the Aged and nursing facilities. The ability of older adults to move, when present housing is unsuitable, is often adversely affected by the reality of high market rentals and unavailable alternate options.

Interim Alternatives

The older adult who seeks housing assistance from the community and is advised that there is a two-year waiting list for the type of facility he presently requires, becomes frustrated, sometimes hostile and withdrawn or he may stoically face each day resigned to "stick-it-out". Such resignation is breeding ground for emotional and physical illness. A number of communities (Philadelphia, Baltimore, St. Louis, New York) having taken note of this "locked-in" elderly group, have developed out-reach programs providing critical resources and services which make living somewhat easier and more pleasant for these aged individuals. A variety of community services (as noted earlier) can help relieve much of the mental anguish and the physical handicaps of the environment. However, by the time more appropriate housing facilities are available, the older adult may very well need a more protective setting; perhaps a permanent one. The transitional characteristics of the older adults' independence status requires an approach to providing housing facilities which can accommodate their changing requirements.

As an expedient to relocate a group of elderly Jews living in a changed neighborhood in Philadelphia who requested such help, the author located a number of suitable apartments in more desirable neighborhoods. Working in close cooperation with the Jewish Family Service, these apartments were offered to a number of clients over a period of time (with a rent supplement, as an additional inducement, as needed). These apartments were rejected by a majority of these clients for a variety of reasons, but it was apparent that an underlying factor appeared to be their desire to retain their social relationships with their friends and Jewish neighbors of long standing in the old neighborhood. This need obviously was greater than their expressed need for a safer, more wholesome physical environment.

Opportunities to move into public housing projects met with the same rejection from these and other elderly clients. Only when there was assurance of a significant nucleus of Jewish tenancy at the project, did a few of these older adults consider public housing. In the same vein, the acquisition of a small apartment building to accommodate a small group of these aged in separate, independent units, as contrasted with single apartment referrals, sparked their interest and their desire to relocate. Their social needs and cohesiveness as an ethnic group must be noted carefully and supported in considering their housing needs. At the same time, it is important to avoid isolating them from the general community.

Differentiated Housing

In planning housing for older adults, facilities should reflect, as closely as possible, the independence level at which the individual can best function. This calls for an appraisal of those characteristics which provide indices of independent activity and the kinds of facilities needed to sustain such activity.

Some guides to measure the physical and mental capabilities of older adults would undoubtedly be helpful in determining the most suitable type of housing to meet their needs at the time. Facilities and services within a particular housing environment can be provided to meet a wide range of needs without changing the character of the housing environment with time. The multi-dimensional needs of older adults can be met by a coordinated approach to service; one which respects the self-determination of the individual yet allows for an adequate flow of services, as they are needed, from the respective agency sources most effectively equipped to provide them. This calls for a systematic referral process and a clear determination of function within each agency.

As a guide to appraising the most suitable type of housing for older adults at any point in time, it is necessary that there be periodic evaluation of their continued ability for self-care. Four basic types of facilities are generally required; independent apartment units, semi-independent units, protective housing and nursing home care. Ideally, the move from one type of facility to another should be related to the individual's ability to function.

The housing facilities and services to meet transitional levels of functioning follows:

Independent Elderly

Physical Characteristics of Those Able to Utilize Independent Housing.

1. *Health.* Physically sound, no serious chronic, debilitating illness; physical impairment does not preclude self-sufficiency.

2. *Mental Health.* Alert, able to handle household finances, no mental or personality aberrations.

3. *Capacity for Self-Care.*
Able to:
   —dress & groom self.
   —prepare own meals.
   —handle household chores.

   —shop (for groceries, etc.)
   —travel to community resources.
   —sustain some outside work, if desired.
   —care for self when ill.
   —care for others.

Independent Housing Units.

(Private living unit with supportive & referral services available as needed.)
High-rise, garden apartment buildings.
The apartment is a completely private, self-contained unit (including sleeping, livingroom & kitchen areas & bath).

Facilities & Services.

1. Community laundry room.
2. Community leisure-time facilities (for social, recreational & educational services).
3. Meals on Wheels and Visiting Nurse services provided as needed.
4. Access to transportation & to other community facilities & services.
5. Counseling services re: employment, personal problems, etc. Possible co-op shopping program.

Semi-Independent Elderly

Physical Characteristics of Those Able to Utilize Semi-Independent Housing.

1. *Health.* No serious illness; physically less mobile but still self-sufficient.

2. *Mental Health.* Generally able to maintain wholesome relationships with others, no mental or personality aberrations. (A bachelor or career female unaccustomed to cooking and housework should be considered for this type of facility.)

3. *Capacity for Self-Care.*
Able to:
   —dress & groom self.
   —prepare limited meals.
   —do limited cleaning but needs help for major housework.
   —shop.
   —travel to community resources.
   —sustain some outside work, if desired.
   —care for self when ill.

Semi-Independent Housing Units.

(Private sleeping unit with one meal served, other supportive services available as needed.)
Boarding House, special unit in apartment building.
Housing consists of a self-contained unit (including private sleeping area, private or shared bath & kitchenette).

Facilities & Services.

1. Community laundry room.
2. Community leisure-time facilities (social, recreational & educational services).
3. Central dining room with one meal per day (optional or mandatory). Meals on wheels as needed.
4. Visiting Nurse service as needed.
5. Access to transportation & to other community facilities & services.
6. Shopping, major housekeeping services available as needed. Sheltered workshop available in area, if possible. Counseling service as needed.
7. Physical conditioning & fitness program.

Semi-Dependent Elderly

Physical Characteristics of Those Able to Utilize Protective Housing.

1. *Health.* Chronic but generally mobile.
2. *Mental Health.* Generally well; may exhibit some memory loss.
3. *Capacity for Self-Care.*
   Able to:
   —dress & groom self.
   —prepare light meals.
   —make own bed, dust, light housework but needs help for major cleaning.
   —travel to community resources with help.
   —needs help when ill.

Protective Housing.

(Private or semi-private unit, with basic food, housekeeping, health & social services provided.)
Modified Home for Aged setting.
Self-contained unit (including private or shared bath & kitchenette).

Facilities & Services.

1. Community laundry room in building; weekly linen service.
2. Community leisure-time facilities in building (with social, recreational & educational services).
3. Meal service with Central Dining Room two times per day; mandatory.
4. Nurse on duty. (Health Center in building for emergencies, preventive check-ups & normal health services; separate care facility for temporary short term illness.) Tenants to have own physician.
5. Access to transportation & other community services. Friendly visiting program as needed.

6. Shopping services & escort services available as needed; major house cleaning weekly.
7. Counseling as needed.
8. Rehabilitation facilities & services as needed.

Dependent Elderly

Physical Characteristics of Those Able to Utilize Home for Aged.

1. *Health.* Chronic illness may be debilitating at times, generally mobile with help, may need help walking and with other physical activity.
2. *Mental Health.* Generally alert, may have memory loss, senility.
3. *Capacity for Self-Care.*
   —may need help with dressing & grooming.
   —unable to prepare food, make bed, do housework.
   —needs care when ill.

Home for Aged.

(Private or semi-private room, with full food, housekeeping, health & social services.)

Facilities & Services.

1. Sleeping room (private or semi-private).
2. Laundry & linen service.
3. Community space for recreational program & leisure-time services.
4. Dining room food service as well as room tray service.
5. Medical & nursing services available as needed. Staff of nurses, aides & house doctor.
6. Visiting program.
7. Shopping service.

Summary

While there are no clearly definitive boundaries of physical functioning with which one could readily place the older adult in his appropriate housing environment, these guide posts may be helpful toward arriving at a suitable setting for them. However, since individuals manage their own physical capacities differently, each must be appraised as to his housing needs in the light of such differences.

Social agencies, providing for the

shelter needs of elderly, often find themselves under pressure to admit or to retain individuals whose personal needs cannot be adequately served in the settings they provide. The character of such a facility may change with time as its residents grow older and become less self-sufficient. The community has the choice of modifying the existing facilities to meet the needs of its tenant population or it can transfer the client at the appropriate time to another facility which can more adequately serve the client's new status. The latter solution appears to be more logical but it is not without drawbacks since each move for the older adult is another trauma in his ending years, marking dramatically a further deterioration of his capacity to function. Such moves must be handled with care, consideration and feeling for the client and for his family.

The inherent value of such a plan is the realization of an established pattern of essential services and facilities to meet these critical and transitional life periods. Appropriate shelter for older adults is essential to their well being. The community has a responsibility to provide each type of housing environment which can enable older adults to sustain themselves in comfort and security and with opportunities for them to be as productive as their abilities and interests will allow.

Home Health Care for the Elderly

JULIANNE S. OKTAY
FRANCINE SHEPPARD

Social workers have much to offer the large and growing population of elderly people in need of home health service. These programs need to be expanded substantially. This article discusses their role in increasing the quantity and quality of home-care services.

SEVERAL RECENT TRENDS have begun to focus the attention of social workers on home-care services for the elderly. First, the growing power of the elderly population has begun to sensitize society to its special needs. Second, alarm about the skyrocketing cost of medical services is widespread in the general population. Finally, the human service field has moved away from the use of institutions to deal with people who cannot care for themselves. Social workers and other professionals in the health field, then, are viewing home health services from several angles: as a way of expanding services to the elderly, as a way of keeping health costs down, and as a more humane way of solving the problems of functional limitation.

This article presents an overview of the population in need of home health care and a description of the development and content of such services in the United States. It will demonstrate the need for social work services in this area and give recommendations for the role of social workers in home health care.

There has been a dramatic increase in the size of the elderly population in the United States during the 20th century. Persons over 65 years now make up over 10 percent of the total population. In addition, not only is the older population growing faster than those under age 65, but the oldest group, 75 years and older, is growing at the greatest rate.[1]

Although the majority of elderly persons report good or excellent health, the elderly are more likely than younger persons to have some form of disability or chronic illness. From 12 to 17 percent of older persons are disabled, about 80 percent have a chronic illness, and many elderly persons suffer from two or more chronic conditions simultaneously.[2] Contrary to popular belief, only 5 percent of the elderly population reside in institutions at any one time. However, the figure rises to 20 percent for those 85 years and older. Of the noninstitutionalized aged, about 18 percent are limited in mobility, and about one-third of these are home bound.[3] Thus, the growth of the elderly population has greatly increased the number of persons who are in need of long-term health services because of chronic disease or functional limitation.

GROWTH OF HOME CARE

Although there is evidence of the existence of home health care in the United States as early as 1796, home

> **"Perhaps the most powerful [reason why home health services should be expanded] is that the majority of elderly persons prefer to stay at home."**

health agencies were not given an impetus for growth until 1965, with the passage of Medicare or federal health insurance for the aged. Medicare covers up to 100 visits for home health care per illness under hospital insurance (Part A) and 100 visits per year under supplementary medical insurance (Part B). In 1970, under the provision of 1967 amendments to the Social Security Act, home health care became a mandated service for every state participating in Medicaid, stimulating its further growth. Today, any state-certified home health agency may receive reimbursement for services provided to patients who are eligible for Medicare or Medicaid. According to these laws, covered services include, in addition to social services, intermittent nursing care, physical therapy, occupational therapy, speech therapy, home health aides, housekeeping services, laboratory investigation, and medical equipment and supplies as ordered by the physician. In 1974, 2,329 home health agencies were certified by Medicare in the United States. Of these, about half were official health agencies, such as city health departments, one-fourth were Visiting Nurses Associations, and one-eighth were hospital-based agencies.[4]

The types of patients eligible for home health care are those with acute illness, the disabled, those with exacerbations of chronic illness, and those recovering from surgery. In spite of Medicare and Medicaid coverage, however, the vast majority of persons in need of home health care do not receive this service from any federal program, often because of gaps in coverage. For example, patients may be ineligible for the federal programs but unable to afford the cost of numerous home-care visits, or they may be excluded because they need more than the 100 visits provided for in the Medicare legislation.

Another problem is that the services actually covered vary from state to state. Only two states provide complete coverage. In fact, 70 percent of Medicaid expenditures for home health care are in New York State.[5] The lack of available home-care services is an even greater problem. Only 450 of the nation's 6,000 hospitals provide any type of home-care program. The sad fact is that most communities do not have home services to offer to their populations in need, whether they are eligible for coverage or not.[6] Thus expenditures for home-care services come to no more than 1 percent of both Medicare and Medicaid budgets. Out of an estimated 5–10 million persons in need of long-term care, less than 300,000 are receiving home-care services. In addition, a great many persons are being maintained at home through health care provided by family, friends, and neighbors.[7] A study of all persons receiving health services in the home shows that 80 percent are receiving care from relatives and not from health agencies.[8]

WHY HOME CARE?

Advocates of home health services often argue that such services are less costly than institutional alternatives. This argument is based on the difference in the cost of a nursing home ($45 per day) and that of maintaining a patient through home-care services ($12–14 per visit). However, although there is some evidence that home-care services can prevent institutionalization, home care does not appear to be a viable alternative for the majority of nursing home patients. Assessments indicate that no more than 15–25 percent of these persons could be maintained in their homes. Home care is cost effective primarily for cases in which the disability is not severe. In addition, expansion of home-care services to the large number of persons in need of long-term care who are not in institutions and who are now receiving no services would undoubtedly increase expenses rather than conserve them.[9]

Although the cost argument has not been settled, in part because of the extreme difficulty of doing experimental research in this area, there are other reasons why home health services should be expanded.[10] Perhaps the most powerful is that the large majority of elderly persons prefer to stay at home. Clearly there are psychological and social benefits for the patient who can avoid the disruption, isolation, and impersonalization of institutional placement. Another question is how the quality of health care offered by home health agencies compares to that in nursing homes or hospitals. Although there has been little careful research on this issue, there is some evidence that patients maintained in home health care have better health outcomes than those in more traditional medical settings.[11] There is a critical need for more research in this area.

ROLE OF SOCIAL WORKERS

In sum, there is a large population in need of long-term services, and home health services are desirable for

> **"Although there is some evidence that home-care services can prevent institutionalization, home care does not appear to be a viable alternative for the majority of nursing home patients. Assessments indicate that no more than 15–25 percent of these persons could be maintained in their homes."**

quality if not also for cost reasons. Social workers have several roles to play in providing this care. The first is as advocate regarding the quantity and quality of services. Social workers can be effective in their local communities as well as at the national level in encouraging the expansion of home-care services. Appropriate activities might include conducting research to demonstrate the need for these services, bringing evidence of this need to the attention of social action groups and legislators, and generating public support for home health services. Furthermore, there has been general concern that the proprietary agencies in the home field will repeat the scandals of the nursing home industry, in which quality of care is too often sacrificed for increased profits. Social workers must help communities develop high standards and serve as watchdogs to insure that home health agencies are carefully regulated.

It is well known that the needs of home-care patients extend beyond those directly related to health. The loss of almost all social roles is an important problem for any elderly or disabled person. Unemployment can result in a loss of self-esteem as well as in financial problems. Inability to maintain contact with friends and family members brings increasing isolation. Physiological and psychological changes resulting in increased dependency on others cause difficult adjustments for both patients and their families. When their condition deteriorates over time, patients need increasing support from family, friends, and community agencies to prolong independent functioning and to maintain a high quality of life. Financial resources must be stretched to cover ongoing medical expenses. Resources for housing, income, food, transportation, and recreation, as well as health care, are frequently needed. Thus the homebound elderly need many services that social workers traditionally provide.

As mentioned earlier, social services are covered by Medicare and Medicaid as part of home health services. According to guidelines of the Department of Health, Education, and Welfare, the social worker's functions in home health services include the following:

1. Working with other members of the health team to assess the social and emotional factors related to the patient's health problems, and participating in the development of the patient care plan,

2. Helping the patient and his family to understand, accept, and follow medical recommendations and providing services that are planned to restore the patient to optimum social and health adjustment within his capacity,

3. Assisting the patient and his family with personal, emotional, and environmental difficulties which predispose toward illness or interfere with obtaining maximum benefits from health care,

4. Utilizing resources, such as family and community agencies, to assist the patient to resume life in the community and to learn to live within his maximum capacity,

5. Participating in alternative and appropriate discharge planning.[12]

Unfortunately, the same problems that cause inadequate levels of home health services apply to social services. Although many communities have no home health agencies at all, the majority of the home health agencies that do exist provide no social services. Out of the total of 2,329 home health agencies certified by Medicare, only 607 provide social services. About 75 percent of hospital-based home health programs provide social services, but only about 15 percent of state or local health departments do.[13]

Even in agencies that do offer social services, the social worker is often involved only in initial assessments. In some cases, one social worker is expected to serve the entire caseload, which may involve hundreds of patients. Clearly, this limits the service to crisis situations only. Thus, although social work services are badly needed by the home health care population, and although social services are covered by federal programs, their availability is currently limited.

CASE ILLUSTRATIONS

Three case descriptions illustrate the importance of social work services in home health care and provide examples of some typical home health patients. Fortunately, these cases were all cared for by one of the few home health agencies that provides ongoing social work services.

Mrs. F was a 77-year-old woman who had high blood pressure, edema of the legs, and was suffering from loss of memory. She lived in a two-bedroom apartment with her son and his five children. She was home-bound but could get around with the aid of a walker. The home health aide visited the patient twice a week to do personal care, take vital signs, and aid her in the use of the walker. The home-care nurse visited every other week and provided health services.

Mrs. F and the children were dependent on her son for the supply and preparation of food. The social worker discovered that the son was a chronic alcoholic, that there was often no food in the house, and that the patient and children were frequently hungry. The social worker was able to work in close conjunction with the son's social worker to insure adequate nutrition for the dependents.

Mrs. W, also 77, suffered from cancer of the colon and heart disease, and spent every day in bed on the second floor of her house. Mrs. W said it was impossible for her to get out of bed—she was in too much pain. However, her physician said there was no reason that she could not walk. The home health aide visited twice a week to take vital signs and to do personal care.

The social worker explored the situation of the patient's husband and found that he had recently retired and was deriving great satisfaction from his role as caretaker for his wife. Because of this, he was not anxious to see her gain independence. In this case, the social worker was able to help the other members of the health team understand the situation. The social worker was then able to begin work with Mr. W, assisting him to realize that he would be helping in his wife's health care by encouraging her to walk.

Mr. S, an 81-year-old man, had been recently released from the hospital. He was admitted because he was physically weak. His diagnosis after testing was severe malnutrition. The home-care nurse visited Mr. S once a week to teach him about nutrition. Mr.

S lived alone in an 85-year-old house with no electricity.

The social worker learned that Mr. S was living on a small amount of savings and had not applied for any benefits because he "didn't want to take handouts." With the social worker's help, Mr. S was able to apply for Social Security, food stamps, and a home repair grant to provide electricity for his home.

In each of these cases, the social worker was able to help the home health agency to meet its goals by contributing directly to the health and social welfare of the patients.

TECHNIQUES AND TRAINING

To be optimally effective in the home health field, social workers will need to develop techniques that are effective in this setting. For example, many home-care patients have difficulties that stem from inappropriate behavior. A logical behavioral approach combined with humane behavior modification techniques could be helpful in situations in which patients' behavior is detrimental to their health. Another area that is often overlooked is the needs of the family members who share the responsibility for patients' care. Social workers could be important sources of support for these people. As social workers gain more experience in the home health field, it will be important to determine which techniques are most effective. In addition, social work schools will need to begin training students to be effective workers in this field.

Another important role for social workers will be involvement in the education of other members of the home health team, for example, in training physicians, nurses, and new health practitioners to recognize the importance of social problems and to utilize social resources effectively. This may occur within the agency itself or in institutions of medical education.

SUMMARY

Home health services must be expanded and must include ongoing social work services. In addition to the provision of direct service, social workers are encouraged to advocate for quality home health services, to develop effective techniques for providing social services to home-care patients, to incorporate these techniques into social work education, and to become involved in the education of their medical colleagues. In this way, the home health field can begin to fulfill its goals by providing patients with quality care in the home setting, thus allowing them to remain independent and at the same time meeting their health and social needs.

About the Authors

Julianne S. Oktay, Ph.D., is Assistant Professor, Johns Hopkins School of Health Services, Baltimore, Maryland. Francine Sheppard, MSW, is Director, Howard County Rape Crisis Center, Columbia, Maryland. An earlier version of this paper was presented at a meeting of the American Public Health Association, Washington, D.C., November 1, 1977.

Notes and References

1. Mary Grace Kovar, "Health of the Elderly and Use of Health Services," *Public Health Reports* (January–February 1977).

2. Phillip W. Brickner et al., "The Homebound Aged: A Medically Unreached Group," *Annals of Internal Medicine,* 82 (January 1975); and U.S. Congressional Budget Office, *Long Term Care for Elderly and Disabled* (Washington, D.C.: U.S. Government Printing Office, February 1977).

3. Kovar, op. cit.

4. *Medicare: Health Insurance for the Aged, 1972–74 Participating Providers* (Washington, D.C.: U.S. Social Security Administration, Office of Research and Statistics, 1976).

5. U.S. Congressional Budget Office, op. cit.

6. Isadore Rossman, "Options for Care of the Aged Sick," *Hospital Practice* (March 1977), p. 113.

7. U.S. Congressional Budget Office, op. cit.

8. Mary H. Wilder, "Home Care for Persons 55 Years and Over," *Vital and Health Statistics,* Series 10, Number 73 (Rockville, Md.: National Center for Health Statistics, Department of Health, Education & Welfare, July 1972).

9. U.S. Congressional Budget Office, op. cit.

10. *See* Fredrick W. Seidl, Carol D. Austin, and D. Richard Greene, "Is Home Health Care Less Expensive?" *Health and Social Work,* 2 (May 1977), pp. 5–19; and Sonia Conly, "Critical Review of Research on Long-Term Care Alternatives" (Washington, D.C.: Office of Social Services and Human Development, Department of Health, Education & Welfare, June 1977).

11. U.S. Congressional Budget Office, op. cit.

12. *Federal Health Insurance for the Aged, Conditions of Participation: Home Health Agencies* (Washington, D.C.: Department of Health, Education & Welfare, September 1971).

13. *Medicare: Health Insurance for the Aged.*

Innovative Roles for Social Workers in Home-Care Programs

TERRY B. AXELROD

———

Home care has become recognized as an effective means of preventing or postponing costly institutionalization. In order to provide more comprehensive programs, home health agencies will require the services of professionally trained social workers. The author describes several roles for social workers trained in clinical services, administration, and planning.

THE COMPREHENSIVE HOME-CARE PROGRAM, which is an outgrowth of the more traditional home health agency, offers a major source of potential employment for social workers. As home-care programs expand and diversify their activities, social workers with training in human services, administration, planning, and organizational development must be able to demonstrate to administrators of these organizations specific roles that are appropriate to their talents.

This article will discuss the experiences of one home-care program in developing innovative roles for social workers. After a brief review of the evolution of service delivery in the home, it will describe the program's inception, including its underlying philosophy, the patient population, and sources of referral. Three key roles for social workers will be explained, and, looking ahead to the time when social workers become more firmly established in comprehensive home-care programs, issues for future consideration will be suggested.

BACKGROUND

The provision of services in the home has been the cornerstone of social work practice in this country.[1] In the past century, the preferred treatment setting for the physically, emotionally, or financially disadvantaged client has shifted between community-based and institutional care.[2]

Two pieces of legislation that were passed which greatly influenced the trend toward community care were the Community Mental Health Act in 1963 and the Medicare (Title XVIII) amendments to the Social Security Act of 1965. The Community Mental Health Act mandated that each local community must provide services to meet the basic mental health needs of its residents. Although the criterion of providing crisis outreach services to persons in their homes was not well defined, such services were among those required of a community if it were to qualify for federal funding.

The passage of Medicare legislation has provided a clearer mandate for service delivery in the home. It allowed for the reimbursement of health care and social work services when provided by trained professionals working within a certified home health agency. Within this context, social work was defined as a secondary service, which meant that workers could become involved only after a case had been referred from a primary service such as nursing, physical therapy, or speech pathology. This legislation also defined the requirements for providing the services of a social worker and social work assistant, stating explicitly the previous education and experience considered essential. The Medicare home health program is administered by several private insurance programs that serve as intermediaries between home health agencies and the federal government. These intermediaries are given considerable discretion in determining when social work services are needed and appropriate.

Although the passage of this legislation was heralded within the social work profession, by no means did it guarantee social workers a role in the delivery of home health services. For several decades, nurses working in public health departments or privately sponsored visiting nurse associations had been providing generalized nursing and social services to persons of all ages with psychiatric or medical problems. Many preexisting and newly formulated home-care programs were unable to identify a distinct role for social workers and therefore, despite the availability of Medicare reimbursement, chose not to provide this service.

Social work services were further jeopardized in the late 1960s when the federal government tightened the scope of reimbursable services to exclude maintenance or long-term care and imposed retroactive denials on requests for such services. Many organizations were forced to cut back their programs to the most basic services only or to close down entirely. In most cases, social work was one of the services that was dropped. It has only been within the past five years that home-care programs have begun to take a creative look at the possibilities for offering more comprehensive service delivery and have thus envisioned a broadened role for social workers.

Community Home Health Care is a private, non-profit organization, which has been certified by Medicare as a home health agency in the state of Washington. The organization was started in 1975 to provide the spectrum of health and social services—including professional nursing, physical and occupational therapies, speech pathology, social work, dietary consultation, and paraprofessional homemaker–home health care—that would enable individuals to continue to live in their own homes. Each service conducts its own assessment of the patient's personal and home situation and develops an individually designed plan of care to promote independence. These plans are encapsulated on a form that includes a list of the individual's problems and goals for treatment and are coordinated by an interdisciplinary team. A typical home visit lasts one or two hours.

Because many individuals require assistance for several hours during the day, or on a 24-hour-a-day basis, Community Home Health Care offers two additional services to supplement the intermittent visits of staff members. Trained volunteer "visitor advocates" provide home visits to allow the family temporary relief from patient care. In addition, an employment service assists patients in obtaining untrained housekeepers or companions who are paid privately or through public assistance.

PHILOSOPHY

The philosophy behind the development of Community Home Health Care as a comprehensive program is that each consumer of service is entitled to the right of self-determination. This means that the individual has the choice to continue to live at home, receiving treatment and services that will facilitate his or her attainment of the highest possible level of independent functioning.

Even the professionally trained home-care worker may find it difficult to support an individual's decision to continue to live at home. Frequently the home situation is hastily judged as unsafe or unhealthy and the recommendation is made for a more closely supervised living situation. Members of the home-care staff must be able to recognize each individual's right to remain in a living situation that they consider less than ideal and to receive instruction in the necessary skills to improve that situation. Indeed, the predictions of home-care workers are frequently defied, because the patient's motivation and response to rehabilitation and treatment may be enhanced by the familiar surroundings of the home environment.

A related philosophical tenet is that the home is the domain of the patient and is respected as such. Thus, the patient maintains the right to request or reject the services of the home-care program. Home visits are scheduled at times that are convenient to both the patient and the family, and staff members are required to telephone to reconfirm visits so that they do not arrive at the patient's home unexpectedly.

A comprehensive home-care program has a responsibility to recognize that if the patient is to remain at home, he or she may require assistance in a number of areas of basic functioning. The home environment, in contrast to the traditional outpatient clinic, provides a rich milieu in which each member of the team can observe firsthand the integration of all aspects of individual and family functioning. Before a suitable treatment plan is developed, medical, emotional, social, and environ-

"Many preexisting and newly formulated home-care programs were unable to identify a distinct role for social workers and therefore, despite the availability of Medicare reimbursement, chose not to provide this service."

mental needs must all be taken into consideration and an assessment of the individual's ability to manage at home must be made. Staff members will have to look beyond the limits of their professional training for symptoms of problems that would normally be the concern of another discipline. For example, a physical therapist should be alert to symptoms of depression or of alcoholism, just as a social worker should be able to notice edema or skin deterioration. A comprehensive home-care program must acknowledge this overlapping of roles and be prepared to provide team members with ongoing training to enable them to learn how and when to utilize staff from other disciplines.

As a community service organization, the comprehensive home-care program must take responsibility for identifying other complementary programs and services and for helping individuals make use of these services. In addition, by conducting an ongoing assessment of a patient's unmet needs, the home-care program may be able to participate in community planning processes and to help develop new services to expand its own scope. A well-integrated mental health component is a single example of a service that distinguishes comprehensive home-care programs from traditional home health programs.

As with the other philosophical tenets discussed

earlier, the provision of comprehensive social work services requires the solid backing of the organization's administration. At Community Home Health Care, this process has been facilitated by the professional background of the program administrators and cofounders, as well as by the organizational structure and areas of responsibility. The executive director, a nurse, is experienced with and committed to expanding the role of social workers as part of the interdisciplinary team. One of her primary responsibilities is to oversee all the medically related health care services. The associate director is a social worker who has had previous experience as a member of an interdisciplinary home-care team. She oversees all the social work and mental health services, including social work counseling and advocacy services, a volunteer program, an employment service, and a planning and program development unit.

SERVICE DELIVERY

Community Home Health Care provides services to patients whose primary problem may be either medical or psychiatric. Approximately 70 percent of the individuals receiving services have been referred because of medical problems, and 30 percent are referred for emotional or psychiatric problems.

Over 90 percent of the individuals referred for medical reasons are elderly. The remainder of this population are middle-aged or younger adults who are physically disabled or terminally ill. The majority of patients have just returned home from a hospital or nursing home following surgery or have required treatment for a stroke, heart attack, or bone fracture. Many have been recently diagnosed as having chronic degenerative or terminal illnesses. Although nearly all the patients are highly motivated to return to their own homes, members of their family are generally apprehensive about their ability to provide the necessary care. It is to this nonpatient group that the teaching-oriented services of Community Home Health Care are directed. Another group of patients are those still living at home, who have not been hospitalized recently, but whose medical condition has been deteriorating gradually. These persons not only need to have their present situation assessed, but some stabilization or improvement in their physical condition is required.

Individuals referred to Community Home Health Care for assistance with emotional or psychiatric problems are generally high-risk candidates for admission to a psychiatric hospital, either for the first time or for rehospitalization. They may require treatment for paranoid or schizophrenic behavior, profound depression, confusion, or alcohol or chemical dependence. For the most part, they require the outreach services of a home-care program because they have proved to be unable or unwilling to make use of mental health facilities on an outpatient basis. Frequently, they have been hospitalized and have failed to report back for outpatient treatment, or they may have kept one or two appointments at the local community mental health center and then have dropped out.

Referrals are made by medical and psychiatric units in hospitals, nursing homes, community-based social service agencies, or by private individuals, family members, or physicians. Patients accepted by the program must be confined to their homes because of a physical or emotional problem and must have a physician's approval when medical services are needed at home.

Services are reimbursed on a fee-for-service basis by the Medicare or Medicaid plans or, less frequently, by private health insurance plans. A limited amount of state, county, and city funds are available in the form of grants, thus enabling the program to use a sliding-fee scale for mental health services in the home.

Social workers function in three major roles in the Community Home Health Care program. Their primary responsibility is to provide casework services to individuals in their homes. A second role is in program coordination and supervision. In addition, social workers assume administrative responsibility in the areas of planning and program development.

CASEWORK

Social workers providing casework services in the patient's home are, for the most part, professionally trained workers at the master's degree level, although MSW students also take on casework assignments as part of their field experience. In addition, undergraduate social welfare students serve as office-based patient advocates and assist social workers and other staff in processing patient referrals.

In all cases, social work intervention includes an assessment of the individual's current level of functioning in the home and the development of a problem-oriented treatment plan. The primary goal of intervention is to assist the patient to develop the skills and to use the environmental supports necessary to continue living independently. A related activity is to provide supportive or therapeutic counseling to help the patient and family cope with the emotional impact of illness. For example, an elderly man who has just received a diagnosis of metastatic cancer during a hospital stay may need an opportunity to talk with an outsider about his impending death and his feelings that he is a burden to his family. In such a situation, the wife, who has become exhausted and frustrated from providing round-the-clock care to her husband, might also benefit from supportive counseling. As part of the treatment plan, the social worker could help her set limits on the care she can provide and make sure that she develops outside sources of support and relief.

Other examples of patients are the middle-aged woman who has just returned home following a mastectomy and who needs counseling for ongoing depression, or an elderly man who has recently suffered a recurrent episode of congestive heart failure and returns home from a convalescent center to learn of his wife's sudden death. The social worker may also be asked to visit to help the individual make plans for the future. For example, a young woman with multiple sclerosis may need assistance in planning for transportation and child care for a daughter who is to enter kindergarten. An older man who has suffered a recent stroke may request help in obtaining continuing assistance with bathing and housekeeping. An elderly woman with a terminal illness may ask for help in planning for the additional assistance she needs in order to remain at home until she dies. In the case of patients who are unable to maintain such independence, a social worker can assist them in making arrangements for the move to a nursing home or retirement home.

The social worker, in collaboration with office-based patient advocates, assists individuals in securing financial or social services from other community organizations. The criteria for eligibility and referral processes for programs such as meals on wheels, Medicaid, and Supplementary Security Income are confusing and awesome to the physically or emotionally disabled person. The social worker is able to assess the patient's ability to initiate a self-referral and follow through with it and can suggest appropriate resources and be available to help the individual work through the "system."

COUNSELING AND ADVOCACY

The majority of cases referred for social work intervention require both counseling and advocacy services. A young woman who has just returned home following her third psychiatric hospitalization in a year will need assistance in building a network of support in the community. This may include help in finding a more centrally located apartment with greater accessibility to neighbors, shops, and the community mental health center where she is to attend a day program. The social worker might also help the woman to identify early symptoms of psychiatric breakdown and a plan of action to be followed at these times.

One critical component of home-based social service delivery is the way in which the social worker is introduced to the patient. If a patient is referred to the organization for services covered by Medicare, the primary health care professional making the referral—the nurse or physical therapist, for example—has already established a relationship with the patient or family. Patients are generally more receptive to the tangible, health-related services offered by a nurse or other health care professional than they would be to the talk-oriented services of the social worker. Generally, a member of the referring team will already have discussed the role of the social worker with the patient, focusing on one or two particular problem areas in which the social worker can offer assistance. In introducing himself or herself on the first visit, the social worker can follow this lead. In some situations, the nurse or therapist may request assistance from the social worker in determining a means of introducing social work services to the patient. Clearly, this process of case identification and referral for social work intervention is dependent on the team member's understanding of the role of the social worker and demands skill in assessing the need for social work intervention.

In the case of a patient referred to the organization for assistance with emotional or psychiatric problems, the person making the referral takes on the responsibility for preparing the patient for the social worker's first visit. However, in spite of the most careful planning and preparation, social workers are occasionally still refused entry into the home—another reminder of the delicate host-guest relationship in home care. Creative methods for gaining the patient's trust have included holding interviews over fence posts or through open windows or doors left slightly ajar until the patient felt comfortable enough to allow the "stranger" to enter.

Such creativity and flexibility on the part of social workers are prerequisites to providing services in the home. The social worker must be ready to adapt treatment plans and interviewing techniques to meet the unpredictable nature of the home visit. For example, the practitioner may have planned a visit to talk with the patient's spouse, only to discover on arrival that other members of the family or neighbors have come to visit as well. Because medical crises can occur during home visits, all social workers are required to have completed basic training in cardiopulmonary resuscitation and to have learned techniques for safely moving physically disabled persons.

The duration of social work services to the homebound population is generally on a short-term basis, ranging from one to eight visits. However, if a patient's fluctuating psychiatric condition needs to be monitored, or if a social worker is providing counseling for profound depression or because of a patient's terminal illness, additional visits are frequently necessary.

In calculating the cost of social work intervention with individuals in their homes, it must be remembered that the time spent in actual home visits to the specific patient is only one component of total service delivery to that patient. A large amount of time is also devoted to telephone calls and direct interviews with family members and resource persons in the community. In addition, the worker must coordinate activities with other members of the interdisciplinary team and keep accurate case records. Social workers are also available to visit patients in the hospital or nursing home to plan for their discharge and maintain contact if reinstitution-alization is necessary.

PROGRAM COORDINATION

Another social work task is to coordinate the activities of the various members of the interdisciplinary team that provides counseling and advocacy services and to supervise various program units within the organization. This mental health coordinator is responsible for the selection, orientation, and supervision of staff. Supervision focuses primarily on staff development and administrative issues, whereas case management and is-

> "Patients are generally more receptive to the tangible, health-related services offered by a nurse or other health care professional than they would be to the talk-oriented services of the social worker."

sues regarding treatment are handled in peer-review sessions with small groups. The coordinator also attends the organization's weekly case-review conference in which more complex cases are discussed by the entire interdisciplinary team. The mental health coordinator also takes the lead in establishing departmental objectives, preparing a departmental budget, and helping to develop new policies and procedures, and soliciting staff participation.

Another role for a social worker is that of coordinator of volunteers. The volunteer coordinator is responsible for the overall operation of the volunteer program, including recruitment, screening, training, and supervision of volunteers. The primary direct-service role for volunteers is as visitor-advocate, which includes friendly visits and companionship for homebound patients as well as client advocacy. Visitor-advocates also function as part of the home-care team by attending team meetings and assisting in carrying out the treatment plan. A subgroup of visitor advocates has received special training in working with persons suffering from life-threatening or terminal illnesses. Another group of volunteers serve as rehabilitation assistants to help the patient to practice walking and follow through with the plan prescribed by the physical therapist. The social service background of this coordinator has been especially valuable in helping volunteers, individually and in groups, to express their feelings about the client population and in providing the necessary supervision regarding case management.

A third example of a social worker's responsibilities in program coordination is as employment service coordinator. The employment service provides assistance to patients and families in assessing and securing any nonprofessional services in their own homes that they need to supplement the services of Community Home Health Care. Although funding to employ such helpers is often available to low-income persons, finding a reliable worker is especially difficult for the elderly and disabled. The coordinator accepts all requests for this type of help and is responsible for recruiting and screening all workers and for maintaining an up-to-date record of their availability. In order to carry out this responsibility successfully, extensive coordination with the various staff members is essential. Follow-up is done on all requests to determine whether the placement is satisfactory. Because of the skills and judgment involved in screening and interviewing both the untrained workers and the patients requesting this service, a social work background is a prerequisite for this position.

PLANNING

The third major role for professionally trained social workers in a home-care program is in the area of planning, development, and evaluation of new programs. The development of a comprehensive home-care program requires a commitment to planned growth in accordance with stated organizational goals. At Community Home Health Care, unmet needs among patients may be identified by staff, administration, the board of directors, or even the consumers themselves. An informal assessment is then conducted by the director of planning and program development to determine the need for the service and the extent to which it is already being provided in the community. The proposed program or service is also evaluated in terms of its impact on the health delivery system as a whole as well as on the existing organizational structure. Examples of unmet needs that have been identified and fulfilled in this manner are the need for the paraprofessional services of a homemaker–home health aide and the need for mental health and alcoholism services to persons in their homes.

The director of planning and development assumes responsibility for exploring suitable funding sources and preparing necessary applications for grants. This department guides the grant through the funding process and, once funded, internally monitors new programs to see that standards are complied with. The director of planning and development also supervises the staff person responsible for all private fund-raising efforts.

In addition, the program director assumes responsibility for monitoring state and federal legislation related to the organization's services and prepares testimony for legislative hearings. Community Home Health Care strives to influence proposed legislation by joining coalitions with other home-care programs. The director of planning and development has a master's degree in social work with special training in health systems planning and organizational development and has an additional background in home care and gerontology. This professional training has also been used in a special assignment to develop and staff several committees that link the board of directors, the advisory board, and the organization's consumer. Social work students in community and organizational development have been assigned projects in this area.

Essential to the development of diverse roles for social workers within the same home-care organization is their mutual understanding of one another's roles, responsibilities, and training. Furthermore, each social worker must be able to explain these functions to staff members and students in other disciplines as well as to individuals in the community.

As social workers become increasingly involved in home-care programs, more complex issues in terms of program and service delivery will need to be addressed. Some examples of such issues are (1) the development of professional standards of practice in leading to a mechanism for peer review, (2) the need to make social work services available on a full-time basis, 24 hours a day, 7 days a week, (3)) the development of group work approaches with isolated, home-bound individuals, (4) the differentiation of responsibilities between bachelor's and master's level social workers, and (5) the development of roles for clinicians who have particular areas of specialization, such as work with alcoholics, the aged, or persons with physical disabilities.

CONCLUSION

The development of comprehensive home-care programs provides a unique setting for social workers. The national trend toward preventing or prolonging costly institutional care suggests that, increasingly, social service funds will be spent on keeping individuals in their own homes for as long as possible. As existing home health programs become more responsive to the needs of the homebound population, they will provide additional social and mental health services to supplement their medically related health services.

This article has described the way in which one home-care program has developed a comprehensive range of services and has outlined several roles for professionally trained social workers. In addition to functioning as direct providers of mental health and advocacy services, social workers assume administrative roles as program coordinators and planners. The primary challenge to the profession is to prepare practitioners who can demonstrate to administrators of home-care programs the usefulness of their skills. Social workers need to accept this challenge readily.

About the Author

Terry B. Axelrod, MSW, is Associate Director, Community Home Health Care, Seattle, Washington. A version of this article was presented at the Seventh Annual Meeting of the National Association of Home Health Agencies, Portland, Oregon, October 1977.

Notes and References

1. Ralph E. Pumphrey and Muriel W. Pumphrey, eds., *The Heritage of American Social Work* (New York: Columbia University Press, 1961), pp. 27–49.

2. Ibid., pp. 137–239.

In an earlier study it was found that very few Mexican-Americans applied for public housing for the elderly. One obvious reason was lack of information about the facilities. Such lack of information may hold true for other community services. Therefore, it seemed important to learn more about the ways in which the older Mexican-American acquires information and to consider how traditional news media might be adapted to his use and other channels of communication opened to him. This is the report of an investigation into the means by which these older people obtain information, a comparison of their communication habits and capabilities with those of other elderly persons, and consideration of some ways in which the community might improve communication with its older Mexican-American members.

Communicating with Elderly Mexican-Americans

Frances M. Carp, PhD[2]

Communication is a critical problem today.

The most remarkable paradox of our time is that, in proportion as the instruments of communication have increased in number and power, communication has steadily declined. Mutual intelligibility is probably a rarer phenomenon now that at any time in history (Hutchins, 1967).

Even "scholars of communication" have difficulty in exchanging information (Gerbner, 1966).

Social scientists long overlooked the extent to which communication is "the cement that binds" society together (Wiener, 1967). "Until recently, communication pathology has been almost entirely the domain of psychiatry" (Ruesch, 1967). Now communication failure is seen to be pervasive in our society and is recognized as dangerous to it. All too clear is the evidence that age groups, ethnic groups, economic groups, and national groups "talk past" one another. Persons at different socioeconomic levels and in different ethnic groups have different access to mass communication media (Asheim, 1956; Gray, 1956; Schramm, 1956; Westley & Severin, 1964), and they are affected differently by these media

which now are dominant agents of socialization (Gerson, 1966).

Listening is one of the most important phases of communication. Various ethnic and socioeconomic groups have different patterns and different capabilities of listening. Alienation and hostility derive from and feed upon communication failures (Baldwin, 1963; Brody, 1966; Cleaver, 1969; Grier & Cobbs, 1968; Jacobs, 1967).

Society . . . continues to exist . . . by communication. . . . Men live in a community in virtue of the things which they have in common; and communication is the way in which they come to possess things in common (Dewey, 1916).

The old (Rosow, 1967), the poor (Friedman & Phillips, 1967; Smith, 1967; Stringfellow, 1966), and members of ethnic minority groups (Ellison, 1952) have relatively little in common with the mainstream of society and are in poor communication with it. The separation is wider and the information transmission even more difficult when there is no common language. All four factors —age, poverty, ethnicity, and language—impede communication between society and its elderly Mexican-American members. How well informed are they about the larger society with-

1. Supported by research grant No. Aa-4-68-061-01 from the Administration on Aging.
2. Langley Porter Neuropsychiatric Institute, 401 Parnassus Avenue, San Francisco, 94122.

in which they live? How do they usually obtain information about it? How might the majority society communicate more effectively with them?

Background of the Study

The need for special efforts to reach older Mexican-Americans (MAs) became apparent during a study of applicants for public housing for the elderly. Information about the special housing reached older people sufficiently well that before the first facility was built there were more than twice the number of legally qualified applicants who could be accommodated. Only 3% were MAs although they comprised approximately half the population and an even larger proportion of persons eligible for public housing. Most (97%) of the applicants were Caucasian (Anglo-Americans) although they made up only about 40% of the population (Carp, 1966). Integral to plans for the next facility were efforts to recruit MAs. Nevertheless, when it was built 9 years later, application rates were essentially the same. Of the first 500 applicants, only 4% had Spanish surnames.

Reasons for non-application were explored with elderly MAs (Carp, 1969a; 1969b; 1969c). One glaring factor was lack of information. Only 5% of those interviewed had ever heard of the facility for which applications were being taken; less than one-third had heard of the one which had been in operation 8 years. At least in this area of knowledge, the elderly MAs were very poorly informed about the community in which they lived. Furthermore, a special effort to inform them had failed. Parry (1968) and many others have pointed out that "Many failures in daily communication spring from the absence of any means to bring potential senders and receivers into contact" and that the sender may be "in effect talking to himself."

Therefore it seemed important to learn more about the ways in which the elderly MA acquires information and to consider ways in which traditional news media might be adapted to his use and other channels of communication opened to him. This is the report of an investigation into the means by which elderly MAs obtain information, a comparison of their communication habits and capabilities with those of Anglo-American (AA) elderly, and consideration of some ways in which the community might improve communication with its old MA members.

Hypotheses

News media.—The usual channels of information dissemination—newspapers. magazines, radio, and television—probably are not "open" to most older MAs.

In the first place, most information is "sent" in English, and probably few old MAs use it. Clark (1959) found that "About 65 percent of the people five years of age or older speak some English, but most of these are children and young adults." If the MA elderly resemble their AA counterparts, the majority have radio and television sets and use them (Carp, 1966). However, if they do not understand English, it is doubtful that they learn much about their communities by means of radio and television. Their program preferences and the times of day they habitually listen and watch may further reduce their chances of obtaining community information.

Telephone contact has been recommended in any special effort to reach older persons (Proceedings of the International Convention at the Centre de Gerontologie Sociale, 1968). The telephone is critically important to older AAs, and they zealously guard access to it (Carp, 1966). Older MAs distrust the telephone, somewhat as they do banks. They do not want to appear incompetent and feel embarrassed by dialing a number or answering a ring only to be confronted with a voice speaking a "foreign" language. In addition, they are averse to the telephone because of the high value they place on immediate personal contact. When they speak with anyone they want to watch his facial expressions and gestures. In general, "Social intercourse is greatly strengthened by habits of gesture" (Cherry, 1966). This may be especially important to the older MAs. The nonverbal communication enriches the verbal and it provides a sense of interpersonal warmth which they do not deem possible at the end of a telephone line. AA elderly need a telephone for contact with their children (Carp, 1966). MA elderly live closer to their children and see members of their families more frequently (Carp, 1969b). Their other social contacts tend to occur within their own neighborhoods and therefore can be carried out in the highly preferred face to face manner (Carp 1969b). Writing of the importance of the telephone in modern society in general, Pierce (1967) says:

We use the telephone because we have interests that lie outside the home, the family, and the neighborhood.

The MA has little need of learning telephone technique in order to maintain valued interpersonal bonds.

In regard to printed materials, the problem of language may be even more serious than it is with auditory media. Not everyone who speaks and understands English can read it. Published materials may be too difficult for those who can. Education is the most important determinant of literacy (Gray, 1956; Greenbert, 1966; Schramm, 1956). The formal education of elderly MAs tends to be quite limited. For Clark's (1959) subjects over the age of 17, the average number of years of school completed was 4.8. No doubt there is an age differential (Asheim, 1956), and the schooling of the elders must be much less than this average. Furthermore, while, in general, education is a valid index of literacy, "those who leave school before the fifth grade tend, as adults, to read below the expected level" (Gray, 1956).

Elderly MAs may be little better educated or more literate in Spanish than in English. There are wide dialectical differences from state to state within Mexico, so that the Spanish in which an individual was educated may not be the Spanish used in publications. Available Spanish-language newspapers and magazines may be published in Mexico. If so, they probably carry little news of the local community. All in all, the capability of older MAs to obtain information from published materials must be extremely poor. Also, "persons who have had only grade-school education, and persons in the lower economic groups are more likely to read crime and disaster news than any other broad class of news" while "Reading of public affairs news and editorials increases with education . . . and economic status" (Schramm, 1956). Old MAs probably use printed materials, whether in Spanish or English, more for entertainment than for information, and it is likely that they attend primarily to the pictures.

Other sources.—It is unlikely that MA elderly receive much information through the channels which have become the traditional ones "in a world where primary experience has been replaced by secondary communications—the printed page, the radio, and the picture screen" (Gerth & Mills, 1967). Most of their knowledge about the world in which they live probably comes to them in more immediate and more personal ways. "In a simple society where specialized information is rare, everyone can talk to and learn from everyone else" (Dale & Chall, 1956). Membership of the MA elderly in such a "simple" society may be more relevant to their communication patterns than is their residency within a modern culture almost totally converted to secondary communications.

Interpersonal bonds within kin-groups and among friends (compadres) are close and strong in the MA community (Beals, 1951; Carp, 1969b; Clark, 1959; Moore & Holtzman, 1965, Saunders, 1954). This is consistent with Latin-American tradition, and it may be reinforced by segregation and ghetto residence. The world of the older MA is probably no larger than the eight or ten blocks around their own homes (Carp, 1969b). Members of the MA community are strongly interdependent and they are relatively isolated from the majority society; therefore old members of the MA community probably depend to a considerable extent upon family and friends for information.

MAs tend to work at low-level jobs (Saunders, 1954). This tendency probably is exaggerated among those who are now old. Because they are a working-class group, old MAs would be dependent upon their neighborhoods for socialization (Rosow, 1967). This social-class factor reinforces the importance of relatives and neighbors in providing information. It suggests also that neighborhood institutions may play an important information-giving role. Public and private agencies which have local offices may be important sources of information and advice about "the world outside."

The church might be an important source of information and advice. Its parish organization gives it neighborhood visibility and identity. There is a strong religious tradition in MA culture. Broom and Shevky (1952) and Clark (1959) emphasize the importance of the church as an influence on MAs' acceptance or rejection of dominant-culture patterns, but they observe that the influence of the church is to deter assimilation. This suggests that religious institutions do not serve as channels of information from the broad society to old MAs. It was not expected that other institutions would be used as information sources. As Madsen (1964) and others have pointed out, seeking help from institutions is felt to be humiliating because it reflects adversely upon family solidarity and competence.

Subjects

Subjects were 100 MAs who probably would qualify for public housing for the elderly[3] and 100 AA applicants for it. MA subjects were located by MA interviewers who started at a point in the heart of the MA community and moved out, attempting to contact every person

3. Housing Authority standards for eligibility are complex. This study makes no pretense to determine eligibility for public housing, but selected as subjects were persons in age and income ranges similar to those which characterize legally qualified applicants for public housing on whom data were collected for another study.

whose age and income fell within the appropriate ranges. AA subjects were applicants to a public-housing facility for the elderly on whom data were being collected for another study.[4] The 100 for this study were selected by eliminating all applicants under the age of 62[5] and making a random selection of 31 men and 69 women to match the sex distribution of the MA group.

All subjects lived in the same metropolitan county. Data on both groups were collected at the same time, in interviews in subjects' homes. The groups were matched on sex and present income (monthly median = $100, mean = $113). All subjects were aged 62 or over, but the average age of the AA group (72.25) was higher than that of the MA (70.19). This difference (Table 1) may reflect a sampling bias or the difference in longevity between AAs and MAs.

It is patently impossible to match minority and majority groups on more than a few characteristics at a time. Inevitably there are important discontinuities. No doubt some of the differences between these groups are related to patterns of communication with the large society.

---

4. Supported by research grant No. 1 R01 HD03643 from The National Institute of Child Health and Human Development.

5. At the time of the study 62 was the normal age requirement for public-housing for the elderly. Handicapped persons or dependents of family heads who apply may be below that minimum.

Table 1. Comparison of MA and AA Subjects.

Variable	χ^2	t-test
Age		2.25**
Marital status	12.69**	
No. of living children		7.95**
Live alone-with others	25.06**	
Country of birth	80.69**	
U.S. citizenship	45.01**	
Use of English	161.34**	
Education	77.30**	
Job level		3.72**
Home ownership	47.63**	
Time at current address		4.45**
Cost of housing		7.95**
Food costs		5.53**
Health	21.33**	
Last contact with doctor	11.10**	

**Indicates a significant difference between the MA & AA subjects at the .01 level of probability. A difference this large would occur by chance alone only once in 100 times.

Table 2. Use of News Media by AA and MA Elderly.

	Frequency of Usage	
	MA	AA
Newspaper (daily)	14%	89%
Magazines (weekly)	16%	70%
Radio (daily)	87%	85%
Television (daily)	81%	85%
Telephone (weekly)	0%	71%

N=200

In general, MAs had closer and warmer family relationships. More had married, and fewer of their marriages had been broken by separation or divorce. A larger proportion of them had children, and their families tended to be larger. The MA elderly were less likely to be living alone. A much larger proportion of them were foreign-born, but all had lived in the United States most of their lives. Nevertheless, the majority had never been naturalized, and few could communicate in English. Spanish was the mother tongue of every one, and three-quarters still spoke very little or no English. By the most generous estimate, no more than 15% could have been interviewed in English, and even these were much more comfortable with a Spanish-speaking interviewer.

Education, either in English or in Spanish, was much less for the MAs, and the jobs they had held during working years were at lower levels. Many more MAs owned their own homes, and they had lived at the same address far longer than had the AAs. Probably because of home-ownership, housing costs were lower for MAs (Goldstein, 1968). Perhaps as a result, they spent more on food. No medical data were available, but the MAs rated their health less favorably than did the AAs, and they consulted a physician more frequently.

Results

Use of mass media.—Frequency of use of the various news media differed for these old AAs and MAs (Table 2). About one-third of the MA said they sometimes read a newspaper. Less than half that number read one daily, compared to about 90% of the AAs. Newspaper reading habits of these AAs were similar to those of the adult population in general (Asheim, 1956). All newspapers mentioned by AAs were local and English-language. So were the majority (75%) of those mentioned by MAs. One carried a Spanish-language digest of national and international news. One-quarter of the newspapers mentioned by MAs were Spanish-language and published in Mexico.

One local paper popular with the MAs was made up totally of advertisements and was distributed free of charge. Another named by them had been out of publication for 10 years. Their broad use of "read" also included listening to a child, grandchild, or other young member of the family read aloud from the paper. Often this was a school assignment and in English. One MA had learned about public housing for the elderly from a newspaper.

Forty percent of the MAs reported reading magazines. However, fewer than one in six read a magazine as often as once a week, while nearly three-quarters of the AAs did. Again the AAs are similar to adults in general (Asheim, 1956). Most MAs who read magazines read "none in particular" or "any that is given me." Magazines with many colored pictures were the most acceptable. The majority (57%) of magazines mentioned by name were in Spanish. Religious magazines were popular. The favorite news magazines were heavily pictorial and most were published in Mexico. No MA had learned of public housing for the elderly in a magazine.

The differences between MAs and AAs in reading habits are not surprising in view of literacy rates. About half the MAs (46%) had had no formal education, and over two-thirds (70%) had never attended a school in which English was used. Whether in Mexico or the United States, two-thirds were out of school by the time they were 10 years old. MA children in this country tend to be retarded in grade placement (Ott, 1967). Therefore, even those who went to school would be expected to read, as adults, well below the literacy (fifth grade) level. This expectation was borne out in the interviews. Only 8% of the MAs could read and write any English, and most could read and write only the simplest, if any, Spanish. Every AA was literate in English. Most had completed at least the eighth grade, which is typical for their generation (von Mering & Weniger, 1959).

Nearly all members of both groups (93% of MAs and 87% of AAs) listened to the radio, most of them (87% and 85%) every day. AAs listened exclusively to English-language stations. There was considerable use of the radio for background noise as a substitute for companionship. Attention was paid regularly to news broadcasts and religious programs, and many people had favorite entertainment shows. The majority (80%) of MAs listened only to Spanish-language stations, and all preferred them. They listened primarily for entertainment. However, some news of the local community reached them: 5% had heard about public housing of the elderly on the radio.

Most of both groups (MA 81%, AA 85%) regularly watched television. Again the groups were totally unlike in regard to language. All AAs watched only English-language programs; all MAs preferred programs in Spanish, and two-thirds watched them exclusively. Evening was the favorite viewing time for both groups, and variety shows the favorite program type. AAs consistently watched one or more newscasts; MAs did not. However, 4% of the MAs had learned of public housing for the elderly by means of television.

The most startling difference between groups appeared in use of the telephone. No MA used the telephone as often as once a week, and most of then "never" used it. Nearly three-quarters of the AAs used the telephone at least once a week, and over one-third used it every day. A telephone was available to nearly all MAs; they did not want to use it. Not one had learned of public housing for the elderly over the telephone.

Other sources of information.—After discussion of their use of the mass media the MA respondents were asked: "Where else do you hear about what is going on?" As predicted, most named family members or friends and neighbors (Table 3). The church was relatively unimportant. Work was mentioned by a few. There is the suggestion that some of these people felt the lack of information; over one-fifth answered "Nowhere."

They were then asked "Where do you (would you) go when you need information or advice about an important matter?" Again the family played a major role. Most of these old people had gone or would go to members of their families. Daughters were most often mentioned. This is what one might expect from old people in general (Rosow, 1967; Shanas, 1968), but it is somewhat surprising in a subculture which is said to be male-dominated (Beals, 1951; Clark, 1959; Moore & Holtzman, 1965; Saunders, 1954). However, daughters are in the home and therefore more available to parents, and their role includes sympathetic attention to and care of elders and children. Therefore it is not surprising that they are the ones to whom elders turn. Unfortunately, these daughters have more limited information and narrower perspective than do their husbands and brothers, who work out in the community and therefore are in contact with a broader world.

As sources of information or advice, sons were next in importance, then spouses. More distant relatives and in-laws were consulted less fre-

Table 3. Sources of Information for MA Elderly (%).

	News	Advice	Secondary Source
Family	41	65	49
Friends, neighbors	36	7	23
Church	13	18	19
Work	5		
Nowhere	21		
N = 100			

quently. The priest was a rather poor second to the family. Fewer than one subject in five had gone or would go to him for information or advice.

No one mentioned an agency. After the free response the respondent was asked: "Might you go to the staff of some agency?" and if so, "Which one?" Thirty percent responded affirmatively. Some named more than one. The most frequent choice was an excellent privately supported settlement house in the neighborhood (15%). However, public agencies were mentioned more frequently than were private ones, and in this order: Social Security (13%), Medicare (7%), Old Age Assistance (5%), and Civil Service (1%). All the public agencies have offices outside the respondents' neighborhood and in the central downtown area. The problem was always specific to the agency: one would go to the Social Security office if the monthly check was late, to the Medicare office if the doctor had not been paid, or to the Old Age Assistance staff if supplementary income should be necessary. The privately supported neighborhood agency was perceived as a source of somewhat broader assistance. MA elderly would turn there with health problems, for community service and self improvement, and perhaps with personal and family problems.

Secondary sources of information are also given in Table 3. These are responses to the question: "If (the person or agency named) were not available, where would you go for information or advice?" Another member of the family was the most common choice. Friends were more prominent as secondary sources than as primary ones. Priests maintained about the same position. They were consulted only upon spiritual matters and, if one was not available, a different priest would be contacted. Again, no public or private agencies were named.

The subject was then asked if he might go for information or advice to the staff of some agency if none of the resources he had mentioned so far was available or met the need. About a quarter (27%) said they might. The same privately supported settlement house was most often named. Seventy percent of those who might turn to an agency as a last resort mentioned this one. As back-up resources, private agencies were named more frequently than were public agencies (31 to 9). In context, the question asked them to name an agency to which they might go for information or advice which normally they would obtain from a relative, a friend, or priest.

Patterns of information reception in regard to public housing for the elderly were consistent with the general tendency of MAs to use informal and personal rather than formal and secondary channels. Twenty MAs (60% of those who knew of the special housing) had heard of it from kin or friends. Two had seen the facilities themselves. One person had learned of them at church. The only agency which had informed any of these people about public housing for the elderly was the San Antonio Housing Authority, and its only channel to them was the staff of age-heterogeneous public housing in their neighborhood.

Implications

Newspapers and magazines are not effective for disseminating information to elderly Mexican-American people. Two-thirds of those interviewed said they never read a newspaper; 60% that they never read a magazine. Much of the "reading" consisted of looking at illustrations. Real reading was more for entertainment than for information. Little published material was available to these people, and many of the publications they saw carried little information about the community in which they lived. For this generation of old people there is little hope of improving information dissemination through the printed word, because their reading skills are very poor, both in English and in Spanish. The outlook for the telephone seems equally bleak. It is possible that a carefully planned campaign by Spanish-speaking callers might change their attitude, but there is some question whether they could be persuaded to attempt communication by telephone.

Other media hold more promise. Nearly all the MAs interviewed listened regularly to the radio, and over 80% watched television frequently. Ninety percent of those who had heard of public housing for the elderly had learned of it through television or radio. Television should be particularly useful.

As **the** most widely influential institution in the land, television has become the god of the common man's idolatry, his oracle, and the principal source of his news and entertainment (Montagu, 1967).

According to Pierce (1967), television is "the greatest unifying force ever to act upon man." The MA should warm to the television personality because he is seen as well as heard, and the communication experience is more personal and immediate. Among a national probability sample of Latin-Americans (Costa Ricans), television affected view of the world more than did radio listening (Waisanen & Durlak, 1967). Television may be an excellent means of informing elderly MAs about the broader society and about their potential role in it and use of its resources. To reach these people, information should be spotted between variety shows during evening hours. It must be given in the Spanish language and by MA announcers because "mass media messages will be most effective when they are . . . presented by trusted persons" (Dale & Williams, 1960).

Radio should not be ignored: nearly as many of these subjects had heard of public housing for the elderly on the radio as on television. Most listened to the radio, but very few to newscasts. To reach the large group, information should be inserted between entertainment programs on Spanish-language stations.

Far more important than all the mass media were family and friends. Because of the warmth and closeness of kinship and friendship ties, it is likely that elderly MAs will continue to learn most of what they know about the broader society from relatives and neighbors. Then, as the MA community in general becomes informed, so will its elder members. Young-adult MAs (25-36 years of age) in this community tend to be competent in both written and spoken English.[6] Perhaps through these young persons society can inform their parents and grandparents of what that society has to offer older adults. It might even be possible to send information home to elders with school children. One woman said that if she had a problem she would have her grandchildren take it up with their school counselor.

Running a rather poor third after family and friends as sources of information comes the church. Its role was restricted to religious problems. The church was not perceived as a source of information or advice in regard to mandane matters.

Other private and public institutions played a minor role. No respondent spontaneously mentioned an agency as a source of information or advice. When directly asked, about a third of them expressed willingness to go to an agency. Public agencies would be consulted in regard to specific matters relevant to their missions. None was viewed as a source of information more generally. These perceptions were valid; these agencies are not community-information bureaus.

However, it does seem that some agencies within the community should accept responsibility for gathering information of potential interest to old members of minority groups and of finding ways to communicate it to them. Unlike the public agencies, the privately supported neighborhood service agency was perceived as a place one might go for information or advice on a variety of issues. Unfortunately, the private agency, like the public agency, did not immediately come to mind; willingness to go to one was expressed only in response to the direct question. There is no evidence that the private service agencies in the neighborhood of these respondents had assumed an information-giving role; no subject had heard of public housing for the elderly through one of them. It is quite possible that members of the staffs deemed it unnecessary, irrelevant, or improper to discuss public housing, or that they know too little about the special facilities.

It seems possible that the neighborhood service center has an important advantage when it accepts responsibility for information dissemination. At the time these data were collected, more of the MAs were enrolled in Medicare ($\chi^2 = 37.28$, $p < 0.01$). This probably was due to a special effort on the part of the favorite neighborhood agency to inform the elderly MAs about the program.

The advantage of being within the neighborhood is clear. The old MA is a creature of his immediate locale. Primary sources of information were kin and friends, all of whom tended to live close by. Church parishes were local. The frequently mentioned private agencies were in the neighborhood. The facilitating effect of proximity is supported by another line of evidence. While very few of the elderly MAs had ever heard of the local public-housing facilities for the elderly, both of which were located outside the MA part of town, most (85%) knew quite a bit about ordinary public housing, some of which was in their neighborhoods. A few had learned of the special facilities there. Also indicative of the importance of neighborhood location, the MAs used to even a greater extent than did the AAs, medical and senior center services which were available in their own neighborhoods (Carp, 1969b).

The most frequently mentioned service center had other traits which facilitated its relationships with elderly MAs. Like their AA counterparts (Carp, 1966) the elderly MAs prized privacy and independence (Carp, 1969c). They took advantage of the services available at the

6. According to data on a sample of 200 collected in a study supported by research grant No. I R01 HD03643 from The National Institute for Child Health and Human Development.

230

center because the staff treated them "like persons, not cases."

> The right to accept or reject services freely is threatened by aggressive caseworkers intent upon applying remedies to persons who do not seek them. . . . And the most fundamental of all rights of the person—that of living his own life and pursing happiness in his own way—is increasingly endangered by workers and administrators proceeding on assumptions of the irrationality and incompetence of the human person (Matson, 1967).

The agency which undertakes to provide communication between the community and its elderly MAs will probably function best in this role if it accords them respect as persons and does not invade the privacy of their individual lives.

Despite the fact that the MAs used medical and senior center services to a greater extent than did the AAs, medical contact is ordinarily too infrequent to insure up-to-date information, and the majority of elderly MAs do not attend other senior center activities. The best strategy to inform them of something of importance to them probably is a house-to-house campaign by MA informers. MA organizations seem ideally suited to this task. The tradition of the "machismo" suggests that male informants would be more effective because they have higher prestige. The results of this study suggest that women might be as effective: daughters were the most frequently mentioned sources of information and advice. The differential effects of informant age and sex should be clarified.

Older MAs pose a difficult communication problem. Usual techniques for disseminating information are relatively ineffective, even when special efforts are made to reach them. New techniques must be developed, implemented, and evaluated. These efforts should result in improved flow of information to members of this subgroup of the population. Because these people represent an extreme example of inaccessability, efforts to provide them information will also cast light on some of the more general problems of communication in present-day society.

References

Asheim, L. What do adults read? In N. B. Henry (Ed.), **Adult Reading,** Fifty-fifth Yearbook of the National Society for the Study of Education, Part II. Chicago: University of Chicago Press, 1956.

Baldwin, J. **The fire next time.** New York: Dial Press, 1963.

Beals, R. **Culture patterns of Mexican-American life.** Proceedings of the Fifth Annual Conference, Southwestern Conference on the Education of Spanish-Speaking People. Los Angeles, January, 1951.

Brody, E. B. Cultural exclusion, character and illness. **American Journal of Psychiatry,** 1966, **122,** 852-858.

Broom, L., & Shevky, E. Mexicans in the United States: A problem in social differentiation. **Sociology & Social Research,** 1952, **36,** 150-158.

Carp, F. M. **A future for the aged.** Austin: University of Texas Press, 1966.

Carp, F. M. Housing and minority-group elderly. **Gerontologist,** 1969, **9,** 20-24. (a)

Carp, F. M. Some determinants of low application rate of Mexican-American for public housing for the elderly, in press. (b)

Carp, F. M. Use of community services and social integration of the aged. In Proceedings of the Duke University Council on Aging and Human Development, 1969, in press. (c)

Cherry, C. **On human communication.** Cambridge: Massachusetts Institute of Technology Press, 1966.

Clark, M. **Health in the Mexican-American culture.** Berkeley: University of California Press, 1959.

Cleaver, E. **Soul on Ice.** New York: McGraw-Hill, 1968.

Dale, E., & Chall, J. Developing readable materials. In N. B. Henry (Ed.), **Adult reading,** Fifty-fifth Yearbook of the National Society for the Study of Education, Part II. Chicago: University of Chicago Press, 1956.

Dale, E., & Williams, H. A. Audience—size and characteristics. In **Encyclopedia of Educational Research,** 3rd ed. AERA. New York: Macmillan Co., 1960.

Dewey, J. **Democracy and education: An introduction to the philosophy of education.** New York: Macmillan Co., 1916.

Ellison, R. **The invisible man.** New York: Random House, 1952.

Friedman, P., & Phillips, G. M. Toward a rhetoric for the poverty class. **Journal of Communication,** 1967, **17,** 234-249.

Gerbner, G. On defining communication: still another view. **Journal of Communication,** 1966, **16,** 99-103.

Gerson, W. M. Mass media socialization behavior: Negro-White differences. **Social Forces,** 1966, **45,** 40-50.

Gerth, H. H., & Mills, C. W. Symbol spheres in society. In F. W. Matson and A. Montagu (Eds.), **The Human Dialogue.** New York: Free Press, 1967.

Goldstein, S. Home tenure and expenditure patterns of the aged, 1960-1961. **Gerontologist,** 1968, **8,** 17-24.

Gray, W. S. How well do adults read? In N. B. Henry (Ed.), **Adult reading,** Fifty-fifth Yearbook of the National Society for the Study of Education, Part II. Chicago: University of Chicago Press, 1956.

Greenbert, B. S. Media use and believability: some multiple correlates. **Journalism Quarterly,** 1966, **43,** 665-670.

Grier, W. H., & Cobbs, P. M. **Black Rage.** New York: Basic Books, 1968.

Hutchins, R. M. Education and the Socratic dialogue. In F. W. Matson and A. Montagu (Eds.), **The human dialogue.** New York: Free Press, 1967.

Jacobs, P. **Prelude to riot.** New York: Random House, 1967.

Madsen, W. **The Mexican-Americans of South Texas.** New York: Holt, Rinehart & Winston, 1964.

Matson, F. W. The communication of welfare. In F. W. Matson & A. Montagu (Eds.), **The human dialogue.** New York: Free Press, 1967.

Montagu, A. Television and the new image of man. In F. W. Matson & A. Montagu (Eds.), **The human dialogue.** New York: Free Press, 1967.

Moore, B. M., & Holtzman, W. H. **Tomorrow's parents.** Austin: University of Texas Press, 1965.

Ott, E. **Basic education for Spanish-Speaking disadvantaged pupils.** Austin, Texas: Southwest Educational Development Laboratory, 1967.

Parry, J. **The psychology of human communication.** New York: American Elsevier Publishing Co., 1968.

Pierce, J. R. Communication. **Daedalus,** 1967, **96,** 909-921.

Proceedings of the International Convention at the Centre de Gerontologie Sociale: Report of Groupe II. Paris: Caisse Nationale de Retraite de Ouvriers do Bâtiment et des Travaux Publics, 1968.

Rosow, I. **Social integration of the aged.** New York: Free Press, 1967.

Ruesch, J. Clinical science and communication theory. In F. W. Matson and A. Montagu (Eds.), **The human dialogue.** New York: Free Press, 1967.

Saunders, L. **Cultural differences and medical care: The case of the Spanish-speaking people of the Southwest.** New York: Russell Sage, 1954.

Schramm, W. Why adults read. In N. B. Henry (Ed.), **Adult reading:** Fifty-fifth Yearbook of the National Society for the Study of Education, Part II. Chicago: University of Chicago Press, 1956.

Shanas, E. The family and social class. In E. Shanas, P. Townsend, D. Wedderburn, H. Friis, P. Milhøj, & J. Stehouwer (Eds.), **Old people in three industrial societies.** New York: Atherton Press, 1968.

Smith, D. H. Communicating with the poor. **Journal of Human Relations,** 1967, **15,** 169-179.

Stringfellow, W. The representation of the poor in American society. **Law & Contemporary Problems,** 1966, **31,** 142-151.

von Mering, O., & Weniger, F. Social-cultural background of the aging individual. In J. E. Birren (Ed.), **Handbook of aging and the individual.** Chicago: University of Chicago Press, 1959.

Waisanen, F. B., & Durlak, J. T. Mass media use, information source evaluation and perceptions of self and nation. **Public Opinion Quarterly,** 1967, **31,** 399-406.

Westley, B. H., & Severin, W. J. Some correlates of media credibility. **Journalism Quarterly,** 1964, **41,** 325-335.

Wiener, N. Cybernetics and society. In F. W. Matson and A. Montagu (Eds.), **The human dialogue.** New York: Free Press, 1967.

1970 Postdoctoral Institute on Retirement and Aging: The Psychological Aspects

The first half of this Institute will be concerned with organizational retirement practices, the meaning of retirement, retirement in occupational groups, employment of the retiree, the use of leisure time, and the psychological aspects of living in retirement facilities. The second half will include personality theories and aging, changes with age in various psychological functions, and the psycho-pathology of aging.

September 1 through September 3, 1970, Sheraton Four Ambassadors Hotel, Miami. Harold Geist, leader.

The days of our age are threescore and ten; and, though men be so strong that they come to fourscore years, yet is their strength then but labour and sorrow—so soon passeth it away, and we are gone.

The last words of this passage are the one consolation for the failure of our powers before physical death. Affliction with these infirmities is, like life itself, a limited liability. The time-limit set by death makes even mental derangement bearable. Yet, to my mind, this is a far more formidable affliction than death is, and, like death, this failure of our powers brings us up against the startling misfit between our capacities and our limitations.

Experiences
Arnold Toynbee

Moreover, to be mortal is not by any means wholly disadvantageous. When I catch myself resenting not being immortal, I pull myself up short by asking myself whether I should really like the prospect of having to make out an annual income-tax return for an infinite number of years ahead. Should I also really like the prospect of having, **ad infinitum,** to suffer the pressure of the ceaselessly turning screw of inflation?

Death does eventually release each of us, in turn, from the burdens and injustices of this life. Death is, in fact, our eventual saviour from the tyranny of human society in this world—a tyranny that is tolerable, if at all, only because it has an inexorable time-limit. At the moment of death the Inland Revenue authorities and the inflaters will suddenly become impotent to afflict me any further. I now put out my tongue at them anticipatorily on behalf of my corpse. I am grieved that these human oppressors will still be able to afflict people, loved by me, who will survive me; but death is going eventually to come to the victims' rescue—and to the oppressors' rescue too. Death limits life's liabilities. This boon that death confers is supremely valuable, and ought therefore to be immensely consoling, as has been pointed out, manfully, by Lucretius and, plaintively, by Housman.

Experiences
Arnold Toynbee

Sharon M. Fujii

Elderly Asian Americans and use of public services

Changes, including the elimination of sociocultural
barriers, must be effected both within the groups
requiring services and within service delivery systems

Sharon M. Fujii, Ph.D., is senior vice president,
Gerontological Planning Associates, Santa Monica,
California.

Elderly Asian Americans[1] have received
very little attention in the literature and as
consumers of public services. They have
been omitted from any serious consideration because of adherence in the larger society to a false premise which maintains
that Asians take care of their own. This
premise inaccurately assumes that the elderly have families with sufficient resources to meet their needs.

Perhaps, too, Asians have been overlooked because their numbers are small
relative to other racial minorities and to
the majority population. Only 1,369,412
Asian Americans were recorded in the
1970 census, which was equivalent to .7
percent of the total population and 5 percent of the nonwhite population in the
United States.[2] At the same time, there
were 95,264 Asian Americans age sixty-
five and over.[3] By comparison, there were
over 18 million Caucasian and 2.4 million
nonwhite (black, Indian, or Spanish-
speaking) older persons. Thus, the
number of aged Asian Americans, in the
aggregate, is exceedingly small.

In recent years, as the number of elderly
have increased and as the influence of cultural norms and traditional structures has
diminished, the problems of older Asians
have multiplied. Inadequate income, reduced physical capacity, and social isolation often make old age a period of degra-
dation and suffering. Because of cultural
differences, Asians have encountered difficulty in adjusting satisfactorily to the
dominant society. They may be deprived
of their right to participate socially and to
receive services which are necessary for
a meaningful and extended life. Those
minority aging Americans who experience
difficulty adjusting to the "American Way
of Life" either because of their customs
and language or because of institutional
racism directed at them find themselves
further isolated because they are identified
as minority aging Americans.[4]

[1] "Asian Americans" refers to "those who reside in
the United States, who share either Mongoloid or
Malayan racial characteristics, and whose ancestors
originated from the East Asian continent and its
immediate surrounding areas." Bok-Lim C. Kim,
Asian Americans: No Model Minority, *Social Work*,
18:45 (May 1973). Among the predominant groups
of Asian Americans in the United States are the
Chinese, Filipinos, Koreans, and Japanese.

[2] U.S. Department of Commerce, Bureau of the
Census, 1972b:1-293. Supplementary Report, *Race
of the Population of the U.S. by States 1970*
(Washington, D.C.: U.S. Government Printing
Office, 1972).

[3] U.S. Department of Commerce, Bureau of the
Census, 1972a. *General Population Characteristics, U.S.
Summary* (Washington, D.C.: U.S. Government
Printing Office, 1972).

[4] Arthur E. Raya, Social Policy and the Minority
Aging, paper presented at the Institute on Minority
Aging, sponsored by the Center on Aging, School
of Social Work, California State University, San
Diego, Calif., June 6, 1973.

Paucity of knowledge

There are very few current data which would be helpful in acquiring a contemporary view of Asian elderly. "The literature concerning elderly Asian Americans . . . is sparse to the point of being virtually nonexistent."[5] The absence of materials that accurately portray their problems does not mean that elderly Asians are free of difficulties, but rather suggests that these have not been adequately studied and documented. The nature and extent of their problems have largely been ignored or superficially reviewed. Hence, systematically collected information is needed to fill the gaps and extend the knowledge base so that services and social policies will be responsive to the problems of elderly Asian Americans.

Census data on Asian elderly

From census figures, it is possible to acquire a general profile of elderly Japanese, Chinese, and Pilipinos.[6] It should be carefully noted, however, that Asian elderly are very often "apt to be underrepresented because they are among the most mistrustful of government agencies, suffer the greatest language handicaps, and are often poorly informed."[7]

The 1970 census enumerated 588,324 Japanese Americans, of whom 47,159 were sixty-five years of age and older. The elderly comprised 8 percent of the total Japanese population. Of those over sixty-five, about 57 percent were women and 43 percent were men. The median annual income in 1970 was $2,542 for Japanese men and $1,348 for Japanese women in this age group. Ninety-four percent of them were reported as being married or having been married. Additionally, the majority of elderly Japanese were primarily urbanites, with 85 percent living in metropolitan areas. They were concentrated primarily in Honolulu, Los Angeles, San Francisco, Chicago, New York, and Seattle.

Chinese elderly (age sixty-five and over) numbered 26,856 according to 1970 census estimates. This was equivalent to 6.2 percent of the total Chinese population (413,583) at the time. In this age group, 57 percent were men and 43 percent were women. The median annual income for the latter was $1,188; and for elderly Chinese men, it was $1,943. Ninety-two percent were either married or had been married, and 97 percent resided in urban areas such as San Francisco, Boston, Los Angeles, New York, Philadelphia, Seattle, and Portland.

Census statistics reported 21,249 Filipinos who were sixty-five and over in 1970. They comprised 6.3 percent of the total Pilipino population (336,731) in the United States. Nearly 82 percent were males and 30 percent of them had never married. The median annual income for men was reported at $2,528, and for women it was $1,130. Almost 78 percent of the elderly Pilipinos resided in ethnic enclaves of Los Angeles, Seattle, Portland, San Francisco, and New York. The others resided in rural areas, particularly around San Jose and Stockton, California.

Growing concern

The growing concern for older Asians has been expressed in the recent writings of Richard A. Kalish and Sam Yuen and Kalish and Sharon Moriwaki. It is exemplified by the appearance of ethnic service projects specifically designed for the aged.[8] Interest in their plight was also expressed at the Special Concerns Session on Elderly Asian Americans of the 1971 White House Conference on Aging and the Asian American Mental Health Con-

[5]Richard A. Kalish and Sharon Moriwaki, The World of the Elderly Asian American, *The Journal of Social Issues*, 29:187-209 (1973).

[6]The elderly of other Asian groups have been omitted from this discussion not because they are less important or because they have fewer problems, but because such data are not available.

[7]Richard A. Kalish and Sam Yuen, Americans of East Asian Ancestry: Aging and the Aged, *The Gerontologist*, 11:36-47 (Spring 1971).

[8]Examples include the Chinese Golden Age Center in Boston, Self-Help for the Elderly in San Francisco, and the International Drop-in Center in Seattle.

ference in San Francisco. The former occasion signified the first time that persons of Asian ancestry had assembled to deliberate on the problems confronting the elderly.

Interest in older Asians in part reflects the cultural heritage which has stressed veneration and care of the aged. Traditionally, "the Asian aged had a position of respect and to an appreciable extent he perceived growing old as a blessing, as a period in life when he could sit back and enjoy the fruits of his labor."[9] Moreover, the growing interest represents a response to their current conditions—poverty, isolation, racial discrimination, poor health—and the realization that the influence of cultural traditions has diminished. Finally, concern for the aged represents an outgrowth of emerging ethnic awareness among Asians throughout the United States. The struggle for ethnic identity and equality is enmeshed within social concerns, including the plight of the elderly.

Like all older persons, elderly Asian Americans experience various changes related to advancing age. They encounter declining physical strength, increased leisure time, and the imminence of death. They must also adjust to changing values, new life styles, and challenges to established practices. In short, there is not a single difficulty faced by elderly Anglos that is not also faced by elderly Asian Americans. Yet many of the latter's problems are more acute, and arise from a unique personal history and a present milieu that is shared neither with younger persons of similar national origins nor with elderly cohorts from dissimilar national backgrounds.[10]

Limited use of public services

Of the many problems confronting Asian American elderly today, there is one which seems to command major interest. As expressed during the Special Concerns Ses-

sion for Elderly Asian Americans at the 1971 White House Conference on Aging, they face the problem of exclusion from public social and health services presumably available to all older persons.[11] Persons of Asian ancestry appearing before the Subcommittee on Long-Term Care, the United States Senate Special Committee on Aging, attested to the absence of elderly Asians in nursing homes, extended care facilities, hospitals, and community mental health programs.[12] Comparable sentiments were voiced by participants at the first National Asian American Mental Health Conference in San Francisco.[13]

Exclusion from public social and health services has been attributed to barriers such as language, culture, racism, and the structure of delivery systems. It may be *externally* imposed upon the aged by service-providing institutions, through overt acts of racism or insensitivity to cultural differences, or it may be *self-imposed* by Asian elderly who resist using services largely because of culture, language, and lack of familiarity with established practices.

Consciousness of these concerns is founded largely upon impressionistic or experiential observations rather than upon empirical evidence. The lack of systematically collected data reflects the paucity of knowledge about aged Asians—their problems and conditions. However, limited data document the problem of exclusion by exposing low service utilization patterns.

Several related surveys recently completed in Seattle conclude that aged Asian

[9]Kalish and Moriwaki, the World of the Elderly Asian American, p. 201.

[10]Ibid., p. 190.

[11]*The Asian American Elderly*, White House Conference on Aging, 1971 (Washington, D.C.: U.S. Government Printing Office, 1972).

[12]Subcommittee on Long-Term Care of the Senate Special Committee on Aging, Supporting Paper No. 8, Access to Nursing Homes by U.S. Minorities (Washington, D.C.: U.S. Government Printing Office), forthcoming.

[13]Asian American Mental Health Coalition, National Asian American Mental Health Conference Recommendations, San Francisco, April 27-29, 1972.

Americans fail to use social service agencies to any significant extent. These findings were based upon a survey of 132 Asians aged fifty and over.[14] For example, one aged Asian was served daily by a home-delivered meals program, and two others were assisted over a year by an area-wide model project on aging.[15] From a companion survey of fourteen social service agencies in Seattle, Asian elderly were assisted only 643 times out of an estimated 205,156 times, which is equivalent to .3 percent.[16]

From another survey of 131 Issei[17] pioneers, which was conducted in Los Angeles, the findings support the impression of limited service utilization. Responses to two questions are especially revealing. Seventy-eight percent of those interviewed were enrolled in Medicare at the time, but only 30 percent admitted to using benefits.[18] Similarly, only 23 percent of the forty elderly informants enrolled in Medi-Cal[19] claimed to be using the program.[20]

The first attempt to systematically document the health conditions of Filipino aged residing in Seattle's International District revealed that they failed to use public and private health services with any fre-

quency, and certainly not in relation to their needs.[21] Aged Filipino men (N=86) were asked to indicate whether they had used eight nearby health resources (that is, county hospital, public health department, community clinic, and multiservice center). With the exception of the public health department, the county hospital, and a multiservice center, they used the five remaining health services very little or not at all.[22]

Stuart H. Cattell's study of a segment of the Chinese in New York City noted that nearly 33 percent of the older unattached males in the Community Service Society caseload had no prior contact with any agency, either public or voluntary.[23] The figure is astonishing when one considers the multiple problems of this group. Many are eligible for public welfare support, "but refuse to apply or withdraw their applications when they discover the sort of personal information required."[24] Others have been denied welfare assistance for failure to provide documentary evidence of financial need.[25]

Sociocultural barriers to service utilization

Preliminary attempts have been made to ascertain why older Asian Americans do not participate in programs intended to serve all elderly. The Special Concerns Session on Elderly Asian Americans deliberated on the issues and constraints which adversely affect the aged. Also, persons of Asian ancestry testified about the factors

[14]Training Project for the Asian Elderly, *On the Feasibility of Training Asians to Work with Asian Elderly: A Preliminary Assessment of Needs and Resources Available to Asian Elderly in Seattle* (Seattle, Wash.: Training Project for the Asian Elderly, March 1973).

[15]Ibid., p. 4.

[16]Ibid., p. 63. This figure represents the total number of clients of all ages who were served by fourteen agencies over a year.

[17]Issei is the Japanese term for first generation immigrants from Japan.

[18]Council of Oriental Organizations, *A Study of Issei Pioneers Residing in Little Tokyo*, mimeographed (Los Angeles, 1968).

[19]Medi-Cal is comparable to Medicaid plans used in other states, and provides medical assistance for low-income persons of all ages.

[20]Council of Oriental Organizations, *A Study of Issei Pioneers*, p. 5.

[21]Demonstration Project for Asian Americans, *Health Assessment of Elderly Filipinos in the International District* (Seattle, Wash.: Demonstration Project for the Asian Elderly, 1972).

[22]Ibid.

[23]Stuart H. Cattell, *Health, Welfare and Social Organization in Chinatown, New York City.* Report prepared for the Chinatown Public Health Nursing Demonstration of the Department of Public Affairs (New York: Community Service Society of New York, 1962), p. 56.

[24]Ibid., pp. 56-57.

[25]Ibid., p. 57.

236

which are believed to obstruct "the accessibility of nursing homes to minority elderly" in hearings before the Senate Subcommittee on Long-Term Care.[26] On both occasions food preferences, language, cultural differences, and racism were identified as reasons why elderly Asians fail to participate in public social and health service programs.

Elsewhere, these and other factors have been stressed repeatedly as barriers to service utilization for the aged. The Demonstration Project for Asian Americans specified cultural barriers including language, food differences, alienation and isolation from the dominant society, the stereotyped image that Asians take care of their aged, and the fear of government bureaucracies.[27] A recently issued research report from the Training Project for the Asian Elderly surmised "there is strong sentiment that Asian elderly do not receive social services because of language, racial, and cultural barriers."[28] Additionally, the report concluded: "health and welfare agencies have few bilingual staff, haphazard provision for non-English-speaking clients, and very little publicity to the Asian community about their services."[29]

Referring to Chinese Americans, Frederick P. Li and associates identified language and cultural barriers to medical care which aggravate health problems. They noted that the Chinese are often poorly informed about the availability of services or find existing facilities to be inaccessible because of their language handicap.[30] Hospitalization is feared because it accentuates language and cultural gaps, so that "Chinese patients feel utterly helpless and isolated in a strange environment which may be insensitive to their anxieties."[31]

Bok-Lim C. Kim has similarly observed that Asian Americans fail to seek and use existing services to which they are entitled because of language and cultural barriers, and unfamiliarity with the institutional arrangement of a community.[32] She comments: In the past, the major barriers to utilization of community services . . . have been not only the language barriers, but also ignorance of the community with respect to the availability of such services and the culturally bound reluctance to expose their problems and frustrations to "outsiders."[33]

Conclusion

The problems of service utilization will not disappear with the passing of today's elderly Asian American. There will be increasing numbers of older persons among succeeding cohorts and generations. Because of changing family traditions due to acculturation and assimilation, many will not be cared for in old age as they once had provided for their own parents. Moreover, ethnic service programs will be less able to satisfy increasing demands for assistance.

Even though succeeding generations are able to communicate in English, they have inherited a legacy from their parents and grandparents where service utilization has been restricted if not minimal. Many who are approaching old age have lived through periods of violent anti-Asian agitation and are acutely aware of racial discrimination. Therefore, they may prefer ethnic services even though they are not handicapped by language barriers or lack knowledge about American customs.

Changes, including the reduction and elimination of sociocultural barriers, will

[26]Special Senate Committee on Aging, August 10, 1972.

[27]Demonstration Project for Asian Americans, *DPPA Project Effectiveness Evaluation Report* (Los Angeles, Ca.: June 1973), p. 22.

[28]Training Project for the Asian Elderly, *Training Asians to Work with Asian Elderly*, p. 1.

[29]Ibid., p. 7.

[30]Frederick P. Li et al., Health Care for the Chinese Community in Boston, *American Journal of Public Health*, 62:537 (April 1972).

[31]Ibid., p. 538.

[32]Bok-Lim C. Kim, A Study of Asian American Communities in Chicago, unpublished paper, Chicago, Ill., 1972, p. 51.

[33]Ibid., p. 5.

have to be effected both within the groups requiring services and within service delivery mechanisms. The initial source for exposing and dealing with the problems of exclusion from and resistance to the use of public health and welfare services lies within Asian American communities. Future responses—whether directed toward enhancing access to public services, conducting research, or formulating social policies relevant to minority aged—must be performed by persons of Asian ancestry and by non-Asians who understand the ethnic groups and their respective subcultures. Future responses—services and social policies—must be built on accurate knowledge of current conditions. By attempting to understand today's older Asians, who were yesterday's pioneers and folk heroes, we may be better prepared to provide for those who will be elderly in the future.

CHARACTERISTICS OF THE BLACK ELDERLY

by Duran Bell, Patricia Kasschau, and Gail Zellman

Demographic Characteristics

In 1970, blacks represented approximately 11 percent of the U.S. population, numbering 22,580,289 (U.S. Department of Commerce 1973). According to the same census, blacks comprised 8 percent of the 20 million persons 65 years and older residing in the United States. Since 1930, the aged black population has been increasing much more rapidly than the aged population in general, primarily because of higher birth rates among blacks from 1875-1884 relative to the Civil War period and earlier (Smith 1967). In 1970 the elderly constituted 7 percent of the total black population, an increase of 34 percent over 1960. The majority of blacks of all ages still live in the south (53 percent in 1970), and an even higher proportion of black elderly (61 percent) reside in the south, largely because of the relatively greater movement of younger southern blacks to northern cities (Hill 1972).

Elderly blacks who did leave the south most often migrated to areas with a large black population—the northeast and the north central areas. Only 5 percent of blacks in the west are elderly, although 7.5 percent of all blacks are elderly (Sears and McConahay 1973). In general, blacks live in urban areas as compared to 72.4 percent of whites (U.S. Department of Commerce, Bureau of the Census 1973); 58 percent of the black population 65 and over lived in metropolitan areas and 48 percent of this population lived in central cities (Hill 1972).

Data from the 1970 census indicate that in general, elderly blacks do not represent a highly mobile population. Among those blacks 55 years and older, 74 percent reported living in the same residence for the last 5 years. As for all groups, the statistic was lower among urban dwellers: 71 percent of the elderly in this group reported living in the same house since 1965. Naturally, mobility rates are even lower in rural areas. In rural nonfarm areas, 78 percent reported living in the same house since 1965; the percentage for rural farm dwellers was 84 percent.

Social Characteristics

The literature about the family structure of black families has tended to focus on problems associated with female-headed families and on the presumably high incidence of matriarchy in the family structure (Frazier 1966). J. J. Jackson (1972b) provides the only study on the black elderly that addresses these issues. She examined both young and old black couples to determine the relative extent of matriarchal relationships. Subjects were asked to respond to a hypothetical decisionmaking question in order to determine who was primarily responsible for a range of decisions that are generally made in families. The findings indicated that males and females both tended to feel that decisionmaking was a joint venture. Among those who did not report shared decisionmaking, twice as many reported male rather than female dominance. These data lead Jackson to conclude that matriarchy does not prevail in the homes of black aged, which implies that matriarchy was not a common pattern in the past either. But since Jackson's research followed the intraracial research strategy, it provided no comparison groups from which one could evaluate the prevalence of matriarchy in this study; nor is it clear that expectations of matriarchy would be independent of other socioeconomic variables.

It is generally accepted that the family unit becomes more important to the elderly as work roles, professional contacts, and parental and community roles decrease in importance. Hence, the lack of extended family households, or at least of spatial contiguity of extended family members, is more problematic to the elderly than to members of other age groups. Solomon (1970) cites a number of factors that may decrease the viability of the family unit as a source of support for black elderly: increased urbanization, the migration of young blacks to the north, upward mobility on the part of middle-aged adults, and harsh stereotypes of the aged by young, politically militant blacks. However, most of these issues also arise in the discussion of family-related difficulties of nearly all elderly groups. Research has not established the dimensions on which blacks are more disadvantaged, vis-à-vis other groups, on various aspects of family structure and familial relationships. Among others, Billingsley (1969) argues that blacks are relatively advantaged in this regard.

Some of the literature contends that extended families and family solidarity are more relevant to black than white elderly because fewer elderly blacks than whites are married and living with spouses (Rubinstein 1971). Additionally, more of the black population have never been married than is true among whites (Hill 1972). The reasons for this are usually assumed to be based on the lower earnings of black males (J. J. Jackson 1972b). In any case, there is strong evidence that fewer black elderly are likely to live with spouses. They are also less likely to live alone than their white counterparts (Rubinstein 1971; our census tabulation). Of those who are not living with spouses, black elderly are more likely to be in a family setting, rather than living alone or with nonrelatives. Billingsley (1969) contends that the extended black family is a source of considerable strength and stability, and he cites a variety of data to support his contention—e.g., lower incidence of child abuse among blacks than among whites in similar socioeconomic status. Lindsay (1971) cites data indicating that adult children of elderly blacks visit their parents more frequently than do adult children of elderly whites.

The dynamics of these extended families are nowhere discussed in the literature in a way that would provide answers to questions of how satisfied the elderly in such families really are. Hill (1972) contends that extended black families are strong and supportive. However, data from J. J. Jackson (1969) suggest that strength and support may be conditional. In her study of aged parents and their adult children, it appears that among working class parents, affective involvement with adult children is positively related to the receipt of goods and services. Although Jackson does not discuss it, one implication of this finding is that in extremely poor black families, extended or otherwise, the mutual support and strength that may characterize these structures are contingent on the ability of the adult children to provide economic and other necessities and services to the elderly.[2] When adult children are unable to provide economic support, the family structure may fail to be supported. On the other hand, it has been suggested that one of the bases of the widespread occurrence of extended families among blacks is that the black elderly are desirable family members because they have a small but steady income from social security. Hill (1972) rejects this argument as a motivation for the development and widespread occurrence of extended family structures among blacks. Rather, he emphasizes the open, warm, and loving nature of blacks as a motivating force. Such issues would require psychological studies to clarify the incentives and motivations that surround and support the black family.

[2] See Viscusi and Zeckhauser (1974) for a similar argument about the elderly in general.

Quite aside from the question of motivating factors, the psychological outcomes of alternative living arrangements are not clear. In general, living with one's spouse is associated with the most positive outcomes in terms of morale, health, etc. However, when this is not possible because of death, separation, or never having been married, it is not clear whether it is better for an elderly person to live with his or her family, or alone. A variety of studies produced data that provide some information about motivations to live alone and its effects. An analysis by Chevan and Korson (1972) indicates that the percentage of elderly living alone increases linearly with income in the 0 to $4000 range. This suggests that in general, when at all financially feasible, the widowed prefer independent living. However, in the same sample, large race differences emerge. As compared to whites, members of "other races" are much less likely to live alone. But these differences may be partly a reflection of differences in income, which were not controlled in those data, or differences in the availability of housing, or nursing homes, and/or other factors. In any case, there is no question that at very low levels of income, the feasibility and/or desirability of living alone is diminished substantially, especially in the urban setting; if it is economically or physically feasible, the Anglo elderly do tend to live alone. Certainly among the group of elderly who live alone, one would tend to find those who were wealthier and in better functional health. However, comparable data on the preferences and behavior of black elderly are not available.

Data on mental health support the assumption that with the exception of those who live with their spouses, the elderly population living alone are healthier and generally better off than other groups. Hirsch (1974a) found that low functional health was least likely to be found in those who live alone. Data from Palmore (1971) support this observation; living alone was related to decreased disability needs, and those with such needs were likely to seek some form of congregate living. In their multiracial sample (which was not broken down by race), Cantor and Daum (1974) found that the level of psychological vulnerability was moderate for those living alone, but that those living alone were more vulnerable than those living with a family.

Similar studies containing interracial comparisons have yet to be conducted. There is very little information on the actual preferences of black elderly for living arrangements. J. J. Jackson (1969) reports that most elderly parents preferred their current living arrangements, whether they lived alone or with children; such responses, however, indicate little more than the ability of black (and other?) elderly to accommodate themselves to available options. In another study, however, Jackson (1971d) reports that grandparents generally preferred to live near, but not with, grandchildren.

Our census tabulations show that black males 60 years old and over are about 50 percent more likely to live alone than white males. This finding holds for each of the four census regions, and for the age cohorts 60-64, 65-72, and 72 and over. Black women are slightly less likely, on the whole, to live alone than white women. However, for elderly males and females, the black/Anglo differences in the tendency to live alone are affected by the probability of being without spouse. Elderly blacks are much more likely to be without spouse, and this factor is responsible for the greater likelihood of older black males to live alone.

On the other hand, elderly black males and females are significantly more likely than comparable Anglos to live in "irregular groups" with other individuals (not in families with whom they are not related). Black elderly are also more likely to live as "lodgers" within family groups to which they are not related. For Anglo elderly, the status of "lodger" is not greater than 1 percent in any age group or region, but for elderly black males the percentage in lodger status is generally greater than 2 percent in each age group and region; for elderly black females the incidence of lodger status tends to be 1-2.5 percent.

These differences are, of course, gross differences, not controlled for education, income, and health status. But they raise questions about the effectiveness of the black family in supplying the psychosocial needs of black elderly. The available literature on the black family contains contradictions, does not control for SES variables, and suffers from an effort common to writers from most ethnic groups to use family structure as a symbol of the superiority of their ethnic values.

Income and Employment

It has frequently been alleged that the most basic and severe problem of black elderly is low income (e.g., Hill 1972). In 1969 the median income for husband-wife elderly families was $4884 for whites; $3222 for blacks. And among aged families with a female head the median income for blacks was $2511, compared to more than twice that for similar white families. Elderly blacks who live alone have less income. Nearly a third lived on less than $1000 a year. The white elderly living alone were not very well off, but in general had nearly twice as much money as their black counterparts. According to 1970 census data, for the total black population, the median 1969 income for males 65 and over was $1725; for females, $1079.

In 1969, 9.5 percent of all whites and 32.3 percent of all blacks were at or below the poverty level. Among the aged, 23 percent of whites and 50 percent of blacks were in poverty. Elderly blacks are likely to arrive at old age with fewer accumulated assets (Goldstein 1971) and lower social security benefits, if any.

Elderly black males are also more likely to seek social security benefits prior to age 65 in every census region except the south (where the difference is negligible). For females, the tendency toward early benefit status does not differ significantly by race. But after age 65, Anglos are significantly more likely to receive social security benefits (Tables 5.1 and 5.2). In addition to having a higher incidence of receiving social security, Anglos also receive larger payments, on the average, than blacks. This finding holds for each age group and every region, except for those 60-64 in the central and northeast regions (Tables 5.3 and 5.4).

According to Double Jeopardy (1964), in 1960 blacks were three times more likely than whites to receive old age assistance; 1970 census data support that assertion. Elderly blacks are much more likely to receive public assistance; the difference is by a factor of three, or more, in each age and census region category (Tables 5.1 and 5.2). However, among those receiving public assistance, elderly blacks receive larger average payments in some regions and not in others. No pattern of differences in benefit levels seems to dominate (Tables 5.3 and 5.4). Multivariate techniques need to be applied to these data to obtain better controlled observations of black-Anglo differences in both social security and public assistance.

Education

Relative to society at large, the black elderly are clearly at a disadvantage with

Table 5.1

INCIDENCE (AS PERCENTAGE OF AGE GROUP) OF SOCIAL SECURITY AND PUBLIC
ASSISTANCE BENEFIT STATUS BY RACE, AGE,
AND GEOGRAPHIC REGION FOR MALES, 1970

Age	South		Northeast		Central		West	
	Black	Anglo	Black	Anglo	Black	Anglo	Black	Anglo
				Social Security				
60-64	21.4	22.4	15.3	14.0	21.8	16.6	22.7	18.8
65-72	67.1	72.9	59.2	67.6	64.8	74.6	68.1	74.8
72 +	72.9	84.9	75.2	87.7	73.4	88.9	79.1	86.4
				Public Assistance				
60-64	9.0	3.0	6.4	2.0	9.4	2.2	13.6	3.2
65-72	19.9	6.5	11.6	2.7	11.3	3.2	25.8	5.9
72 +	28.2	10.1	13.4	3.8	16.3	4.7	34.0	9.5

SOURCE: 1970 census files.

Table 5.2

INCIDENCE (AS PERCENTAGE OF AGE GROUP) OF SOCIAL SECURITY AND PUBLIC
ASSISTANCE BENEFIT STATUS BY RACE, AGE,
AND GEOGRAPHIC REGION FOR FEMALES, 1970

Age	South		Northeast		Central		West	
	Black	Anglo	Black	Anglo	Black	Anglo	Black	Anglo
				Social Security				
60-64	27.6	27.5	22.0	26.8	28.2	29.0	26.1	29.1
65-72	60.1	69.8	64.8	72.0	62.0	74.4	63.4	73.3
72 +	57.4	71.9	69.4	79.6	64.3	80.3	57.8	78.2
				Public Assistance				
60-64	12.0	3.5	15.0	2.3	13.7	1.9	20.8	3.8
65-72	27.7	8.6	17.3	4.0	18.9	3.6	34.5	7.8
72 +	40.4	16.7	19.9	7.8	25.3	8.2	44.6	15.8

SOURCE: 1970 census files.

Table 5.3

BENEFIT LEVELS (IN DOLLARS) FROM SOCIAL SECURITY AND PUBLIC ASSISTANCE, BY RACE, AGE, AND GEOGRAPHIC REGION FOR MALES, 1970

	South		Northeast		Central		West	
Age	Black	Anglo	Black	Anglo	Black	Anglo	Black	Anglo
Social Security								
60-64	961	1138	1396	1320	1244	1181	1073	1212
65-72	983	1264	1289	1431	1306	1400	1220	1375
72 +	955	1270	1332	1399	1321	1376	1158	1385
Public Assistance								
60-64	686	645	1272	1077	864	877	1206	915
65-72	579	638	1216	932	813	792	1008	893
72 +	593	648	871	1039	737	909	596	947

SOURCE: 1970 census files.

Table 5.4

BENEFIT LEVELS (IN DOLLARS) FROM SOCIAL SECURITY AND PUBLIC ASSISTANCE, BY RACE, AGE, AND GEOGRAPHIC REGION FOR FEMALES, 1970

	South		Northeast		Central		West	
Age	Black	Anglo	Black	Anglo	Black	Anglo	Black	Anglo
Social Security								
60-64	690	770	811	873	968	829	708	826
65-72	692	863	916	991	917	929	894	967
72 +	695	850	910	931	890	896	896	913
Public Assistance								
60-64	683	658	1087	922	865	740	1123	987
65-72	574	583	1079	891	790	767	1094	952
72 +	641	676	875	898	780	869	1224	1023

SOURCE: 1970 census files.

regard to educational attainment and literacy. Many had little opportunity to attend school, and therefore the rate of illiteracy is high. Hill (1972) states that the illiteracy rate among elderly blacks is 16 percent as compared to only 2 percent among elderly whites. According to the 1970 census, 38 percent of blacks aged 65 and over had failed to complete five years of school, while the comparable figure for elderly whites was 11.1 percent. Additionally, only 10.4 percent of elderly blacks had completed high school in 1970, compared with 30.8 percent among elderly whites.

The prevalence of illiteracy may have serious consequences in reducing access to services, especially among those who cannot call on friends and relatives for assistance. The major consequences of low educational attainment, however, are probably indirect, affecting the occupational placement, lifetime earnings, current asset accumulation, and the general socioeconomic conditions of elderly blacks.

The average level of education in the black population has risen greatly since World War II. In 1940 black men aged 25-29 averaged 6.5 years of education; by 1962 the average was 11.0 years. The racial difference has not been eliminated, but it has been reduced. In 1940 whites had, on the average, 4.0 more years of education than blacks; by 1962 the difference was only 1.5 years (12.5 versus 11.0) (Taeuber and Taeuber 1965). By 1970 the median difference was less than half a year. In that year, the major discontinuity occurred after age 35; below that, the racial difference in education was a half year or less in every age group, while racial differences increased with increasing age. Hence, it can be anticipated that the currently observed racial differences in general socioeconomic status will be mitigated in the future, thereby reducing the extent to which elderly blacks have special social services needs.

Life Expectancy and Mortality

Most available health statistics (collected by government agencies) are disaggregated by "color," white and nonwhite, rather than ethnicity. "Nonwhites" include Indians, Asians, and others, as well as blacks. While blacks constitute 92 percent of the nonwhite population, the inclusion of other groups in such health statistics is unfortunate because, as data from Breslow and Klein (1971) confirm, nonwhite groups are markedly heterogeneous in terms of health status. In comparison with whites, Asians—particularly Japanese—consistently rank highest on all indices of health, producing an upward bias on most health and life expectancy indicators. Inclusion of these other nonwhite groups in health statistics may contribute to findings such as that reported in a 1973 article,[3] which found that the lowest mortality rate among nonwhite males aged 35-74 was registered in the Pacific states, the area that contains most of the Asian population of the country. It should be kept in mind that health data generally do combine all nonwhite groups. Where this is not the case, it will be noted.

Nonwhite longevity gains in this century have been more rapid than those for whites. Among males, the gain in the expectation of life at birth for nonwhites surpassed that for whites by 9.0 years. Among females, the corresponding figure was 9.2 years. Despite the more favorable improvement for nonwhites, however, their expected future lifetime is still distinctly below that of whites, as noted above. The

[3] "Regional Variations in Nonwhite Mortality," *Statistical Bulletin*, Vol. 54, 1973, pp. 7-9.

narrowing of the longevity gap between the races reflects the greater reductions in nonwhite mortality.

In recent years (1967-1972), however, age-specific death rates have increased among nonwhite men in the age groups between 15 and 64 years, while declining for most age groups among nonwhite women. Also, nonwhite males did not experience increased life expectancy during the 1967-1972 period, while nonwhite females and whites of both sexes showed measurable increases (U.S. Department of Commerce 1974).

Death rates for nonwhites have been affected by increases in their standard of living and by progress in the prevention and treatment of infectious diseases, especially tuberculosis and pneumonia. On the other hand, a number of contrary factors have tended to raise death rates. For nonwhite males the death rates from all causes increased between 1965 and 1972. Death rates increased for the following causes: malignant neoplasms, accidents, cirrhosis of liver, suicide, and homicide. For nonwhite women, there was a large decrease in death due to cardiovascular diseases. This decrease (440.8 to 366.4) more than compensated for increased death rates from most other causes. Causes of death among whites have all shown stability or reduction in rates, except for homicide, suicide, and cirrhosis of the liver.

In general, however, health data presented by the National Center for Health Statistics and the Public Health Service suffer serious deficiencies. A major shortcoming of these reports is the failure to discuss the etiology and significance of the differential prevalence of various diseases across racial groups. In particular, the absence of such control variables as income, occupation, location, and a number of behavioral variables means that racial differentials cannot be meaningfully interpreted, and the measures that might be taken to moderate these differences cannot be developed.

Data from the National Center for Health Statistics (Bauer 1969) indicate that when income and age are controlled, blacks report substantially fewer chronic conditions than whites. These findings further reinforce the importance of similar controls on mortality and morbidity data. In the absence of socioeconomic control variables, the nonwhite population averages a greater number of days of bed disability, restricted activity, and work loss than whites with age adjustments; and nonwhites are more likely to be injured at work. However, when income is controlled, the relative incidence by race of these health indicators is reversed: low income nonwhite males have lower rates than their white counterparts, and nonwhites earning more than $7000 have lower rates of all types of disabilities than whites.

The finding that nonwhites have fewer chronic conditions, given SES controls, has often been suspect, since most of the relevant data have relied on the self-reports of individuals. However, these self-reports data have been confirmed by a major study of chronic conditions among a Baltimore sample (Commission on Chronic Illness 1957) where the incidence of conditions was determined by intensive medical examinations of each person. The Baltimore study found that the prevalence of chronic conditions was eight times greater than suggested by health survey statistics and that underreporting of conditions has been common for all groups. Only moderate white/nonwhite differences in the prevalence of chronic conditions were found; and among the elderly, nonwhites manifested fewer chronic conditions, even in the absence of SES controls (Table 5.5).

Table 5.5

PREVALENCE OF ALL CHRONIC DISEASES, BY AGE AND COLOR
(Rates per 1000 persons)

Age	White	Nonwhite
All ages	1,635.1	1,386.5
Under 15	373.8	472.4
15-34	1,295.0	994.3
35-64	2,109.0	2,471.7
65 +	4,119.9	3,316.9

SOURCE: Commission on
Chronic Conditions (1957), p.53.

Hence, the data suggest that when relevant controls are applied, race differences tend to be severely mitigated. According to Bauer (1969, p. 5):

> If ... one could control simultaneously for age, income, education, family size and other variables which contribute to differences in medical care, the differences in general level of health, and the differences in reporting, there probably would be little or no difference attributable to color alone.

Subjective and Functional Health

Functional health, or "body age," is another variable that has been used in the study of ethnic differences. This construct has been measured by such factors as glucose tolerance, systolic blood pressure, hearing level, peridontal index, and number of decayed-missing-filled teeth. By using the relevant statistics from the National Health Survey, Morgan (1968) found that black and white males are equal in body age at 21; by 30 years, black males have an older body age than their white counterparts. In fact, the biggest jump in body age is between 21 and 30. After this time, blacks hold a five-year body age differential until 60, at which point the race difference increases even further.

Data presented by Hirsch (1974a) appear to be inconsistent with those of Morgan. He found that fewer black males in his group of inner city residents reported poor functional health when compared with white males on a subset of items from the Rosow Functional Health Scale. However, white females were better off with regard to functional health than men.

Further data were provided by Hirsch's findings using the Brody-Lawton Instrumental Activities of Daily Living Scale (subset of items). Among both males and females, blacks reported themselves to be more capable than whites of performing the specified activities of daily living. However, these findings were developed in the absence of socioeconomic and other controls.

Functional age measures are likely to be of increasing importance in the coming years in the wake of laws against age discrimination. A construct based on a selected list of physical indicators may be inefficient, however, because the relevance of specific components of the index to human behavior varies among individuals and among activities. Self-reports, on the other hand, are fraught with biases of indeterminant direction and magnitude: persons of different ethnic groups and life circumstances may have quite different standards by which to evaluate specified activities of daily living. Hence, only a construct based on objective measures has promise of being useful in the context of interracial comparisons. Such a measure will require considerably more research.

Health Services

Hammonds (1974) contends that the poor—particularly poor blacks—do not receive adequate physician services. The geographic distribution of physicians is uneven; physicians tend to congregate in larger industrial states; and, within these areas, they tend to locate in affluent suburban areas. Moreover, there is a relatively greater shortage of black physicians—physicians who could be expected to have a greater inclination to locate in areas of black population. Hence, poor elderly urban blacks are likely to be deprived of proper medical services.

There is considerable evidence that the *pattern* of medical service sought by blacks is different from that sought by whites. In their sample of Medicare enrollees, Green and Scharff (1971) found that race did not influence the proportion of persons using services; however, average annual charges and average number of visits per person were significantly higher for whites than nonwhites. The average charge for whites ($157) was nearly double that for nonwhites ($86). This was partly because the white group had a significantly higher number of physician visits while nonwhites tended to frequent clinics and outpatient facilities of hospitals.

Medicare was intended to substantially reduce or even eliminate financial barriers to utilization of health services among older Americans. To some extent it has been successful in meeting this goal. Fairchild, Liang, and Kahana (1974) report that while recent studies show that socioeconomic variables continue to have substantial power for predicting use of medical services, the relevance of socioeconomic determinants has been reduced with the inception of Medicare and Medicaid.

The persistent relevance of SES to medical services *utilization* has been further demonstrated by Bice et al. (1973), who found that even though the relationship between use of physician services and SES has decreased substantially in recent years, large differences in utilization rates for some services remain. The literature on the relationship between SES and utilization of medical services is relevant to the analysis of services delivery to the black elderly, but most of the studies do not examine differences among the elderly, per se, or even use age as a stratification variable. Moreover, many studies do not consider the possible independent effect of race on services utilization rates.

In general, whites visit physicians more often than blacks. Bauer (1969) finds that whites average more physician visits at all income levels even with age adjustments. While whites show increasing physician usage with increased income, this trend is not apparent among nonwhites. Within each age group, more whites report extended stays in hospitals; but nonwhite males tend to be hospitalized for much longer periods than their white counterparts. Differences in length of stay by race are nonsignificant for females.

Bauer reports that whites are more likely than nonwhites to consult with physicians at home, at the physician's office or by phone, whereas nonwhites tend to see doctors in hospital clinics or emergency rooms. These findings are confirmed by Berman and Luck (1971). The utilization patterns that seem to be typical of blacks are likely to result in a lower level of care. Emergency room personnel may be irritated by the inappropriate use of their services and skills by blacks and others with nonurgent problems. Additionally, emergency rooms are not equipped to provide and will not provide any sort of continuing and preventive care. Rather, persons are likely to be treated and then referred to a clinic with which subsequent contact may be unlikely. Problems that could be discussed on the phone with a physician are more likely to be ignored.

Davis (1973) notes that in some states there is no provision for a program like Medicaid to pick up the deductible and coinsurance amounts required by Medicare. In these states, the cost-sharing provision of Medicare may represent a substantial deterrent to the use of medical services. Green and Scharff (1971) report that in their Medicare sample, the source of payment of deductible and coinsurance costs varied with race; more whites than nonwhites used private insurance as source of payments of these costs. The greater likelihood that whites have and will use private insurance to pay deductible and coinsurance costs tends to increase their use of medical services relative to nonwhites. These findings all suggest that blacks are less likely to use medical services. Even when services are available, barriers to their use occur when fees must be paid (Bice et al. 1973), or when discontinuity of care is promoted by use of clinics and emergency facilities.

Mental Health

There is very little literature on the use of psychological and mental health services among black elderly. Solomon (1970) contends that blacks are more psychologically vulnerable than other groups. However, she presents no data to support her contentions, and most of the arguments she puts forth are true of other ethnic groups. Data from Cantor and Daum (1974) indicate that when income is controlled, blacks are no more vulnerable than whites. As discussed above, blacks tend to be higher in morale and more accepting of life's difficulties. Hence, it is unlikely that blacks would feel a greater need than comparable Anglos to seek psychological and mental health services. Finally, it is often alleged that mental health and counseling services tend to have a middle-class orientation and clientele. Hence, it would not be surprising to find that most elderly blacks make less use of such services.

Double Jeopardy (1964) contends that leisure programs for older people are often not available to blacks; however, there is no research literature on recreational activities for the black elderly. Tissue (1971) suggests that senior citizens groups and services should serve a single social class. Barg and Hirsch (1974) note the importance of neighborhood social organizations in the lives of working class individuals. Such groups serve as a communication network and provide the individual with a sense of identity. Given ingrained lifelong patterns and decreasing mobility with age, the need becomes apparent for delivery systems of all types to be restricted in terms of neighborhood, class, or ethnic group orientation. H. Jackson (1971b) contends that choices and options should be available to black elderly with regard to the delivery of programs and services and that we should provide aged blacks the option of participating in integrated or segregated activities, since they typically grew up at a time when segregation was the rule. Jackson suggests that most blacks would choose segregated facilities, since they would be more comfortable participating in such facilities, and since segregated programs may be better able to provide recreational and various other services for them.

Housing

While housing is a serious problem for all elderly, it is particularly so for blacks. Elderly blacks are much more likely than their white counterparts to live in substandard and dilapidated housing (Double Jeopardy 1964; Rubinstein 1971). Fewer blacks own their own homes, but as Lambing (1972) notes, *within* his black sample, ownership of comfortable homes was most likely to be found among blacks whose preretirement work could be classified as professional. Palmore (1971) found that those with less education and less income, and who lived alone tended to have less adequate housing. Interestingly, race per se was not found to be associated with the incidence of substandard housing in this sample.

In her study of blacks who applied for admission to integrated public housing in Durham, North Carolina, J. J. Jackson (1972a) found that, in general, applicants who were accepted for admission were more likely to be married, more satisfied with their current income, subjectively healthier, and reported fewer physical complaints. Unsuccessful applicants were more involved in passive and isolated leisure activities and were more dissatisfied with their present housing. From these data, Jackson deduced that successful applicants were those whose characteristics were preferred by the larger society for minority group members. In the absence of interracial comparisons, however, one could presume that higher income, sociability, and good health would be desired characteristics of applicants, regardless of race.

BARRIERS TO SERVICE USE

A number of barriers that interfere with the use of services by the black elderly are manifest in the attitudes and behavior of service delivery organizations and potential clients of those organizations. Solomon (1970) contends that government agencies and institutions do not reflect the black experience and, hence, are less appealing to blacks. A similar observation has been made concerning Mexican American and other minority groups who frequently find Anglo mannerisms and presuppositions discomforting and/or humiliating. The sources of humiliation are often quite subtle; for example, physicians may prescribe special diets that are entirely too expensive for poor persons to maintain. Printed menus passed out by doctors and nurses are often inconsistent with black culture and/or the abilities of poor patients to pay.

Sears and McConahay (1973) contend that agencies' "routine procedures which constitute business as usual" are generally designed by middle-class Anglos with their own values (moral, business, personal convenience, or whatever) foremost in mind and not with consideration of the interests of potential consumers. In Los Angeles, for example, working hours for most social agencies are from 9 a.m. to 5 p.m. Social services offices are placed near freeways for easier access to and from suburban areas, rather than near areas of more serious social need. In recent years, urban blacks have reacted to such routines and procedures with anger and eventual hostility by refusing to cooperate with such agencies (Sears and McConahay 1973). This is in contrast to the more traditional southern pattern wherein blacks were predisposed to avoid, rather than to confront, situations or agencies that were not meeting their needs.

There tend to be two separate services delivery systems: a publicly supported one for the poor and a private system for the nonpoor (H. Jackson 1971b). Those who are more likely to demand a more responsive services system—well-educated, articulate individuals—are largely outside the public system. Among the low-income elderly in particular, complaining is unlikely to occur; rather, various indignities are greeted as yet another of the discomforts of old age. Yet such discontent has its effects, and usually on the individual. For example, Hyman (1970) found that discontent with physicians in an outpatient clinic mediated the relationship between SES and utilization of medical care: medical-social discontent is associated with the presence of untreated illness and appears to account entirely for the relationship between SES and untreated illness. He also found that untreated illness and medical-social discontent are both more prevalent among the poor.

Data from Kent and Hirsch cited in Lindsay (1971) indicate that people fail to apply for old age assistance benefits because of fears of governmental imposition on their personal lives and on the lives of their children; fear of losing their homes; inadequate transportation to government offices; fear of red tape involved in applying for assistance; and uncertainty about eligibility.

The anxiety and discomfort associated with contact with Anglo medical specialists may be one important reason for underutilization of services.[4] Another may be the possibility that blacks do not label many symptoms as serious, but view them as natural consequences of life and aging. Koos (1954) demonstrated that the poor are less likely to deem symptoms serious enough to require medical treatment and to obtain such treatment for their ailments. But these findings may simply reflect the tendency for persons to demand fewer costly services when incomes are low. For example, because dental care is inaccessible to them, persons of lower SES tend to attach less stigma to missing teeth.

Data from Billingsley (1969) and J. J. Jackson (1972c) suggest that some blacks may not utilize public services because they receive sufficient support through their ties to an effective kinship network. Billingsley contends that lower class black families are generally organized in such a way that the members have access to the resources of kin. Where such family support is not available, various forms of support and assistance are enhanced by a network of interrelationships of mutual aid with neighbors. Solomon (1970) suggests that structures such as the augmented family provide services for the elderly which preclude the necessity of their seeking support from the public sector. However, she also contends that society should not continue to rely on family resources to meet the needs of the elderly. Rather, there should be some form of aid to families for the care of the elderly so that the elderly and their kin will have a wider range of options available.

There is no conclusive evidence that the inclination toward family support would manifest strong black/nonblack differences when socioeconomic variables are controlled. The issue of encouraging (or at least not penalizing) families who care for the elderly is an important issue for all ethnic groups.

[4] It has been reported (Bauer 1969) that when blood pressure was measured three times during the physical examination associated with a health survey, differences between blacks and whites were smaller on the final measure, indicating a higher initial level of tension among blacks associated with the circumstances of the physical examination.

RECOMMENDATIONS

Lower Social Security Eligibility Age

One of the most controversial proposals for improving the economic status of older blacks is that blacks should become eligible for full social security benefits at an earlier age than Anglos. This argument rests on the well-established fact that blacks have lower life expectancies and hence fail to receive their fair share of the benefits earned during their working lives. As used by J. J. Jackson (1971b, 1972a), however, the argument is severely weakened by a proposal to restrict such special privileges to black elderly, since life expectancies of Mexican American and Indian elderly are also shorter than that of Anglos. Surely, the validity of the argument must rest on the issue of life expectancey—*independent of race.*

But do blacks, or other ethnic groups, have lower life expectancies independent of locale, occupation, or income? That is, is there a *genetic* basis for the observed differential life expectancy? To this date, no evidence has been offered by J. J. Jackson or others to indicate that this is so. Indeed, morbidity data suggest the dominant importance of SES or occupation, not race.

Terris (1973) contends that breakdowns for epidemiological purposes are more appropriately made on the basis of occupation than on the basis of race, since occupation has been found to be unequivocally associated with mortality, longevity, and disease. Indeed, Terris contends that breakdowns on the basis of race may mask economic causes and falsely suggest that inherent racial differences account for variations by race.

On the other hand, it is not clear that differences in eligibility age should be a function of occupation. From the perspective of economic analysis, findings of differences in longevity and mortality as a function of occupation would not be sufficient grounds for advocacy of differential eligibility age by occupation. Those who choose riskier, or more arduous, occupations, *other things equal,* should expect higher pay, or some other form of compensation, during their work lives. Only if some groups of persons are restricted by law or discrimination to jobs that present a health hazard can there be a reasonable claim that they deserve special early retirement. And, clearly, not all occupations available to blacks are dangerous.

On the other hand, blacks have been limited historically to poorly paying occupations, and low income has been associated with lack of proper nutrition, poor housing, and lack of financial and physical access to medical care. Apparently the only proposition deserving of consideration is that low income workers (persons whose highest earnings fall below some threshold) should be allowed earlier eligibility, regardless of race. But then it could be claimed that such a reward for having low earnings represents an undesirable disincentive to work effort.

Community Control

Anglo domination of most services delivery agencies has prompted the suggestion that services delivery to black and other minority elderly should be community controlled and operated. It has been argued that such a system could provide services consistent with the cultural values of minorities. It may even be found that equity for all groups requires multiple systems, one for each ethnic group.

H. Jackson (1971b) contends that an open society is one that offers choices and options and that some blacks, particularly the elderly, may prefer to have their own separate programs and services. Aged blacks grew up at a time when social segregation was more complete; hence they continue to be uncomfortable in racially mixed settings. For these individuals, segregation may be essential to providing services. An obvious but unstated corollary of Jackson's contention, however, is that elderly whites, who are similarly accustomed to social segregation, should have the option to choose racially segregated nursing homes and other services. Such arguments would represent a return to the separate but equal policy of earlier years. On the other hand, it is not clear that social integration should be reserved largely for the most vulnerable and dependent groups in our society (that is, young children in school and the elderly in nursing homes).[5]

Another issue that emerges in considering recommendations for community-operated services is the cultural uniqueness of blacks. Unlike Asian American elderly, or Mexican American elderly, blacks in general speak the same language as Anglos and tend to eat similar foods. The issue, then, is whether a history of segregation and discrimination which has affected the interpersonal relationships between blacks and whites should be regarded as important and as legitimate as language, religion, and food preferences in justifying separate institutions and service delivery systems.

More Black Gerontologists

Although J. J. Jackson (1967, 1971a), the most vocal supporter of the need for training more black gerontologists, acknowledges (1967) that the best executed studies reviewed were generally those of white investigators, she writes, "...occasionally, however, a few of their interpretations may have varied had they had greater knowledge of and sensitivity toward aging Negro subgroups" (p. 175). Her repeated recommendation of the need for more gerontologists and more training in gerontology for blacks emphasizes the issue of the uniqueness and independence of race as a policy relevant variable. Aside from allusions to greater sensitivity among black gerontologists, Jackson fails to clarify just what she would expect them to contribute. One argument, of course, is that a minority gerontologist would be more likely to pay attention to racial issues in his or her research. But, of course, there is no guarantee that this would be the case.

On the other hand, there should be no special *impediments* to the entry of blacks into gerontological research. The extent to which racial bias in the admission process, or Anglo-oriented subject matter in curricula, act as barriers to a balanced representation of blacks and other minorities in such research should be ascertained.

CONCLUSIONS

This discussion of the literature on the black aged has focused on delineating those factors related to race, per se, that have consequences for housing, health,

[5] H. Jackson's major objective in posing a free choice model is not to increase racial separation, but to put an end to the current system whereby there is one system of care for the rich (largely white) and another for the poor (often black). He seeks a single system that is not class differentiated.

income, and other characteristics, and that have consequences for the delivery of services to elderly blacks.

We believe that race may be important in the design and implementation of a services delivery system for elderly (and nonelderly) blacks; the relevance of race, however, does not arise from the higher incidence of blacks among lower SES categories, because the persistence of serious needs *among the poor* is largely independent of race. Rather, race is relevant because of cultural, historical, and locational factors that affect the extent to which "race neutral" programs can be effective in actually providing services to *similarly situated persons* from different racial groups.

The literature that best illustrates this point pertains to health status and health care delivery: in the absence of SES controls, blacks exhibit a much greater incidence of chronic conditions than whites; and when age and SES controls are applied, blacks appear to be less subject to chronic conditions than whites. Yet, the health services needs of blacks may be less adequately provided to blacks by the existing health delivery system, due to a variety of race-linked factors.

There are two major implications of these findings:

1. Future research on minority elderly should pose implicit interracial comparisons with a recognition of the importance of entering SES variables.

2. Minority elderly will be better served by research that is oriented toward problems of services delivery, rather than research that purports to demonstrate a greater relative magnitude of need.

BIBLIOGRAPHY FOR SEC. V

Alston, J. P., and M. J. Knapp, "Intergenerational Mobility Among Black Americans," *Journal of Black Studies*, Vol. 4, 1974, pp. 285-302.

"An Improved Outlook for the People Left Behind?" *Geriatrics*, Vol. 28, 1973, pp. 22-24.

Ashford, Norman, and Frank Holloway, "Transportation Patterns of Older People in Six Urban Centers," *The Gerontologist*, 1972, pp. 43-47.

Barg, Sylvia K., and Carl Hirsch, "A Successor Model for Community Support of Low-Income Minority Group Aged," *Aging and Human Development*, Vol. 3, 1972, pp. 243-252.

Barg, Sylvia K., and Carl Hirsch, "Neighborhood Service Support Networks: An Alternative for the Maintenance of Active Community Residence by Low Income Minority Group Aged in the Inner City. Paper presented at the Gerontological Society Meetings, Portland, Oregon, November 1974.

Barron, Milton, "Minority Group Characteristics of the Aged in American Society," *Journal of Gerontology*, 1973, pp. 477-482.

Bauer, M. L., *Differentials in Health Characteristics by Color, U.S., July 1965-June 1967*, National Center for Health Statistics, Series 10, No. 56, October 1969.

Beattie, W. M., "The Aging Negro: Some Implications for Social Welfare Services," *Phylon*, Vol. 21, 1960, pp. 131-135.

Berman, J. T., and E. Luck, "Patients' Ethnic Backgrounds Affect Utilization," *Hospitals*, T.A.H.A., Vol. 45, No. 14, July 1971.

Bice, T., D. Rabin, B. Starfield, and K. White, "Economic Class and Use of Physician Services," *Medical Care*, Vol. II, 1973, pp. 287-296.

Billingsley, Andrew, "Family Functioning in the Low Income Black Community," *Social Casework*, Vol. 50, 1969, pp. 563-572.

Binstock, Robert, Carolyn Cherinton, and Peter Woll, "Federalism and Leadership-Planning: Predicators of Variance in State Behavior," *The Gerontologist*, Vol. 14, 1974, pp. 114-121.

Bourg, Carroll J., "A Social Profile of Black Aged in a Southern Metropolitan Area," *Proceedings, Research Conference on Minority Group Aged in the South*, Durham, North Carolina, April 1, 1972.

Braver, Ruth, "Chicago Nutrition Program for Older Adults," Mayor's Office for Senior Citizens, Chicago, Illinois, January 1972.

Breslow, Lester, and Bonnie Klein, "Health and Race in California," *American Journal of Public Health*, Vol. 61, 1971, pp. 763-775.

Brostoff, Phyllis, Roberta Brown, and Robert Butler, "The Public Interest: Report 6. 'Beating Up' on the Elderly: Police, Social Work, Crime," *Aging and Human Development*, Vol. 3, 1972, pp. 19-122.

Cameron, Sandra, "The Politics of the Elderly," *Midwest Quarterly*, Vol. 15, 1974, pp. 141-153.

Cantor, Marjorie, "The Elderly in the Rental Market of New York City," New York City Office for the Aging, 1970.

Cantor, Marjorie, "The Reduced Fare Program for Older New Yorkers: Some Effects and Implications of the First Year of Operation," in E. J. Cantilli and J. L. Schmelzer, eds., *Transportation and Aging*, Administration on Aging, Office of Human Development, Department of Health, Education, and Welfare, 1970.

Cantor, Marjorie, and M. Daum, "Extent and Correlates of Mental Health Vulnerability Among the Inner City Elderly Population," Paper presented at Gerontological Society Meetings, Portland, Oregon, November 1974.

Carp, Frances, "The Mobility of Retired People," in E. J. Cantilli and J. L. Shmelzer, eds., *Transportation and Aging*, Administration on Aging, Office of Human Development, Department of Health, Education, and Welfare, Washington, D.C., 1970.

Carp, Frances, "Public Transit and Retired People," in E. J. Cantilli and J. L. Shmelzer, eds., *Transportation and Aging*, Administration on Aging, Office of Human Development, Department of Health Education, and Welfare, Washington, D.C., 1970.

Carp, Frances, "The Mobility of Older Slum-Dwellers," *The Gerontologist*, 1972, pp. 57-65.

Carter, James, "Psychiatry, Racism and Aging," *Journal of the American Geriatrics Society*, Vol. 20, 1972, pp. 343-346.

Chevan, Albert, and J. Henry Korson, "The Widowed Who Live Alone: An Examination of Social and Demographic Factors," *Social Forces*, Vol. 51, 1972, pp. 45-53.

Cohen, Elias S., "Welfare Policies for the Aged Poor: A Contradiction," in *Minority Aged in America*, Institute of Gerontology, University of Michigan, Ann Arbor, 1972, pp. 1-14.

Commission on Chronic Illness, *Chronic Illness in a Large City*, Vol. IV, Harvard University Press, Cambridge, Massachusetts, 1957.

Davis, K., *Lessons of Medicare and Medicaid for National Health Insurance*, Hearings of the subcommittee on Public Health and Environment Committee on Interstate and Foreign Commerce, U.S. Congress, December 12, 1973.

Demeny, P., and P. Gingrich, "A Reconsideration of Negro-White Mortality Differentials in the United States," *Demography*, Vol. 4, 1967, pp. 820-837.

Double Jeopardy: The Older Negro in America Today, National Urban League, New York, 1964.

Dreger, R., and K. Miller, "Comparative Psychological Studies of Negroes and Whites in the United States," *Psychological Bulletin*, Vol. 57, 1960, pp. 361-402.

Economics of Aging: Toward a Full Share in Abundance. Hearings before the Special Committee on Aging, 91st Congress, Part 8: National Organizations, October 29, 1969.

"Efforts at Improving Transit Services for Special Groups," Sec. III in E. J. Cantilli and J. L. Shmelzer, eds., *Transportation and Aging*, Administration on Aging, Office of Human Development, Department of Health, Education, and Welfare, Washington, D.C., 1970.

Fairchild, Thomas J., Jersey Liang, and Eva Kahana, "Utilization of Ambulatory Services Among an Urban Aged Population." Paper presented at the Gerontological Society Meetings, Portland, Oregon, November 1974.

Farrar, D., and J. Haritatos, "Needs and Characteristics of Aged 'Single Room Only' Hotel Occupants." Paper presented at the Gerontological Society Meetings, Portland, Oregon, November 1974.

Frazier, E. Franklin, *The Negro Family in the United States*, Chicago University Press, Chicago, 1966.

Garrison, W. L., "Limitations and Constraints of Existing Transportation Systems as Applied to the Elderly," in E. J. Cantilli and J. L. Shmelzer, eds., *Transportation and Aging*, Administration on Aging, Office of Human Development, Department of Health, Education, and Welfare, Washington, D.C., 1970.

Gelwicks, Louis E., and Robert Newcomer, *Planning Housing Environments for the Elderly*, National Council on Aging, Washington, D.C., 1974.

Goldstein, Sidney, "Negro-White Differentials in Consumer Patterns of the Aged, 1960-1961," *The Gerontologist*, Vol. 11, 1971, pp. 242-249.

Green, Jerome, and Jack Scharff, "Use of Medical Services under Medicare," *Social Security Bulletin*, Vol. 34, 1971, pp. 3-16.

Hammonds, Carl, "Blacks and the Urban Health Crisis," *Journal of the National Medical Association*, Vol. 66, 1974, pp. 226-231.

Harel, Bernice, and James Stilson, "Problems and Promises of Coordinated Services to the Elderly: A Comparative Organizational Perspective." Paper presented at the Gerontological Society Meetings, Portland, Oregon, November 1974.

Hays, David S., and Morris Wisotsky, "The Aged Offender: A Review of the Literature and Two Current Studies from the New York State Division of Parole," *Journal of the American Geriatric Society*, Vol. 17, 1969, pp. 1064-1073.

Hearing Levels of Adults by Race, Region, Sex and Area of Residence, U.S. 1960-1962, National Center for Health Statistics Series 1, No. 26, September 1967.

Hearn, H. L., "Career and Leisure Patterns of Middle Aged Urban Blacks," *The Gerontologist*, Vol. 11, 1971, pp. 21-26.

Helland, R., and P. VanMatre, "Legislative Constraints on the Provision of Housing for the Elderly in the Los Angeles Area." Paper presented at the Gerontological Society Meetings, Portland, Oregon, November 1974.

Henderson, G., "The Negro Recipient of Old-Age Assistance: Results of Discrimination," *Social Casework*, Vol. 46, 1965, pp. 208-214.

Herz, Curt G., "Community Resources and Services to Help Independent Living," *The Gerontologist*, Vol 11, 1971, pp. 59-66.

Heyman, Dorothy, and F. Jeffers, "Study of the Relative Influences of Race and Socio-Economic Status Upon the Activities and Attitudes of a Southern Aged Population," *Journal of Gerontology*, Vol. 19, 1964, pp. 225-229.

Hill, Robert B., "A Profile of the Black Aged," in *Minority Aged in America*, Institute of Gerontology, University of Michigan, Ann Arbor, 1972, pp. 35-50.

Himes, J., and M. Hamlett, "The Assessment of Adjustment of Aged Negro Women in a Southern City," *Phylon*, Vol. 23, 1962, pp. 139-147.

Hirsch, Carl, "Health and Adjustment of Inner-City Black and White Elderly." Paper presented at the Gerontological Society Meetings, Portland, Oregon, November 1974(a).

Hirsch, Carl, "Social and Physical Environment Effects on Utilization of Services by Older People in Working Class Neighborhoods." Paper presented at the Gerontological Society Meetings, Portland, Oregon, November 1974(b).

Hochschild, Arlie Russell, "Communal Life-Styles for the Old," *Society*, Vol. 10, 1973, pp. 50-57.

Housing and Environment for the Elderly: Proceedings from a Conference on Behavioral Research Utilization and Environmental Policy, Gerontological Society, December 1971.

Hyman, Martin D., "Some Links Between Economic Status and Untreated Illness," *Social Science and Medicine*, Vol. 4, 1970, p. 387.

Jackson, Hobart, "National Caucus on the Black Aged: A Progress Report," *Aging and Human Development*, Vol. 2, 1971(a), pp. 226-231.

Jackson, Hobart, "National Goals and Priorities in the Social Welfare of the Aging," *The Gerontologist*, Vol. 11, 1971(b), pp. 226-231.

Jackson, J. J., "Social Gerontology and the Negro: A Review," *The Gerontologist*, Vol. 7, 1967, pp. 168-178.

Jackson, J. J., "Negro Aged and Social Gerontology: A Critical Evaluation," *Journal of Social and Behavioral Sciences*, Vol. 13, 1968, pp 42-47.

Jackson, J. J., "Negro Aged Parents and Adult Children: Their Affective Relationships," *Varia*, North Carolina College Faculty Research Committee, Spring 1969, pp. 1-14.

Jackson, J. J., "Aged Negroes: Their Cultural Departures from Statistical Stereotypes and Rural-Urban Differences," *The Gerontologist*, 1970, pp. 140-145.

Jackson, J. J., "Negro Aged: Toward Needed Research in Social Gerontology," *The Gerontologist*, 1971(a), pp. 52-57.

Jackson, J. J., "Aged Blacks: A Potpourri in the Direction of the Reduction of Inequities," *Phylon*, Vol. 32, 1971(b), pp. 260-280.

Jackson, J. J., "The Blacklands of Gerontology," *Aging and Human Development*, Vol. 2, 1971(c), pp. 156-171.

Jackson, J. J., "Sex and Social Class Variations in Black Aged Parent-Adult-Child Relationships," *Aging and Human Development*, Vol. 2, 1971(d), pp. 96-108.

Jackson, J. J., "Compensatory Care for the Black Aged," in *Minority Aged in America*, Institute of Gerontology, University of Michigan, Ann Arbor, 1972(a), pp. 15-24.

Jackson, J. J., "Marital Life Among Aging Blacks," *Family Coordinator*, Vol. 21, 1972(b), pp. 21-27.

Jackson, J. J., "Social Impacts of Housing Relocation Upon Urban, Low-Income Black Aged," *The Gerontologist*, Vol. 12, 1972(c), pp. 323-337.

Kahana, Eva, "Service Needs of Urban Aged." Paper presented at the Gerontological Society Meetings, Portland, Oregon, November 1974.

Kalish, Richard, "A Gerontological Look at Ethnicity, Human Capacities and Individual Adjustment," *The Gerontologist*, 1971, pp. 78-87.

Kendig, Hal, "Identification of Supportive Neighborhoods for the Aged." Paper presented at the Gerontological Society Meetings, Portland, Oregon, November 1974.

Kent, Donald P., "The Elderly in Minority Groups: Variant Patterns of Aging," *The Gerontologist*, 1971(a), pp. 26-29.

Kent, Donald P., "Social and Family Contexts of Health Problems of the Aged," in C. O. Crawford, ed., *Health and the Family*, Macmillan, New York, 1971(b), pp. 161-174.

Kent, Donald P., "The Negro Aged," *The Gerontologist*, Vol. 11, 1971(c), pp. 48-52.

Kent, Donald P., "Changing Welfare to Serve Minority Aged," in *Minority Aged in America*, Institute of Gerontology, University of Michigan, Ann Arbor, 1972, pp. 25-34.

Kiefer, Christie W., "The Limitations of Theory: A Case Report on the Japanese American Elderly." Paper presented at the Annual Meeting of the Gerontological Society, Portland, Oregon, October 1974.

Koos, E. L., *Health of Regionville*, Columbia University Press, New York, 1954.

Lacklen, Cary, "Aged, Black and Poor: Three Case Studies," *Aging and Human Development*, Vol. 2, 1971, pp. 202-207.

Lambing, M., "Social Class Living Patterns of Retired Negroes," *The Gerontologist*, Vol. 12, 1972, pp. 285-288.

Lawton, M. Powell, "Social Ecology and the Health of Older People," *American Journal of Public Health*, Vol. 64, 1974, pp. 257-260.

Lawton, M. Powell, Morton Kleban, and Diane Carlson, "The Inner-City Resident: To Move or Not To Move," *The Gerontologist*, 1973, pp. 443-448.

Lewis, Myrna I., and Robert N. Butler, "Why Is Women's Lib Ignoring Old Women?" *Aging and Human Development*, Vol. 3, 1972, pp. 223-231.

Leyhe, D., F. Gartside, and D. Procter, "Medical Patient Satisfaction in Watts," *Health Services Report*, Vol. 88, 1973, pp. 351-359.

Lindsay, I., *Multiple Hazards of Age and Race: The Situation of Aged Blacks in the United States.* A report by the Special Committee on Aging, U.S. Senate, November 12, 1971.

Maddox, Geroge L., "Some Correlates of Differences in Self-Assessment of Health Status Among the Elderly," *Journal of Gerontology*, Vol. 17, 1962, pp. 180-185.

Margolius, S., et al., *The Aging Consumer*, Institute of Gerontology, University of Michigan, Ann Arbor, 1969.

Markovitz, J. K., "Transportation Needs of the Elderly," *Traffic Quarterly*, Vol. 25, 1971, pp. 227-253.

Martin, W. C., "Activity and Disengagement: Life Satisfaction of Inmovers into a Retirement Community," *Gerontologist*, Vol. 13, 1973, pp. 224-227.

McGuire, Marie, "The Status of Housing for the Elderly," *Gerontologist*, 1969, pp. 10-14.

Metropolitan Life Insurance Company, "Trends in Mortality of Non-Whites," *Statistical Bulletin*, Vol. 51, 1970, pp. 5-8.

Monk, Abraham, "Social Policies for the Aged: A Parsonian Interpretation," *Social Work*, 1971, pp. 97-103.

Monk, Abraham, and Frank Endres, "Black Elderly in Public Housing: A Case Study in Community Planning." Paper presented at the Gerontological Society Meetings, Portland, Oregon, November 1974.

Morgan, Robert F., "The Adult Growth Examination: Preliminary Comparisons of Physical Aging in Adults by Sex and Race," *Perceptual and Motor Skills*, Vol. 27, 1968, pp. 595-599.

Nahemow, Lucille, Constance Shuman, and Leonard Kogan, "Findings from a Study of Participants in a Reduced Fare Program," in E. J. Cantilli and J. L. Shmelzer, eds., *Transportation and Aging*, Administration on Aging, Office of Human Development, Department of Health, Education, and Welfare, 1970.

Nutrition and the Elderly, Hearings Before the Select Committee on Nutrition and Human Needs, U.S. Senate, Part 1, *Feeding the Elderly*, May 30, 1973, and Part 2, *Elderly Americans' Nutritional Needs*, March 18, 1974.

Older Americans in Rural Areas, Hearings Before the Special Committee on Aging, U.S. Senate, Parts 1-12, September 8, 1969-October 27, 1970.

Orshansky, M., "The Aged Negro and His Income," *Social Security Bulletin*, Vol. 27, 1964, pp. 3-13.

Palmore, Erdman, "Variables Related to Needs Among the Aged Poor," *Journal of Gerontology*, Vol. 26, 1971, pp. 524-531.

Prevalence of Osteoarthritis in Adults by Age, Sex, Race and Geographic Area, U.S., 1960-62, National Center for Health Statistics, Series II, No. 15, June 1966.

"Recommendations of the Workshop Committees," in E. J. Cantilli and J. L. Shmelzer, eds., *Transportation and Aging*, Administration on Aging, Office of Human Development, Department of Health, Education, and Welfare, Washington, D.C., 1970.

"Regional Variations in Nonwhite Mortality," *Statistical Bulletin*, Vol. 54, 1973, pp. 7-9.

Rice, Carolyn, "Old and Black," *Harvest Years*, Vol. 8, 1968, pp. 38-45.

Rubinstein, D., "An Examination of Social Participation Found Among a National Sample of Black and White Elderly," *Aging and Human Development*, Vol. 2, 1971, pp. 172-182.

Schmiel, Calvin F., and Charles E. Noble, "Socioeconomic Differentials Among Nonwhite Races," *American Sociological Review*, Vol. 30, 1965, pp. 909-922.

Sears, David W., "Elderly Housing: A Need Determination Technique," *The Gerontologist*, Vol. 14, 1974, pp. 182-187.

Sears, D. O., and J. B. McConahay, *The Politics of Violence*, Houghton-Mifflin, Boston, 1973.

Shanas, Ethel, "Making Services for the Elderly Work: Some Lessons from the British Experience." A report to the Special Committee on Aging, U.S. Senate, November 1971.

Shore, Herbert, "The Current Social Revolution and Its Impact on Jewish Nursing Homes," *The Gerontologist*, Vol. 12, 1972, pp. 178-180.

Smith, T. Lynn, "The Changing Number and Distribution of the Aged Negro Population of the United States," *Phylon*, Vol. 18, 1967, pp. 339-354.

Solomon, B., "Ethnicity, Mental Health and the Older Black Aged," in *Proceedings of Workshop on Ethnicity, Mental Health and Aging*, April 13/14, 1970, sponsored by University of Southern California Gerontology Center, Los Angeles.

Stephens, Joyce, "The Aged Minority," in *Minority Aged in America*, Institute of Gerontology, University of Michigan, Ann Arbor, 1972, pp. 59-63.

Sterne, Richard S., "Exploring Bureaucratic Hurdles to Serving the Elderly." Paper presented at the Gerontological Society Meetings, Portland, Oregon, November 1974.

Stone, Virginia, "Personal Adjustment in Aging in Relation to Community Environment," in F. C. Jeffers, ed., *Proceedings of Seminars*, Duke University, 1959-1961.

Stouffer, S. A., et al., *The American Soldier: Adjustment During Army Life*, Vol. 1, *Studies in Social Psychology*, Princeton University Press, Princeton, New Jersey, 1949.

Suchman, Edward, and A. Allen Rothman, "The Utilization of Dental Services," *Milbank Memorial Fund Quarterly*, Vol. 47, 1969, pp. 56-63.

Swanson, William C., and Carl L. Harter, "How Do Elderly Blacks Cope in New Orleans?" *Aging and Human Development*, Vol. 2, 1971, pp. 210-216.

Taeuber, K. E., and A. F. Taeuber, *Negroes in Cities*, Aldine Publishers, Chicago, 1965.

Terris, Milton, "Desegregating Health Statistics," *American Journal of Public Health*, Vol. 63, 1973, pp. 477-480.

Thomas, George, "Regional Migration Patterns and Poverty Among the Aged in the South, *Journal of Human Resources*, Vol. 8, 1973, pp. 73-84.

Tissue, Thomas, "Social Class and the Senior Citizen's Center," *The Gerontologist*, 1971, pp. 196-200.

Torda, Theodore S., "The Impact of Inflation on the Elderly," *Economic Review*, 1972, pp. 3-19.

Trent, R., "The Color of the Investigator as a Variable in Experimental Research with Negro Subjects," *Journal of Social Psychology*, Vol. 40, 1954, pp. 281-287.

U.S. Department of Commerce, Bureau of the Census, *The Social and Economic Status of the Black Population in the United States: 1971*, Current Population Reports, Series P-23, Vol. 42, U.S. Government Printing Office, Washington, D.C., July 1972.

U.S. Department of Commerce, Bureau of the Census, *Subject Reports: Negro Population*, U.S. Government Printing Office, Washington, D.C., May 1973.

U.S. Department of Commerce, Bureau of the Census, *Current Population Report*, Series P-23, July 1974.

U.S. Senate Special Committee on Aging, Hearings Before the Subcommittee on Long-Term Care, *Access of Minority Groups to Nursing Homes*, August 10, 1972.

U.S. Senate Special Committee on Aging, Hearings Before the Subcommittee on Housing for the Elderly, *Adequacy of Federal Response to Housing Needs of Older Americans*, August 2-4, 1971.

U.S. Senate Special Committee on Aging, *Housing for the Elderly: A Status Report.* Working paper, April 1973.

U.S. Department of Health, Education, and Welfare, Public Health Service, *Blood Pressure of Adults by Race and Area, 1960-1962*, PHS Publication No. 1000, Series 100, No. 5, Washington, D.C., July 1964.

U.S. News & World Report, "Day Care Centers for the Elderly," March 5, 1973.

"Utilization of Short-Stay Hospitals by Patients 65 Years of Age and Over: United States 1965-1967," *Monthly Vital Statistics Report*, National Center for Health Statistics, Vol. 20, 1971, pp. 1-4.

Viscusi, W. Kip, and Richard Zeckhauser, *Welfare of the Elderly*, Vol. II, prepared for the Department of Health, Education, and Welfare, Washington, D.C., September 1974.

Wahl, Dorothy, "The Volunteer Protective Service Board: A Framework for Action." Paper presented at the Gerontological Society Meetings, Portland, Oregon, November 1974.

Weiss, James E., and Merwyn Greenlick, "Determinants of Medical Care Utilization: The Effect of Social Class and Distance on Contacts with the Medical Care System," *Medical Care*, Vol. 8, November-December 1970, pp. 456-462.

Wilder, Mary, *Disability Days, U.S. 1968*, National Health Survey Series 10, No. 67, January 1972.

Wylie, Floyd, "Attitudes Toward Aging and the Aged Among Black Americans: Some Historical Perspectives," *Aging and Human Development*, Vol. 2, 1971, pp. 66-70.

Youmans, E. G., "Family Disengagement Among Older Urban and Rural Women," *Journal of Gerontology*, Vol. 22, 1967, pp. 209-211.

Youmans, E. G., "Objective and Subjective Economic Disengagement Among Older Rural and Urban Men," *Journal of Gerontology*, Vol. 21, 1966, pp. 439-441.

LIFE STRENGTHS AND LIFE STRESSES:
Explorations in the Measurement of the Mental Health of the Black Aged

Audrey Olsen Faulkner, Ph.D., Marsel A. Heisel, M.A., Peacolia Simms

This paper describes an attempt to understand the self-concept, social characteristics, personal strengths, and frailties of a group of older black men and women, in order to tailor mental health and social work services to their needs. Difficulties inherent in obtaining such information were minimized by a methodology that integrated the research and service aspects of the project. Results of the pilot study, and service implications, are discussed.

The problems of aging and the aged have recently caught the attention of investigators and practitioners in the mental health professions, with considerable research and a number of service projects being aimed both at gathering information about old people and at alleviating their plight. However, the segment of this population that probably has the greatest need for services of all kinds—aged blacks—are not benefiting as much as whites from this increase of interest and effort. In a survey of social gerontological literature concerned with blacks, Jacquelyne Johnson Jackson [7] noted that, in spite of an increase in absolute bulk, there is a definite, continuing need for additional concrete data.

If we are to offer mental health or social work services to aged blacks, we should have some understanding of the population being served, their life styles and social characteristics, and beyond that, their strengths and their perceptions both of self and of their relationships to the environment. There are tremendous difficulties in getting this in-

Presented, in part, to the annual meeting of the Gerontological Society, San Juan, Puerto Rico, December 1972. The project described is financed by NIMH Grant MH18051.

Authors are: Professor (Faulkner) and Assistant Professor (Heisel), Graduate School of Social Work, Rutgers University, New Brunswick, N.J.; and Family Consultant, Rutgers-Friendly-Fuld Aging Project (Simms).

formation. Besides inherent distrust and possible racial animosity, there is the subject's fear of being used for the benefit of others with no apparent self advantage when there is a very real need for immediate assistance. It must be well known to all by now that this population most often lives in deplorable conditions, trapped in the inner city and prey to the more agile young predator, unable and perhaps unwilling to join the racial movements of the young, suffering from inadequate assistance and the lack of those services that many groups in our population take for granted. There may be little patience with research in such a situation.

In this atmosphere of need for immediate service plus a real dearth of information, we undertook a service-research project in a highly urbanized area of New Jersey. In addition to giving social work service and extending the opportunity to participate in recreational and community service activities similar to those available at other senior centers, the project aims at evaluating the effectiveness of its program in terms of improving or maintaining the mental health of the recipients. It has also undertaken to provide material about the life styles, attitudes, and social functioning of the black aged. This paper deals with the initial phases of the research and gives the results of the pilot study undertaken as the first endeavour in the measurement of self-concept and delivery of needed services.

THE SAMPLE

The sample for the overall research consists of a random selection of 143 men and women, aged 55 and over, who reside in two census tracts of a northern New Jersey urban center. The pilot group, on which the present results are based, consists of a similar sample of 25 men and women. In the case of subjects 55 to 59 years of age, only those no longer in the work force are included. Two-thirds of the research population live in a large housing project, and one third inhabit the half-razed area surrounding it. Although the social services are aimed primarily at the research sample, they are extended to other elderly people in the area who request help. However, the aggressive outreach service is given only to those individuals who make up the research sample.

THE PROGRAM

The program was designed as an ongoing, multi-level process, with both service and research components complementing each other. Information obtained from the initial stages of the research would be used to guide the service portion of the project; the feedback from actual service, plus hypotheses derived from initial research phases, would guide the next steps in the inquiry. Needless to say we made every effort during the pilot phase of the program to keep both elements of the project, research and service, open and flexible so that they would both be in a position to respond and hopefully to innovate.

THE QUESTIONNAIRE

One of the first tasks to which we applied ourselves was that of constructing a questionnaire to assess the characteristics and mental health of this group: to find out how the older black views himself or herself, how he or she responds to his health, economic, and social situation, and how he or she views that response. It was necessary to do this in order to establish a bench-mark of present mental health, including social and psychological functioning, against which to evaluate the effective-ness of the program at a later date, independent of the service record and the impressions of the service staff.* There were four areas we decided to tap: 1) concept of self and feelings of self worth; 2) feelings of satisfaction or dissatisfaction with life in relation to actual life situation; 3) degree of social participation or isolation; and 4) knowl-edge about and facility in using environ-mental supports.

Although much has been written in the last decade on personality and men-tal health in old age, empirical data come mainly from white, and often middle-class, respondents.[1, 3, 5, 8] Those studies dealing with the effect on the self-concept of being black are for the most part the results of research with children, and it is questionable whether the findings—that racial attitudes learned early in life negatively affect feelings of self esteem—are applicable to the individual past sixty. In addition, a researcher overly concerned with the "oppressed minority syndrome" may focus undue attention on a simple causal relationship between the self-concept and oppression, concentrating only on negative self perceptions and ignoring indications of character strength and positive self values. The black low-in-come person who has survived to reach old age has had to have unusual psycho-logical and physical stamina. We need to know more about these strengths.

Our aim, therefore, was to devise a questionnaire that could assess self-concept and give as clear a picture as possible of the distinctive features of the black aged, while minimizing any interference that might be the outcome of adverse cultural and interviewer fac-tors. It would have to be an instrument as "culture-fair" as possible, depicting the population from within its own sub-culture and refraining from the implicit or explicit humiliation of measuring "deviation" from white society. Such a comparison would be grossly unfair to the individuals themselves and would run counter to the pride of the entire black community. Aside from this, we were deeply ideologically committed to the belief that there was no norm from which there were deviations; there were only diverse patterns of living, resulting from differing adaptations to life situa-tions, which had to be understood be-fore either social or mental health ser-vice could be effectively given.

In addition, the research instrument had to be one with which paraprofes-sionals coming from the neighborhood adjacent to the center could feel com-fortable. They were the service person-nel for the project, and we planned to use them in the interviewing process. Indeed, we carried this integration of service and research one step further; the questionnaire itself, a semi-struc-tured instrument, was developed jointly with these Family Consultants who were intimately familiar with the values and idioms of the neighborhood. Together we discussed and decided upon the substantive areas to be covered in the research and on the ways in which the items would be presented to the respon-

---

* There is also a control group—a random sample from a population having the same characteristics who do not receive service—for additional evaluation.

264

dents. In this manner we hoped to solve some of the problems we had earlier perceived—those that made a "culture fair" instrument so difficult to devise—and also to involve the interviewers, enabling them to feel secure in the later interviewing situation by developing the greatest familiarity with the research schedule. If, during the pilot study, the paraprofessionals found that certain questions were not "working," they alerted us and helped us to reword or change the items.

INTERVIEWING

Fully aware of the risks involved, we decided to use the paraprofessional Family Consultants as the interviewers in the project. It was hoped to thereby create an easier and more relaxed atmosphere during the interviewing session, which would facilitate the exchange of ideas and feelings. Certainly the interviewers would have to be black and familiar with the neighborhood culture, for otherwise the results obtained could be substantially distorted.[6] It was our impression that the population would be less guarded, would respond with greater confidence and trust if interviewed by black paraprofessionals from the neighborhood whom they had already met in initial visits and who would be offering them help with their problems. The service personnel fulfilled all these requirements.

On the whole, the service personnel cooperated extremely well with the research team in carrying out the interviewing task. They felt comfortable with the schedule, especially with those parts upon which considerable time had been spent jointly with the research staff. These portions included questions regarding age-specific self-concepts, self-referent statements, and attitudes towards the young. On the other hand, they were less comfortable regarding items that seemed somewhat academic, with the result that the number of "no responses" increased in those instances.*

RESULTS

The pilot study, undertaken to test the questionnaire and to guide the course of service, was set up so that the Family Consultants administered the schedule after making two visits to the client's home and writing their own assessment of the client's mental health status.** As we have already noted, the population consisted of a random sample of 25 black seniors living in the aforementioned public housing project and surrounding neighborhood. Most of the sixteen women and nine men were born in the Southeast, and migrated to New Jersey as adults. At the time of the interview, 60% were mobile (defined as the ability to get around and independently care for one's daily needs), about half were living alone, and four of them were working. Most of the people were poor, and all had been members of the labor force.

Our data on self appraisal reveal a predominantly positive self-concept. The majority of the respondents compare themselves favorably with their peers, most saying they are doing fine for

---

* A case in point is Cantrol's self anchoring scale. An entire day was spent talking about the scale and rewording it; however, only 50% of the respondents in the pilot project answered the question, a result we consider attributable to the discomfort of the interviewers.

** A comparison of the two assessments and a discussion of the risk and advantage of our methodology will be the subject of a future paper.

their age (56%), that they look younger (43%) or about the same (39%) as others their age, and that they are able to do as much (44%) or more (16%) than their contemporaries. Those who live alone and are mobile are much more likely to say they feel younger than their age and see themselves as being able to do more than their age mates. Interestingly, men say they feel younger than their age almost twice as often as women.

When asked what they like most about being their age, they most often agree that it is "being alive;" the next most common answer is "not having to work so hard." Generally, they dislike their aches and pains and the inability to do things for themselves, but while 20% say they like nothing at all about being old, 44% reject the premise of the question and respond by stating that there is nothing bad about it. Those who find nothing negative about being old tend to be mobile and live alone. Ratings on a set of self-referent statements show that they see themselves as being good, helpful, neighborly, and worthwhile individuals. Well over half describe themselves as very happy, or pretty happy individuals. Happiness seems to be the result of good health, independence, and the fact that their families—children and grandchildren—are doing well. Bad health and dependence make them unhappy; it is no coincidence that the ones who say they are "not too happy" tend to be the individuals who live with others and have restricted mobility. All the "very happy" people are mobile.

In questioning perceptions of their life situation, we had to first make note of the actual conditions under which they live. Grim, ugly, and dangerous, the inner city neighborhood continuously poses risks to their personal safety and meager belongings. It is not surprising, then, to find that they feel they are to some extent the victims of others, that they must continuously be on guard and rely upon themselves, and that they cannot trust their neighbors. A third of the sample reports feeling all alone in the world. Men, more often than women, report this feeling of loneliness. They are more suspicious of their environment, but on the other hand, more eager for contact with others. Twenty-five percent of the respondents—mostly men—feel that their children have let them down.

Almost all of the pilot sample are afraid to venture outside their homes. Half of them have already had trouble in the neighborhood, and over a third have been mugged, beaten or robbed in the past three years. Women, more often than men, express fear of young people, related to robbery, dope, and knifing. In spite of this, three-fourths of them do not believe that life in the neighborhood would be better if there were no young people around. Over half of the respondents feel that young people of today are worse than past generations, saying that they have no respect, no obedience, exhibit criminal behavior, use dope, and so forth. Three-fourths of the sample feel that parents are responsible, declaring that child-rearing practices and teaching in the home are at fault. "Turning to God" on the part of youth, and "proper training by parents" are the cures most frequently proposed.

An important element we wished to measure was the extent to which old people living in the ghetto are in touch with the rising racial consciousness stirring in their community. The race related questions were by far the hardest to formulate and ask, even though the Family Consultants were on hand to help in the task, and therefore, we have less confidence in the reliability of these answers. Nonetheless, we will report some of our findings.

When we asked what they would like to be called, the majority of the women said, "Colored," the majority of men said, "Black." Most of them think life is harder for a black person their age than for a white, that they have been denied rights or oppressed during their lifetimes, that life has been harder with fewer chances of getting ahead because of their race. They are about equally divided as to whether they would have had a better life if they had been white. Yet only two respondents blame white society for some of the bad things that happened to them in life; surprisingly, most of them blame themselves.

A majority of the respondents feel that it used to be easier for a black woman than a black man to make a living; however, a third of the women disagree. Women think life is easier for men now; men think it is easier for the women.

To assess the degree of social participation or isolation of those in the pilot study we asked people who they had seen or talked with in the recent past, how they spent holidays, and so forth. Sixty percent of the respondents had gone out the day before the interview. We found that visiting is by far the most important reason given for leaving the apartment, while shopping is a poor second. Attending clubs or club type recreational activities is almost nonexistent. Our data show that women,

people who live alone, and those who are mobile do more visiting than others.

Women and those who are not mobile receive more visitors in their homes. Most of the recent visitors were friends rather than relatives; indeed, none of the visits of the previous day which were recorded had been to or from children or relatives (the interviews were carried out Tuesday through Friday). Men express more feelings of loneliness and an eagerness for social contact, although they are more likely than women to say that they are keeping busy. Women hold more telephone convertstations than men, often with their children, which is a rarity for men. Men watch television, listen to the radio, and specifically to the news, more often.

While half of the respondents have children in the immediate area, few have close relatives of about the same age living nearby. Our findings were that women maintain contact with relatives more often than do men.

Both sexes seem to depend more upon friends for companionship than upon relatives. These findings are substantiated by workers serving this population, who report that their clients are unwilling to ask children or relatives for favors or companionship and seem to prefer an outsider's aid when they require help in their daily lives. According to the Family Consultants, clients must be very ill before they are willing to ask relatives for support.

About a third of the respondents to the pilot study report very little interaction with others. However, we believe it is not accurate to think of this in terms of disengagement since so many of these same people indicate that they are lonely, wish people would visit them more often, and are sorry that they do not have close friends. If this were a true pattern of disengagement no desire for social interaction would be exhibited.

The pilot questionnaire ended by asking the respondents about their wishes for the future. To our surprise, we found that, while women wish for health, money, and better housing, the men could not choose between health and a wish to help others. Males seem to be a lonely group who have few family and informal social ties and who consequently wish to be of help. Indeed, they may be an important new source of service in the elderly black community.

DISCUSSION

The pilot study, although small, utilized feedback to the maximum and was thus instrumental in enhancing both practice and research aspects of the project.

Where there were indications from data that the clients were eager for social contact but unwilling to venture out of their home or be the initiators, Family Consultants have taken it upon themselves to form social groups. These gatherings are kept small, meet in living rooms, and engage in activities of the group's choice. Service workers report that clients have responded very positively to this program. Questionnaire information also led us to scrap the erroneous assumption that elderly blacks are surrounded, served, and supported by a network of concerned, extended family. This just was not so for our population, not because of family breakdown, but because of the absence of relatives. Consequently, we saw the need for service workers to act as family surrogates, going into the clients' homes as if they were close relatives or friends

and helping them make use of available community resources and personal relationships. Family Consultants help the client shop, cash checks, go to church, find help with personal or home care, host visitors, give volunteer service to others, avoid spending holidays alone, and of course are always there to lend a sympathetic ear to troubles or triumphs.

It must be noted that service was quickly and easily directed in this pattern not only because of interview findings but also because the workers became keenly aware of the need for family surrogates while administering the questionnaire. Because we began both service and research with a small pilot project, it was possible for us to conceive of and carry through the family substitute mode. Had the entire target population been involved in service from the beginning, or had all the interviews been initially analyzed without the benefit of exploratory service strategies, the idea would most probably have appeared impossible to attempt. It would have seemed too ambitious, too time consuming and too costly. The first steps in this direction have proved not only that this approach is rewarding but also that it is quite possible to enlarge the program to cover the entire service population.

While not an entirely new idea, utilizing the service personnel in construction of the questionnaire and in the interviewing of respondents is still unusual enough to merit discussion. When we look at the wording of the questionnaire the results of this effort at cooperation are rather difficult to judge. Would we have come up with the same instrument if we had written it at our desks at Rutgers University? Surprisingly, it would probably have been quite similar, for there is not as much use of the vernacular as we had initially expected. However, many questions are worded differently from what one would anticipate, and, in fact, some seem awkward and badly phrased to the academic ear. This is the result of our having opted for the empirical approach, in which the actual experience of the pilot study decided the fate of the eventual phrasing.

While we do not know whether the questionnaire elicited a better response than one that would have been written exclusively by the research staff, it must be emphasized that the advantage of writing it with the Family Consultants was that of heightening their motivation to explore the needs of their clients and subsequently to utilize the findings in the service portion of the project. As we have indicated before, there was considerable ease felt in use of the schedule, and it has aided client-worker interaction. The Family Consultants report that they gained a great deal of insight and understanding as a direct result of being the interviewers. Collecting data in this way served as a spur to service. Workers learned quickly and in detail about their clients and their needs, and consequently, service could be adapted to need with little loss of time.

The research instrument was also found to be helpful in the actual delivery of service. By examining the data, Family Consultants became aware of how little the clients (and sometimes the workers themselves) know about existing services or of the experience which the population has had with various agencies.

With at least part of the research having immediate consequences upon the quality of the service being rendered, the initial resistance to data collection which the paraprofessional staff had exhibited weakened. The pilot group experience defused much of the negative feeling towards research that had been in evidence in the community as well. After the first two initial contacts with clients, the Family Consultants were eager for an instrument that would help them understand the population better, and in this enthusiastic climate researchers were encouraged to devise a comprehensive and thorough instrument.

SUMMARY AND CONCLUSION

The results show that in spite of a life full of stress and difficulties, the majority of the black men and women in this group have a highly positive self-concept, compare themselves favorably with other people their age, and express relatively high satisfaction with life and themselves, all indices which show their strength, and which we consider highly relevant to mental health. They do, however, tend to feel victims of their environment (which, in view of the very high crime rate in the area they live in, is a realistic appraisal) and some seem socially isolated in spite of their eagerness for contact.

The findings, based on a very small sample, are of course tentative, and should be treated as hypotheses to be tested in further research. Our subsequent study, already in progress, is a step in that direction.

REFERENCES
1. BRADBURN, N. AND CAPLOVITZ, D. 1965. Report on Happiness. Aldine, Chicago.
2. CLARK, K. AND CLARK, N. 1952. Racial identification and preference in Negro children. *In* Readings in Social Psychology.

3. CUMMING, E. AND HENRY W. 1961. Growing Old: The Process of Disengagement. Basic Books, New York.
4. GOODMAN, M. 1964. Race Awareness in Young Children. Collier Books, New York.
5. GURIN, G., VEROFF, J. AND FELD, S. 1960. Americans View Their Mental Health. Basic Books, New York.
6. HYMAN, H. 1954. Interviewing in Social Re-search. University of Chicago Press, Chicago.
7. JACKSON, J. 1971. Negro aged: towards needed research in social gerontology. Gerontologist 11:52–57.
8. NEUGARTEN, B. 1964. Personality in Middle and Later Life. Atherton Press, New York.
9. PORTER, J. 1971. Black Child, White Child. Harvard University, Cambridge.

For reprints: Dr. Audrey Olsen Faulkner, Graduate School of Social Work, Rutgers, The State University, New Brunswick, N.J. 08903

A SUCCESSOR MODEL FOR COMMUNITY SUPPORT OF LOW—INCOME MINORITY GROUP AGED[1]

Sylvia K. Barg, Director and Carl Hirsch, Deputy Director

Philadelphia Model Cities Senior Wheels East

ABSTRACT—Experience in research and community outreach work with low-income urban aged led to the development of a multifocal program approach. The program approach includes case referral and advocacy work with the target population as well as the organization of neighborhood-based groups of elderly residents. The two approaches are intended to achieve both treatment of extant social symptoms of age discrimination and social and political power by the aged to eliminate discrimination on the basis of age. The two approaches provide mutual reinforcement for the success of each, and are based on tenets of social interaction theory as well as an analysis of the social and political powerlessness of the aged in the Model Cities Neighborhood of Philadelphia.

Experience in the Model Cities Senior Wheels East has led to considerations involving cross-generational ties between worker and client to achieve senior power, the role of indigenous community workers in social welfare agencies working with the aged as well as the successful application of the approach to the black, Puerto Rican, and foreign-born white aged residing in the area.

Although perfection in program operation is not claimed, the validity and appropriateness of the approach is raised for consideration following the National Conference of the National Caucus on Black Aged and the White House Conference on Aging.

INTRODUCTION

In previous work the authors, in collaboration with others, have focused attention upon low-income minority group aged in the urban communities in which they reside (Kent, Barg, 1969). This focus has included an emphasis upon the role of indigenous community workers as liason agents between the members of the deprived minority and the social welfare system functioning to serve them. Positive results have been reported in training programs to heighten communication skills of indigenous workers, as well as to develop referral and advocacy skills among community workers with the aged (Kent, Hirsch, Barg, 1969, 1971; Kent, Hirsch, 1971).

In a further development Kent (1970) and Brody, Finkle, and Hirsch (1972) report on an experimental program designed to foster outreach by the Philadelphia County Board of Assistance to insure public supportive services to minority group aged in low-income areas of the city including populations of black ghetto areas. While the program focused on the referral and advocacy skills of community workers to insure the elderly residents' rights to minimal supports for community living, attention was also given to the development of "gatekeepers" in the community. The gatekeepers are persons who in resident or work roles in these communities are in touch with the elderly populations in their normal role activities and who, through program contact, are informed of the supportive services and procedures for obtaining social, health, and economic supports for

---

[1] An earlier version of this paper was presented at the Twenty-fourth Annual Meeting of the Gerontological Society, Houston, Texas. October 28, 1971.

the aged. Ideally, the result of concentrated program inputs would have resulted in both (1) the invigoration of the aged population through close contact with the skilled community workers who provide a role model for aged individuals and (2) the development of legitimate community advocates for the aged within the social structure of the low-income community. Unforeseen developments in program administration led to the abortion of advocacy procedures and inhibition of gatekeeper development as reported by Brody, Finkle, and Hirsch (1972).

However, some conceptual gaps in the structure of the experimental program did not become obvious until the process was underway. Failure to recognize the impact of long isolation for some aged and the decline in social integration through role loss for many others among the deprived minority groups comprising the target population placed unrealistic demands upon aged individuals. They were expected to move from states of fear and dependency (Kent, Hirsch, 1971; Kent, 1970) to confident self-representation with respect to the service bureaucracies existing and functioning in their communities. The goal of institutional change in these areas was to have been accomplished with support for the aged that was too meager considering the nature of both the aged groups' status in the community and the resistance to change by service institutions and government itself. While the support and positive role model provided by the community workers and the potential role of the gatekeeper could have led to improved conditions among the aged in low-income communities, the outcome still conceptualized a state of dependency by the aged on community agents vigorously acting in advocacy roles. Overlooked was (1) the need for structured roles for the aged fostering interaction among peers in their community and (2) the role of interaction as a theoretical prerequisite for both personal integrity or personality coherence and social activity, including self-representation in the community.

While building upon previous positive experience with community workers in work with the aged, Model Cities Senior Wheels East incorporates both case and group work techniques in urban neighborhood applications to form a model for an approach to meet the critical needs of individual aged. At the same time, it provides the basic means for alleviating the social conditions contributing to the reoccurrence of individual problems, i.e., self-representation of the aged themselves through group participation and group advocacy to gain service rights.

INTERACTION THEORY: THEORETICAL UNDERPINNINGS OF THE MODEL CITIES SENIOR WHEELS EAST APPROACH[2]

Arnold Rose (1964) refers to the implicit acceptance of symbolic interactionist theory in social gerontology from inception of the field in the work of Ernest Burgess and others. However, this orientation became formalized only as late as 1961 and 1962 when disengagement theory had already been introduced. To both Rose (1961) and Cavan

---

[2] In adopting the program, the Model Cities Administration in Philadelphia placed operational responsibility with two delegate agencies. The Model Cities Senior Wheels West Program is operated by the Wharton Centre, a long-established multiprogram agency. Model Cities Senior Wheels East is operated by the Olde Kensington Redevelopment Corporation, a recently established nonprofit organization of community residents working for the physical rehabilitation of housing and social change. While sharing program goals the two delegate agencies follow somewhat different approaches in their work in their respective communities.

(1962), adjustment of the individual to himself in his own old age is interdependent with adjustment to the persons and groups in his social world. Both authors agree on the importance of retirement or loss of occupation, decline in physical powers, and a new adjustment to the family and/or other primary groups, such as peer and friendship groups, as crucial to understanding and appreciating the situation of the aged. Reevaluation by the aged of themselves in the context of changed roles results. The difficulty of this adjustment is increased when we appreciate that the aged person is moving from a set of structured roles, positively evaluated within the society, to a set of ill-defined roles that receive less powerful positive evaluation, if not distinctly negative evaluation, in the social world. To Kent, the aged are "structured out" (1968).

Both Rose and Cavan would agree with Clark (1967) in her reference to Benedict's finding that " . . . cultural discontinuities . . . always involve strain for the individual; however, when persons confronted with such discontinuities are fortified by 'a solid phalanx' of social grouping, they can often swing between remarkable extremes of opposite behavior without apparent psychic threat" (Clark, 1967, p. 442). This assertion is supported by data from Clark's San Francisco study as is its alternative: " . . . where the aging individual is released from earlier adult roles without either real or symbolic inter-relationships upon which to build self-esteem he often suffers a serious, stress-ridden discontinuity" (Clark, 1967, p. 442).

The situation of the aged person is then seen to be dependent on the interrelationship of his ties to formally organized and positively evaluated structures and of the degree of firm supportive ties he experiences in the more informally structured groups of which he is part. Cavan discusses the inability of recreation clubs to substitute for lost occupation or child-care activity in provision of equivalent roles since the positive self-conceptions developed through interaction or participation in these latter groups " . . . are often limited . . . in that they may not be capable of expression in any group except the club itself" (Cavan, 1962).

Rose sees a more effective alternative for the development of equivalent roles in the process of development of a subculture of aging. The process of development of the subculture described by Rose can be seen to represent an interactionist perspective. Rose identifies the interaction of aged with one another on the bases of affinity, as a key factor in the potential development of a subculture. Second, the exclusion of the aged from interaction across age-grades reinforces the affinity within the old age group (Rose, 1962, p. 29). With the development of positive subcultural evaluations of new roles substituting for the neutral or negative evaluation of such roles in the wider culture, the aged person is helped to reestablish a positive self-concept in a changed context. While the approach to be described here recognizes the validity of the tenets of interaction theory as providing a viable perspective within which work with minority group aged residents of low-income neighborhoods can be carried out, there are further considerations of the special status of minority group aged that make the conceptions of individual-group adjustment presented in interaction theory even more compelling.

LOW-INCOME MINORITY GROUP AGED AS AN OPPRESSED MINORITY: POLITICAL CONSIDERATIONS IN THE MODEL CITIES SENIOR WHEELS EAST APPROACH

The problems which have occurred in the lives of those aged people identified and served in the first year of the program and the emergence of new problems among them following first contact are not seen as random events which will be unlikely to reoccur. They are seen as typical events in the lives of the aged poor and especially of those who are members of racial and ethnic minority groups as well. The assertion of the normality of reoccurring crises in the lives of the target population of the program is based on a view which decidedly does *not* see the cause of these problems resulting from failures of the older people themselves. The assertion stems from a view of the aged as members of a minority group which is discriminated against and systematically cut off from access to the resources of society which allow younger residents of these same areas a somewhat greater degree of independent functioning and greater control over their circumstances. The degree to which both younger and older members of this community are members of racial or ethnic minorities complicates the difficulties experienced by all age groups in their efforts to control their own lives and the conditions which serve as parameters of their social existence.

We then see the problems existing in the lives of the target population of this program resulting from the identification of the *individual* aged as members of a *disadvantaged group.* They are disadvantaged especially in terms of role loss and reduced economic means as discussed above. However, disadvantage also stems from the passivity of these persons. Passivity may have been present in previous life activity, but it becomes especially reinforced when "old age," as society defines it, is reached; social and economic incapacities are increased while physical health resources tend to decrease. Passivity extends throughout the life of the aged as citizens. It is unreasonable to expect that the low-income minority group aged can successfully serve in their citizen roles since political participation generally means group participation and the aged increasingly lose group identification and opportunities for interaction. This passivity is especially limiting since what is required to resolve the problems of the aged is a basic shift in values and national priorities so that the aged do not continue to be consigned to a second-class citizenship. They must be as highly valued as a group as any other within the society if the disadvantages they now suffer are to be removed. This is generally recognized as an outcome achievable only through political self-representation and consequent political power.

In this view we have a situation in which the aged—as members of a minority group per se,—lack resources to cope with changes in their social, economic, and physical health conditions. Their situation is then compounded by their placement in a community that has been characterized by low-income minority populations for many years. Concomitant with this is an absence of adequate social, economic, and health resources to meet the needs of the population and an absence of political power to gain the necessary resources.

We must anticipate the development of crises or problems in the lives of these older people under these conditions. Although many problems existing during the first year of the program of individual aged persons were dealt with, we recognize that these problems are only symptoms of the underlying individual and community disability reinforced throughout the years. Continued treatment of the problems alone is one alternative for program activity which would guarantee a busy workload for the staff. Service, however, would remain at a treatment level where only the symptoms and not the underlying conditions were dealt with. The program can attempt to confront and attempt to overcome the underlying conditions, at the same time that the painful social symptoms experienced by the older persons are treated, through the combination of case and group work techniques applied in the neighborhoods of residence of the deprived minority groups.

THE MODEL CITIES SENIOR WHEELS EAST PROGRAM

Conclusions concerning the role of interaction and group involvement in adjustment and functional ability levels achieved and maintained by the aged, together with social-political analysis of the present situation of low-income minority group aged provide the conceptual bases for this outreach program which deals with critical personal problems of aged in the target area and attempts, through community organization and group work techniques, to eliminate the personal vulnerability of individual members of the aged group.

In the first year of program activity, community workers canvassed the total target area on a door-to-door basis from the mobile office unit and uncovered numerous cases of aged persons with critical problems. Community workers participated with the aged in referral and advocacy capacities and placed pressure upon service institutions to respond to client needs. As well as having contributed to worker acceptance in the neighborhoods of the target area, this technique served to move many aged from a level of mere subsistence to more firm existence within the community as incomes increased, housing conditions improved, health problems received regular treatment, and personal or family problems were confronted. Where institutionalization was the only solution to the plight of some individual aged, the transition out of the community was facilitated.

While 7,620 contacts with households were attempted or completed, only 460 aged persons were served during the first nine months of activity. Fifty-two agencies were utilized and a total of 1,591 follow-up contacts were made to achieve satisfactory resolution to case problems.

Two citations from casework files illustrate two different outcomes relevant to the basic goals ofthe approach used. The first illustrates the movement of an aged woman to increased activism at the community level.

Mrs. A is seventy-three years old and has been elected to several community board positions with various community-based organizations. Her activity had been limited to attending meetings when it was convenient. She first came in contact with M. C. Senior Wheels East when she was invited to attend an Elders' Council meeting. Gradually she became more interested in the discussions of problems of senior citizens and then requested assistance to obtain Food Stamps. Although she had been receiving Social Security and Public Welfare Supplement (total = $138/month), she was not aware of the benefits of the Federal Food Stamp Program. Mrs. A knows nearly every senior citizen living within a three block radius of her home, and soon began referring others to our program for assistance.

Over the past months of association with Senior Wheels East, Mrs. A's community involvement has escalated. She participates fully in discussions of community problems, she has taken petitions and flyers to neighbors to alert them to certain actions or recommendations, she has been a key person in the formation of a new Senior Citizens group which has sponsored fund-raising events, and she attends other meetings of senior citizens as an information resource for them. She is taking a leadership role which she had not previously assumed—and is assuming corresponding responsibilities for action. She is now a regular member of the Elders' Council and recently was one of three who represented the council at a meeting with the governor of Pennsylvania to report the recommendations and demands of senior citizens.

The second case illustrates the success of the program in enabling continued community residence of an aged man who otherwise might have been institutionalized in his later years.

Mr. B expressed desire for employment and social activity to the Senior Wheels East worker during a regular door-to-door outreach effort of the program. Recognizing that Mr. B was depressed by his feelings of uselessness and isolation, the worker made arrangements for him to be employed as a maintenance man in the Senior Wheels East office. By having been offered this employment opportunity, he again felt useful and productive. Surrounded by people who cared about him, he was able to respond by caring about someone other than himself. His four weeks of employment also gave him the opportunity to evaluate his dreams and desires within the perspective of additional limitations which had come with age.

Although his missing finger on one hand had been his only physical limitation during his employment years, he now found that his general health could not withstand the demands of a regular part-time job. He did, nonetheless, begin attending and participating in every senior citizen meeting held in his neighborhood and derived tremendous joy just from anticipating the mailman's delivery of another meeting invitation. Several months after he made the decision that he was not well enough to work, following weeks in the hospital, he began to talk more openly about his living conditions and alternatives to working as means by which he could feel like somebody.

He had developed a good working relationship with his D.P.A. caseworker, as well as the hospital social worker. We held an interagency conference to discuss alternatives which Mr. B might consider. Shortly thereafter, he decided that foster home care placement under D.P.W. would be his first choice. This program places elderly in home/family settings where the elderly person is treated as "one of the family." Since the placement he has gained weight, is healthier, and is thoroughly pleased with his new family. Although it was necessary for Mr. B to make a transition from a familiar neighborhood, he was given every support to remain in a community setting. Through frequent case contact he became known as an individual with strengths and limitations, and his strengths were reinforced through the case contact as well as through the group contacts, even after employment. He was given supports which enabled him to select an alternative at a time when he was still able to do so, and thereby prevent the very imminent reality of institutionalization if a transition to more protected living was not made.

Although a major portion of community worker time in the first year was spent on outreach, referral, and advocacy on individual case problems, the community organization specialist on staff devoted full time to the organization of several neighborhood groups, establishment of liason and staffing relationships with some groups already existing, as well as organization of thirteen neighborhood meetings preparatory to an area-wide forum focusing on development of recommendations for the White House Conference.

Movement of individuals from client caseloads to social activity in the group structures was encouraged on the initial visit with clients, as well as on one-week, one-month, three-month, and six-month follow-ups with individual clients. Similarly, aged persons participating in group activity often moved to the client caseload after establishing rapport with the group worker and raising individual problems that required worker assistance for resolution. In the first nine months of program activity, 41 group activities were conducted with a total attendance of 657. This figure represents repeated participation by a large proportion of group members.

Fostering group participation by the aged through program activity is primarily based on the recognition of both the group nature of human social life and the losses in this regard experienced by the aged. Forced movement to social participation, or to social action following initial group participation, is *not* a practice of the program. Recognizing the variation in personal adjustment to social deprivation which exists among any large group of aged community residents, the basic approach of the program is to provide social alternatives for the aged within their social life space as well as the provision of activity alternatives, which range from bingo to social action within the groups.

A secondary goal of group initiation in the communities in which the program is active is the development of skills to maintain dynamic interaction within the groups which can enable their continuation beyond the life of this program. Included in this latter category of skills is both leadership development and transfer of techniques to achieve financial independence by the groups through their own efforts. Intergroup contact has been established through the formation of an Elders' Council consisting of representatives of each of the eleven functioning groups. The Elders' Council meetings serve as a monthly forum for the exchange of group experiences as well as an active advisory board to the program.

An example of group movement towards self-direction and operation of activities may be seen in the residents' club at an apartment house for the elderly which includes a large portion of Ukrainian Americans, many of whom are fluent only in Ukrainian. From an initial meeting in January of 1971 this group moved to committee structure and responsibility for the conduct of monthly meetings four months later. While not directly involved in social action programs outside of the apartment dwelling, the group has identified certain resident needs within the facility and has acted to provide resources to meet those needs. Participation by residents of this facility in Elders' Council meetings, joint trips with members of other racial and ethnic groups, and attendance at area-wide conferences on the mutual problems of the aged and workshops to develop action agendas have served to introduce the potential for externally oriented social action among members of this and other groups. Joint concern for lack of public transportation adequate to the needs of the elderly among members of all groups illustrates one potential area for collective social action by aged community residents who recognize the limited role that can be played in this respect by the mobile unit, the "wheels," of the Model Cities Senior Wheels program.

In another instance a neighborhood group, brought together through the joint efforts of Model Cities Senior Wheels East staff and Model Cities Housing Information Center staff decided to emphasize both their concern for deteriorated housing in their immediate neighborhood and their identity as senior citizens in their group name. Continued staffing by both programs of the Philadelphia Model Cities Administration has contributed to increased skills in group self-representation on the housing issue as well as recognition of potential social rewards from expansion of group interest to recreational activities as well as to other social issues on which action is possible. The community leadership potential of the group has been secured by their persistence and success in eliminating some housing hazardous to the community. The reintegration of the aged as a group into community decision-making processes has been begun in this one neighborhood by the activities of these concerned seniors.

RELATED CONSIDERATIONS FROM PROGRAM EXPERIENCE

Three issues concerning the community-workers staff's activity with the aged in this multifocus program are of special interest to the authors and deserve greater attention than can be given in this brief report.

(1) Inability to hire part-time community workers together with the strenuous nature of job tasks made the employment of elderly community workers impossible, although the need for the creation of such employment opportunities among the aged was fully recognized. Field work experience in previous community work with the aged (Kent, Barg, 1969; Kent, Hirsch, 1971; Kent, 1970) demonstrated the burden placed upon older workers by daylong door-to-door activity. Although performance of individual elderly workers was adequate, the perceived unpredictability of work demands at the initiation of this program led to a decision to forestall employment of the elderly.

However, the predominantly young and younger middle-aged community worker staff have not reported incidents of resentment from the target-aged population on the basis of age disparities. Indeed, group experiences involving younger workers have been extremely rewarding and dynamic. The experience of the program suggests that the demonstrated concern of younger people with the social problems of the aged group contributes to an enthusiastic commitment to confronting these problems through organized social action by the aged to a degree that might not be achievable if the community staff were composed only of the elderly. The potential for cross-generational alliances perceived by the aged activists might allow for greater optimism among them and this, in turn, can be seen to be related to the degree of activity undertaken. Similar observations of the role of young staff in group therapy sessions with institutionalized aged in stimulating improvement in personal appearance and willingness to participate actively have been reported by Dr. Maurice E. Linden (1954), consultant to Model Cities Senior Wheels East. Psychiatric explanation of increased enthusiasm in the group therapy setting involves a revitalization of libidinal energy on the personality level.

(2) In other work, the authors (Kent, Hirsch, Barg, 1969, 1971) have recognized concern expressed in the literature for the integration of indigenous community workers in professionally staffed agency settings. The maintenance of the workers' community perspective on issues of social policy while developing increased skills for the achievement of social change is accepted as a necessary combination if the rigidity of the social welfare establishment is to be successfully challenged by the incorporation of community workers in structured roles within agencies and if profound social change is to occur. However, if the agency continues to view the client population as composed of essentially atomized, dependent individuals and the agency approach is founded in this conception, the ability of the community workers to remain in work roles and maintain the perspective of their community, founded in their experience within that community, is seen to be minimal. Agency acceptance of a view of the target population as a politically powerless group, oppressed in their group identity, and an agency commitment to contribute to the liberation of that population will, on the other hand, lead to a

resolution of the apparent conflict suggested above. The attempt to achieve self-representation through group organization of the aged in this instance is viewed as a technique which will, at the same time, provide community workers with feedback from the community that is at least equivalent to feedback received from professionally oriented personnel, and can serve to contribute to the maintenance of their community perspective.

(3) A third consideration based on program experience with three groups of elderly in the target area who differ in racial and ethnic identity leads to conclusions that the basic approach utilized is appropriate to all three groups. We accept that cultural differences among black, Puerto Rican, and foreign-born white aged lead to differences in some patterns of adjustment to aging. However, impressionistic evaluations support the view that the common experiences of economic deprivation, loss of social roles and group supports associated with sociological aging, and declines in physical health associated with physiological aging combine to obviate cultural differences which each group brings to the experiences of sociological and physiological aging. Research findings from a study of black and white aged residents of low-income neighborhoods in Philadelphia (Kent, Hirsch, 1971) do point to differences between the two groups in terms of supports available in later life which can, in turn, be seen to result from differential access in earlier life to employment—security when employment was achieved, economic rewards of employment, and other opportunities associated with economic status. The role of racism in limiting access in earlier life can not be disregarded when evaluating the effects of early life experience found in later life. However, other minority groups in the same society and with whom the Model Cities Senior Wheels East has worked have endured similar oppression on social, economic, cultural, and personality levels, and the Model Cities Senior Wheels East approach has been effective in work with each group.

While the observations included in this section of the presentation were introduced with a statement recognizing the limited time and space for full discussion, it must be further conceded that the issues raised also require further well-documented study.

SUMMARY AND CONCLUSIONS

The bases of this multifocus approach to community work with low-income minority group aged in urban neighborhoods has been presented in the discussion of social theory and political ideas concerning the location of the aged in contemporary American society. The program's success has been suggested in the impressionistic material presented. However, limitations of information-referral-advocacy work with the aged when adequate services to support the aged in the community are only available in restricted quantity must be confronted.

The group work-community organization component of the work already undertaken is directed at achievement of political power by the aged to secure the necessary supportive services on a permanent rather than demonstration basis in all neighborhoods of the urban community. However, the achievement of appropriate levels of human services requires the elevation of human priorities in governmental structures nationally and the positive evaluation of the aged as a social group in the ideological segment of the social structure of the society. Work among the aged can contribute to the change in priorities, values, and material inputs to this group in the community but the involvement of other age groups within the society in this struggle must be seen as another force necessary to the achievement of the goals represented in this one service program.

Efforts to achieve funding to increase levels of necessary service to be delivered by the program are underway—but efforts to achieve this goal in other urban neighborhoods and in other cities where the aged reside must also be undertaken.

REFERENCES

Brody, S. J., Finkle, H., Hirsch, C. Benefit alert: Outreach program for the aged. *Social Work* 1972, *17, 1.*

Cavan, R. S. Self & role in adjustment during old age. In Arnold Rose, *Human behavior and social processes: An interactionist approach* Boston: Houghton Mifflin Co., 1962.

Clark, M. The anthropology of aging: A new area for studies of culture and personality. In *Middle Age and Aging: A Reader in Social Psychology,* Bernice L. Neugarten (ed.) Chicago and London: The University of Chicago Press, 1968, pp. 433-443.

Kent, D. P. Aging within the American social structure, *Journal of Geriatric Psychiatry,* 1968, *II,* 1.

———. *Benefit Alert Final Report.* Sociology Dept., The Pennsylvania State University, Spring 1970. Case studies presented in this report reveal the hesitancy of clients to request greater supports for fear of losing present supports.

Kent, D. P., Barg, S. K. From "N" to ego, *Social Casework,* April 1969.

Kent, D. P., Hirsch, C. *Needs and Use of Services Among Negro and White Aged: Volume I Social and Economic Conditions of Negro and White Aged Residents of Urban Neighborhoods of Low Socioeconomic Status.* Sociology Dept., The Pennsylvania State University, July 1971. Appendix D has interviewers' comments on respondents fears of losing present supports through challenging the status-quo.

Kent, D. P., Hirsch, C., & Barg, S. K. An antagonistic model of the role and training of indigenous workers with low-income aged. Paper presented at the 8th International Congress of Gerontology, Washington, D.C., August 1969.

———. Indigenous workers as a crucial link in the total support system for low-income minority group aged; A report of an innovative field technique in survey research, *Aging and Human Development, II,* 3, 1971, *2,* 189-196.

Linden, Maurice E. The significance of dual leadership in gerontologic group psychotherapy: Studies in gerontologic human relationships. *The International Journal of Group Psychotherapy, IV,* 3, 1954, *4,* 262-273.

Rose, A. Mental health of normal older persons. *Geriatrics,* September 1961, 459-464.

———. The subculture of aging: A topic for sociological research. *The Gerontologist, 2,* 123-127.

———. A current theoretical issue in social gerontology. *The Gerontologist, 4* 1964, *4.*